Seventh Edition

Reading Difficulties

Their Diagnosis and Correction

Guy L. Bond

Miles A. Tinker

Barbara B. Wasson
Moorhead State University

John B. Wasson
Moorhead State University

Allyn and Bacon
Boston • London • Toronto • Sydney • Tokyo • Singapore

Series Editor: Virginia C. Lanigan
Series Editorial Assistant: Nicole DePalma
Production Administrator: Annette Joseph
Production Coordinator: Holly Crawford
Editorial-Production Service: Laura Cleveland, WordCrafters Editorial Services, Inc.
Cover Administrator: Linda K. Dickinson
Cover Designer: Suzanne Harbison
Manufacturing Buyer: Megan Cochran

Copyright © 1994, 1989 by Allyn and Bacon
A Division of Simon & Schuster, Inc.
160 Gould Street
Needham Heights, MA 02194

Library of Congress Cataloging-in-Publication Data

Bond, Guy Loraine
    Reading difficulties : their diagnosis and correction / Guy L.
Bond ... [et al.]. — 7th ed.
        p. cm.
    Includes bibliographical references and index.
    ISBN 0-205-15091-8
    1. Reading—Remedial teaching. 2. Reading disability. I. Title.
LB1050.5.B6 1993
372.4′3—dc20   93-6583
                                                                  CIP

Printed in the United States of America
10 9 8 7 6 5 4 3 2 1   98 97 96 95 94 93

Contents

Preface

Deficiencies in reading ability among children and adults have become a serious national concern. Severe disability in reading, in modern times, makes finding employment difficult, changing employment problematical, and advancing in employment nearly impossible. The seventh edition of *Reading Difficulties: Their Diagnosis and Correction* has major changes in emphasis from the previous editions.

Current research exploring the many causes of reading difficulties is discussed. Areas of exceptional importance include research on linguistic abilities, phonological abilities, cognitive functioning, and home environmental factors. New reading diagnostic methods are presented and evaluated, along with an extended description of observational methods.

The use of good literature with students who have reading difficulties is emphasized, as is the value of integrating reading and writing with these students. Instructional methods are presented that promote independence as well as skill in reading, that encourage active, engaged learning, and that facilitate cooperation among students and among the professionals who serve them.

As in the past, this book is written with the knowledge that learning to read is a dynamic, continuing process. It is also written with respect for the dedicated professional teacher.

The aim of the book is to help classroom teachers, resource teachers, and reading specialists diagnose and correct the various kinds of problems involved in preventing and correcting reading difficulties. The authors are keenly aware of the fact that learning to read is complex and that there are many possible confusions along the route. If the classroom teacher can detect and correct these difficulties early, many minor problems that could lead to a major reading disability may be prevented. This book is designed to give the teacher specific help by describing how to diagnose and correct reading difficulties in their formative stages.

Certain children will persist in their reading difficulties to the point that they will need more detailed diagnosis and individualized remedial training. The classroom teacher cannot be expected to make these more detailed and complex analyses, but the book discusses the various reading disabilities in a sufficiently detailed and direct manner that a thorough understanding of the most complex cases is possible. Finally, there are specific suggestions for diagnosing and correcting even the most stubborn kinds of problems, so that all who are concerned with readers with disabilities will have the information necessary to understand the adjustments required.

We have drawn heavily on our own and many coworkers' experiences in helping children overcome reading difficulties. For their contributions to this book, we specifically want to thank Leslie Crawford, Virginia McKinnon Deitz, Elynn Severson, and Carol Sibley. We also want to thank the many in-service teachers who presented their insights while discussing the problems of reading instruction in advanced courses and seminars. We also want to thank the reviewers of the manuscript: Roger J. DeSanti, University of New Orleans; Desmond V. Rice, Lamar University; and Molly M. Wilson, Idaho State University. Finally, we want to thank the numerous classroom, reading, and learning disabilities teachers who invited us into their classrooms and resource rooms so that we could share knowledge concerning the reading problems of their students.

Chapter 1

Introduction

Being able to read well is a valuable attribute. At work, at home, at school, and even at leisure, reading is required to some extent. Reading is a needed channel of communication with the global community.

Consideration of the daily activities of almost any adult reveals a need for reading. These activities are made possible or are aided by information gained from reading. Magazines, newspapers, books, maps, directories, pamphlets, signs, and catalogs all assist the reader in making plans and in carrying them out. People read to obtain information, to buy wisely, to solve problems, for pleasure, and for many other reasons. More people read now than ever before.

Nature of Reading Development

Preparation for reading does not start when a child enters school for the first time. It has begun long before this. Even before an infant talks, there is communication among parents, the infant, and others. From infancy until the child enters school, a multitude of experiences and the child's reactions and adjustments to them help to prepare each youngster for the demands of learning to read. In a few short years, children progress from the point at which they can only pat the pictures in their books to learning to point out and name familiar objects in the pictures. Soon they willingly listen when read to and then recite little rhymes and talk about the stories in books. These steps are gains in verbalization and in recognition of form and meaning. Progress in *readiness* for reading can be extensive and significant during the preschool years.

When taught with any of the usual approaches used in learning to read, the child must understand the relationship of printed language to oral language— must understand that a printed word stands for a spoken word and has the same meaning as the spoken word. In beginning reading, the printed word should be in the child's speaking and meaning vocabulary, so the child will associate the printed word with both the sound and meaning of the spoken word.

The printed words in any writing are merely symbols for the meanings intended by the author. These symbols serve as cues to the reader, who must organize an understanding of what is meant. The ease with which a reader can do this depends largely upon his background of experiences. For a beginning reader, these meanings are acquired through the reader's previous experiences and previously acquired facility with language. The child reads using his experience and language skill, interrelating them to derive meaning from printed symbols.

To a large degree, a child's thinking requires verbal manipulations. When the child begins to read, this is important to consider, for thinking is essential to reading at all stages of development. In fact, reading as a tool for learning will be ineffective unless it is accompanied by thinking. Learning to read and reading to learn should develop together throughout the school years.

Reading is both a subject of instruction and a tool for studying. Special skills should be taught as they are needed, and they should be taught in the appropriate context. For example, the special skills needed for reading science text should be taught with material similar to that used in science instruction. Although this emphasizes reading as a tool, it also teaches reading.

Growth in reading abilities is developmental. New learning is an addition to or an expansion or refinement of a previous attainment that facilitates the learner's participation in meaningful communication through reading. Growth in reading involves the gradual acquisition of skills that synchronize together to enable the learner to interpret printed symbols correctly. These skills are developed concurrently with their use in the act of reading itself. Reading development is the result of the completion of tasks that are neither easy nor simple. Each new learning rests upon a child's previously acquired achievements. Each new learning requires that the child apply newly developing skills to increasingly more complex reading tasks. Instruction must maintain balances among the various skills and abilities that are essential to effective reading and must be geared to the needs and characteristics of the children being taught.

Definition of Reading

Our definition of reading is as follows: *Reading is the recognition of printed or written symbols that serve as stimuli to the recall of meanings built up through the reader's past experience.* New meanings are derived through the manipulation of concepts already in the reader's possession. The organization of these meanings is governed by purposes that are clearly defined by the reader. In short, the reading process involves both the acquisition of meanings intended by the writer and the reader's own contributions in the form of interpretation and evaluation of and reflection on those meanings.

Description of Normal Reading Growth

To identify those children who have failed to make satisfactory progress in reading, it is necessary to have in mind some standards of reading growth. There are marked individual differences in rate of reading attainment. Some children begin to read early and progress rapidly. Others start late and move forward slowly. Between these are the average learners. It should also be noted that a child may progress at different rates during different stages in the development of reading abilities. Generally, however, growth in reading tends to be continuous and developmental in nature. At each stage, the skills essential to success at the next level are acquired. When this progress is continued without serious interruption, the child eventually becomes a mature reader.

The Prereading Period

Soon after birth, the child begins to acquire experience essential to learning to read. When, in addition, the child matures in mental ability and emotional adjustment and acquires increasing interests, she becomes ready to begin reading. A listening and speaking vocabulary develops gradually. In time, sentences are understood and properly used. Meanwhile, the child develops skill in auditory and visual discrimination. Varieties of concepts are formed. Under favorable circumstances, the child is able to focus attention, enabling her to listen to and comprehend stories. If the child's experience has been extensive, if many clear concepts have been acquired, and if adequate facility in the understanding and use of language has been achieved, the child has a distinct advantage in getting ready for reading.

A child's experiences affect the rate of development of skills up to the time reading instruction is begun. To acquire auditory and visual skills and facility with language, a child must have both appropriate experiences and guidance. The child must be encouraged to discriminate sounds and visual details and to listen to and use words. It is important for adults to talk to and with the child. Stories should be read with the child while she looks at the pictures and talks about them. Crayons and paper should be provided so that the child can express her own thoughts through drawings and scribblings. The child who is accumulating experience with such items as picture books, crayons, and paper is also preparing for reading.

Under favorable circumstances, provided that mental growth, personal adjustment, and physical development are normal, the child will not only be *ready* to read, but should also be *eager* to read. There are marked differences in the rate at which children acquire reading readiness. A few are ready even before entering kindergarten, others by the time they enter first grade. Many become ready soon after beginning first grade, but a few are not ready until later.

Progress in Reading Readiness

The child is ready to begin a reading program only after reaching sufficient mental maturity, achieving satisfactory classroom adjustment, maintaining normal physical development, acquiring an adequate background of experiences, and developing positive attitudes toward reading. As already noted, there are many degrees of readiness among children at the beginning of Grade 1. After an evaluation of each child, the teacher provides instruction to compensate for whatever deficiencies in reading readiness he discovers.

It should be pointed out here that the concept of readiness is basic to the development of reading ability at all levels, from kindergarten on. With each new unit of instruction, the child should be prepared to accomplish the reading and thinking activities involved in it. For success in any specific reading task, the child must possess the necessary concepts, the vocabulary, and the ability to handle the language relationships involved. The child must also select and organize ideas and details related to her purpose. All this implies instruction and guidance so that the student will be *ready to read* each new unit proficiently.

Introduction to Reading

After proper preparation, the child is introduced to reading in Grade 1. The child begins to accumulate a sight vocabulary and at the same time learns that printed and written symbols stand for meanings in a variety of situations. Training in auditory and visual discrimination continues. New word meanings are acquired. The teacher helps the child use elementary techniques and clues for word identification. Meanwhile, the child is progressing naturally from reading labels, words standing for actions, short signs, and notes to reading a book, the preprimer. Such systematic training in reading a book leads to success at the primer level and so on to the first reader. All along, learnings are practiced through the judicious use of exercises suggested in manuals, through selected work sheets, and through supplementary materials such as storybooks for beginning readers.

There will be noticeable individual differences in the reading progress made by first-grade students. By the end of the first grade, the average learners will have acquired a considerable stock of sight words, some independence in using techniques of word recognition, and much skill in both oral and silent reading of easy materials, including those in the public library.

Progress in the Primary Grades

To a great extent, the reading instruction in Grades 2 and 3 consists of extension, refinement, and amplification of the program begun in Grade 1. New techniques of reading are introduced, and the child begins to learn them when she is ready. Throughout the primary grades, there are no abrupt distinctions in progressing from one part of the program to the next. Under favorable circumstances, the average child will have achieved the following goals by the end of Grade 3: (1) marked progress in mastering techniques of word recognition and the other fundamentals of reading, (2) considerable independence in reading, (3) a degree of flexibility in the use of reading skills, (4) a sound basis for study-type reading, (5) greater speed in silent rather than oral reading, and (6) positive attitudes toward reading. With normal progress, by the end of Grade 3 the child will have acquired a sound foundation for future reading, although there will be many skills in word recognition, comprehension, and techniques of study to be developed later.

Reading instruction in Grades 4 through 6 is an extension of the developmental program begun in the primary grades. Besides improving the basic abilities, it focuses on developing the specialized abilities and study skills required for reading subject matter in the content areas and other work-type materials. Beginning in Grade 4, children move into a phase of increasing diversification of learning in which reading is the essential tool. To an accelerating degree, reading becomes a means of gathering information and achieving pleasure. When there has been normal progress in the earlier grades, the consolidation of basic reading abilities and the extension of these abilities in specialized directions in the intermediate grades proceeds at a relatively rapid pace. The child reads more independently and more widely. Although the relative emphasis upon silent reading increases, oral reading should not be neglected. By the time the sixth grade is finished, the child who has made normal progress will have achieved the basis for reading in later years. Additional instruction in reading in the junior and senior high school years is necessary to assure proficiency. This is especially true in perfecting the special skills needed for serious study and for the comprehension of difficult materials.

Progress in the Basic Reading Abilities

Throughout the grades, there tends to be a steady growth in the acquisition of words, word-recognition skills, and comprehension skills. Progress is developmental or sequential, and each learning provides a basis for learnings similar to it. Reading readiness plays an important role. A child is ready to advance to a more complex level of a learning sequence only when mastery of previously taught skills is sufficient to ensure success in more mature learning. In word recognition, for example, the child learns letter and phonogram sounds in the early years. This equips the child for the more mature features of word recognition taught in the intermediate grades, which include syllabication and recognition of prefixes, suffixes, and word roots. Basic reading abilities are acquired, not in isolation, but as part of a well-integrated sequential reading program.

Progress in the Special Reading Abilities

Acquisition of the special abilities necessary for proficient reading in the content areas, such as reading to organize, begins early and progresses at a gradual pace for most students. Since the reading of some content material is introduced in Grade 1 in many reading programs, it is necessary to teach the elementary features of the special abilities during the primary grades. By Grade 3, such guidance receives a good deal of emphasis. When the special abilities are stressed, the progress of the average pupil in reading to learn has advanced far enough by the end of the primary grades that a smooth transition to the major reading tasks in the intermediate grades will be achieved.

As the child moves through Grade 3 and through the intermediate grades, the study skills are added to the special reading abilities. Mastery of the basic reading skills, together with continuing improvement in special reading skills and study skills, is coordinated into proficient reading. With normal progress, the child will have developed much flexibility in adapting these skills to the purposes and subject-matter requirements of each of the content areas. The child will also have learned the supplementary skills necessary for dealing with reading programs unique to a particular subject. Although complete mastery of the special reading abilities cannot be achieved by the end of Grade 6, there will have been good progress in this direction. The child will have a sound foundation for further progress in the reading tasks in the junior and senior high school years. However, a sound foundation is not enough. Because the materials read in high school are more mature than those used in elementary school, the child must be taught how to meet more advanced reading demands.

Goals of Reading Instruction

An effective reading program does more than develop the abilities and skills, both basic and special, outlined in the preceding section. Nevertheless, the broader goals of the reading program are built upon these foundations. Reading is more than skill in identifying and recognizing words, in grouping words into thought units, and in noting details and following directions. It is more than the sum of all reading skills and techniques.

The overall goal of reading instruction is to help each pupil become as able and diversified a reader as his capabilities, the available facilities, and the instructional program permit. To achieve this, certain subgoals must be considered. These goals are present during early reading experiences and become more apparent as reading develops through the grades. It should be recognized that there is interdependence among the goals of reading instruction. One goal is not necessarily more important than another. These goals will be discussed in the paragraphs that follow.

Basic Understanding of Words, Sentences, Paragraphs, and Entire Selections

Growth in understanding words, sentences, paragraphs, and whole selections is essential if the student is to develop into a mature reader. Word meanings are derived from experience. As language facility increases and words are used with newly experienced situations, concepts are clarified and enriched. Growth is continuous but gradual. The instructional program for developing a child's understanding and use of words to express meanings provides a variety of appropriate firsthand and vicarious experiences, wide and extensive reading, and study of words in context. It also develops the habit of attending to the meaning of words, so that if an unusual or expressive word is used, the child will note it and its meaning. An understanding of words is basic to an understanding of sentences, paragraphs, and selections.

The understanding of sentence structure affects reading comprehension. Besides knowing the meanings of words in a sentence, the reader must grasp the relationships between words and between groups of words. The kind and amount of instruction are determined by individual needs. With one child, the instruction may involve proper phrasing and interpretation of punctuation. Another child may need instruction in interpreting figures of speech and using a word whose meaning fits the verbal context. A third may need help in sorting out and properly relating several ideas incorporated in one sentence.

Along with understanding words and sentences, comprehending a paragraph requires understanding the relationship among sentences in that paragraph. The instructional task involves guiding the student in identifying the topical sentence containing the key idea and in interpreting its relationship to the explanatory or amplifying sentences. In a similar manner, attention should be devoted to the relationship between paragraphs in longer selections.

Understanding words, sentences, and paragraphs is essential to comprehending reading selections. Also involved is a child's ability to listen to and understand a selection read aloud. Some children, when they begin school, are skilled at listening to and understanding stories. Others have acquired little or no story sense by that time. These will need guidance and instruction in how to listen carefully to what is said and in how to follow a sequence of events in stories. Story sense is never completely developed for any child by the time reading instruction is begun, and guidance in listening attentively and in following sequences of events should be an integral part of reading instruction at least through the primary grades. After the primary grades, because of the more complex plots and more complicated organization of ideas encountered, the child must learn to sense the author's organization in order to grasp the meanings of the longer selections.

Maturity in Reading Habits and Attitudes
Developing reading habits and attitudes begins early and continues for as long as the child is growing in reading capability. The child learns to appreciate and to care for books. The child develops intellectual curiosity and comes to realize that books can help satisfy the need to know, to solve problems, and to contribute to group enterprises. The habit of attending to words and demanding an understanding of their meanings should be encouraged at all levels. Finally, the habit of relying on one's own resources and energetically attacking reading material should be encouraged early, to establish a realistic amount of independence throughout the instructional program.

Independence in Reading
To begin to read well and to be able to continue developing as a reader after formal education is finished, the child must develop independence in reading. There are several aspects to achieving this independence. The child must be able to recognize words quickly and easily in order to understand and consider content. Independence in reading depends on the ability to work out the pronunciation and understanding of new words. The independent reader also knows appropriate sources where new information can be found, is able to select rele-

vant subject matter from these sources, and can judge the suitability of that subject matter. Independence in reading is also shown by the ability of the child to initiate reading activities, to appreciate reading problems, and to set reading purposes. Reading programs organized into major experience units that require related reading and cooperative group activities promote independence in reading and encourage cooperation among students. The teacher's guidance plays an important role in the development of independence in reading.

Efficiency in the Use of Basic Study Skills

A number of skills are involved in this goal. The ability to locate information through such aids as tables of contents, indexes, and glossaries is one example. Instruction in the elementary techniques of finding information begins early. The more complex skills are taught in sequential order. Proficiency in the use of general reference material is a second example of a basic study skill. Beginning with simple alphabetizing, the child progresses to being able to use such reference sources as dictionaries and encyclopedias.

Additional skills include abilities in the interpretation of pictures, maps, graphs, and charts. Teaching begins in kindergarten and progresses in a developmental manner through the school years.

Finally, organizational skills must be included as essential study skills. This important group of skills includes the ability to outline, classify materials under main headings and subheadings, organize sentences in experience charts in sequential order, and order selected materials in sequence. Being able to construct time lines, two-way charts, and classification tables are other examples. The ability to organize materials is essential to well-rounded growth in reading proficiency.

Maturity in Essential Comprehension Skills

The development of five interrelated comprehension skills is a major goal of reading instruction. These skills are the abilities to (1) read for specific information, (2) read to organize, (3) read to evaluate, (4) read to interpret, and (5) read to appreciate. They are ever-present goals of reading instruction and they should not be postponed so that they have to be initiated in the more advanced grades.

Maturity in Choosing Suitable Strategies for Various Reading Purposes

To communicate their ideas to readers, authors write in ways appropriate to their goals. To mature in reading proficiency, a child must learn to adjust his reading to the requirements of the specific type of material being read. An example is the contrast between how a child reads and solves an arithmetic story problem and how a child reads and enjoys a standard short story. Such adjustments are made through coordinating the basic reading proficiencies, the different abilities involved in comprehension, and the study skills. The reader must choose, from his repertory of skills, those that are best for reading a particular selection effectively for a specific purpose.

A young child starts to develop different strategies for reading various types of material as soon as he reads a science unit in his basic reader or reads scientific writing in a supplementary book. Versatility in this sort of adjustment improves from grade to grade. The teacher should instruct the child in why these adjustments are needed and when and how to make them. The achievement of facility in using different strategies for different reading purposes is a goal of reading instruction at all grade levels.

Breadth of Interest and Maturity of Taste in Reading

To be successful, a reading program must go beyond developing the basic and special abilities and the study skills. The child must also want to read widely. The amount, the variety, and the quality of what is read reflect the quality of the teaching program.

Point of View

We, the authors of this book, believe that reading problems develop because one or more factors within the child or in the environment, or both, prevent her from reaching her learning capacity. Reading difficulty may occur at any stage of a child's school career, from the first grade throughout the grades. We also believe that reading difficulties can be corrected through proper diagnosis and remedial instruction. Nothing is accomplished by blaming the difficulty on low intelligence, lack of interest, laziness, or the home. For one reason or another, school instruction has not capitalized on the child's mental ability or developed motivation by appealing to the child's interests.

If all the skills and abilities necessary for growth toward reading maturity are to be acquired, the learner must be motivated and energetic, work smoothly at her own level of accomplishment, and also be a comfortable learner. Each child must be able to sense that her proficiency in reading is increasing and that the enterprise is worth the effort.

In recent years, the teaching of reading has gained an important position in our schools. Research has been carried out, teachers are better trained, reading materials have multiplied, and techniques and devices for teaching have improved. Nevertheless, a surprising number of students fail to make the progress in reading expected from their potential.

The presence of reading difficulties in our schools is a serious problem at all grade levels. Many reading difficulties can be prevented altogether. The classroom teacher can correct others in their initial stages, when correction is relatively easy. A sound preventive program stresses at least three kinds of instruction: (1) a thoroughgoing reading readiness program to prepare the child for beginning reading and for reading at successively higher levels; (2) proper adjustment of instruction to individual differences; and (3) systematic developmental programs at all levels.

A well-organized instructional program works to prevent reading difficulties. If it were possible in day-to-day classroom teaching to instruct each student according to her exact instructional needs, there would be less need for remedial work. Even with the best teaching and the best organized, systematic program, certain children will experience serious difficulties. With less than the best teaching, the incidence of reading difficulties will increase. In any case, there will be an appreciable number of students who have serious difficulties with their reading, and there must be remedial help available to correct those difficulties.

View on Causes

We know that the causes of reading difficulties are multiple and tend to be complex. In the more difficult cases, a pattern of interacting factors usually operates, each contributing its part to the difficulty and each impeding future growth. The reading specialist must search out as many as possible of these limiting conditions operating in a particular case and apply the proper corrective measures.

In general, we believe that most reading difficulties are created and are not inherent. Reading difficulties are sometimes the result of unrecognized, predisposing conditions within the child, but for the most part they are caused by elements of the child's environment at home, at play, and at school. Without appropriate guidance or proper instruction, the child fails to acquire the skills needed to develop normal reading ability.

Reading difficulties vary from minor to very severe. When minor difficulties occur and are not recognized and corrected promptly, their deleterious effects become cumulative and may result in a severe disability.

Although we emphasize educational factors as causes of reading difficulties, we also recognize that there are other factors that may and often do contribute to a complex pattern of causes. These include immaturity, associated sometimes with low socioeconomic status; personal adjustment problems; physical deficiencies; and excessive pressure for achievement from home or school. There seldom is a single factor that causes reading difficulty, but one factor may be relatively more important than others.

We are aware that failure to recognize a child's handicaps and failure to adjust instruction to lessen their effects upon learning can contribute to a reading difficulty. Unless all educational, physical, and behavioral factors that can hinder normal progress in learning to read are identified early and corrected if possible, along with making proper instructional adjustments, reading difficulty is apt to develop.

View on Remedial Instruction

We maintain that remedial instruction in reading is essentially the same as good classroom teaching, but is more individualized. The teacher works with the child, using essential regular teaching methods, but concentrates on the skill in which the child is deficient. Effort is concentrated on the child's needs, assuming that there has been a thorough diagnosis of his strengths and weaknesses.

We believe that the best results in remedial instruction are attained by designing an *individual instructional plan* that utilizes a combination of approaches. The remedial plan, however, should include any one approach or any combination of approaches suggested by the results of the diagnosis.

Effective remedial instruction is given by a good reading teacher—a teacher who is familiar with the principles and practices of sound reading instruction. Above all, the teacher must be versatile in adapting materials and techniques to specific needs based on formal and informal diagnosis and on the specific events of daily instruction. Instructional tasks may need to be broken down into small, manageable units. Extra effort is usually needed to give clear introductions to activities for students who have difficulty understanding what to do and to ensure that students are actively involved in learning. The teacher must employ patience, understanding, and empathy.

Success in remedial work is achieved only when there is a positive interaction between teacher and child and when the student is strongly motivated toward reading improvement. Even in group remediation, some individual attention by the teacher is important. To help the student view reading as enjoyable and worthwhile, the teacher must present lessons and activities that are as pleasant, interesting, and meaningful as possible. Sufficient variety helps maintain interest. However, it is not simply instructional methods that impart positive attitudes and motivation for reading improvement to children. Of great importance are the expressed attitudes and observed actions of the teacher; enthusiasm is essential.

A good many poor readers dislike reading due to previous failures. The wise remedial reading teacher knows how to dramatize progress in order to demonstrate success. Spoken remarks, written comments or evaluations, and even the use of stickers or stars provide valuable information to the child about progress and success. Such feedback should be frequent and honest and should always stress what the child has done well or any evidence of improvement. Progress charts may be used on which units of improvement are small enough that progress can be frequently recorded. Take-home samples of the child's work, sight-word files, progress charts, and similar materials that illustrate to parents the child's improvement in reading also help demonstrate success.

We are convinced that well-conceived remedial instruction results in improved reading. Theoretically, the instruction should bring the child up to the reading grade that is consistent with her learning potential. This should be possible, except in those cases that are complicated by factors beyond the ability of the teacher to correct. It is, however, most unusual when a skilled teacher is not able to bring about a significant improvement in reading, given a reasonable amount of time.

Plan of This Book

This book discusses a practical approach to reading based on research findings and sound instructional procedures. Our chief concern is the child who experiences difficulty in his attempts to learn to read. We are convinced that both the classroom teacher and the reading specialist must be equipped to diagnose and correct reading deficiencies whenever they arise.

We will present the treatment of learning problems in ways that apply to both the classroom teacher and the reading specialist. Chapter 2 is concerned with the extent of individual differences and the problems of adjusting instruction to meet those differences.

The next four chapters deal with diagnosing reading difficulties. Chapter 7 discusses the principles and levels of diagnosis and treats questions to be answered by the diagnostician in analyzing reading difficulties. Chapter 8 describes specific standardized and informal diagnostic procedures. Chapter 9 examines the principles involved in using the diagnostic findings to formulate an appropriate educational plan of remediation.

The techniques used in the treatment of word-recognition difficulties are described in the next four chapters. The techniques used to overcome deficiencies in basic meaning clues necessary for successful word recognition are discussed in Chapter 10. Remedial techniques used to correct faulty decoding skills in word recognition are presented in Chapter 11. Chapter 12 concentrates on the remedial teaching necessary to deal with the complex reading problems of children with extreme reading difficulties, and Chapter 13 presents the adjustments needed to assist the child with reading difficulties who is disabled physically, emotionally, intellectually, or environmentally.

The last four chapters focus on the problems of basic comprehension abilities and more specific types of disabilities related to comprehension. Chapter 14 identifies remedial techniques for correcting basic comprehension difficulties. Chapter 15 deals with remedial treatment for weaknesses in specific comprehension abilities and basic study skills and with reading materials in several fields of endeavor. Chapter 16 is concerned with improving inefficient rates of comprehension and overcoming ineffective oral reading, and Chapter 17 covers ways to encourage continuous growth in reading by expanding interests in reading, increasing independence, and providing follow-up help.

To help the readers of this book identify antecedents, we have used the labels *remedial teacher* and *reading specialist* according to the phase of work being done, whether it be by resource teachers, reading specialists, or classroom teachers. Also, although we have tended to use the word *child* in our writing, the principles of diagnosis and treatment are equally applicable to all persons with reading difficulties, from the early grades to adult.

Chapter 2

Adjusting Instruction to Individual Differences

The teacher's goal is to provide instruction and learning opportunities in the classroom that will encourage maximal growth in reading development and in achievement in all the other outcomes of the curriculum for each child she instructs. The organization of classroom activities and the adjustment of methods and materials to the wide variations found among children are two of the most crucial and complex problems that education must solve.

In any plan of school organization, the teacher is the main contributor to adjusting instruction in reading to the individual differences among the children she teaches. The teacher must know the nature of reading growth, the types of reading difficulties that might impede growth, and the characteristics of each child that might predispose the child to reading difficulties.

Individual Differences in the Classroom

The classroom teacher needs to be a keen observer and student to follow the reading growth of all the children. The knowledge she has of each child's general level of reading capability, while important, is not sufficient for maximum accomplishment or for preventing serious reading problems. The teacher must also study the attainment of specific skills and abilities, so that any faulty learning can be detected and corrected early and so that any omissions or overemphasis can be avoided.

A class made up of 25 to 30 children cannot be taught as though all members of the class had the same interests, desires, intellectual capabilities, or physical characteristics; nor can it be taught as though they had reached the same levels of attainment in reading or possessed identical instructional needs. Each child must be given material that is as nearly suitable to his level of reading growth as is possible. The child must be taught by methods compatible with his characteristics and capabilities. For him, those phases of reading instruction that demand immediate attention must be emphasized. Reading instruction, to be effective, must proceed on an individual basis.

The teacher, however, is teaching a class and not just one child. It is her responsibility to organize instruction so that a class may be taught as a community, with all of its members engaged cooperatively in educationally worthwhile activities. At the same time, instruction must be adjusted to meet the needs and characteristics of individuals. It must be organized so that, for at least part of the time, the teacher is free to devote attention to those children needing special guidance. Adjusting instruction to individual differences in large classes is probably the most difficult instructional problem faced by the teacher.

Improved Methods and Materials

Fortunately, today's teachers are better prepared to adjust instruction to individual differences in reading than were teachers in the past. As a result of research and classroom practice, the teacher of today is equipped with more and better teaching techniques. The teacher is an effective caring professional who realizes that reading growth is developed gradually over the years in an orderly, systematic manner and is facilitated by businesslike, energetic, and organized instruction.

Today's teachers are more aware of the individual instructional needs of children than were teachers of the past because there is an ever-increasing diversity of instructional needs in every classroom. Fortunately, children's individual needs can be diagnosed far better today than formerly. As a result, many serious reading problems are prevented, and those reading problems that do develop are corrected more successfully. It is also true that more information is available to teachers so that they may adjust instructional programs to meet the known needs of the class.

Basic reading programs, supplementary reading materials, and library and media center materials, as well as opportunities to work with computers and other special equipment, provide the resources needed for carefully planned systematic instruction and for attention to individual needs.

Reasons for Increased Attention to Differences in Reading

The contemporary teacher is better equipped to adjust instruction to individual differences than was the teacher of the past. There are several reasons why this is good. First, awareness of the importance of education and of reading ability in modern society has caused a greater concern for the reading capability of the growing child than there has ever been before. Second, children who have difficulty reading are no longer allowed to drop out of school. Every child who enters the first grade is expected to go on developing reading proficiency up to the level of her capabilities as the child progresses through the elementary and secondary schools. Third, because the great majority of children progress through secondary education, reading ability is no longer used as the sole criterion for promotion. Children now, for the most part, are promoted in school so that they will be with other children of their own age, interests, and stage of development. This policy, in some respects, makes the problem of adjusting reading instruction to individual differences more difficult. Fourth, improved instruction has increased the need for adjusting instruction to individual rates of growth. The only way to make children equal in reading ability is not to teach any of them. Then they would all have the same stature in reading—none of them would be able to read. But instruction that allows each child to grow as rapidly as she is able encourages differences in reading capability. Under improved instruction, a wide range of reading ability can be expected at any grade level. It would be unrealistic to expect children with divergent interests, with different backgrounds, and with unequal linguistic ability, physical stamina, hearing ability, vision, and intellect to grow at the same rate in a complicated set of skills and abilities such as those used in learning to read.

Range in Reading Ability to Be Expected

At any grade level, then, it is reasonable to expect that there will be a wide range in reading ability. In the fifth grade, for example, it is quite normal to find a 6- or 7-year difference between the least and the most competent reader. This range of reading ability within a fifth-grade class cannot and should not be prevented, but it must be recognized and adjustments must be made.

Failure to adjust the material and the instruction to the range of reading capabilities found within the classroom is a major cause of reading difficulties. This failure limits the usefulness of the printed page as a tool of learning throughout the curriculum. The teacher must know how to make appropriate adjustments in class organization and in instruction to meet the range of reading talent and the variety of instructional needs.

Every teacher is aware that children grow in reading capability at different rates and that in any class there is a wide range of reading capabilities. Teachers know that there is a vast difference in the difficulty of a paragraph that can be read and understood by the most able and the least able within the class. Teachers know that some children read extensively and that others read very little. They know that many children initiate their own reading activities and that others must be urged to read. They know that some read books of high quality and others appear to be satisfied with relatively immature writing. They are aware that some children read broadly and others confine their readings to a single type or to what satisfies a single interest.

It is little wonder that children grow at different rates. A child learns to read with his eyes, ears, energy, background of experience, interests, drives, emotional stamina, and intelligence. Any differences found within children in any of these traits will affect the rate at which they learn to read. Teachers know that it is quite normal for children to have differences in auditory acuity, in physical stamina, and in intelligence. The problem of adjusting to individual differences is one of recognizing these differences and their varying rates of growth and, thus, of adjusting materials and instruction so that the child may be an energetic, comfortable learner absorbed in the learning situation. The instructional program should allow the child neither to dawdle nor to be placed in situations that are so difficult that the child may become confused and discouraged.

Most teachers quickly recognize that individual differences in reading exist within their classroom. Teachers are also aware that each child varies in his own reading capabilities. They know that just because a certain child excels in reading and understanding science, it does not necessarily follow that the same child will also excel at oral reading of poetry. It is often evident that a child, by grasping the overall meaning of a sentence, is able to recognize unfamiliar words, even though his knowledge of phonics remains limited. Another child may have a high degree of independence in working out words but is unable to group them into thought units. The extent of these variations, the ways of diagnosing them, and the importance of making adjustments for individual differences are frequently not fully understood.

Figure 2–1 illustrates the range of reading abilities found within selected classrooms at various grade levels for students whose reading instruction was the responsibility of the classroom teacher. As the graph shows, the range of reading capabilities increases as students progress through school. The total range between the best and the poorest reader in the second-grade class is 2 years and 5 months. In the third grade the range is 3 years and 6 months, in the fourth grade 4 years and 8 months, in the fifth grade 6 years and 1 month, and in the sixth grade 7 years. At the secondary school level, the range of reading becomes very large indeed. These data approximate the range of reading abilities that is usually found and that the teacher must be prepared to handle at the various grade levels.

Probably the most important information about a typical class is *the great range in reading talent that is to be found in the upper and lower third of the class.* Also, the fact that the middle third is relatively homogeneous in reading capability is important. In Grade 5, for example, the difference between the best and the poorest reader in the upper third of the distribution is spread over about 2 years and 6 months. Some members of this upper third will find themselves comfortable with books suited to typical students halfway through the fifth grade, while others can profitably read books appropriate to the early months of Grade 8.

The problem of adjusting to this wide range of reading capabilities makes it important for the teacher to diversify instruction for the superior readers. Similarly, the lowest third of a fifth-grade class has a great range of reading abilities— about 2 years and 5 months. A few of the pupils in this third will find material suited to the typical beginning second-grader somewhat difficult. Others within this lowest third will profitably read material suited to pupils halfway through

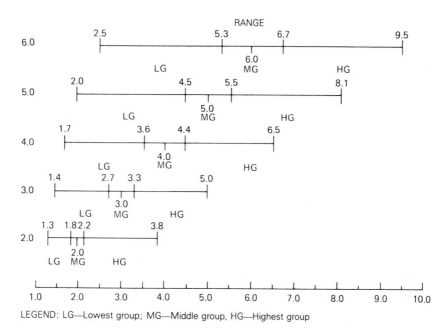

LEGEND: LG—Lowest group; MG—Middle group, HG—Highest group

FIGURE 2–1   Range of Reading Ability Found in Selected Classrooms of Grades 2 through 6 at the Beginning of the School Year

the fourth grade. Thus, the lowest group also needs diversification of instruction to meet its wide range of reading capabilities.

The problems of adjusting instruction to fit the large range of reading capabilities found in the upper third and in the lowest third of a fifth-grade class are, however, quite different. The pupils in the upper third of the distribution are competent, independent readers, and the teacher, in adjusting to their individual differences, can depend upon their proficiency and their independence. Adjustment to the large range found in the lowest third of the distribution is complicated by the fact that these pupils are somewhat less than competent and are not independent readers at all. The problem is still more difficult in planning for the poorer readers because there are not as many reading materials suitable to their age and interest level or to their reading level. The teacher is fortunate that superior readers are easily guided to select materials suitable to their reading abilities, interests, and intellectual capabilities.

Most teachers who use grouping to adjust to individual differences vary the number of pupils in the reading groups. A teacher might make the middle group the largest because it is more homogeneous than the other groups, the advanced group next largest because it is more independent, and the lowest group quite small because it needs closer diagnosis and more help.

Basic Considerations in Adjusting to Individual Differences in Reading

The problem of adjusting to the wide range of reading capabilities resulting from the different rates of growth found in any classroom has many dimensions. Each of these dimensions must be considered in formulating programs for adjusting to individual differences in reading. Among the more important facts to be considered when formulating an instructional approach are the following:

1. Children are alike in many ways.
2. Children develop in ways other than in reading attainment.
3. Children's development in reading is not always uniform.
4. Reading is a complex learning process.
5. Adjustments to individual differences change through the grades.
6. Adjustments to individual differences change according to the type of reading performed.
7. Adjustments to individual differences change with changes in school organization.
8. Adjustment to individual differences must be realistic in the time required.
9. Teachers' energy and time for preparation must be considered.

These facts must be recognized in formulating classroom organization and procedures to adjust to individual differences in reading. They are so crucial that neglecting any one of them limits the adequacy of the adjustment. Quite obviously, an adjustment that so dissociates one child from another so that learning is no longer a shared experience is unwise, an approach that takes more of the teacher's time in preparation than is reasonable must be rejected, and a method that freezes a child in a less advanced group so that she cannot advance if her rate of learning accelerates cannot be recommended. Adjustments to individual differences in reading, then, must recognize and provide for the many dimensions of the problem.

Children Are Alike in Many Ways

A program of adjustment to individual differences in reading must recognize the similarities as well as the differences among children. Each child in the classroom is an important individual. Each child has many drives, motives, and desires. Children of any given age are likely to be interested in many of the same things. Each child in a class needs to be recognized as an important member of the classroom community. The poor reader, as well as the good one, must have friends and be an integral part of the class, must make contributions to the class, and must not be forced into a position of inferiority. Every child should be helped to preserve feelings of personal worth. All children need to feel that they are progressing and continually becoming better readers, even though some may recognize that their rate of growth in reading is somewhat slower than that of other children. When each child is of recognized personal worth, each will have a feeling of confidence, security, and well-being that will encourage comfortable and efficient growth in reading for all children.

Children Develop in Ways Other than in Reading Attainment

Any adjustments must take into account the many characteristics of child growth and development besides level of attainment in reading. Children are changing in physical size, in social adaptability, and in interests. They are developing proficiencies in many skills and abilities.

It is sometimes suggested that within a school system, children could be grouped placing all those with the same reading needs in the same classroom. The teacher could then use more uniform approaches in teaching them. The problem with this grouping plan is that differences between children within classrooms would soon become apparent. The children might be equal in reading capability at the onset of instruction, but they would soon become heterogeneous. The differences in rates of reading growth would show up almost immediately. Moreover, children grouped according to reading ability would not be similar in many other characteristics. There would be almost as great a range in chronological age within a group classified according to reading ability as there is now in reading ability among children classified according to chronological age. Methods of adjustment, then, that place children of different ages and interest levels within the same classroom are unfortunate. Programs of adjustment that keep children, as nearly as possible, with others at their own levels of *overall* development are the ones that are most likely to succeed. Adjustment to individual differences in reading will have to be done in ways other than homogeneous grouping according to reading ability at any level of instruction.

Childrens' Development in Reading Is Not Always Uniform

Any adjustment that does not provide for moving the child from one group to another is unwise. One child, for example, may find reading a very difficult undertaking at the outset, but as the child progresses, his rate of growth may be accelerated. This child may have high general intelligence but be limited in auditory acuity. At the beginning, the child would find the establishment of word-recognition techniques somewhat difficult. As a result, his growth in reading would be slow. But as the program advanced and as the role of reasoning became increasingly important, his rate of growth in reading would accelerate. Another child might start out being relatively good in the reading program, as long as building basic sight vocabulary and word-recognition techniques was the important determinant of success. But if this child was somewhat limited in the more complex reasoning abilities, such as the ability to make accurate judgments and to visualize what is read, his rate of growth would taper off as the program, at more mature levels, began to emphasize these abilities.

The correlation between intelligence and reading ability at the end of the first grade is approximately .50 (Bond & Dykstra, 1967). The relationship rises through the grades (Rubin, 1982, p. 50), to approximately .70 at the upper elementary level and .80 at the high school level. To the extent that organization within the classroom allows the child to grow comfortably and energetically in reading, and remains flexible enough to adjust to varying rates of growth, progress can be optimized.

Reading Is Complex Learning

Reading ability is not a specific or single attribute. It is made of a hierarchy of many skills and abilities, attitudes, and tastes. A well-rounded basic reading program encourages relatively uniform growth in the many components of reading ability. Nonetheless, a study of reading profiles indicates that no child develops skills, abilities, attitudes, interests, and tastes in the same manner. There will be marked differences in degree of maturity of reading development in the various outcomes of reading instruction.

A fifth-grade child, for example, may show as great a difference as 3 or 4 years between her most mature reading capability and her least mature one. She may have a high degree of proficiency in using word-recognition techniques, but her ability to read or to understand the fundamental idea in a selection may be relatively immature. Or the child may, given an unlimited amount of time, be able to work out words independently as well as the usual seventh grader, while her efficiency in understanding what the passage is about may only be equal to that of the beginning third grader. Another child may be relatively efficient in reading material of the narrative type, but may be relatively inefficient in reading expository materials in particular content areas. Uneven profiles of reading, produced by the complex nature of learning, are unfortunate and indicate the need for corrective work.

The child is rare whose areas of best and worst performances in the complex task of learning to read are separated by less than a year. The reading program must be flexible enough to adjust to the differences in reading capabilities found in the individual child. The program cannot be so formalized that the adjustments cannot vary according to the type of reading done at a given time. The child who has difficulty understanding the general idea of a passage should get considerably more emphasis on that type of reading than she does on the development of word recognition in the basic program. Similarly, the child who reads narrative text satisfactorily but is poor at reading text from a particular content area must have the level of difficulty of the latter material adjusted to the development of her comprehension abilities and to the application of these to reading material in that area.

A reading program designed to meet the individual needs of children must take into account not only the range of general reading achievement found within a classroom, but also the characteristics of each child's reading growth pattern. Undoubtedly, the complex nature of reading and the resultant unevenness in children's growth in reading make adjusting to individual differences in reading difficult. Teachers who are successful in meeting the individual reading needs of their students must be aware of the reading attainments of each student and must employ teaching methods that allow for individual adjustments.

Adjustments to Individual Differences Change through the Grades

The problem of adjusting to individual differences changes in at least three ways during the school years. First, the range of reading capability found within any classroom increases as the pupils become more and more proficient in reading. Recall that a beginning second-grade class has a range of reading capability of about 2½ years, while a beginning sixth-grade class has a range of approximately 7 years. The range increases at each higher grade level, through high school and beyond. This difference in range does not necessarily mean that the teacher at higher grade levels has more difficult problems adjusting to individual differences than do teachers at lower grade levels. It does mean, however, that there will have to be a greater difference between the levels of difficulty in the materials used. An inspection of the difference between the material that the average fourth grader can read and the material that the average sixth grader can read will not be as apparent as the difference between the material that an average second-grade child can read and the material that a child approximately halfway through the first grade can read. The rate of reading growth during the early grades is very rapid, and the fineness of adjustment required to meet the reading capabilities within a second-grade class is more demanding than the adjustment needed to meet the range of reading capabilities in the sixth grade or beyond.

The second way in which adjustment to individual differences changes through the grades is found in the relative independence of students at the higher levels, as contrasted with children in the second grade. Teachers in the first and second grades have very few who can be called independent readers, while teachers at higher grade levels find an increasing proportion of independent readers. Although there are many independent readers at upper grade levels, this does not mean that adjustment to individual needs is not necessary, but it does mean that teachers can rely more upon individual assignments and small-group activities that can be completed independently of assistance. In the basic reading program, however, in which skills and abilities are developed, the problem of the sixth-grade teacher is similar to that of the second-grade teacher.

The need for basic reading instruction is not diminished as the child advances. The teacher of the intermediate grades must be alert to the need for adjusting to the level of development in each child's reading skills and abilities. The teacher must be aware of the need for adjusting to the child's range of capabilities, of the importance of identifying his reading needs, and of giving systematic instruction to ensure balanced growth. It cannot be overemphasized that a systematic, well-organized program of instruction in reading is essential to the intermediate grades. Incidental reading instruction with, for example, social studies material will not suffice.

Another way in which adjustment to individual differences changes as students progress is in the amount of available and suitable reading material. The teacher in the intermediate grades has more material, at various levels, for the range of reading talent found within these grades than does the primary teacher. The secondary teacher has an even wider range of materials from which to choose. It must be remembered that even the poorest group of readers in a sixth-grade class are just as mature readers as the most competent readers in a beginning second-grade class.

In formulating programs for adjusting to individual differences, it is essential to recognize the changes that occur throughout the school years. It is fortunate that as the range of reading capability increases, the independence of the children in the class is increasing and that there is a wider selection of suitable materials available. It also should be remembered that at all levels of instruction there is an abundance of materials suitable for the capable readers. The problem is difficult only for the poor readers. Fortunately, the number of materials suitable for poor readers increases in the higher grades.

Adjustments to Individual Differences Change According to the Type of Reading Performed

The child, at all levels of advancement, must have at least four types of reading experiences to become a proficient reader. First, the child must progress through a systematic set of reading experiences designed to show her how to read. Second, the child must participate in those reading experiences in which reading is used as an aid in gaining understanding and knowledge within subject matter areas. Third, the child must have reading experiences designed to enhance personal development, interests, and tastes. These are experiences that give broad contacts with children's literature, enhance understanding of self, enlarge awareness of social relationships, and develop aesthetic appreciations. Fourth, the child must have experiences designed to correct reading faults. This phase of the program can be described as reeducative or corrective. There is probably no child who, from time to time, does not have reading faults or who does not need more practice in some reading skill or ability.

The adjustment to individual needs and capabilities in each of these phases of the reading program is a different problem. Adjustments suitable for one phase of the reading curriculum are not necessarily good for another. If the child's goal is to develop skills and abilities in reading, the adjustment to individual differences in reading is different than if the goal is to understand content. The goals set by the teacher in these two situations are different. When the teacher is teaching social studies, his primary concern is developing the outcomes of social studies instruction, even though the children are using books for that purpose.

When the teacher is teaching reading, his primary concern must be the development of skills and abilities in reading, even though the children may be reading material of the social studies type in their basic readers. It would be unfortunate if teachers thought that reading skills and abilities could be learned incidentally when the basic purpose is learning the subject matter of any given content area. It would be equally unfortunate if the basic reading program failed to give systematic instruction in the skills and abilities necessary to read materials in those areas.

In sum, adjustment in the four types of reading experience is dictated by the results expected and the use of reading. In the basic reading program, some form of group instruction is advisable. In the second type—reading in other branches of the curriculum—it is desirable for groups of children to work cooperatively on topics within a unit of the curriculum. In reading for personal development, a highly individualized approach emphasizing the "right book for the right child" is most feasible. When children who have similar interests form a reading circle to share comments on the books they are reading, they will expand and enrich their enjoyment of reading.

In the reeducation or corrective phase of the program, the skill that needs attention prescribes the type of instruction needed and who among the children should work together. Much of the controversy over the most effective way to adjust to individual differences stems from the fact that proponents of one type of adjustment over another are actually concerned with one particular phase of the reading program that especially interests them. It should be remembered that the phases are not completely discrete. For example, when the children have a social studies lesson, the teacher may discern that certain of them are having difficulty finding places on a map and may surmise that the cause of their difficulty is that they are ineffective in interpreting the marginal key numbers and letters. The teacher would then call these children aside and reeducate them in the skill needed in map reading. Although this skill was covered in the basic reading program, these children failed to learn it.

Adjustments to Individual Differences Change with Changes in School Organization

As the child progresses through the grades, the school organization changes. The usual type of organization in the primary grades is a self-contained classroom. A single teacher is responsible for learning activities in the primary class. This changes in the intermediate grades. In most school systems, there are special teachers for music, art, physical education, and other specialized areas. In some school systems, there are departmentalized arrangements in which teachers devote their entire day to teaching arithmetic, reading, or some other subject. In most secondary schools, the students have different teachers for each subject.

In the secondary school, understanding a student as fully as is necessary for adjusting to his reading needs is more difficult than in the primary grades. This is so because the secondary school teacher may be teaching as many as 150 different students in five classes for an hour a day, while the primary teacher lives rather closely with some 25 or more children during the day. It is fortunate that reading growth begins when the teacher and children live and work together throughout the entire day, because a detailed understanding of the child's interests, needs, drives, and levels of reading competency is necessary if proper provision for his reading needs is to be made. The application of this detailed information is crucial when the child is a relatively immature and dependent learner.

As stated, differences in school organization can complicate the problem of recommending adjustments to individual differences. In the secondary school, the need for guidance programs to collect information about the students and to see that it reaches the teachers who must make the adjustments has to be fulfilled. This is not so essential a recommendation in the primary grades, for the teacher in this case can observe the children throughout the year.

Adjustment to Individual Differences Must Be Realistic in the Time Required

In considering suitable methods of adjusting to individual differences in reading, the time required becomes exceedingly important. The time that can be devoted to basic instruction in reading, for example, is limited. At all levels of instruction, other learning is taking place during the school day, and the efficient use of time in all school activities is fundamental. Reading is no exception. Those methods of adjustment, then, that make undue demands on either the teacher's instructional time or the class's working time must be rejected. A teacher must organize her class in the most efficient way. She cannot, for example, devote her entire time to developing reading skills and abilities for just one child at the expense of the other members of the class, no matter how urgent the child's need.

Programs that recommend that each child have a different book for her individual needs for basic instruction are unrealistic. It is necessary for the teacher, in developing reading skills and abilities, to introduce the material, to establish purposes, to develop a background, to introduce new vocabulary, to guide reading through pertinent questions, and to discuss the selection after it is read. The new words must be related to previously learned words in order to develop word-recognition techniques, and the selection must be used creatively so that the children feel they have completed the experience. Faced with such instructional demands, it is apparent that the teacher cannot have each child reading a different book while she is teaching the class to develop skills and abilities in reading. There simply would not be enough time. If we assume that the teacher devotes an hour a day to systematic instruction in reading development, she would have somewhat less than 2 minutes in which to accomplish the fundamentals of reading instruction for each different selection that some 25 children were reading.

Because of the time factor, some form of grouping for basic reading instruction is recommended. It must be recognized that even if the class is divided into three groups, each reading a different topic, the teacher who devotes an hour a day to basic reading instruction must divide her time among each of the three groups. Whatever method of adjusting to individual differences in reading is adopted, the efficient use of the teacher's and the class's time must receive careful consideration.

The Teacher's Energy and Time for Preparation Must Be Considered

Methods of adjusting to individual differences and of adopting a class organization must be realistic in their demands on the teacher. Sometimes it is suggested, for example, that teachers prepare the exercises to correct faulty learning or to reinforce skills and abilities that the children have only partially learned. These recommendations are justified. But if the teacher were to prepare materials to meet all of the reeducative or practice needs of a class of 25 pupils, he would need more than a 24-hour day. The use of commercially prepared supplementary materials suitable to the child's level of development is recommended as one means of saving the teacher's energy and preparation time.

In certain methods of group instruction in the basic reading program, the teacher is expected to teach three discrete sections in reading and therefore is expected to make three preparations. These involve the collection of pictures and other means of developing readiness, background, interest, and understanding of word meanings. They also include analyses of the stories or selections to be read by each group and the preparation necessary to develop the specific comprehension abilities and word-recognition techniques for three separate lessons. They entail finding three separate sets of related reading materials and planning three separate activities related to what is being read.

Although there are many plans for adjusting to individual differences in reading, whichever is used, the fact that the teacher is a person whose time and energy are not unlimited must be taken into account. The fact that children like to work and do things cooperatively must also be recognized. It must be remembered when formulating the approach to basic reading instruction that they are growing in many ways other than in reading capability, that their reading development is not necessarily uniform, that reading is very complex learning, and that class time is limited. All these considerations have to be taken into account when planning adjustments to individual rates of growth in reading.

Meeting Individual Differences in Reading

A major responsibility of the school is to help each child develop to the limit of his capabilities. Any failure in the instructional program to adjust to individual differences in reading has two effects: First, failure to adjust materials and methods in reading instruction to the range of reading capabilities found within any classroom impedes growth in reading; second, failure to adjust the difficulty of reading material to the known reading capabilities of individual pupils in the classroom reduces the usefulness of printed material as an aid to learning in all areas. In addition, material that does not challenge the capable learners in the various subject matter areas limits the possibility of superior achievement in those areas for the brighter children and also limits their growth in reading. Exposing the less able readers to materials that are too difficult reduces the usefulness of printed material as an aid to learning for them, and it can cause serious confusions and rejection of reading, thereby causing reading difficulties.

The entire reading curriculum of the children in a classroom must be adjusted to their individual reading capabilities if the printed page is to become an effective tool of learning and if reading problems are to be prevented. A fifth-grade child, for example, who can read material of seventh-grade difficulty with ease and accomplishment should have many reading experiences at that level of difficulty. A fifth-grade child who is unable to read third-grade material comfortably will not accomplish much from holding a fifth-grade book in his hands and staring at it. This child would accomplish much more by reading a book more appropriate to his reading capabilities.

Individual differences in reading must be provided for throughout the curriculum if textual material is to become an effective aid to learning for all the members of the class and if maximum growth in reading is to be achieved. The adjustment of instruction to individual differences in reading is more than just an approach: It is a combination of approaches and adaptations of methods of instruction that encourages individual rates of growth.

The various approaches to meeting individual differences in teaching reading are difficult to discuss and evaluate, because each phase of the reading curriculum has special problems. The basic program in reading is probably the most complex in the curriculum in adjusting to individual differences. This phase of the curriculum must assume responsibility for developing, in an orderly, sequential manner, the skills and abilities needed for success in all other reading activities. Adjustment to individual differences in the basic reading program must be such that there is little chance for gaps in learning, for overemphases resulting in loss of balance among the skills and abilities, and for the persistence of faulty habits with consequent confusion and deterioration of reading progress. When reading is used as an aid to learning, adjusting to individual differences is considerably less complex and resolves itself into bringing children and books together realistically so that the topics under consideration can be studied effectively. In reading for personal development, the problem is still less complex. This phase of the reading curriculum can be individual, with guided reading programs in which children and books are brought together according to each child's level of reading maturity, interests, personal growth, and needs. Neither an orderly sequence of skill development nor the knowledge and understanding of a curricular field needs to be considered. The sole problem here is that of guiding each child into books that can be read comfortably and with pleasure and that develop him as a person.

The importance of finding suitable material for every situation cannot be overemphasized. In all reading, the child must have material that he can read effectively. At times there should be material with which he must struggle, but he must be able to win. In this way, the child will increase stature in reading. More often, the child must read material that causes little or no difficulty. It is through such reading that the child gains fluency and the ability to understand the ideas of the author.

In the basic reading program, the difficulty of the material is ever increasing. As soon as the child is comfortable reading, the difficulty is increased so that the learner is continually challenged. Fortunately, material is introduced well, difficulties are anticipated, and instruction on how to proceed is given.

Material that the child reads independently in other phases of the curriculum should be somewhat less difficult than those in his basic reading program. This is especially true of the guided reading program. The teacher does not have time to give the necessary instruction in reading for 25 different references. The materials for learning subject matter and those for personal development should be at such a level of difficulty that they can be studied and read independently without faulty reading.

There are many ways in which the problem of adjusting to individual differences in the program of basic instruction in reading can be attacked. Many administrative and curricular plans involving schoolwide adjustments have been tried. Some of the better known are *ability grouping* among the classes according to intelligence, reading capability, or average achievement; yearly *retention or advancement* based upon overall educational advancement or reading achievement; *continuous growth* or *ungraded primary* plans in which the child is advanced to a higher reading level upon completion of the current reading program; *team teaching,* which involves a large group of children taught together by several teachers in one large room for many lessons and then separately for reading instruction according to level of advancement; and *special rooms,* where children of like reading maturity are taught reading, but for the rest of the day are in the regular classroom with other children of their own ages. As yet, an adequate solution to the problem has not been found, and maybe it never will be.

Flexible grouping plans are very likely the best and most widely used approaches in adjusting to individual differences in reading. In the basic reading program, in which an orderly introduction of reading skills and abilities is essential and a gradual expansion of vocabulary is demanded, it is likely that for certain parts of the instruction, three reading groups are desirable. There can be no method of promotion or any static method of grouping that will solve the problem. When grouping is flexible, many of the difficulties are avoided, and grouping becomes one of the best single means of individualizing instruction in reading.

Grouping procedures must be flexible in three ways. First, the group formed for basic reading instruction should be used for that phase of the curriculum only, and the children should be regrouped according to need in other phases of the curriculum. Second, the children who need instruction in a certain reading skill or ability should form a temporary instructional group, even if they come from different basic reading groups. Third, a child should be able to move readily from one group to another if he improves in reading ability enough to be better suited to a more advanced group. A child also should be able to move to a less advanced group without stigma if he has been absent or if, for any other reason, he needs to be with a less mature reading group. A child may even meet with two groups for a time.

When the children use reading as an aid to learning subject matter, the class often benefits by working together as well as by working in cooperative interest groups. There is a continuing need for material, differentiated in difficulty, in learning subject matter, so that the individual differences in reading can be met realistically and practically. When reading children's literature, it is often wise to have the entire class working together. A book shared by the teacher or librarian through reading aloud or through a book talk could involve the entire class. In the reeducative phase of the reading program, the entire class might profit from a demonstration of a word-recognition technique and could be taught together.

Instruction with multiple, flexible grouping and with materials that allow each child to participate actively while working with material he can read will do much to allow children to grow in reading at the best rate for each. When adjustments to levels of reading capability are combined with attention to individual needs, the teaching of reading can be adjusted to individual differences. This instruction will do much to prevent minor misunderstandings from accumulating to the point at which the child becomes confused and develops reading difficulties.

This administrative plan for meeting individual differences is designed to give a good teacher a more reasonable chance of making the necessary adjustments. But no matter what arrangement is adopted, the crux of the adjustments lies in the ability of the teacher to diagnose the needs of the children and to be ready to provide whatever corrective help is needed.

Diagnostic Teaching in the Classroom

The effectiveness of diagnostic teaching is based on the extent to which the teacher knows each child within the classroom. In order to attain maximum growth in reading and to avoid confusions in learning, the teacher must be aware of and adjust to each child's capacities, physiological condition, emotional and social adjustments, interests, attitudes, and general level of reading ability.

Besides these personal, cognitive, and physical characteristics, the teacher must know the child's reading development. It is to the child's growth in the specific skills and abilities in reading, above all else, that the instructional program must be geared. Diagnostic teaching is based on an understanding of the *reading* strengths and needs of each child. This knowledge must be used to modify instructional procedures so that teaching, adjusted to the changing needs of the children, can be maintained. Such teaching centers on continuous diagnosis of the skill development of each child and on flexibility in instruction so that the teacher can alter the general procedures or methods to meet the specific needs of the individual.

One child may find most learning relatively easy, but some difficult and time consuming. Another child may find the knowledge of sound-symbol relationships relatively easy to learn, whereas she may acquire little skill in using meaning clues to recognize words. In the same class with the same instruction, yet another child may quickly develop too much dependence upon meaning clues and too little skill in sound-symbol relationships. Fortunately, most children maintain a rather consistent balance among the essential skills and abilities of reading and need only a small and infrequent amount of attention to maintain growth. Even for these children, however, the teacher should be alert to neglected skills or knowledge. Sometimes, serious disabilities are simply the result of minor confusions that have been allowed to continue.

Most children maintain consistent, reasonable achievement in reading. These children are helped if the teacher recognizes their minor deviations from effective, balanced reading growth and gives added or modified instruction to overcome any faulty or inadequate learning. Some children require more careful and continuous diagnosis than do others. Children who have more complex difficulties learning to read make up only a small percentage of those being taught. Usually there are no more than 2 or 3 in a classroom of 25 children. In these instances, more thorough and time-consuming appraisals may be needed. Such children may also require a more intensive program of remediation. Some of their difficulties may be too time consuming or too complex to be diagnosed and corrected by the classroom teacher. However, a thorough diagnosis of a particular child's reading problem, accompanied by an *appropriate individual educational plan of remediation* made by a reading specialist, will enable the classroom teacher to correct the difficulty without interfering with the progress of the rest of the class. In other cases, the child can be served best in a reading center. These are decisions that must be made cooperatively by the classroom teacher and the reading specialist.

Every child's reading growth must be appraised continuously if her progress is to be at a high level and if any confusion is to be detected before the more stubborn problems develop. Work samples, always present in the day-by-day teaching and learning activities of a class, enable the expert teacher to gain familiarity with each child's needs. More systematic observations may be made through informal diagnosis or standardized testing. In studying the children's reading patterns, the teacher uses many sources of information to decide on the instructional modifications. These sources will be discussed later in the book.

Many teachers keep a diagnostic notebook in which they list the children within each instructional group. As the teacher studies each child's reading pattern, he makes a notation of any reading characteristic that might limit the child's reading growth and of any indication of visual difficulty, auditory limitation, negative attitude, tendency toward fatigue, or anything else he observes. For example, a teacher might notice that one child, poor in comprehension, is a word-by-word reader; another child, good in using analytical skills, is ineffective in using context clues as an aid to word recognition; a third child has a limited meaning vocabulary; another reads rapidly, but with many inaccuracies, because of uncertainty about initial blends and digraphs; still another child reads slowly because he overarticulates as he reads; and another has excellent word-recognition capabilities and is able to comprehend all the details in a passage, but is relatively ineffective in organizing, evaluating, and reflecting on what she has read. The teacher rightly feels that all of these types of problems can be corrected while teaching the group as a whole.

The expert teacher makes individual adjustments in the regular reading lessons. As the children progress through the reading lesson, the teacher has many opportunities to give each one the experiences needed to overcome particular problems.

Knowing the results of all the appraisals, including his daily observations, the teacher is able to modify the general approach to reading so as to adjust instruction. The more diversified the approach, the greater is the opportunity for the teacher to make such adjustments. This may be one reason why combined approaches to reading prove more effective than do narrow programs.

Most reading lessons can be separated into introductory, guided reading, and follow-up phases. During the introductory phase, which includes introducing the lesson, developing concepts and word meanings, introducing unknown word patterns, and setting purposes for reading a selection, instructional adjustments can be made to help children with certain types of reading problems. In the guided silent reading and discussion phase, other types of instructional modifications are possible. During the follow-up phase of teaching the lesson, which includes exercises to develop specific skills and abilities and related recreational and self-selected reading, there are many other opportunities for fulfilling individual needs.

During the introductory phase of teaching a selection, the teacher gives the child who is weak in the use of context clues more opportunities to select, from among the new words being introduced, those that fit the context of oral sentences or those presented on the chalkboard. The teacher gives the child having difficulty with initial blends more opportunities to work on those presentations that emphasize the similarity of initial blends in known and unknown words. The child with a limited meaning vocabulary should discuss the pictures and concepts for clarification of word meanings. She should be encouraged to attend to the meanings of all words introduced, so that the habit of attending to words and their meanings is fostered. When the purposes for reading are being developed, children limited in specific types of comprehension should be given more opportunities to discuss how to read for a specific purpose. The teacher might even adjust the purpose for reading. For example, the child who reads to note details, but is poor in reflecting on what is read, might be asked to read a selection in order to tell in one sentence what it was about or to write a title for it.

During the guided reading and discussion phase, the teacher might call upon the children to relate some of the content of the selection. If there is a misconception, the teacher should use this as an instructional opportunity to correct the faulty reading, instead of calling upon another child for the correct response. The teacher should have the child who made the mistake find the place where the idea was presented and then determine with her how the error came about. In this way, the error could be used to help the child overcome the problem.

In the follow-up phase, the teacher has unlimited scope in adapting to individual needs. In the skill and ability exercises prepared by the teacher, emphasis can be placed where it is needed. In the skill development workbooks, the teacher may excuse a child who depends too much on context clues from those exercises emphasizing their use. Or the word-by-word reader may be excused from word-drill exercises and be encouraged to prepare a conversational selection for reading aloud, stressing reading the selection the way people talk.

Most of these adjustments are made by the classroom teacher who is sensitive to the needs of each child and who makes modifications to correct any confusion before it becomes seriously limiting to the child's future growth. Such a teacher is a *diagnostic teacher*. If this kind of teaching is coupled with a flexible grouping plan, the broad use of children's literature, and a stimulating learning environment in which children feel free to participate and express themselves, the reading program will provide maximum growth for all and will limit the frequency of reading difficulties, because *it is the teacher who makes the difference* in adjusting to individual differences. The classroom teacher, however, cannot be expected to solve all problems in reading instruction. His work must be supplemented, for each child who needs it, with a diagnostic and remedial program. The classroom teacher cannot spend the time necessary to correct the more complex reading problems. Therefore, every school should have the services of a reading specialist. The reading specialist has three responsibilities: being a consultant, a diagnostician, and a remedial teacher. The classroom teacher's responsibilities are to prevent reading problems, to aid in their early detection, and to carry out those corrective procedures appropriate to the classroom. It is our fervent hope that this book will aid both the classroom teacher and the reading specialist in helping all pupils to become more effective readers.

Summary

One of the most complex problems confronting the teacher is that of adjusting instruction to individual differences in reading. The children within any classroom vary greatly in reading maturity, reading habits, intellectual capabilities, and physical characteristics. The teacher must organize the class and the instruction so that each child can work up to capacity. The teachers of today are better equipped, with better professional training, improved materials, and more effective assessment procedures necessary for making adjustments, than were the teachers of the past.

The range of reading abilities found in any classroom is large. The better the instruction and the longer it continues, the greater will be the range in reading achievement. If the instruction is excellent, not only will the average reading performance of the class be raised, but also, the range of reading achievement within the class will become greater. Each succeeding year of instruction increases the range of reading achievement within the class. There will be extensive over-lapping in the reading capabilities found in the various grades. Indeed, there is so much that the teacher, at any grade level, must be able to fulfill the reading needs of the children for grades above and below the one she is teaching. If the teacher organizes the class into three instructional groups, the range within the upper and the lower groups will still be so great that further grouping is required. Adjustment to the upper group is somewhat easier than it is to the lower group because of the reading competence and independence of the children in the upper group and the greater availability of appropriate materials for them.

Among the more important considerations in meeting individual differences in reading are the similarities and differences in children, the nature of individual reading development, the complexities in learning to read, the changes of ap-proach due to differences in curriculum and school organization, the differences at the various grade levels, and the need for realistic use of class time and teachers' energies.

The need for adjusting to individual differences in reading throughout the entire curriculum makes adaptation somewhat more complicated than adjusting to the basic reading program alone. The methods and class organization effective for one type of reading will not always be good for another. The types of reading may be classified roughly as basic instruction in reading, reading and study in other phases of the curriculum, independent personal development or recrea-tional reading, and reeducative or remedial reading. These phases of reading are not completely separate. In general, the approaches to individual differences used in them are different, and much of the controversy over methods stems from the fact that the proponents of one approach over another are emphasizing different phases of reading instruction.

Some approaches that have been tried include retention, curriculum adjust-ment plans, fixed grouping plans, and flexible grouping plans. Among these, the flexible grouping plans, utilizing materials written on many levels of difficulty, seem to have the most promise. Whatever approach is used, the teacher should be sure that groups are not fixed, but can be adjusted to facilitate the outcomes expected from the instruction. Also, the number and size of the groups should be compatible with the maturity and independence of the children. In many in-stances, the groups should be reading about a topic of concern to the entire class, and the best and the poorest readers should have opportunities to work together.

Notwithstanding the type of school and classroom organization used to aid the teacher in adjusting to differences in reading growth, the skill of the teacher is the most important factor. The crux of meeting the individual differences found among children lies in the ability of the teacher to diagnose the needs of the children and to correct their minor confusions in reading before these confusions become major. Even under the best classroom instruction, a limited number of pupils develop reading difficulties that can be solved only by special diagnostic and remedial procedures.

Study Questions

1. Why is adjusting to individual differences important?
2. Why might accommodating individual differences in reading be easier for a teacher in the higher grades than for a teacher in the lower grades, even though the range of reading achievement is much greater as the students reach the higher grades?
3. If students were grouped according to their reading achievements, why would individual differences still be an important concern?
4. What are the four types of reading experiences necessary for proficient reading? For each type, describe a whole-class and a small-group activity that would provide a helpful reading experience.
5. Why should children be grouped for reading instruction?
6. What is a diagnostic teacher?

Selected Readings

Gillet, J. W., & Temple, C. (1990). *Understanding reading problems: Assessment and instruction* (3rd ed.) (pp. 1–8). Glenview, IL: Scott Foresman.

Harris, A. J., & Sipay, E. R. (1990). *How to increase reading ability* (9th ed.) (pp. 117–149). New York: Longman.

Jewell, M. G., & Zintz, M. V. (1986). *Learning to read naturally*. Dubuque, IA: Kendall/Hunt.

National Institute of Education. (1985). *Becoming a nation of readers*. Washington, DC: Author.

Rupley, W. H., & Blair, T. R. (1989). *Reading diagnosis and remediation* (3rd ed.) (pp. 3–17). Columbus, OH: Merrill.

Chapter 3

Description of Children with Reading Disabilities

Most children grow in reading in a reasonable fashion, with a relatively desirable pattern of reading abilities. Their reading achievement is, in general, consistent with their overall learning capability. These children's instructional needs can be met effectively by the classroom teacher using the approaches suggested in Chapter 2 for adjusting to individual differences in reading. There are some children, however, whose reading growth is so atypical, so different from that of the usual child, that they may be said to have a reading disability. These children constitute an instructional challenge. Often, the classroom teacher can assess their disability and give them the corrective or reeducative help that they need, so that they can continue to progress in reading. At other times, these children become so confused that they require more time for individual help than the classroom teacher can devote to them. In both instances, the nature and severity of the disability determine whether or not individual help is warranted.

In considering the nature of a reading disability, it is necessary to isolate the group of children to be discussed, define them, explain the characteristics that set them apart from the general population, and describe the categories into which they fall.

The child with a reading disability cannot be described as one whose reading ability is below his achievement in other school subjects. Although some such readers can be so described, the majority will be low both in reading and in general achievement. This is true because poor reading ability so limits other achievement, that it is the rare child who can attain success in school in spite of having a reading disability. It also is important to note that the child who is low in both reading and general achievement may or may not have a reading disability. A child may be poor in reading and poor in the other school subjects for reasons other than a disability in reading.

The child who has a reading disability jeopardizes his educational career. Not only is the child's educational growth impeded, but frequently, his reading patterns are so confused that future growth in reading becomes improbable. Such a child is ineffective in using print as an aid to learning. He is often a discouraged student who thoroughly dislikes reading. In many cases, he becomes so frustrated over his inability to read that his personal adjustment suffers. He may feel quite anxious while reading or may sometimes demonstrate maladaptive adjustment in general.

Alberto illustrated his dislike of reading when he said, "I don't want to read about a boy that has a boat. I want to have one myself." Many children who have trouble reading complain about the material not meeting their needs, but when they can read the same material with ease, they find a new interest.

Amy displayed a functional disorder when it became apparent that she could not read even for 2 or 3 minutes without developing a headache and an upset stomach. She claimed to have eye trouble, although this could not be detected by thorough examination. She would work on puzzle-type material and numbers for long periods of time with no signs of visual discomfort or stomach unrest. After she attained success in reading by careful, individually planned work based on a complete diagnosis, she showed no signs of her former disorders. Not all children who both read poorly and have poor personal adjustment can be said to be that way as a result of poor growth in reading. Sometimes the child is disturbed for other reasons, and reading suffers along with other achievements.

Typically, the child with a reading disability is a child of intellectual capability who has (for reasons to be discussed in the chapters that follow) failed to grow in reading. The child is not living up to potential as a learner in reading. He is likely to be ineffective in all that is expected in school and may reject reading, become discouraged, acquire maladaptive adjustment patterns, and become increasingly less able to learn. He is in need of educational help.

Identifying Children with Reading Disabilities

The problem confronting us here is different from the one discussed in the preceding chapter. The identification of children with reading disabilities is much more complicated than sectioning a class into reading groups or even finding the right level at which to start instruction for each child in a class. A reading test alone is not enough to identify these children in a school. There are many poor readers in every class who cannot be classified as having a reading disability, and there are some seemingly adequate readers who nonetheless do have such a disability. Therefore, we must discuss the factors that need to be considered in order to determine whether a pupil has a reading disability or is just a poor reader.

Opportunity to Learn

The child who is classified as having a disability must be distinguished from the child who has not had an opportunity to learn. If we did not take into account the opportunity a child has or does not have to learn, we would have to say that nearly all children have a reading disability before they enter the first grade. Although, at that time, it is true that their ability to find meaning in the printed page is negligible and in no way in keeping with their ability to listen, they cannot have a reading disability, because they have not yet been taught to read. They have had no opportunity to learn. They may have a relatively large listening vocabulary, but the typical child entering the first grade cannot read many more words than her own name. Most children, for example, cannot read the word STOP if it is taken off the octagonal sign on which they are accustomed to seeing it. They seem to have had the opportunity to learn, because there has always been printed matter before them. But they did not receive systematic, organized instruction, so, in reality, they have not had the opportunity to learn. Even though the child entering the first grade is not able to read as well as she can listen, she does not have a reading disability, because she is doing as well as could be expected of her.

The older child who has come from a non-English-speaking country to the United States would not be considered to have a reading disability either, even though he does have an instructional problem. He may need to start learning to read elementary English, but he cannot be said to have a reading disability. He should have material different from that for the 6-year-old beginner, and he will need special methods of instruction. But he does not have a reading disability. He is a child who cannot read English because he did not have the opportunity to learn.

The lack of opportunity to learn is even more complicated than is indicated in the case of the child who has not yet entered school or is non-English speaking. Some children will be poor in reading in comparison to their other intellectual achievements because they did not start to learn to read as early as they started other verbal learnings. A gifted child, for example, who is just entering the third grade may have the verbal facility of the usual sixth-grade child. However, he could not be expected to read as well as a typical sixth-grade child, because he has received reading instruction for only 2 years, while his general language has developed over a period of 8 years.

Verbal Competency

The listening ability of a child is frequently used to indicate the level at which we can expect her to read. If a child has a superior listening vocabulary, she may be expected to read at a higher level than can other children of her age. If the child is able to understand paragraphs of more than usual difficulty read aloud to her, she should be able to read better than those children who have less listening ability. The child's verbal ability is measured by a test such as listening comprehension on the Diagnostic Reading Scales (Spache, 1981).

There are two considerations the diagnostician must recognize in using the child's general verbal competence as an indicator of the reading level she can be expected to attain. The first is that it may not be safe to assume that a child who is low in both reading and verbal ability does not have a reading disability. Poor performance on listening comprehension tests may indicate that the child has had one avenue of developing verbal ability closed to her. A child, for example, who has been a poor reader from the first grade to the sixth will not have had an opportunity to develop language equal to that of a peer who has always been a good reader. In general, poor readers will not have had as much experience with words, because they have not read as widely as good readers (Siegel, 1989a; Torgesen, 1989). Nor will they have had as much experience understanding paragraphs.

Children with reading disabilities have been found to score lower on the verbal scale of the Wechsler Intelligence Scales (Revised) than they do on the performance scale (Brock, 1982; Moore & Wielan, 1981; Nichols, Inglis, Lawson, & MacKay, 1988; Roberts, 1983). These findings could indicate either that these children have native limitations in verbal ability compared with their general intelligence and are therefore poor readers (Bowers, Steffy, & Tate, 1988; Leong, 1989) or that they are limited in developing language because they are poor readers and therefore lack verbal experience. Data presented by Nichols et al. (1988) confirming a progressive deterioration in verbal ability, but not nonverbal ability, among 224 poor readers suggest the latter, as do results obtained by Sinatra (1989) from his study of 14 disabled readers. An able child who is a poor reader cannot be expected to develop as extensive a vocabulary and other verbal abilities as can a good reader. Accordingly, the use of a discrepancy between verbal ability and reading level as a criterion in diagnosing reading disabilities might classify certain children as merely verbally inept, although, in truth, they have a reading disability and would benefit from remedial instruction.

The second problem in using a discrepancy between verbal ability and reading level to classify a child as a disabled reader is that it does not take into account the opportunity the child has or has not had to learn. Two children, for example, may have the same measured verbal ability. One, however, is only a second-grade child, while the other is a sixth-grade child. The second grader has had only 1 year of reading instruction, while the other child has had 5. The younger child cannot be expected to read as well as the older child, who has had five times as much reading instruction, even though they measure the same on an oral vocabulary test or a test of ability to understand paragraphs read aloud.

Verbal competency certainly should be one consideration in classifying a child as having a reading disability, but it will often mislead the teacher or diagnostician if used as the only criterion. The length of time in school and the opportunity to learn to read must also be considered. The accuracy of the estimate of verbal aptitude also must be taken into account if all the children who are in need of specific help in reading are to be located and if a child is not to be misjudged.

In identifying the child with a reading disability, teachers often compare the child's reading achievement with his degree of success in subjects requiring a minimum of reading. Frequently, arithmetical computation is used as one subject in which success is less influenced by reading achievement. If the child is doing well in arithmetic and poorly in reading, the child is likely to have a reading disability. Such information adds to the accuracy of locating children with reading disabilities, rather than poor readers who are doing almost as well as can expected.

Success in fields that do not require much reading does indicate in most cases how well children are able to apply themselves to learning situations other than reading. If they are not motivated to achieve, they are likely to show ineffective learning in those fields as well as in reading. If they have limited ability to learn, they will also do poorly in those fields as in reading. But when children are successful in such fields, yet have difficulty reading, they are likely to be able, motivated children who have reading disabilities because of faulty learning. These children can usually be helped a great deal by remedial instruction in reading. Although success in fields that require minimal reading is insufficient evidence by itself to classify children as having a reading disability, it is often used as one fact to be considered in making such a classification.

Monroe (1932), also cited in Harris and Sipay (1990, pp. 171–172), used arithmetic achievement as one of the criteria for selecting children who would profit from remedial instruction in reading. She used a reading index (R.I.) to find those children who were farther behind in reading than was reasonable to expect. The index was determined by using the child's average reading age (R.A.), chronological age (C.A.), arithmetic age (A.A.), and mental age (M.A.). The reading index (R.I.) can be calculated with the formula

$$R.I. = \frac{R.A.}{(C.A. + M.A. + A.A.) \div 3}$$

Experience shows that a child with a reading index of 0.80 or below practically always has a reading disability. Those with indexes between 0.80 and 0.90 tend to be borderline. Some of the latter will need remedial instruction, while others will not. All of those who are borderline should be tested further to see whether irregularities in their reading profiles indicate serious problems.

Mental Ability

Mental ability is related to reading achievement. The mere fact that the child has high intellectual ability does not itself guarantee that she will be successful in reading, especially in the early years. Nor does the fact that a child has trouble in reading indicate that the child is mentally limited. Evidence shows that the relationship between intelligence and reading success becomes greater when populations are sampled at successively higher grade levels (Bond & Dykstra, 1967; Rubin, 1982, p. 50). The relationship ranges from approximately .50 at the end of the first grade to .80 at the high school level. Torgesen (1989) reports relationships between word reading and intelligence of about .40 for children in first through third grade and of about .80 for children in fourth through sixth grade. These correlations indicate that factors in addition to mental age influence a child's success in reading. Some children, who begin relatively slowly in the primary grades, later increase their rate of learning and surpass some of their contemporaries. Thus, early floundering does not necessarily indicate ultimate reading failure.

These comparative relationships seem reasonable. In the early stages of their reading development, children are concerned with the mechanical aspects of reading. For instance, word-recognition skills lean heavily upon visual and auditory discrimination. In the higher grades, the complexities of reading and study demand fine verbal discrimination, logical reasoning, abstract analysis, and other comprehension skills that require a high level of mental ability. It is not surprising that mental age and reading capability become more and more closely related as the reader progresses into more and more mature materials and reads for more and more mature purposes.

The mental ability of the child is often used as the basic measure with which to compare reading capability in order to judge whether a reading disability exists. The customary method of making this comparison is to use the mental age of the child as the key to reading expectancy. When the child's average reading level is felt to be significantly lower than that appropriate for his mental age, the child is thought to have a reading disability. While undoubtedly, the true mental ability of the child should be used as a basic consideration in classifying a child in this manner, caution is necessary for two reasons: First, the determination of the mental capacity of a poor reader is difficult; second, the problem is complicated by the fact that although mental age is calculated from birth, the child is not introduced to systematic instruction in reading until he is 6 or more years old.

In an attempt to consider chronological age as well as mental age, Harris and Sipay (1980) proposed the following formula for reading expectancy age:

$$\text{Reading Expectancy Age (R Exp A)} = \frac{2MA + CA}{3}$$

Thus, using a division process, one can compare a child's present reading level with his expected reading level, to assess whether or not the child has a reading disability.

Assessing Mental Age

Among the many types of tests that may be used to assess mental age, four are common: group verbal mental tests, group nonverbal mental tests, individual verbal mental tests, and individual performance mental tests. Each of these tests has its advantages and limitations. In classifying a child as having a reading disability, the particular test used must be considered carefully.

Group Verbal Mental Tests.   These are of little use in selecting children who will profit from remedial work in reading. They are, to a great extent, reading tests, and therefore, the poor reader cannot demonstrate her true mental ability. Clymer (1952) has shown that at the fifth-grade level, certain group intelligence tests give no valid measure of the mental ability of the children reading in the lowest 40 percent of the class. To show the extent of misinterpretation possible by the uncritical use of such tests for children with reading disabilities, consider the following example. At the end of kindergarten, Bianca was given an individual intelligence test which indicated that she had an I.Q. of 115. In grade four, she was given a group verbal mental test that assessed her I.Q. as 80. Inasmuch as her reading achievement and general school performance were consistent with the 80 I.Q., no mismeasurement was suspected. She went into junior high school and, in the ninth grade, was given a group verbal mental test. Because of her reading difficulties, Bianca could read neither the questions nor the answers. She marked her answer form mostly by guessing. She received an I.Q. of 56. This result, while somewhat consistent with her scholastic performance, seemed unreasonable to the counselor, so a complete assessment of Bianca was made. When an individual intelligence test was given, the results indicated that she had an I.Q. of 104. Bianca, in reality, had a marked reading disability. Her reading achievement measured at a third-grade level. She had ineffective decoding skills. She could comprehend but little and therefore could not show her true mental ability on a test that required reading.

Group verbal mental tests are often inappropriate for making comparisons between reading growth and mental growth. The one advantage to such tests is that they can be given to large groups. The results are useful in making comparisons among typical students. But they are worse than worthless in the case of poor readers, because the results are often considered accurate.

Group Nonverbal Mental Tests.   These tests can be used as a criterion for determining reading expectancy. They can be given to large groups and therefore save a great deal of testing time. They are useful in identifying children who have a notable discrepancy between their mental age and their reading age. Although these tests are paper-and-pencil tests, they do not require reading matter as a means of presenting the items on them. Therefore, the child with a reading disability can take them unhampered by his poor reading. The major difficulties with these tests are two: First, they are not as accurate in measurement as is desirable for individual diagnosis; second, they do not appear to measure the type of mental ability needed for success in reading. They are, to some degree, performance tests rather than tests of reasoning ability. Nonetheless, they have merit as screening tests and can be administered by the classroom teacher, thus saving testing time. When a reading disability is suspected, however, the results should be checked by more accurate, individual tests.

Individual Verbal Mental Tests. These are the most suitable measures of mental growth to be used with children with reading disabilities. The Wechsler Intelligence Scale for Children, Revised (WISC-R), and the revised Stanford-Binet Intelligence Scale are popular and useful tests of this type. They give an accurate measure of mental ability for able readers and have been shown to be affected only slightly by the lack of reading ability of children with reading disabilities.

Individual Performance Mental Tests. These tests are useful in diagnosing certain types of reading problems. They aid in measuring the mental ability of children who are hearing impaired, those who have marked oral-expressive problems, and those who have other handicaps. They have the same limitations as other individual tests, being time consuming and requiring trained examiners. Also, they do not fully consider the verbal aspects of intellectual growth.

Relating Mental Growth to Reading Expectancy

The problem of relating a child's mental growth to reading growth in order to estimate the level at which the child should be able to read is a complicated one. The usual way in which this judgment is made is to consider that the child should have reached a reading age or grade roughly comparable to her mental age or grade. Then, if the child's reading grade is significantly lower than her mental grade, the child is classified as having a reading disability. The amount of discrepancy between reading grade and mental grade considered significant increases as the child grows older. In the primary grades, from one-half to three-quarters of a grade difference is taken to be enough to classify the child that way. In the intermediate grades, a difference of 1 to $1\frac{3}{4}$ grades is used. Thus, a second-grade child whose mental grade is 2.8 and whose reading grade is 2.2 would be thought to have a reading disability. Similarly, in the second grade, a very able child whose mental grade is 4.0 and whose reading grade is 3.4 would also be considered to have such a disability. There is a serious question, however, as to whether this latter conclusion is justified.

For example, the child with an I.Q. of 150 who enters the first grade at age 6.5 cannot be expected to read at a 4.3 grade level, even though that would be about her mental grade. As a matter of fact, this child would be able to read little, if anything, because she has not yet been taught. The child has had no real opportunity to learn to read.

There are many possible ways of using the general intelligence of the child as a yardstick against which to judge reading growth. The results of mental tests in classifying a child as having a reading disability have been used with the mental age or grade as the level at which the child is expected to read. Most studies of overachievement and underachievement have used the mental age criterion to estimate who were the good and who were the poor achievers. These studies universally found that bright children underachieve and dull children over-achieve in comparison to their mental age.

The assumption that a child should be achieving up to his mental age thus needs careful inspection. Although it is true that certain kinds of learning, such as listening or speaking vocabulary, can be so judged, other learning cannot be expected to be related in the same way. The child with a 150 I.Q. who is 10 years old has a mental age of 15. This means that he should, for example, on the basis of his mental grade, be doing mathematics equal to that of about a tenth grader instead of a fifth-grade child. But it is doubtful if such a child would know algebra and geometry, because the child has not yet met them. Reading achievement acts in much the same way.

Systematic instruction in reading is usually not begun before the first grade. The typical child, regardless of I.Q., has little if any measurable reading ability when starting the first grade. At this time, the child would be said to read at the 1.0 grade level. If we assume that the I.Q. is, in one respect, an index of rate of learning, we can estimate the reading potential of each child by means of the *reading expectancy* formula:

$$\left(\frac{\text{I.Q.}}{100} \times \text{years of reading instruction}\right) + 1.0 = \text{Reading Expectancy}$$

The 1.0 is added because the child who is just starting to learn to read is given a 1.0 grade score, and after 1 year of instruction the typical child will be classified as a 2.0 reader.

By this formula, the typical child with an I.Q. of 70 could be expected to read at the level of 1.7 at the end of 1 year of instruction, and at the end of 2 years of reading instruction, she should read at the 2.4 grade level. Still using the same formula, the child with a 100 I.Q. would be expected to read at the 3.0 grade level after 2 years of reading instruction, and the able child with a 150 I.Q. would be expected to read at 4.0. At the end of 3½ years, a child with a 130 I.Q. could be expected to read at a 5.6 grade level [(130/100 × 3.5) + 1.0 = 5.55]. To the extent that all other elements that influence reading success are favorable, she could learn somewhat faster, thus exceeding her reading expectancy. If, on the other hand, these other conditions were unfavorable, she would not read up to her expectancy level and might even be so far behind that she would be considered to have a reading disability.

Experience and research have shown the foregoing formula to be surprisingly accurate in estimating the potential reading ability of the typical child. As can be seen, the formula is easy to calculate, but the following considerations should be kept in mind:

1. The time of reading instruction is the number of years and months in school from the time systematic reading instruction was started. This typically begins with first grade. (Some slower learning children may have a delay of a year or so in starting to learn to read.)

2. Readiness training in kindergarten is not counted, even though such instruction does much to diminish the chances of disabilities from occurring once reading instruction has started.
3. If an I.Q. obtained from a Binet or Wechsler intelligence test is not available, it is suggested that a Slosson Intelligence Test given by the teacher or a group performance intelligence test score be substituted temporarily.

We must now consider the extent of the discrepancy between the child's reading expectancy grade level and actual average reading grade that would indicate that he is a disabled reader. Table 3–1 shows that this discrepancy increases grade by grade. In the first grade, for example, 1 half-year is a sufficiently large difference between reading expectancy and reading achievement to indicate a serious problem. Even children who are three-tenths of a year lower in reading achievement than we would expect them to be are considered seriously enough behind to be studied further as possibly having a disability. At Grade 7 or above, the difference must be 2 or more years to be classified as a disability, and there must be a 1.3- to 2-year lag to indicate a possible disability if supported by other evidence.

A child of superior intellect with a possible reading disability may appear to be progressing reasonably well in reading in comparison with the other children in her grade. The child may appear, for example, to be an efficient reader of third-grade material, even though she is only just finishing the second grade. Her achievement in reading in comparison with her reading expectancy would place her in the region of doubt (possibly having a disability), but not significantly low enough to classify her as disabled. A study of her reading skill development might show irregularities, indicating that she was using faulty skills that, if allowed to persist, would limit her at more advanced levels.

Many reading disabilities that could have been discovered early do not become apparent until faulty reading techniques have become so entrenched that they interfere with reading at a more mature level. The tasks involved in reading change as materials become more difficult in structure and content and increasing demands are placed upon the reader. A reader's dependence upon the use of

TABLE 3–1   Discrepancies Between Reading Expectancy and Achievement That Indicate Disability at Each Grade Level

GRADE SCORE DISCREPANCY	GRADE IN SCHOOL						
	1	2	3	4	5	6	7 and Above
Indicating Disability	0.5 or more	.66 or more	.75 or more	1.0 or more	1.5 or more	1.75 or more	2.0 or more
Indicating Possible Disability	.3–.5	.4–.66	.5–.75	.7–1.0	.9–1.5	1.1–1.75	1.3–2.0

immature skills can preclude the development of more advanced skills, eventually resulting in a reading disability. Yet such a disability might have been avoided easily if faulty reading techniques were identified and corrected early.

The child with a reading disability is, in general, a child who has had an opportunity to learn to read, but who is not reading as well as could be expected according to verbal ability, mental capacity, and success in nonreading learnings. She is, in reality, the child who is at the lower end of the reading distribution when compared with other children of the same age and general capability. She is at the lower end for reasons that will be discussed in the chapters that follow. It should be noted, however, that there are other equally capable children who are as far advanced in reading as she is behind. These advanced readers have been fortunate and probably have been favorably endowed in other ways that influence effective reading growth.

Categories of Reading Problems

Children with reading problems can be classified into four categories:

1. *General reading immaturity.* This category is composed of children who are significantly behind in reading, compared with other children of their general reading expectancy. There are no unusual characteristics about their reading patterns. Although these children are immature in reading, there is nothing especially wrong with the reading they do.

Juan, a fifth-grade boy of average intelligence, has always been disinterested in reading. As a result, he has read very little—far less than most of his classmates. Currently, he has great difficulty reading fifth-grade material, but reads third-grade material well and possesses reading skills typical of a normal third-grade child. Juan may be classified in the general reading immaturity group. Many children with reading disabilities show general reading immaturity due to a variety of causes.

Remediation. Instruction should involve giving more experience in reading and systematic instruction at the child's level of reading achievement. These children do not require a reeducation in reading, but they do need adjustment in materials and instruction. If they are asked to read books that are too difficult for them, or if they are not given systematic instruction in reading at their level, they will very likely develop more complex reading disabilities.

2. *Specific reading immaturity.* This classification is used for children who have specific limitations in their reading patterns. For example, Joan is able to read and understand the general significance of paragraphs difficult enough to challenge the reading skill of children of her age and intelligence. She cannot, however, read to follow directions or to organize longer selections. She has acquired general basic reading skills, but she has not learned to adapt them to all her reading purposes.

Remediation.   Instruction should involve specific training in the areas in which the child is weak. Other adjustments will depend on the child's overall reading achievement. Many children with specific reading immaturity read at an acceptable level in general and require few adjustments other than the provision of specific training. Others may require adjusted materials.

3. *Limiting reading disability.* This classification concerns those children with reading disabilities who have serious deficiencies in their basic skills that limit their entire reading growth. Children who have a word-recognition deficiency, limiting mechanical habits, or inability to sense thought units, for example, fall into this category.

David has a limiting disability. He is a capable fifth-grade boy who scores quite low in all types of reading. His intelligence enables him to grasp the significant ideas in a passage relatively well, even though he reads less well for specific detail. His ability to recognize words is even more immature. He often does not recognize words in isolation, although in reading sentences and paragraphs, he does pick up on contextual clues. His basic problem, as detected through his oral reading and written work, appears to involve an inadequate approach to attacking words. This limitation not only is the probable cause of David's reading disability, but also threatens to impede any future growth unless corrected by careful remedial work.

Remediation.   Children in this group need reeducation. Instruction must serve to help them unlearn some of the reading strategies they are currently employing and to teach them some new basic approaches to reading. Often, these children are compensating in an unproductive manner because they failed to learn skills basic to continued reading growth. They need the help of well-planned, systematic remedial programs to correct their faulty reading approaches and to develop the skills that they lack.

4. *Complex reading disability.* This classification is really a subtype of the limiting reading disability. Not only do children with this disability have deficiencies in their reading that limit further growth in reading, but in addition, instructing them in reading is complicated by their negative attitudes toward reading and by their undesirable adjustments to their reading failure. Reeducating these children may be complicated further when they have sensory, physical, or other disabilities.

Remediation.   Children in this group need careful assessment by a team of professionals in order to provide an appropriate remedial program. These children's learning disabilities must be recognized and planned for in order for successful reading remediation to be achieved. Constitutional and environmental factors involved in reading disabilities will be discussed in the next three chapters. Modifications needed in the remedial treatment of complex reading disabilities are discussed in Chapter 13.

Summary

Children with reading disabilities are more than just children who cannot read well. They are children who are not reading as well as could be expected from their intellectual or verbal maturity. No two such children are the same, and it is likely that no two disabilities are caused by the same set of circumstances. Many of these children become discouraged and frustrated when they read.

The classification of a child as having a reading disability, rather than as just a poor reader, must be based upon learning opportunity, verbal ability, achievement in learning situations other than reading, and the child's general mental ability. The mental ability of the child is used most often in assessing reading expectancy. Care must be taken in measuring the mental ability of a child with a reading disability, because most tests require reading ability. For this reason, individual mental tests are the most suitable instruments.

The problem of using mental growth as a means of assessing reading expectancy is a complicated one. The use of mental age or grade as the sole criterion of expected attainment in reading is of questionable validity. A more sensible and useful approach would be to depend on calculations based on number of years of reading instruction and the child's I.Q.

Children with reading disabilities can be grouped into descriptive categories according to the seriousness of the problem they have and the nature of the adjustment needed. General reading immaturity refers to those children whose reading ability is generally immature but otherwise well balanced. Children with specific reading immaturity are low in one or more types of reading, but are competent in basic reading skills and abilities. Children with limiting reading disability are deficient in basic reading abilities that preclude further growth in reading. Children with complex reading disability cannot grow further in reading because of deficiencies in basic reading abilities. Their problems are complicated by additional learning problems such as rejection of reading, accompanying personality problems, and sensory or physical limitations.

Study Questions

1. How does verbal competency relate to reading competency? How is verbal competency measured?
2. Success in fields that require minimal reading and mental ability are used to predict reading success. What are the advantages and disadvantages of each as a predictor?
3. What is the reading expectancy of a child with an I.Q. of 80 who is just beginning sixth grade and has had 5 years of reading instruction (Grades 1 through 5)? If this child's reading achievement is at a beginning third-grade level, is reading disability indicated?
4. Hiro was a pleasant, cooperative seventh-grade student of average intelligence. He participated in many school activities and had many friends. How-

ever, he seemed to have unusual difficulty understanding and completing reading assignments in social studies. In other course work he did well, especially in math. When the reading teacher assessed Hiro's reading skills, she found that he was excellent in all aspects of word recognition and in understanding the details of his reading. However, he was a somewhat slow reader and was poor in isolating major ideas and themes in longer selections. Which classification seems to suit Hiro best—general reading immaturity, specific reading immaturity, limiting reading disability, or complex reading disability?

Selected Readings

Collins, M. D., & Cheek, E. H. (1989). *Diagnostic-prescriptive reading instruction* (3rd ed.) (pp. 102–149). Dubuque, IA: Wm. C. Brown.

Harris, A. J., & Sipay, E. R. (1990). *How to increase reading ability* (9th ed.) (pp. 150–180). New York: Longman.

McCormick, S. (1987). *Remedial and clinical reading instruction* (pp. 83–163). Columbus, OH: Merrill.

Roswell, F. G., & Natchez, G. (1989). *Reading disability* (4th ed.) (pp. 57–76). New York: Basic Books.

Rubin, D. (1991). *Diagnosis and correction in reading instruction* (2nd ed.) (pp. 124–148). Boston: Allyn and Bacon.

Searls, E. F. (1985). *How to use WISC-R scores in reading/learning disability diagnosis* (pp. 1–3, 42–57). Newark, DE: International Reading Association.

Wilson, R. M., & Cleland, C. J. (1985). *Diagnostic and remedial reading for classroom and clinic* (5th ed.) (pp. 43–89). Columbus, OH: Merrill.

C h a p t e r **4**

Causes of Reading Disability: Physical Factors

Causes of reading disability are numerous. Rarely will a teacher or clinician find that a single factor has caused a child to have a reading disability. It is almost always true that a reading disability is the result of several factors working together to impede progress in reading. Reading is a complex process. Proficient reading depends upon the acquisition and versatile application of many intricately coordinated skills. These skills are acquired only through long, motivated practice under good guidance. Because reading is so complex, there are many opportunities for unfortunate complications to retard its growth. Various factors, operating singly or, more often, together can block further progress in reading until they are discovered and eliminated, or until corrective instructional procedures can be devised to adjust to, or to circumvent, their effects.

Labels, such as dyslexia, sound serious, but do not provide so much as a hint of how to help a child, do not even have an accepted meaning, and certainly do more harm than good. Labeling usually does not provide useful remedial information. Finding out as precisely as possible what is needed to teach a child to read and then providing that help is more valuable. A further complication in some cases is that it is difficult or impossible to distinguish cause from effect. It is easy, for example, to mistake emotional stress or behavioral problems as the cause of reading failure when they are often the effect of a child's awareness of his failures in reading.

This chapter will discuss and evaluate the roles of various physical deficiencies or conditions as contributing causes of reading disability. Visual, auditory, and speech impairments, neurological status, and conditions of general health will all be considered.

Visual Impairment

Rutherford (1967, pp. 503–507) cites an extreme case of visual impairment. Janice seemed to be a well-adjusted child before entering first grade, but then had great difficulty learning to read. Professional examination revealed severe visual impairment. On the way home, after receiving her corrective lenses, she asked her mother about the signboards along the street, the rear lights of cars, and even the leaves on trees. Of course Janice had seen them before, but not in the form and dimension in which they now appeared to her, which made them look so different that she could not identify them. It is no wonder that Janice was not able to learn to read before getting glasses.

It seems axiomatic that ocular comfort and visual efficiency are prerequisite to easy reading. When a child first shows signs of having a reading disability, the tendency of both teachers and parents is to think of visual problems. It is true that a child's eyesight may be so poor that it is practically impossible to read. However, there are a number of less severe eye defects that affect reading. With these defects, when children attempt to read, they become uncomfortable, squirmy, fatigued, and so distraught that they can continue reading for only a short time. They may refuse to read at all. Although certain mild defects may not interfere with learning to read, they may make reading for a lengthy period fatiguing. It is not surprising, therefore, that many studies have concentrated upon visual impairments as causes of reading disability.

Considerable historical research relating visual deficiency to reading difficulty has resulted in conflicting findings. For a selective bibliography of research associating vision problems and reading problems, see Weintraub and Cowan (1982). In general, research does not support a strong relationship between visual problems and reading problems (Poostay and Aaron, 1982). In the midst of disagreement and controversy, however, a few fairly consistent findings have been established:

1. There is a slightly greater percentage of visual defects among children with reading disabilities than among children without reading disabilities.
2. Children with visual defects, as a group, tend to read more poorly than children without visual defects.
3. On the other hand, many children with visual defects learn to read as well as or better than children without visual defects
4. No matter what kind or type of visual deficiency is studied, some children can be found who have that specific kind or type of visual deficiency and who are making good progress in reading.

Most types of visual defects appear to increase the possibility of reading disability, but none appears to be sufficient in itself to preclude reading success. Perhaps the answer is that some children with visual defects fail to learn to read because of the extra effort required of them to master reading, whereas other children with the same visual defects do learn to read successfully because they, for one reason or another, try so hard that they overcome their disability. In any event, children with visual deficiencies who do read well probably have learned under conditions of visual stress and fatigue. The wise teacher is alert to signs of fatigue among visually impaired children when they are required to complete demanding visual tasks and makes appropriate adjustments. The appropriate educational adjustments for these visual problems will be discussed in Chapter 13.

Types of Visual Deficiency

Faulty focus of light rays that enter the eyes—*refractive errors*—may be associated with reading disability. However, certain types of refractive errors are more closely associated with reading disability than others (Eames, 1935; Wharry and Kirkpatrick, 1986; Young, 1963). The farsighted—*hyperopic*—child, who can bring far targets into clear focus easily, but who finds it difficult to focus clearly on near targets, is more likely to have a reading disability than is the child with normal vision. On the other hand, the nearsighted—*myopic*—child, who can bring near targets into clear focus easily, but who finds far targets difficult, is less likely to have a reading disability than is the child with normal vision. According to research by Wharry and Kirkpatrick (1986), even among children with a learning disability, myopic children outperform normal and hyperopic children in reading. This seems reasonable when one considers the nature of the reading task, which involves prolonged periods of close visual inspection of near targets. However, if the teaching method relies heavily on the use of experience charts and chalkboard work, the nearsighted child may have difficulty.

Problems in focusing the two eyes precisely and simultaneously on a target—*binocular difficulties*—are more common among children with reading disabilities than among successful readers. Lack of binocular coordination because of muscular imbalance in one or both eyes—*strabismus*—causes images to be blurred or, in more severe cases, causes two images of a single object to be seen. The result is confusion, fatigue, or suppression of one eye when the child attempts to read. It has been demonstrated that one-eyed students progress better in reading than those with muscle imbalance.

Another binocular characteristic connected with success in reading is precision of focus so that images may be fused into a single, clear picture. Fusion difficulties are associated with reading difficulties (Eames, 1935; Spache and Tillman, 1962). Not only accuracy of fusion, but also speed of fusion, seem to be related to reading success. Ocular images of a fixed target that are unequal either in size or shape in the two eyes—*aniseikonia*—have also been found to be related to reading difficulties.

Many children with visual defects are successful in reading. Although visual defects may contribute to reading problems, even children with very poor vision can learn to read (Martin, 1971). Children with visual defects are more likely to get into difficulty in reading and are more difficult to teach. Correction of visual defects is essential for all children with visual deficiencies, whether they are experiencing reading difficulties or not. Correction of visual defects enables children to learn to read more easily, but rarely, if ever, is such correction sufficient to relieve a reading disability. Once correction has been made, however, most students are able to progress more easily when given appropriate remedial instruction.

Identification of Visual Defects

Accurate identification of all visual defects depends on the cooperation and coordinated efforts of parents, teachers, and eye-care professionals. Beverstock (1991) has published a simple pamphlet for parents, and Jobe (1976) has practical suggestions for organizing visual screen programs in the schools.

Extensive research by Knox (1953) and Kozlowski (1968) strongly suggests that observation by the teacher, combined with visual screening tests by school personnel, provides more accurate identification of children in need of visual care than either factor alone. However, as Jobe (1976) cautions, visual screening tests must be given only for the purpose of identification. Children who already have, or who may develop, problems requiring treatment by an eye-care specialist must be referred to one. Screening tests are not diagnostic, and neither teachers nor school nurses should ever attempt to diagnose or treat visual problems.

Observations by Teachers

Based on extensive research on the identification of children with visual problems through observation, with subsequent validation by an eye-care specialist, Knox (1953) believes that the following behavioral symptoms are most indicative of visual problems:

1. Facial contortions
2. Book held close to face
3. Tenseness during visual work
4. Head tilting
5. Head thrust forward
6. Body tense while looking at distant objects
7. Poor sitting position
8. Head moving excessively while reading
9. Eyes rubbed frequently
10. Tendency to avoid close visual work
11. Tendency to lose place in reading

When two to four of these symptoms are noticeable and persistent, it is the teacher's responsibility to work with the parents, school personnel, and an eye-care professional to ensure that the child receives a proper vision examination. If a visual defect is diagnosed by an eye-care specialist, cooperative efforts must be made to provide proper vision care for the child and to make appropriate educational adaptations within the school. Suggestions in this regard are found in Chapter 13.

Visual-Processing Defects

Research on the relationship between visual perception, visual memory, visual sequencing, and reading disability has been contradictory and confusing (Weintraub and Cowan, 1982). Vernon (1969) concluded, from a review of research relating deficient visual perception to severe reading difficulties, that deficient visual perception is one of the characteristics of children with severe reading disabilities, but that deficient visual perception is so often associated with a general maturational lag, that it may be but one symptom of a general immaturity that also includes language development and personality development.

Robinson (1972) found that students with deficiencies in visual perceptual abilities also had lower I.Q.s than children who did not have such deficiencies. Bryan and Bryan (1978, pp. 169–172) found, from a review of research on visual memory and visual sequencing, that the relationship between these abilities and reading disability was not clear. Two major reasons for the ambiguity were cited. The first was a validity problem, specifically, that researchers could not measure visual-processing abilities convincingly. The second was that among the children studied, visual-processing abilities were so intermingled with other factors usually considered detrimental to reading success, that determining the cause of reading difficulty was not possible. Both Vernon and Robinson also expressed concern about the contamination of results of research on children with visual-processing problems.

Kavale (1982), on the basis of a meta-analysis of 161 studies, concluded that visual perception is an important component of reading achievement, but that its importance varies, depending on the combination of visual and reading variables considered in individual studies. The association between visual perception and reading was also investigated by Spreen and Haaf (1986). These researchers found that children with both reading disabilities and visual problems maintained both of these conditions into their adult years. Further research studying visual perceptual problems and reading problems, conducted by Feagans and Merriwether (1990), revealed that children with reading disabilities who had visual discrimination problems at 6 or 7 years of age performed more poorly in reading throughout their elementary school years than did other children with reading disabilities who did not have visual discrimination problems.

On the other hand, research by Hare (1977) points out that not all children with visual-processing defects are poor readers. According to her research, among beginning readers, individuals can be identified with both visual and auditory disabilities who nonetheless are achieving at grade level in reading.

Training children to use their visual abilities more effectively does not improve their reading achievement, according to research by Seaton (1977), although Feagans and Merriwether (1990) suggest that specific training in visually discriminating letters may be helpful. In the clinic, children who have visual-processing problems, as well as extreme reading disabilities, often benefit from a kinesthetic-auditory emphasis in reading instruction (see Chapter 12).

Auditory Impairment

Sustained hearing loss, even when it is mild, results in poor reading achievement, which becomes increasingly pronounced as children become older (Blair, Peterson, & Viehweg, 1985; Bockmiller, 1981; Quinn, 1981; Serwatka, Hesson & Graham, 1984). In addition, even for children with very slight hearing loss or no hearing loss, but with a history of recurring middle ear disease, reading is affected adversely (McDermott, 1983; Silva, Chalmers, & Stewart, 1986; Zinkus, Gottlieb, & Schapiro, 1978).

The importance of auditory abilities in reading achievement can be appreciated when one considers that children learn to read utilizing the language they understand and use, which is influenced by the language they have heard. Both the inability to pronounce words correctly and the ability to understand what these words mean, as used in various sentences, are based on that part of a child's language ability which has been acquired through listening. The effect of auditory deficiencies on reading depends on the severity and type of auditory impairment; the quickness with which it was detected; the quality of the educational program; the coordination of the efforts of parents, specialists, and others; the desire of the child to read; and other causal factors that all work together to determine the eventual outcome.

Types of Auditory Deficiency

Weintraub (1972) identifies three major areas of concern: auditory acuity (hearing), audition (listening), and auditory processing (working with sounds). Much of the confusion in research, clinical work, and teaching results from the difficulty in separating the effects of hearing loss, listening skills, and auditory processing. Often, a student may have difficulty with all three aspects of hearing, but sometimes the difficulty may be specific. For example, some children with no measurable hearing loss have difficulty hearing sounds in words but no difficulty understanding the meaning of spoken sentences. Other children with hearing loss have difficulty with all the auditory aspects of language, speech, and reading. Still other children have specific difficulty blending sounds into whole words and recognizing the meaning of the words. There are many kinds and types of auditory deficiency, and what is best for one child with an auditory impairment may not be best for another child with a different auditory impairment.

Although research studies disagree, apparently because of dissimilar techniques of measurements and lack of uniform standards for differentiating hearing-impaired from non-hearing-impaired children, it is safe to say that a large number of schoolchildren—about 5 percent—have serious hearing losses. Apparently, many more children have slight hearing losses, which may become more serious unless proper medical treatment is given.

The relationship between hearing loss—especially high-frequency hearing loss—and reading difficulty is well documented (Dechant & Smith, 1977, p. 140; Gillet & Temple 1990, p. 469; Savage & Mooney, 1979, pp. 118–120; Spache 1976a, pp. 49–50). Although children with severe and extreme hearing losses always have great difficulty learning how to read (Erickson, 1987), those with lesser impairments often do reasonably well if the hearing loss is identified early and appropriate medical and educational measures are taken. From the teacher's or the reading specialist's point of view, proper management of instruction in phonics is crucial.

Research shows a direct, though low, correlation between auditory processing and reading success. Kavale (1981) presents a meta-analysis of 106 studies relating auditory perceptual skills and reading ability.

Identification of Auditory Defects

As with vision, successful identification of auditory defects depends upon the cooperation and coordinated efforts of parents, teachers, other school personnel, and auditory specialists. Early screening of very young children has been beneficial in many cases. Auditory screening programs in the schools are important.

Observations by Teachers

An alert teacher notes signs of hearing difficulty through careful observations of children's behavior. Hearing impairment may be suspected if a child shows behavior such as:

1. Inattention during listening activities
2. Frequent misunderstanding of oral directions or numerous requests for repetition of statements
3. Turning one ear toward the speaker or thrusting the head forward when listening
4. Intent gazing at the speaker's face or strained posture while listening
5. Monotone speech, poor pronunciation, or indistinct articulation
6. Complaints of earache or hearing difficulty
7. Insistence on closeness to sources of sound
8. Frequent colds, discharging ears, or difficult breathing

For informal screening, a whisper or low-voice test can be used. Four or five children are lined up in a row in a quiet room about 5 feet from the examiner and with their backs to him. The examiner stays in one place and gives directions to the children, speaking in a distinct, low tone. Directions include items such as "Take five steps forward," "Raise your right arm," "Take two steps forward," and

"Hold up three fingers." By watching the children, the examiner can see those who hesitate, turn to see what other children do, look back at the examiner, or fail to follow directions. The children who get to a position approximately 20 feet from the examiner without signs of seeking help have normal hearing. Hearing-impaired children can be detected readily. Whisper tests may be given by saying single words softly, with the child standing about 20 feet away with one ear turned toward the examiner, or at the distance at which most children can hear in the particular room used. The child tries to repeat each word as she hears it. If necessary, the examiner moves closer until the responses are correct. Each ear is tested separately.

Although whisper or low-voice screening tests are valuable when they can identify a child with a hearing loss, these methods sometimes miss children with less severe hearing losses. For this reason, routine audiometric screening of all children before entering school, and from time to time during the school years, is preferable to total reliance on any informal method.

As with vision, the purpose of identifying hearing loss is to refer the child to a hearing specialist for proper treatment. In addition, educational services and instructional adaptations (see Chapter 13) must be provided.

Speech Impairment

Defective speech is associated with reading difficulty, according to research by Bond (1935), Catts (1986), Lyle (1970), Monroe (1932), and Silva, McGee, and Williams (1985). Research findings demonstrate that inaccurate formation of speech sounds, or *articulation disorders,* are more closely associated with reading disability than is faulty rate of production or repetition of speech sounds, or *fluency difficulties.* It is agreed that in many cases, both inaccurate articulation and reading difficulties are associated with other factors, such as slow intellectual development, neurological involvement, or the inability to discriminate sounds in words. Nevertheless, clinical experience suggests that for some children, defective speech itself is a causal factor.

Monroe (1932) notes that faulty articulation may affect reading directly by causing confusion between the sounds the child hears others make and the sounds the child hears himself make when he is asked to associate printed symbols with sounds in reading. Clinical experience and research by Bond (1935) show that reading methods which require individual letter-by-letter sounding and blending can cause difficulty for a student with faulty articulation. If the student has auditory limitations as well, the difficulty is augmented. Methods stressing visual-mental word analysis enable such a student to progress in reading more successfully.

Confusion may also arise when a student hears words spoken one way when *he* reads orally, but another way when he sees the words in his book while *others* read them aloud. This confusion not only affects sound-symbol associations, but also may interfere with the student's understanding of what is read. The child may thus become increasingly confused both about how words are pronounced and about what they mean.

Some children with speech defects become obviously upset when they are asked to read aloud. This is usually because they are sensitive about articulation errors and dislike displaying them in an oral reading situation. Clinical experience reveals that many children with speech defects—even very minor, barely noticeable problems—insist that they do not want to read aloud, but are willing to read silently. In fact, insistence upon oral reading has been known to turn some children with speech defects against all reading.

Research by Bond (1935) and Monroe (1932) suggests that speech defects are not associated with achievement in silent reading, but are associated with oral reading disability. Some evidence suggests that the strongest association of all may be between speech defects and poor oral reading when it occurs together with adequate silent reading.

The child with speech defects usually needs the assistance of a speech specialist to remedy his speech problem, plus an appropriate reading program. Emphasis on visual-mental word analysis and silent reading usually is best. Planning a suitable reading program for a child with speech defects becomes more complicated when other factors, such as slow intellectual development, neurological impairment, or auditory discrimination difficulties, are also present.

Neurological Impairment

Among children who have not yet acquired the ability to read, there are a very few who have sustained known brain damage before, during, or after birth. Some of these children have severe disabilities, such as aphasia, cerebral palsy, marked mental retardation, or debilitating motor problems. Obviously, they require highly specialized medical assistance and educational programming. Other children with known brain damage are much less disabled. They, too, require medical assistance and educational programming. However, in their reading instruction, appropriate educational programming may or may not be much different from good reading instruction for the typical learner, depending on the needs of the individual child. Case studies from the Geneva Medico-Educational Service (1968) suggest that known brain lesions, unless very severe, often do not retard learning and that many children with verifiable brain damage make good progress in reading. Similar results were obtained by Voeller and Armus (1986) from their study of 43 children with learning and behavior problems. Compared to children with learning problems who showed no evidence of neurological involvement, children with learning problems and neurological impairment scored lower on intelligence testing and higher on reading achievement. Of the 26 children with neurological impairment, the majority were classified as normal readers. Educational adjustments for neurologically impaired students are discussed in Chapter 13.

In addition to the research on children with known brain damage, there has been a great deal of concern, research, speculation, opinion, and clinical data reported regarding suspected brain damage and reading difficulties. Such terms as *developmental dyslexia, primary reading retardation, minimal brain damage,* and *maturational lag* have been used to refer to suspected brain damage in the absence of medically verifiable brain pathology. Bender (1957), Critchley (1970), Denckla (1987), Hynd (1987), and Rabinovitch (1962), among many others, have argued persuasively in favor of some type of neurological impairment, other than known brain pathology, as a probable cause of reading disabilities. A careful and perceptive review of relevant research by Balow, Rubin, and Rosen (1975) suggests that subtle, often undetected neurological impairment associated with complications of pregnancy and birth is a cause of later reading disability among some children. Harris and Sipay (1990) believe that the number of such children has probably increased over the years due to advances in medicine. Rourke (1975) also presents compelling evidence for the view that neurological dysfunction, in the absence of known brain damage, is commonly associated with reading disability.

On the other hand, Spache (1976b) provides a highly critical review of the overwhelming abundance of literature relating suspected neurological impairments to reading disability. He warns that some specialists appear to be attributing almost all reading disabilities to suspected neurological impairment, not only in the absence of known brain damage, but even in the absence of *any* signs of abnormal neurological functioning. Isom (1968) cautions that the assessment of a child's neurological development and its relationship to reading is extraordinarily complex. His thoughtful review of neurological research relevant to reading indicates that among children who show signs suggestive of neurological impairment, some have no reading difficulties, some have moderate reading difficulties, and some have serious reading disabilities. He emphasizes the critical need for competent research comparing the frequency of occurrence of presumably abnormal neurological signs found in children with reading disabilities with the frequency of occurrence of the same signs among their peers who have no reading disabilities. In a somewhat related study, Larsen et al. (1973) found that among a group of 100 children referred to a center for learning disabilities, signs of neurological impairment were no more common among those who had reading disabilities than among those who were making normal progress in reading. Further, Dorman (1985) cautions that the neurological basis of developmental reading disorders remains hypothetical.

In a study comparing children with reading disabilities who had clinical signs of neurological dysfunction with those who showed no such signs, Black (1973) found no real differences among the groups in severity of reading problems, overall cognitive functioning, or behavior. He concluded from his research that suspected neurological dysfunction was *not* an important factor in planning proper remediation of reading disability. Black (1976) also compared children who were suspected of neurological dysfunction with children with known brain damage. Once again, patterns of behavior, cognitive abilities, and academic difficulties noted for these groups were similar enough to suggest that specialized remedial programs differentiating between children with documented brain damage and those with only suspected brain dysfunction are probably unwarranted. Black concluded that remedial programs should be based, *not* on probable neurological causation, but rather on the instructional needs of each child.

In our opinion, a medical referral for neurological assessment should be made when:

1. There is an extreme discrepancy between a child's reading expectancy and reading achievement, in spite of appropriate educational experiences.
2. Despite a wide discrepancy between expectancy and achievement, a child's progress in a carefully planned and well-taught reading program is persistently and unexplainably slow.

Practically speaking, what should the reading teacher or reading clinician do about suspected neurological involvement among poor readers? The best initial referral for neurological assessment is usually to a cooperative pediatrician who has had extensive experience with both normal and neurologically impaired children. Often no real evidence of neurological impairment will be found, sometimes an unexpected physical deficiency of a different sort will be uncovered, and sometimes evidence of neurological impairment will be revealed. If any type of physical condition that requires medical assistance is found, appropriate measures should, of course, be taken. Any suggestions a physician offers that might serve to enhance a child's learning should be followed. However, as with any child with a reading disability, instruction for the child with a reading disability who shows signs of neurological impairment should proceed according to a careful plan based on a diagnosis of the child's particular deficiencies and instructional needs. Methods of proper diagnosis and treatment of reading disabilities are given in Chapters 7 through 17.

Based on an ambitious review of clinical and research evidence concerning neurological correlates of reading disabilities, Duane (1983) suggests that there is a biological preference for verbal tasks to be performed with maximum fluency and accuracy within the left hemisphere of the brain. Yet observation of their learning strategies shows that some children with reading disabilities appear to be using right-hemisphere processing when reading. As Helfeldt (1983) points out, right-hemisphere processing, more typical of boys, tends to be visually oriented and is facilitated through active manipulation of the learning environment. Additional research, conducted by Bakker, Bouma, and Gardien (1990), suggests that tactile instructional methods benefit the reading fluency of these students. Academic learning tasks that demand a great deal of attentive listening and long periods of quiet sitting are not suited to right-hemisphere processing. Neither is a major emphasis on language- or phonics-based methods of reading instruction. Procedures that emphasize the perceptual aspects of words in reading instruction are more beneficial.

According to research by Bakker, Teunissen, and Bosch (1976), early reading proficiency is associated with dominant processing of information in either hemisphere. For children using right-hemisphere processing, reading tends to be slow and accurate, while for those using left-hemisphere processing, reading tends to be more rapid, but less accurate. Eventually, however, advanced reading, which is both rapid and accurate, is favored by left-hemisphere dominance.

General Health Impairment

Learning to read is a difficult, even arduous, task. To succeed, the learner must be an attentive, active participant in the learning process. General health factors such as endocrine disorders, cardiac conditions, allergies, and other physical problems make it difficult for children to be effective learners (Carner, 1981). Any physical condition that lowers a child's vitality makes it difficult for the child to sustain active attention to learning. Nutritional deficiencies, as well, affect learning, according to a research review by Grohens (1988). Caloric deficiency, protein deficiency, iron deficiency, and vitamin deficiency all contribute to impaired learning, as does lead poisoning.

Chronic Illness and Malnutrition

Chronically ill or malnourished children are often unable to sustain attention to demanding learning tasks. These children are likely to miss much instruction due to frequent absences, which makes learning even more difficult. When learning to read becomes a matter of having to catch up on a week's missed work while feeling insecure about how to proceed and feeling tired, unwell, and perhaps hungry, it is little wonder that some children begin to dislike and avoid reading.

What is the teacher's responsibility in regard to poor general health, malnutrition, and frequent absence?

1. When a general health problem is suspected, the teacher, school nurse, parents, and others should discuss the matter and decide what to do. Often, the appropriate action is to refer the child for a medical diagnosis. In this case, it is important to alert the doctor or diagnostic team to the nature of the behavior in the home and in the school that prompted the referral.

2. Although malnutrition is still an important problem for many children, the schools have taken an increasingly important role in combating it through various lunch, milk, and breakfast programs. Teachers should support these programs and encourage good breakfasts at home. Children who eat adequate breakfasts learn more during late morning hours, whereas children who come to school hungry have increasing difficulty concentrating (Grohens, 1988). Some teachers—especially those who use behavior modification techniques—may also provide some students with tiny amounts of nutritious food as part of their teaching procedures.

3. In the case of absenteeism, it is the teacher's responsibility to provide special assistance to ensure that children have not missed essential skill development and that they do not feel confused or insecure about proceeding with their work. Depending upon the circumstances, the teacher can provide this assistance directly, use other resource personnel within the school, or enlist the parents' aid.

General Fatigue

In a reading clinic, it is often discouraging to hear a chronically fatigued child with a reading disability give a detailed rendition of last evening's late, late television movie. It is especially so when follow-up questioning reveals that the student watches a great deal of television, usually far into the night. In this case, the child's television-viewing habits must be discussed with his parents and the child himself. Often, viewing habits will be changed; sometimes they will not. It is tempting to believe that extensive television viewing or other factors that seem to be interfering with proper rest are causing a student's reading difficulty, and in some cases this is true. In other cases, however, overuse of television or overdoing other activities may be a child's way of escaping from the frustrations the child feels, including the frustration of reading failure.

Summary

The survey presented in this chapter suggests that any one of a number of physical conditions may be a contributing factor to a child's reading disability. Much of the evidence is equivocal. It is obvious that a single factor seldom, if ever, causes reading disability. As emphasized throughout the chapter, reading disability tends to be caused by many factors. Several hindering factors combine into a pattern to produce the disability.

Although the evidence concerning the relationship between specific eye defects and reading disability is ambiguous, there are certain relevant trends. (1) Eye defects appear frequently among both good and poor readers and can be a handicap to either group. Comfortable and efficient vision should be provided for all children whenever possible. (2) There is evidence that farsightedness, binocular incoordination, fusion difficulties, and aniseikonia may contribute to reading disability. However, when there is a visual defect, there are usually other contributing causes. (3) Visual examinations are essential in the diagnosis of certain reading disabilities.

Hearing impairment can be a handicap in learning to read. This is particularly true when hearing loss is severe enough to interfere with normal auditory discrimination. There is evidence that hearing impairment is associated with reading disability when (1) the hearing loss is severe, (2) the child has high-tone deafness, or (3) pupils with hearing loss are taught reading by predominantly auditory methods.

Defects in articulation, which complicate word discrimination and recognition, may contribute to reading disability. Any emotional involvement created by speech defects tends to inhibit progress in learning to read. Brain damage is seldom a cause of reading disability, but when it is present, a very difficult instructional problem may exist. Various conditions associated with poor health and malnutrition can be detrimental to normal progress in reading.

Study Questions

1. What is the association between visual defects and reading disability?
2. How can a teacher identify a child with hearing difficulty?
3. How might articulation disorders interfere with reading progress?
4. What generalizations can be made about teaching reading to neurologically impaired children?
5. What do you feel is the proper role of a teacher regarding the health needs of children?

Selected Readings

Harris, A. J., & Sipay, E. R. (1990). *How to increase reading ability* (9th ed.) (pp. 303–353). New York: Longman.

Kirk, U. (1989). Neurological aspects of learning difficulty. In R. Roswell & G. Natchez, *Reading disability* (4th ed.) (pp. 17–40). New York: Basic Books.

McCormick, S. (1987). *Remedial and clinical reading instruction* (pp. 32–58). Columbus, OH: Merrill.

Rubin, D. (1991). *Diagnosis and correction in reading instruction* (2nd ed.) (pp. 91–123). Boston: Allyn and Bacon.

Vernon, M. D. (1960). *Backwardness in reading*. New York: Cambridge University Press.

Westman, J. C. (1990). *Handbook of learning disabilities: A multisystem approach* (pp. 95–190). Boston: Allyn and Bacon.

Wilson, R. M., & Cleland, C. J. (1985). *Diagnostic and remedial reading for classroom and clinic* (5th ed.) (pp. 61–79). Columbus, OH: Merrill.

$$Chapter \quad 5$$

Causes of Reading Disability: Cognitive and Language Factors

In the preceding chapter, a number of physical conditions possibly affecting reading disability were surveyed. In this chapter, various cognitive and language factors and their relationship to reading disability will be considered.

Intellectual Limitations

Although reading achievement is related to intelligence, according to Bond and Wagner (1966), Kirk and Elkins (1975), Siegel (1989a, 1989b), and Stanovich (1989), intellectual development alone does not determine how well a given child will or should read. The precise assessment of reading achievement and intelligence is complex and difficult. Both are influenced by other factors, and both are difficult to measure fairly and accurately. Nevertheless, for proper diagnosis of reading disability, the relationship between intelligence and reading achievement is important. This is especially true for children with below-average intelligence.

As Durrell (1955) cautions, the relationship between intelligence and reading achievement must never be used to set any limit on how much or what a child can learn. Rather, it should be used to identify the child who is failing to progress in reading commensurately with what is most reasonable to expect of him. Discrepancies between reading expectancy and achievement that indicate the presence of a disability are discussed in Chapter 3.

The implication for the intellectually limited child is that if educational adaptations are made which are suited to his needs, he can and will make continuous, appropriate progress in reading. Clinical experience shows that children and youth of quite limited intelligence can and do learn to read if the proper educational adaptations are made. Although their achievement remains very low in comparison with others of their age, they are able to master reading skills useful to them throughout their lives.

But as Buttery and Mason (1979), Cegelka and Cegelka (1970), and Kirk, Kliebhan, and Lerner (1978) point out, low intelligence can be a cause of reading disability when appropriate educational adaptations are not made. For example, if children with low intelligence are expected to read before they have been taught appropriate prereading skills, or if they are expected to progress through sequential reading instruction without an adequate opportunity to make sure that they learn essential reading skills, then they are likely to fail to make reasonable progress in reading. Research by Cummins and Das (1980) suggests that among educable mentally retarded adolescents, poor reading skills may not be entirely attributable to their low intelligence, but may also be due to their failure to apply their intellectual abilities effectively to reading. Such students have reading disabilities not because their reading achievement is low, but because it is unreasonably low. (Methods of adapting reading instruction for the intellectually limited child are described in Chapter 13.)

When a child progresses in reading much more slowly than his peers, it is natural for his teachers to think that he may have low intelligence, especially when there are no other reasons for his slow progress. However, it is not correct to assume that the child's intelligence is low; rather, it is imperative to refer the child to a specialist, such as a school psychologist, for further assessment. Either the Wechsler Intelligence Scale for Children (Revised) (WISC-R) or the Revised Stanford-Binet Intelligence Test should be used for most children for this assessment. Results from group intelligence tests requiring the child to read as a part of the intelligence-testing procedure must not be used, because the child who cannot read well cannot do well on such tests, no matter how well he might have performed if proper testing procedures had been used.

Cognitive Factors

Cognition—the process of gaining knowledge—and reading are related in two important ways. First, specific cognitive abilities are essential for the acquisition of reading skills. Second, for the competent reader, reading becomes a powerful means of acquiring, structuring, and applying knowledge.

Researchers who have attended to cognitive factors in learning emphasize the central importance of the learner in all teaching-learning situations (Reid and Hresko, 1981). From this point of view, effective reading instruction is instruction that facilitates the learner's ability to construct meaning from reading. As Smith

(1978) suggests, "Reading is asking questions of printed text. And reading with comprehension becomes a matter of getting your questions answered" (p. 105). Rystrom (1977) emphasizes the mental activity required in reading when he speaks of readers as "both information receivers and information generators."

Specific Cognitive Abilities

The relationship of specific cognitive abilities to reading disabilities has been investigated through analyzing the performance of children with reading disabilities on individual intelligence tests and tests of cognitive abilities.

According to independent reviews of research on cognitive abilities by Huelsman (1970), Kendler (1972), and Sattler (1982, pp. 394–397), as a group, children with reading disabilities show higher abilities on performance tasks than on verbal tasks. They also tend to have difficulty recalling specific information and working with symbols. A longitudinal investigation conducted by McGee, Williams, and Silva (1984) yielded similar results, but, in addition, found that cognitive factors could not predict which children with a "slow start" in reading would develop long-term reading disabilities and which would ultimately become successful readers.

Cohen (1969), Kaufman (1975), and Bow (1988) present evidence that, whereas successful readers can avoid being distracted during cognitive tasks, unsuccessful readers are less able to maintain concentration. In addition, Horn and Packard (1985) found that freedom from distraction was important in predicting the future reading achievement of kindergarten and first-grade children.

Bannatyne (1974) and Rugel (1974) conducted research which suggests that, as a group, children with reading disabilities are weak in sequencing ability, but strong in spatial abilities, such as understanding quickly how to put together a complex puzzle. More recent research reported by Shapiro, Ogden, and Lind-Blad (1990) suggests that these children have difficulty sequencing two-syllable words, in comparison with age-matched and reading-matched peers. Further, Kirby and Robinson (1987) found that 105 children ages 7 to 15 who had a reading disability had deficits in sequencing on a variety of reading tasks.

From an analysis of the results of research on cognitive factors, Spache (1963) speculated that children with reading disabilities may have unusual difficulty in recognizing that words have meaning and in recalling specific meanings of words. They may also have difficulty recognizing the types of relationships within the structure of a paragraph and summarizing the content of a paragraph in their own words with due attention to order. Research by McConaughy (1985), however, suggests that these children are capable of comprehending a story well when they read structurally simple narrative stories.

Finally, Moore and Wilson (1987) caution against classifying children as having reading disabilities or prescribing instruction on the basis of a pattern of cognitive ability scores.

In teaching, it may be well to keep in mind that for certain poor readers, attention to having them work with activities, games, and other *hands-on* projects would be beneficial. Emphasis on relating reading to discussion and other verbal outcomes puts many poor readers at a considerable disadvantage.

Most teachers would agree that poor readers understand text better through listening than through reading. When Sannomiya (1984) presented the same text to children with good and poor comprehension at a fixed pace using a tape recording or an overhead projector, he found that the tape presentation resulted in better comprehension for the poor readers, for whom the text was difficult, but not for the good readers, for whom it was easy. He suggests that auditory versus visual modality effects arise when text is difficult and when children are not allowed sufficient time to process the text.

Poor readers may be at a special disadvantage when asked to work with the specific symbols used in reading and arithmetic. These symbols must be mastered, but the children may need extra understanding and encouragement as they attempt to learn what is particularly difficult for them. Also, poor readers may find recall of specific information from a story difficult, whereas it may be much easier for them to find information, tell about the story, or draw a picture about it. Certain children need to be protected from too many distractions in the busy classroom, or they will find themselves unable to concentrate on demanding tasks. They may also need instruction that emphasizes order and structure in reading.

Cognitive Style

Cognitive style, or one's preferred manner of intellectual functioning, has been investigated widely in nonreading contexts (Kogan, 1980). As a result of this research, it has been determined that consistent individual differences in cognitive style can be demonstrated. Aspects of cognitive style include field dependence versus field independence, amount of reliance on the learning environment, tendency toward complexity versus simplicity in classification tasks, leveling versus sharpening in memory, focusing versus scanning as an attention strategy, and analytical versus global view of causation.

Recently, research concerning the relationship of several of these aspects of cognitive style and reading has been conducted. Field dependence-independence has been related to reading ability and achievement. Strongly field-dependent children process information in a generally global fashion and appear to be easily influenced by their environment, whereas strongly field-independent children typically process information in an analytical manner and tend to be individualistic.

Field independence was found to be related to higher reading achievement by Blaha (1982), based on his study of 324 inner-city fifth-grade children. On the other hand, Roberge and Flexer (1984) studied 450 suburban children and found that field-independent, analytic, sixth-, seventh-, and eighth-graders did *not* score higher in reading achievement than their field-dependent, globally oriented peers. Their results did show, however, that students' cognitive levels were related to reading achievement. Further research conducted by Blake (1985) involving 121 sixth-grade students similarly failed to find a relationship between field independence-dependence and reading comprehension. She did find a strong relationship between intelligence and reading comprehension, however. Research by Paradise and Block (1984), who studied 200 urban fourth-grade children, suggested that students who closely match their teachers on field dependence-independence make greater gains in reading achievement than students who are dissimilar in that regard.

These conflicting results suggest that the effect of factors such as type of school, grade level, cognitive level, and teacher's cognitive style need to be understood before the relationship of field dependence-independence to reading achievement can be established.

Dunn, Price, Dunn, and Saunders (1979) and Price, Dunn, and Saunders (1981) studied how students prefer to learn when provided with an opportunity to choose from among environmental, sociological, and physical conditions. They argued that the kinds of decisions a student makes concerning instructional choices should be related directly to her learning style, because specific learning style characteristics appear to interact with instructional methods and environmental resources.

In reviews of research on learning style and reading, Carbo (1983, 1985) has characterized poor readers, in contrast to good readers, as learning best (1) under conditions of quiet, (2) when allowed intake of food or drink, (3) if given opportunities to move about, (4) under carefully structured instruction, (5) in informally designed classrooms, (6) when provided chances to work with peers, (7) if provided tactile-kinesthetic learning experiences, and (8) when given major instruction at times during the day other than early morning. Dunn (1988) holds that young children's modalities of learning tend to develop according to age. Kindergarten children are usually tactual-kinesthetic (learning through touching and experiencing). Next, visual learning comes to be preferred, and then, as the learner matures, auditory learning takes precedence.

Another aspect of cognitive style that has been related to reading achievement is conceptual tempo (Kogan, 1980). In most studies, reflexive children—those who respond more slowly than average, but with fewer than average errors—achieve at a higher level in reading than do impulsive children, who respond more quickly than average, but with more errors. In a study of 170 second-grade children, Readence and Baldwin (1978) found that while reflexive children achieved higher levels of reading than did impulsive children overall, the method of reading instruction affected the specific aspects of reading on which the reflexive children performed better. On the other hand, a study of conceptual tempo as a predictor of first-grade reading achievement for a group of kindergarten children (Margolis, Peterson, & Leonard, 1978) did not support the reading superiority of reflexive children. An additional study, conducted by

Halpern (1984), involving 168 second-grade children supported a relationship between conceptual tempo and performance only on some types of word-recognition and comprehension tasks.

Language Factors

The importance accorded listening-speaking language as a basis for reading can be judged from statements made by Wilkerson (1971), who wrote that the ability to read is largely dependent on the skill in spoken language the learner already possesses, by Lundsteen (1976), who believed that reading may depend so completely upon listening that it appears to be a special extension of it, and by Catts and Kamhi (1986), who proposed linguistic deficits as the basis of many types of reading disorders. Research by Blachman (1984), Edmiaston (1984), Fletcher, Satz, and Scholes (1981), Rosenblum and Stephens (1981), and Rosenthal, Baker, and Ginsburg (1983) demonstrates a positive relationship between children's language ability and their reading achievement.

Evidence from longitudinal research (Ruddell, 1979) suggests that primary-grade listening ability may be a better predictor of total reading performance in Grades 8, 9, and 10 than primary-grade measures of reading comprehension and word analysis skills. Additional longitudinal research conducted by Aram, Kelman, and Nation (1984) points to an association between preschool language disorders and later adolescent reading deficits.

Semantic Abilities

Logically, reading is highly related to oral language, since printed words are a graphical representation of spoken language. Myklebust, among others, has contended that proficiency in reading depends on success in listening and speaking (Johnson & Myklebust, 1967). Hammill and McNutt (1980) completed a selective review of studies relating language abilities and reading. In 31 studies relating receptive semantics (contextual listening) to reading proficiency, they found 170 correlation coefficients, with a median value of .44. This suggests a moderate relationship among understanding, listening, and reading performance. On the other hand, of 82 coefficients from 23 studies relating expressive semantics (contextual speech) to reading, the median coefficient was not significant. This suggests only a slight relationship between expressive language and reading proficiency. Taken in its totality, the research suggests that a stronger relationship exists between receptive oral language and reading than between expressive oral language and reading. Additional research conducted by Edmiaston (1984) with third-grade children confirmed this stronger relationship. Her research also supported a stronger relationship between oral language and reading than was obtained by Hammill and McNutt. Edmiaston speculated that the relationship between oral language and reading may increase with age. Gray, Saski, McEntire, and Larsen (1980) found that when intelligence was controlled for, there was no significant relationship between semantic ability in oral language and measures of reading readiness among seventy 4- 5- and 6-year-old children.

An experiment conducted by Howell and Manis (1986) compared the speed with which children with and without reading disabilities in two age groups (second-third and fifth-sixth grades) retrieved semantic information from memory. In each age group, the children with reading disabilities were slower to name both pictures and words than were those without reading disabilities. Felton and Wood (1989) found that children ages 8 to 12 with reading disabilities were slower than average readers in naming depictions of colors, numbers, objects, and letters.

Syntactic Abilities

Language problems are commonly implicated in reading difficulties (Kamhi & Catts, 1986). The complexity of syntax, or sentence structure, has been shown to be highly related to reading difficulty (Dalgleish & Enkelmann, 1979; Evans, 1979). Studies on children's language and reading comprehension have yielded findings about the role of sentence structure in reading. Inability to understand written text is often the result of differences between a child's facility with oral language and the structure of written language (Barnitz, 1980). A review by Evans (1979) of 10 years of research supports a probable relationship between difficulty in reading comprehension and complexity of written syntax.

Although most children are skilled in listening-speaking language before they are taught to read, their ability to comprehend certain syntactic structures of oral language has not yet developed (Barnitz, 1980). Chomsky's classic research (1969) on the acquisition of grammatical structures among children ages 5 to 10 demonstrated that syntax continues to develop among children who are beginning readers. Chomsky also found that the development of syntax is variable from child to child and that errors in syntax persisted even among the oldest children in her group.

Research concerned with the structural difficulty of written materials and the language competencies of children who read them has been done by Glazer and Morrow (1978). In a study of 90 children, the use of syntax by 6-, 7-, and 8-year-olds was compared with the use of syntax in reading material for children of the same ages. It was found that the reading materials were syntactically more complex than was the language of the children.

Studies dealing with good and poor readers' use of syntax, specifically pronouns, indicate that the poor readers are less successful in using syntax in context reading and have less knowledge of English syntax than the good readers. When Chapman (1979) investigated good and poor readers' abilities to deal with pronouns in reading text, he found that good readers were more successful with pronouns than were poor readers, even in materials that did not cause either group difficulty in recognizing words. Dalgleish and Enkelmann (1979) found that poor readers (ages 8 through 12) have less knowledge of syntax than do good readers. Similar results were reported by Morice and Slaghuis (1985) for 8-year-olds and by Fletcher, Satz, and Scholes (1981) for 11-year-olds.

Phonological Abilities

The use of phonological information—information about the sound structure of language—is essential in oral and written communication. According to an extensive research review by Wagner (1986), phonological abilities are important, if not essential, in the acquisition of beginning reading skills. Also, deficiencies in phonological abilities are a probable cause of the difficulty some children with reading disabilities experience in acquiring reading skills.

Phonological awareness—hearing sounds in words—is related to success in reading, according to a number of studies. In a study of first-grade readers, Foorman and Liberman (1989) found that those who were achieving above grade level were more skilled at hearing sounds in words than were those who were achieving below grade level. Similar results were obtained by researchers who studied groups of children from third through sixth grade with and without reading disabilities (Ackerman, Anhalt, & Dykman, 1986; Felton & Wood, 1989; Lenchner, Gerber, & Routh, 1990; Pratt & Brady, 1988). After measuring the phonological awareness of a group of good and poor adult readers, Pratt and Brady (1988) concluded further that phonological awareness appears to be related to reading skill in adults as well as children.

Phonological processing—performing mental operations involving sounds—was found to be less accurate for children with reading problems than for good readers, according to a review of research by Brady (1986). Snowling, Goulandris, Bowlby, and Howell (1986) found that children with reading disabilities were comparable to younger children without reading disabilities at the same reading achievement level and made more errors than the younger children in listening to and repeating nonwords, but not in listening to and repeating real words. This result suggests that the children with reading disabilities had difficulty performing mental operations involving sounds.

Stanovich (1985) concluded, from a review of research, that word-decoding ability accounts for much of the difference in reading ability among children and that decoding ability reflects differences in phonological ability. Success in oral reading of nonwords is a measure of phonological processing in reading. Szeszulski and Manis (1987) studied word recognition in second- through eighth-grade children with reading disabilities, compared with children in the same grades without reading disabilities. Their results suggested that both groups of children used the same processes to identify words, but that the children with disabilities had considerably more difficulty with nonwords. Olson, Wise, Conners, Rack, and Fulker (1989) found that difficulty with reading nonwords as opposed to real words, was a characteristic of persons ages 10 through 30 with reading disabilities, compared with persons of the same ages without reading disabilities. Vellutino and Scanlon (1987) studied second- and sixth-grade good and poor readers and also found that difficulty with reading nonwords was characteristic of the poor readers. Techniques to help students develop phonological awareness and phonological processing are presented in Chapter 11.

Summary

This chapter has considered various cognitive and language factors and their association with success and difficulty in reading. Although a specific deficit may be essential in educational planning for an individual child, no single factor has been isolated as the unique cause of reading disability in general. Some of the most recent and most carefully performed research studies available for review have yielded the most ambiguous results.

Lower than normal intelligence need not be a cause of reading disability, in the sense that reading achievement can be as advanced as is reasonable to expect for the slow-learning child. But when instructional procedures are not adjusted to a child's slow learning ability, an accumulation of partial learnings makes it impossible for him to profit from regular class instruction.

In a review of studies involving specific cognitive variables, a number of factors have been identified as influential in groups of children with reading disabilities. The results of cognitive assessment hold the promise of providing additional information about the individual with a reading disability that will prove useful in planning an appropriate remedial program. Cognitive style also appears to be of promise in planning programs for youngsters with reading disabilities.

Research dealing with language factors and reading suggests that problems with receptive language and with syntax are associated with reading difficulties. A good deal of recent research contends that phonological abilities are related to success in reading and that deficiencies in phonological abilities are characteristic of children with reading disabilities.

Study Questions

1. Under what conditions can a child with low intelligence be considered to have a reading disability?
2. How do cognitive abilities differ from cognitive styles?
3. Why has the search for a single pattern of cognitive abilities as a predictor of reading difficulty proven largely unproductive?
4. Which language factors discussed in the chapter have been shown to be better developed among successful readers and more poorly developed among children experiencing difficulty reading?

Selected Readings

Goswami, U., & Bryant, P. (1990). *Phonological skills and learning to read.* East Sussex, UK: Lawrence Erlbaum.

Harris, A. J., & Sipay, E. R. (1990). *How to increase reading ability* (9th ed.) (pp. 257–302). New York: Longman.

Kirk, S. A., Kliebhan, J. M., & Lerner, J. W. (1978). *Teaching reading to slow and disabled learners.* Boston: Houghton Mifflin.

Richek, M. A., List, L. K., & Lerner, J. W. (1989). *Reading problems: Assessment and teaching strategies* (2nd ed.) (pp. 55–85). Englewood Cliffs, NJ: Prentice Hall.

Singer, M. (1990). *Psychology of language.* Hillsdale, NJ: Lawrence Erlbaum.

Westman, J. C. (1990). *Handbook of learning disabilities: A multisystem approach* (pp. 237–268). Boston: Allyn and Bacon.

Chapter 6

<hr/>

Causes of Reading Disability: Emotional, Environmental, and Educational Factors

In the two preceding chapters, a number of physical, cognitive, and language attributes possibly affecting disability were surveyed. In this chapter, various emotional, environmental, and educational factors and how they may contribute to reading disability will be examined.

Personal and Social Adjustment

When the behavior of children with reading disabilities is compared with that of students making normal progress in reading, it becomes obvious that there are differences in personal and social adjustment. Children who are failing to learn to read well are more likely to show indications of disturbed behavior than are their more successful peers (Gentile & McMillan, 1987; Jorm, Share, Matthews, & Maclean, 1986). Although many children with reading disabilities manifest some indications of disturbed behavior, it is difficult to determine the relationship of behavioral problems and emotional problems to reading problems.

When working with children with reading disabilities in a one-to-one or small-group setting, it soon becomes apparent that they are laboring to learn under stress. In the classroom, children with reading problems also manifest symptoms of stress. According to a substantial review of research reported by Gentile and McMillan (1987), the stress associated with reading difficulties can seriously limit some students' ability to concentrate and can cause a range of behavior, from anger and aggression to avoidance and apprehension. This is why some children with reading problems appear shy or listless, some appear unable to concentrate, and many appear to lack self-confidence. These children become discouraged easily and tend to give up when work becomes difficult. Other children with reading problems appear easily irritated, may argue with the teacher, or even may become aggressive in the classroom. These children actively avoid reading.

It is the teacher's responsibility to aid and assist such children in proper classroom behavior, for their own benefit and for that of the rest of the class. It is crucial, as Gates noted many years ago (1947), not to assume that a child's instability is permanent or unalterable. It is necessary, if the child's emotional or adjustment problems appear severe enough, to seek the aid of professionals, such as teachers of emotionally disturbed or behaviorally disordered children, school psychologists, or social workers. It is important to remember that many children with serious emotional or adjustment problems learn to read and to read well.

When groups of poor readers are compared with groups of good readers, the results usually show a somewhat larger percentage of pupils with signs of personality maladjustment among the poor readers. In most instances, the differences are not great. According to Sornson (1950), children who first manifest reading disabilities in the primary grades develop feelings of insecurity and show less satisfactory forms of personal and social adjustment than do their more successful peers.

A study in which behaviors were used to predict the achievement scores of 90 second graders was done by McKinney, Mason, Perkerson, and Clifford (1975). The results suggest that observable classroom behavior is an important determinant of academic progress. Swanson (1984), who studied 96 first-grade children, found observable classroom behavior to be highly related to reading achievement. In a systematic study of the behavior of 108 students enrolled in Grades 1, 3, 5, 7, 9, and 11, poor readers were off task more and volunteered to participate in class less than did good readers (Wasson, Beare, & Wasson, 1990). Classroom behavior was also observed systematically by Camp and Zimet (1975). Their study of 45 first-grade children revealed that poor readers exhibited more off-task behavior and more deviant behavior than did good readers.

When Harris and King (1982) studied 242 fourth- and fifth-grade children, they found that children who were judged by their teachers to have low achievement were less preferred by their classmates, were less intelligent, and were less emotionally stable than children who were viewed by their teachers as having no academic problems. A major study of over 1,000 New Zealand children who were followed from age 3 to 15 years (McGee, Silva, & Williams, 1984; Stanton, Feehan, McGee, & Silva, 1990) revealed that after first grade, lower reading achievement levels were highly related to teacher-reported behavior problems. In fact, lower reading achievement levels were more highly related to behavior problems than to intellectual level or rating on a family adversity index.

Self-concept, which can be thought of as one's perception of self, also appears to be related to reading difficulty. Eldredge (1981) concluded, on the basis of her review of research, that although a number of studies have shown no significant relationship between self-concept and reading achievement, most of the evidence supports a strong relationship. She also notes that one reason for this may involve the importance of reading in our society. Failure to master reading may interfere with the development of a child's positive self-concept. In a study of 800 nine-year-old children, Chapman, Silva, and Williams (1984) found that poor readers' perceptions of their abilities were significantly lower than normal readers' perceptions. Stevens (1971) found that fourth-grade students identified as remedial readers were less accepted than others in their classrooms and that they had poor self-concepts. Using various measures of self-concept, Herbert (1968) and Prendergast and Binder (1975) reported that ninth-grade students with low reading achievement also tend to have poor self-concepts. Bristow (1985) and Winograd and Niquette (1988) suggest that poor readers are more passive than good readers and that they may demonstrate learned helplessness, a perception that one's actions do not affect outcomes. Learned helplessness may result from the persistent academic failure that accompanies serious reading difficulties.

Some studies have been concerned with the effect of adjustment difficulties on progress in reading. Feldhusen, Thurston, and Benning (1970) identified a group of aggressive-disruptive children for comparison with a group of children who behaved more appropriately. When the school achievements of the two groups were compared 5 years later, the grades of the maladjusted group were found to be significantly lower than those of the normally adjusted children. Harris (1970), in summarizing a study from the Children's Juvenile Court in New York City, reported that "Among those tested . . . 76% were found to be two or more years retarded in reading, and more than half of those disabled five or more years" (p. 37). Wattenberg and Clifford (1966) studied the relationship of the self-concept of kindergarten children to beginning reading achievement. They found that the children's attitudes about themselves were more closely related to success in beginning reading than was intelligence. The researchers suggested that self-concept is causally related to reading achievement. Swanson (1982), however, found a positive, but very low, relationship between attitude toward reading and reading achievement among first-grade students. Black (1974) found that children with reading difficulties tend to hold a negative view of themselves. He also noted that older children with reading problems felt more negatively toward themselves than did younger children.

Although case studies of children often reveal an intimate relation between a child's emotional problems and reading difficulties, most research studies comparing the personality characteristics of poor readers with those of good readers have failed to show any consistent differences between them. Harris and Sipay (1990) suggest that this probably reflects "misguided attempts to find a common personality type or emotional problem in students who have reading problems or disabilities" (p. 363).

Successful reading requires application and sustained concentration. Whatever emotional problems prevent a student from paying attention and concentrating also interfere with the child's learning to read. Harris and Sipay (1990) outline several types of emotional problems that may contribute to reading disability: conscious refusal to learn, overt hostility, negative conditioning to reading, displacement of hostility, resistance to pressure, clinging to dependency, quick discouragement, fear of success, extreme distraction or restlessness, and absorption in a private world (daydreaming). Although in some cases the underlying emotional difficulties may be similar, the symptoms or forms of expression may differ so widely that attempts to place them in useful categories would be futile. It should also be kept in mind that reading problems tend to have several causes rather than just one. The more inhibiting factors present, the greater is the possibility that a reading disability will occur.

Effects of Lack of Success

The inability to learn to read satisfactorily usually means severe frustration for the child. When unsuccessful attempts to read make her conspicuous in a socially unfavorable way, the child is hurt and ashamed. Her continued lack of success, with its attendant frustration and feelings of insecurity, brings on emotional maladjustment (Sornson, 1950). Some children become easily convinced that they are stupid, a feeling that is frequently enhanced by the attitudes of their classmates, their parents, and even the teacher if he fails to understand the real problem. The child with a reading disability comes to dislike reading and seeks opportunities to avoid it. Sometimes failure leads children to become timid and withdrawn; they frequently daydream. In other cases, children show their insecurity through nervous habits such as nail biting or through avoidance-motivated illnesses such as headaches. Still others may compensate for their feelings of inferiority by developing various forms of antisocial behavior.

Most children who enter school with well-integrated personalities are eager to learn to read. Such children thrive on success and approval. For some of them, though, learning to read will mean only the failure and frustration of reading difficulties. When success is denied and approval withheld, as failure and frustration increase, an emotional reaction is a natural consequence. From this, personal and social maladjustment often follow. Reading disability has led to personal maladjustment.

Maladjustment as a Cause

Some children are emotionally unstable even before they begin school. The basis of their maladjustment may be constitutional or environmental, or it may be due to a series of unfortunate incidents during the preschool years. Whatever the basis, some children exhibit impulsive responses, negative attitudes, irritability, difficulty maintaining attention, or lack of energy. These children are unable to achieve the cooperation and sustained effort required in learning to read. Until their maladjustment is dealt with, they make little progress in learning to read.

Several studies suggest that the behavioral problems associated with reading disabilities may precede, and not just be a reaction to, difficulty with reading.

Jorm et al. (1986) studied 453 children from kindergarten through second grade. They found that upon entering school, children who later developed reading difficulties were more likely to exhibit behavior problems than children who progressed normally in reading. The researchers attributed the behavior problems of the children they studied principally to attentional deficits. McMichael (1979) investigated the sequential relationship of antisocial emotional disorders and reading difficulties among 168 boys in their first 2 years at school. Her results indicated that antisocial behavior was apparent from the initial months and was associated with reading difficulties throughout the first 2 years. Horn and Packard (1985) in analyzing 58 studies that explored the association between a number of kindergarten or first-grade behaviors and subsequent reading problems, confirmed that attention problems showed the strongest association. Somewhat unexpected in their analysis was the finding that internalizing behavior problems in the form of anxiety and depression was also a good predictor of later reading difficulties.

The personality patterns of backward readers in two special classes were explored by Frost (1965). He rated 40 percent of the children as maladjusted and another 40 percent as unsettled or likely to become maladjusted. The outstanding characteristic of these children was depression. Weinberg and Rehmet (1983) also found a high rate of depression in children with severe reading difficulties.

In a study of 108 emotionally disturbed boys ages 9 to 14, Graubard (1971) found that their level of reading disability was about as high as for regular students of the same ages. The greatest degree of disability was found for those with behavior problems.

On the basis of research into the relationship between reading achievement and behavioral disorder among 130 children from Grades 2 through 6, Glavin and Annesley (1971) warn that learning problems do not disappear after the treatment of emotional problems, unless the learning problems receive specific attention. These researchers do not feel that behavior problems must be changed before academic achievement can be stressed, and they suggest that academic achievement can be required from children with behavior problems without causing additional problems.

Maladjustment: Cause and Effect

When reading disability is accompanied by emotional involvement, the question arises whether the personality maladjustment is primary or secondary. There is no consensus among writers and investigators on this point. Examination of reported evidence and the views of writers and clinical workers suggest that although in some instances a previous emotional or behavioral difficulty prevents a child from learning to read, in most instances emotional or behavioral difficulties are reactions to reading failure. There are no data available that can assign exact percentages to the proportion of instances in which emotional or behavioral difficulties are causes rather than effects. The view that such maladjustments are most often effects rather than causes is supported by the fact that in most cases, emotional and behavioral difficulties improve as the reading disability is alleviated by remedial instruction.

When emotional and personality maladjustments are interactively causes and effect of reading disability, the interaction tends to become viciously circular. Lack of success during early attempts to learn to read causes tension, stress, and frustration, usually accompanied by feelings of inadequacy and often by negative behavior. The resulting personal and social adjustment difficulties then handicap further progress in learning to read. In effect, the reading disability and the emotional and behavioral reactions to the reading disability interact, each making the other more intense. [For a more in-depth review of stress and reading difficulties, with suggestions for reducing stress while instructing children with reading disabilities, see Gentile and McMillan (1987).]

Environmental Factors

Achievement in reading depends on the child's personal strengths and the demands of the reading program. Children with a background of family tension may approach reading as unhappy and insecure learners. Children from a culture different from that of the teacher and different from that portrayed in the materials they read may experience unusual difficulty in learning. Children who feel comfortable listening to and speaking a language or dialect different from the teacher's and different from that found in their books may find learning to read unusually demanding.

Some children who are from unstable homes, or who must make cultural or language adjustments, do learn to read. Many teachers are sensitive to these students' needs and adapt instruction accordingly. Many of these students can adjust to the school's demands, even though they must try harder than other children.

Home Environment

Some children come from a home environment that provides love, understanding, an opportunity to develop their individuality, and a feeling of security. Others do not. Quarreling parents, broken homes, child neglect, child abuse, overprotection, parental domination, anxiety, hostility, or destructive rivalry among siblings are likely to produce stress and feelings of insecurity. There is more evidence of family conflict in the homes of poor readers than in those of children with no reading difficulties, according to Seigler and Gynther (1960). Similarly, disturbed parent-child relations, marked sibling jealousy, and unfavorable attitudes toward school were characteristic of the poor readers studied by Crane (1950). Thayer (1970) counseled students with reading disabilities and their parents and then compared the reading progress of those students with that of students who had had no counseling. The former had made large gains, while the latter had made none. These results suggest that improvement in conditions at home facilitates improvement in reading.

Neglect or lack of sympathetic understanding may cause a child to feel that he is not loved or wanted. Apparent indifference on the part of a parent or overconcern about a child's difficulties in learning may cause anxiety, lack of confidence, and perhaps attention-seeking behavior.

Overprotection or domination of a child by his parents can lead to adjustment difficulties. Too much parental control can prevent a child from developing initiative and cause him to become so dependent on others that he is unable to learn independently. If a parent attempts to dominate all of a child's activities, including learning to read, the child may rebel against such domination and against reading as well. Pressure for early reading may cause a child to value reading as a means of receiving attention, but not to value reading itself (Werner and Strother, 1987).

When a child's reading achievement is compared unfavorably with that of a brother or sister, it may have a bad effect. A child who cannot compete successfully may attempt to escape from competition and may refuse to continue to learn to read. Any conflict between parents and teachers over a child's reading is likely to have negative consequences. A study by Klein, Altman, Dreizen, Friedman, and Powers (1981) found that parental attitudes, such as being openly critical of the teacher, principal, or school, affect a child's learning. These researchers also point out that some parents believe and communicate to their children the view that it is unnecessary to be concerned about success in school. Learning is viewed as unimportant. Other parents hold the attitude that "high academic achievement is crucial to survival." These parents pressure their children to be outstanding in all school learning.

A child who is under unusual stress from conditions at home may become an anxious, insecure learner or may give up much too easily when reading becomes demanding. Some children react to stress at home by disrupting the classroom. In certain other instances, the result is quite different. Some children find that reading alleviates personal anxiety and insecurity, and they use it and school success as an escape from environmental pressures. But usually, tension and pressures at home hinder rather than help progress in reading.

A French study of family characteristics of 249 children aged 8 through 15 years with severe reading disabilities revealed that low occupational status and low educational level of the head of the household were associated with the children's severe reading disabilities, as was being a younger child from a large family. On the other hand, parental age and marital status were not associated with severe reading disability (Melekian, 1990).

Data collected by McGee, Williams, and Silva (1984) for 790 New Zealand children who were studied from age 7 to 13 years suggested that variables relating to literacy in the home, in contrast to measures of cognitive development, behavior, and family background, were the best predictors of eventual reading success among children who get off to a slow start. Results of a national assessment of educational progress in the United States were reported by Walberg and Tsai (1985). Among the 1,459 nine-year-old students surveyed, home environmental factors most associated with high reading achievement levels were a favorable attitude toward reading, the availability of reading materials in the home, use of English in the home, and kindergarten attendance. Neuman (1986) reports, on the basis of a questionnaire administered to the parents of 84 fifth-grade students, that frequency of reading to young children and availability of magazines in the home were related to the amount of the children's leisure reading. Austin, Bush, and Huebner (1961) point out that, although certain home factors have been shown to be partly responsible for a child's success or lack of success in reading, it is almost never the case that any one of them can be cited as the single causal factor thereof.

Attitudes

It is important that the child develop a favorable attitude toward school, classmates, and reading. While positive attitudes foster progress in learning to read, negative attitudes can result in reading difficulties. Personal and social adjustment, home conditions, peer relationships, teacher-pupil relations, and the instructional program all influence attitudes toward reading.

Although most children begin school eager to learn to read, some do not. Occasionally, there will be a beginner who, for one reason or another, is antagonistic toward learning in general or toward reading in particular. It requires tact, patience, and sympathetic understanding and guidance from the teacher for these children to form positive attitudes toward reading.

In most instances, unfavorable attitudes toward reading come after, rather than before, the child is exposed to reading instruction. That is, achievers form positive attitudes toward reading and school, while pupils who make slow progress and children who have reading disabilities have negative attitudes. Sound reading instruction emphasizing each child's successes does much to ensure that the child will maintain and acquire positive attitudes toward reading and other school activities—in short, that the child will like school.

Cultural and Language Differences

There is little doubt that the child who approaches reading from a cultural or language background different from that of her teacher and different from the material she is expected to read is at a disadvantage. When cultural and language differences are also accompanied by poverty, poor food, poor sanitation, poor housing, and poor medical care, the disadvantage is compounded (Birch & Gussow, 1970). When home conditions prompt the teacher to expect little from the student, the pathway to failure has been prepared (Rist, 1970). Although, as Cohen and Cooper (1972) argue, it is not the role of education to eradicate all social ills, a major contribution can be made by teaching poor children adequate reading skills. The best way to do this, according to Cohen (1969), is to provide intensive, quality instruction, based not on race or social condition, but on the learning needs of each child.

There are many kinds of cultural differences that can affect the teachers' perceptions of their students, the children's perceptions of their teachers, the children's behavior in school, and the nature and importance of reading for each child. For example, there are cultural differences in how a child should behave when an adult is speaking, the desirability or undesirability of answering when unsure, the amount of competition or cooperation displayed to peers, the amount of physical aggression that should be used, and the amount of control asserted over the child's own destiny. A child may be misunderstood by a teacher with a different cultural heritage, unless the teacher is aware of the differences and their implications.

A cultural difference can interfere with a child's comprehension of material because it may cause the child to make inferences that are not suggested by the author of the material (Lebauer, 1985). If reading materials deal with events, activities, ideas, and ideals quite different from those in the child's own experiences, reading itself may seem to be for someone else and may be rejected or considered unimportant for that reason. If a child's books portray people from her culture negatively, the child may reject reading, or may learn to read but develop adverse feelings about herself or her family. Spache (1970) provides a list of realistic, yet positive books from which appropriate selections could be made for children from various minority groups. But, as Vick (1973) points out, there are many excellent materials available with content that is suitable for all children.

Language differences pose an additional problem in instruction. Some children may speak a dialectical variation of the standard English used in the classroom. Other children may speak a foreign language. In many of the nation's largest urban school systems, 10 or more different languages may be spoken by students (Cooper and Sherk, 1989). These language differences increase the difficulty of learning and of teaching reading.

Simons (1973) states that the mismatch between a student's dialect and standard English interferes with the student's reading achievement. He criticizes both unsystematic attempts to teach standard English along with reading and textbooks in which the stories are written in some dialect. On the one hand, teaching standard English as a part of the reading lesson hinders the child as she learns to read. On the other hand, dialectical textbooks are unpopular because not all children who speak a dialect speak the same one. Simons and others, including Venezky and Chapman (1973) and Rystrom (1973), believe that the teacher's knowledge of dialectical differences and her attitude toward children who do not speak standard English are more important than the dialect or the materials themselves. Cooper and Sherk (1989) add that many students need help in the expressive use of English, in using complete sentences, and in learning how to listen carefully. They need a teacher who can translate dialect accurately to standard English, without degrading the language or humiliating the students.

Although dialectical differences interfere with learning to read standard English, language differences create even more serious problems. There is a great need for bilingual teachers who understand the positive qualities and are sensitive to the real needs of the non-English-speaking child. In an extensive review of the literature, Engle (1975) was unable to determine whether minority children in a bilingual culture should be taught to read in their native language or the dominant language. She pointed out that any method that undermines a child's pride in his native language or culture, or that places a child in a situation in which he cannot understand the teacher's instruction, will be unsuccessful. Thonis (1976) presents much valuable information for those teaching Spanish-speaking children.

In sum, most authors agree that teachers of children with cultural or language differences must understand these differences in order to be effective in teaching reading. A positive attitude is also necessary, as is the ability to communicate to each child a sense of his dignity and worth.

The educational problems involved in improving the reading growth of children with cultural and language differences belong to the developmental reading program rather than to the remedial reading program. The educational program of these children should be adjusted to meet their individual needs.

Children from homes in which a language other than English is spoken may know little or no English. They may be unable to understand or to speak English well enough to participate in ordinary classroom activities. These children may appear to be of low mental ability, because it is difficult to obtain a fair estimate of a child's intelligence when he can neither understand nor speak English if the child is tested in English.

Miramontes (1987) assessed the reading levels of a group of fourth-, fifth-, and sixth-grade Hispanic students who were labeled as having reading disabilities by asking them to read English and Spanish text. Her analysis of the results provides strong evidence that the reading difficulties of children who progress from Spanish literacy to English literacy may be based on a lack of overall English proficiency, rather than on a problem with reading.

Because the reading difficulties of children who are learning English as a second language tend to be due to their inability to understand or speak English, procedures used in teaching beginning reading which assume that each child has already learned to understand and speak English will not be beneficial. These children first need a program to strengthen their English. Preparatory instruction ordinarily should have three simultaneous activities: building up a basic vocabulary for understanding and speaking, improving the children's facility in oral communication, and providing a background of meaningful experiences. Words and concepts associated with these experiences must be in English. Thus, the child learns to speak and understand a vocabulary before he encounters it in reading. Probably, much of the training in the understanding and use of spoken English should be carried out in sessions not concerned with reading. In general, lessons in reading should not be complicated by simultaneous training in pronunciation. Of course, all this does not mean that no reading is done while the child is being taught English; but although the two can be done concurrently, they should be in separate class periods.

These children do not acquire any reading disabilities if an appropriate teaching program is organized early in their school lives. Nevertheless, the development of an adequate background in English will be gradual. Until this is achieved, the children are at a disadvantage in all school activities. Hence, the program may need to be continued throughout the elementary school years.

Children from culturally different environments in which a dialect other than standard English is spoken have a somewhat different problem. Preschool-level programming is especially beneficial to them. As Lloyd (1965) points out, language patterns are established firmly by the time a child is 6 years old. Therefore, it is desirable to encourage early language development and build essential concepts in young preschool children. Such development of language and of necessary concepts is especially important for the child from a different culture. This is part of the role of programs for preschool children. Preschool programs are important in helping disadvantaged children prepare for reading and other learning. Special teaching is also needed to help the disadvantaged child progress through the elementary grades.

Continued emphasis upon real experiences, field trips, audiovisual presentations, storytelling, puppetry, and role playing should be maintained throughout the school years. The language used as a by-product of these experiences is beneficial to disadvantaged children and is an important part of beginning reading instruction. The language experience approach may be used in a major or supplemental role in reading instruction. In this approach, children tell a story, immediately tied to a real experience, which the teacher writes down verbatim. The children then review the story and work on activities associated with it, such as reading sentences, matching words, or drawing pictures to illustrate the story. For a child with experiential differences, language differences, or dialectical differences, this approach is useful in that it deals with experiences he has had, and it uses words and language structures with which he is familiar and comfortable.

Some children with dialectical differences, as well as those for whom English is a second language, have reading difficulties that can be corrected by specific remedial training. They should receive immediate help and be treated like others with reading disabilities: Their reading patterns should be diagnosed, their basic reading problems isolated, and individual remedial plans formulated.

The fact that a given child has a dialectical difference itself should be taken into account in the remedial plan, and the techniques used should include the language experience approach. Silent reading exercises should always use interesting, meaningful material. Any oral reading errors related to the child's dialect should be ignored.

It should be remembered that children with dialectical differences understand radio and television well, although when they discuss what they have heard or seen, they tend to use their own dialect, rather than the standard English used in the radio or television programs. This should not be criticized or belittled.

We suggest that these children do much independent reading of material written in standard English. The material should be very easy for each child to read, and the child should be allowed to discuss it as he likes. We also suggest that the child select parts of a story that he liked best, that he found most exciting or most humorous, or that he thought was well written. The child then might choose a part of the story to read aloud to others. The child should read this material as it is written. It might be even more helpful if he pretended to be a television personality and read as he would on a real television program.

Educational Factors

Among all the factors that are considered possible causes of reading disability, the group of conditions classed as educational stands out as tremendously important. Careful consideration of various characteristics that predispose children to experience difficulty in learning to read does not diminish the importance of the educational program as the major cause of reading difficulty. Rather, it shows how necessary it is for each child's instruction in reading to meet her individual learning needs. In the vast majority of cases of reading disability, careful diagnosis reveals that there is faulty learning or a lack of educational adjustment in the student's instructional program.

As discussed earlier, reading is a complex process involving many interrelated skills and abilities. As a child progresses through the reading program, there is constant danger that she may fail to acquire essential knowledge or that she may get into difficulty because she may over- or underemphasize such knowledge. Under the broad category of educational causes, several educational practices must be considered. Although this book discusses them separately, it should be supposed, not that they operate in isolation, but rather, that they are related and interacting.

School Administrative Policies

Success in teaching children to read depends on the teacher. Thus, we must examine the role that certain administrative policies play in determining how effectively a teacher can organize and carry out her reading program. Some of the policies that hinder even the best of teachers will be considered briefly.

Reading versus Child Development
Whether reading or child development should be the chief concern of the school during the early grades is controversial. Some educators believe that the emphasis should be almost entirely on developing reading skills. Others object to this and feel that the school's chief concern should be the happy, balanced development of each child's personality. Many teachers not only are aware of the issue, but also may be under pressure to stress one approach at the expense of the other. The argument of those opposing effective reading in the primary grades is that putting pressure on the children to read may produce maladjustment. They claim

that emphasis upon reading destroys interest in learning since, they believe, reading is an activity foreign to the real interests of children in these grades. Actually, there need be no serious conflict between well-balanced child development and all-around development that includes reading, if reading is taught properly. With individualized instruction, including accounting for reading readiness, developing reading skills can become an integral part of a well-balanced total program. In this program, only those who are ready to do so begin to read early in Grade 1. Other children start later, when they are capable of succeeding. When frustrations arise, it is likely to be because of the method of instruction. Reading instruction suffers when administrative pressure overemphasizes or underemphasizes reading in the primary grades.

Promotion Policy and Curriculum Requirements

In 1938, Cole stated that the reason for the prevalence of remedial reading classes was the failure of schools to adjust the curriculum to the current promotion policy. To some degree, this indictment is still valid. Cole was referring to promoting children mainly by age rather than by achievement, with no accompanying change in curriculum requirements. This produces a wider and wider range of reading abilities in successively higher grades. At the same time, curriculum requirements remain fairly rigid. When pupils are promoted by age, not achievement, and there are no instructional adjustments made, then much of the material assigned to pupils in the higher grades is too advanced for the poorer readers' level of reading competence. The poorer readers also do not receive needed instruction in certain reading skills, because these skills are not usually emphasized in the higher grades. For some students, the result is a reading disability. Yet it is not the yearly promotions per se that have caused the disability, but rather the failure to adjust instruction to the individual needs of certain students. If alternative materials are assigned and if essential skills are taught, then reading disability need not result from promotion by age.

Readiness for Beginning Reading

Success in beginning reading depends largely on the child's overall level of maturity. The pattern of growth entails many types of abilities, acquired behaviors, and specific pieces of knowledge. Although some aspects of reading readiness come with maturation, many of the most important ingredients are learned and can therefore be taught. This means that when a child approaches beginning reading lacking certain essential skills and knowledge, these can and should be taught before or during beginning reading instruction. Research by Spache (1965) has demonstrated the effectiveness of appropriate training in visual and auditory perceptual skills for children who need such skill development to succeed in beginning reading. The evidence suggests that training is effective in developing visual and auditory perceptual skills before beginning reading instruction and that, in addition, such prereading skill development facilitates initial reading success. Other beginning reading achievements, such as knowledge of the meanings of words, attention to oral directions, the ability to work independently, the ability to work cooperatively in groups, and even the desire to read, can be taught.

Many first-grade children are not ready to learn to read in the typical program, and therefore, instructional modifications must be made if they are to experience initial success in learning to read. Reading disability is frequently caused by starting a child in a standard reading program before the child is ready. Because of lack of experience, verbal deficits, poor visual or auditory perceptual development, overall immaturity, or a combination of these features, the child is unable to achieve what is expected of him daily and therefore does not succeed. Instead of learning to read, the most the child can do is acquire only bits of reading skills that he is unable to use. Thus, he falls farther and farther behind. The outcome will not be reading well, but frustration and failure, perhaps leading to feelings of inadequacy, inferiority, insecurity, and even rebellion. Such a child may even come to hate reading and all persons and activities connected with it.

The many failures in reading during the primary grades are due in part to the inability of programs of instruction to adapt to differences in readiness for beginning reading. Any educational program or administrative policy that provides exactly the same formal reading instruction for all pupils at the beginning of Grade 1 causes reading failure for many children.

Adjustment to Individual Differences

Beginning in Grade 1 and continuing in every grade thereafter, reading instruction can be effective for all students only when it is able to adjust to individual differences. Without such adjustment, reading difficulties arise.

Methods of Teaching

Most reading difficulties are caused by children's failure to acquire necessary learning, or by faulty learning, as they go through the reading program. The complexity of the reading process has many points at which children are vulnerable to experiencing difficulties. Sometimes this is coupled with *ineffective teaching*. For one reason or another, there may be a lack of educational adjustment to the needs of certain students, so that they do not acquire essential knowledge.

A number of factors may lead to ineffective teaching. Curriculum requirements may take so much of the teacher's time that the teacher is unable to individualize the program satisfactorily. Concurrently, the methods or materials used may be too difficult for certain youngsters. Under these conditions, it is probable that certain students will be pushed through the program too rapidly to learn what it is designed to teach.

Using materials and methods that seem dull and unimportant *to the student* is another part of ineffective teaching. In beginning reading, for instance, it is important that the child develop the attitude of insisting on understanding what is read. To do this, the reading material should either tell a story (have a plot) or give some information. Neither of these can be done by the excessive use of badly constructed and insipid experience charts, or by reading dull and anemic materials made of almost meaningless sentences, or by isolated drill on the parts of words. One youngster, on being exposed to such material, said to his teacher, "That sounds silly." It is not surprising that some children react to this kind of material by acquiring negative attitudes that become obstacles to learning to read.

Similarly, procedures that do not tie class activities to the reading program can lead to reading disability. When reading is taught separately from activities the child enjoys, it is no wonder that the child sees no reason for learning to read. In contrast, if there is a relationship between reading and class activities, so that reading itself is a tool for those activities, the child becomes motivated to learn to read. It is desirable that reading activities affect some of the important things the child is doing in the class and that many of the class activities grow out of the reading program. Then the child can see a reason for reading, and interest and motivation are maintained at a high level.

It should be emphasized here that interest is not the same thing as entertainment. Real interest backed by strong motivation is not found by flitting from one amusing incident or story to another. Much better is a program in which reading is tied carefully to activities in the classroom. Such a program would imply coordination among the language arts. Interest in and motivation to improve one's skill in speaking, listening, writing, spelling, and reading are interrelated and flow from the desire to communicate with others through language.

Excessive emphasis on isolated drills kills interest. As we shall see later, some drill is desirable and necessary. Sometimes, however, drills are so far removed from the act of reading that the child cannot bridge the gap. Not only is the child unable to transfer what is learned in the drill to actual reading, but she also cannot see the reason for the drill. Methods concentrating on isolated drills, rather than on sharing stories and experiences, lead to loss of interest and inhibit the desire to learn to read.

Insufficient emphasis on basic reading skills can prevent effective reading. For example, children who do not recognize enough words at sight, or who do not possess adequate skills in word analysis, or who do not comprehend what they are reading are not effective readers. Basic skills underlie proficiency in reading, and they must be properly stressed.

Many youngsters have trouble reading because their reading programs are not well thought out. It should not be forgotten that methods that ignore the orderly development of essential skills and abilities are not beneficial to the student. Moreover, indifferent, unorganized, and superficial teaching of various subjects contributes to the reading difficulties of some students. Teaching content subjects can contribute to effective reading if training in necessary skills and abilities is an integral part of the instructional program.

When emphasis upon the mechanics of reading leads to neglect of the meanings of words, children run into serious difficulty. Undue stress on word recognition, perfection of enunciation, and speed may lead to verbalism—the pronunciation of words without understanding their meanings. A girl in one of our remedial reading groups could read fourth-grade materials aloud without error, but she could comprehend practically nothing of what she "read." To pronounce words without understanding their meaning is not reading; it is merely calling out words. The girl had a reading disability.

Overemphasis on phonic analysis as a word-recognition technique frequently causes disability. The child is so intent upon sounding out most of the words she encounters that she cannot attend to meaning. Or she laboriously separates a new word into its component sounds and then is unable to blend the separate sounds into a recognizable pronunciation of the word. Such children usually have an insufficient sight vocabulary and are unable to make adequate use of contextual clues for word recognition.

To progress satisfactorily in learning to read, there must be a proper balance among many skills and abilities. A sight vocabulary, various techniques for word recognition, concepts and meanings of words, reading in thought units, comprehension and study skills, and many other abilities must not be taught separately. They are all part of an integrated sequential program. There is a balanced relationship between them that must be striven for. The student who gets into difficulty is quite frequently the child for whom a balance among these skills has not been maintained.

Granted that it is difficult to imagine a teacher who is able to manage a class of 30 children and at the same time keep account of all the essential balances while carrying out his reading program in a systematic and orderly fashion. But the teacher should never forget the importance of a balanced program and should do what is possible to achieve it. The smaller the class, the greater is the possibility of maintaining balance.

Role of the Teacher

The role of the teacher is important. She can have a positive or negative influence upon progress in learning to read. Students are fortunate if their teacher is so able, well trained, and sympathetic that she maintains good relationships with them and is able to achieve a proper balance in developing skills and abilities in the reading program. When teachers deviate from this combination, reading instruction is apt to suffer. The teacher who is inept because of poor training, lack of experience, or a slavish devotion to inflexible routine is unable to adjust reading instruction to the varied needs of her students.

A teacher's personality—especially when she has a negative attitude toward a particular student—may cause or intensify the stress associated with failure in reading. Apparent indifference, hostility, or obvious anxiety in the teacher when a student has difficulty reading intensifies the child's emotional reactions and feelings of insecurity. We have to face it—too often, the teacher is not without blame when a child develops a reading disability.

Role of the Library or Media Center

The school library or media center also plays an important part in the total reading program. Although the teacher develops the child's reading skills in the classroom by means of the formal program of instruction, it is through the school library or media center that the child's interests in reading are pursued and expanded. The librarian can provide teachers with materials for developmental reading programs, as well as for individual and remedial programs. Within the library or media center, there can be attractive book displays, book talks, and storytelling hours to make reading exciting to the students. The library's varied book collections offer students opportunities for reference reading, research, and additional reading at each grade level.

Secondary schools lead in library services for their pupils; many elementary schools have been much less fortunate in their library facilities. In fact, some elementary schools have no books at all, other than textbooks. Other schools have small classroom collections, while others, fortunately, have a library room or media center with a trained librarian or media expert.

The value of a library or media center to the elementary pupil's advancement in reading cannot be overemphasized. Gaver (1961) evaluated six school libraries and their services, as well as the quantity and quality of reading done by the students who frequented the libraries. She found that higher educational gains were made when there was a school library and that students read more and better books when there was a library.

Summary

The causes of reading disability are numerous; seldom is a single factor the cause. In all but the mildest cases, the difficulty is due to a composite of related conditions. The contributing factors interact in a pattern.

Reading disability is usually accompanied by emotional factors that adversely affect the child's personal and social adjustment and classroom behavior. The maladjustment may be due to constitutional factors, to environmental factors, or to failure in reading. In some cases, a child may be emotionally upset or behaviorally disordered upon arrival at school. Such a child is apt to have difficulty reading. For many children, frustration will then arise. In these instances, the reading difficulty causes emotional upset that is often expressed by a wide variety of reading-avoidance behaviors. Emotional maladjustment may be both effect and cause. When an emotional reaction arises from a reading disability, it may then become a handicap to further learning. There is, in such cases, a reciprocal relationship between the child's emotions, behavior, and reading disability. When maladjustment is due to reading failure, it tends to disappear when the child learns to read satisfactorily. When maladjustment is the primary problem, the child should be served by an appropriate specialist.

For children who are learning English as a second language, ordinary reading instruction is usually not productive until they have made some progress in spoken English. Just as soon as the teacher considers it feasible, however, they can be taught reading concurrently with continued instruction in spoken English.

Disadvantaged children benefit greatly from preschool programming. Good health, sound nutrition, a positive self-concept, and language development are all helpful. In the preschool and school years, opportunities to participate in real experiences and to utilize audiovisual presentations are especially beneficial to many disadvantaged children. The language experience approach can be an important part of beginning reading instruction for many children with experiential, language, or dialectical differences.

Frequently, reading disability is due largely to educational factors. Any administrative policy that hinders the individualization of instruction, including emphasis upon reading readiness, prevents effective progress in reading. Failure to acquire necessary skills or the acquisition of faulty techniques is most frequently due to ineffective teaching. One or more of the following factors may be involved in the ineffective teaching that brings about reading disability: too rapid progress in the instructional schedule, isolation of reading instruction from other school activities, inappropriate emphasis on some technique or skill, or treating reading as a by-product of studying subjects. Frequently, the difficulty occurs because the instructional program has failed to maintain a balance in the growth of the large number of skills and abilities involved in learning to read.

If one conclusion were to be made, it is that there is no cause of all reading disabilities. Each case is unique. Only when there is a valid diagnosis will there be a sound basis for planning an individual remedial program to alleviate a particular child's reading disability.

Study Questions

1. How do emotional and behavioral problems interfere with learning to read?
2. How do problems with reading affect a child's adjustment and behavior?
3. How do parental attitudes affect a child's progress in learning to read?
4. What should the teacher emphasize in teaching children with cultural or language differences?
5. What should be done if a first-grade child is not ready to learn to read in the typical program?
6. Why is it bad practice to emphasize the mechanics of reading to the extent that it leads to neglect of meaning?

Selected Readings

Gentile, L. M., & McMillan, M. M. (1987). *Stress and reading difficulties: Research, assessment, intervention.* Newark, DE: International Reading Association.

Harris, A. J., & Sipay, E. R. (1990). *How to increase reading ability* (9th ed.) (pp. 354–389). New York: Longman.

Maggart, Z. R., & Zintz, M. V. (1990). *Corrective reading* (6th ed.) (pp. 406–442). Dubuque, IA: Wm. C. Brown.

McCormick, S. (1987). *Remedial and clinical reading instruction* (pp. 413–425). Columbus, OH: Merrill.

Richek, M. A., List, L. K., & Lerner, J. W. (1989). *Reading problems: Assessment and teaching strategies* (2nd ed.) (pp. 26–42). Englewood Cliffs, NJ: Prentice Hall.

Taylor, B., Harris, L. A., & Pearson, P. D. (1988). *Reading difficulties: Instruction and assessment* (pp. 32–44). New York: Random House.

Westman, J. C. (1990). *Handbook of learning disabilities: A multisystem approach* (pp. 51–93). Boston: Allyn and Bacon.

Chapter *7*

Basic Considerations in Diagnosing Reading Difficulties

Remedial instruction that is not based on a thorough diagnosis is likely to waste time and effort for both the student and the teacher. Moreover, remedial work done without an adequate diagnosis is likely to fail. A student who has had difficulty with reading may already be apprehensive. Continued failure in a remedial program is apt to intensify this insecurity. Persons responsible for remedial programs should make every effort to ensure that each child will be successful and will sense the success he or she achieves.

General Principles of Diagnosis

An adequate diagnosis determines in no small measure the success of the remedial program. Since reading is a complex process, there is no one single or simple cure for reading difficulties. Remedial training that is effective in one case might be detrimental or wasteful in another. It is only through understanding the underlying factors of any given child's difficulty that an adequate remedial program can be formulated. For example, suppose two students have difficulty reading and appraisal shows that both are low in reading comprehension. Suppose also that further analysis indicates that one student is low in comprehension because of inadequate recognition of words, while the other student is low because she is a word-by-word reader who is so conscious of individual words that she is unable to group them into thought units. Then the first student needs remedial work to build up his awareness of words and his ability to inspect them in detail. This procedure, however, would be detrimental to the second student's need for overcoming her overemphasis on isolated words.

The problem of helping children with reading difficulties is complicated further by the many characteristics children possess and by the learning environments that affect their reading growth. It is necessary to adjust one's plans and methods to some of the variations among the children's physical, emotional, educational, intellectual, and environmental factors if reading growth is to progress smoothly or even at all. Sometimes, these same factors need to be totally corrected before remedial programs can be effective.

It is little wonder, then, that the classroom teacher attempting to correct reading difficulties finds that no two children have the same instructional needs. Any attempt to give a child remedial instruction must be based on a thorough diagnosis of the child's unique reading needs and personal characteristics. The diagnosis is the very core of successful remediation programs, whether they are for the less complex problems addressed in the classroom or for the more complex problems that require a specialist.

The classroom teacher may need special help in diagnosing or correcting the more complex reading problems of some children or when limitations in reading require a diagnosis that is more detailed and more discerning than the teacher has the time or the training to give. Frequently, it is necessary to study a child's reading pattern by means of an individual appraisal that takes several hours to administer. It is thus expedient to have the more detailed diagnoses conducted by someone who can work individually with children over a long period of time. In many cases, it is essential to obtain evaluations and corrective help from other specialists, such as speech pathologists, social workers, school psychologists, or physicians.

Of course, the teacher should diagnose and correct as many reading difficulties as he can. Early detection and correction of these problems will prevent many of them from becoming more complex. There are many diagnostic procedures that the classroom teacher can use in studying the child with a moderate reading disability. In other cases, an outside diagnosis may be needed to help the teacher formulate the kinds of remedial treatment he can provide in the classroom. In some instances, both the detailed diagnosis and the corrective treatment should be given by specialists. But for every reading difficulty, whether simple or complex, a diagnosis is necessary.

Characteristics of the Diagnosis

A good diagnosis:

1. Focuses on improving the child's condition.
2. Provides all essential information to remedy the condition.
3. Is efficient.
4. Uses information from cumulative records.

5. Includes only relevant information.
6. Uses standardized procedures when they exist.
7. Uses informal procedures when standardized procedures do not exist.
8. Bases its decision on patterns of scores.
9. Is ongoing.

Let us examine each of these in turn.

Focus on Improvement

The diagnosis of a child who has difficulty reading should include information necessary for planning a corrective program for the child. There are two types of diagnosis: etiological and therapeutic. An etiological diagnosis finds out what originally caused a child to get into difficulty. Often, this kind of diagnosis is impossible to obtain, and frequently, it is useless for formulating a remedial program. It is of little use, for example, to search a child's records and find that the child is having difficulty in reading in the fourth grade because of an extended absence due to illness in the first grade. Nothing can be done now to give the help the child needed then. This information, collected and summarized for research purposes, might be useful in preventing subsequent reading difficulties, but it is not useful for the immediate task of correcting a reading problem that began several years earlier.

By contrast, therapeutic diagnosis is concerned with conditions that are now present, in order to plan a program of reeducation. The therapeutic diagnostician searches for the child's reading strengths and limitations and for any characteristics within the child's present environment that need to be corrected before remedial instruction can be successful or for conditions that need to be adjusted to before the child can be expected to make progress. As an example, the reading specialist is more concerned about a current hearing loss than about finding out that the child is in difficulty because she had a temporary hearing loss several years ago.

Provision of All Essential Information

The complex nature of a reading disability and the many factors related to achievement in reading make it necessary to explore the child's many traits and reading skills and abilities for an adequate diagnosis. Besides discovering the deficiencies in reading that are at the root of the disability, it is often necessary for the reading specialist to appraise the physical, sensory, emotional, and environmental factors that may be impeding the child's progress. Frequently, the diagnosis requires other expert help. The specialist should be alert to the possible effect of conditions within the child or his environment that require specialized help. All appraisals made in more complex cases should be extensive enough to pinpoint the existence of such limitations. The measurements used in a reading diagnosis will be discussed in the following chapters. It is enough to say here that the diagnosis should supply all the information that is pertinent to correcting the disability.

Efficiency

Although the diagnosis of some reading disabilities may be lengthy and intricate, in other cases a child's instructional needs can be isolated relatively easily and quickly. A diagnosis should proceed as far, and only as far, as is necessary to formulate a remedial program in each specific instance. The diagnosis should proceed from group measurements to the more detailed individual measurements needed for the case under study. The diagnosis should be reached by measuring first the relatively common types of problems and then the more unusual ones.

It would be expected, for example, that for all children suspected of having a reading disability, one would routinely measure their general reading achievement and their general mental ability. It would only be in an unusual circumstance that a complete neurological examination would be required. The procedures in diagnosis are much like successive screenings in which only the more complex and elusive cases are retained for further measurement and study. The three levels of diagnosis are (1) appraisals that are made routinely for all children in the schools or for all children referred for special study, (2) more detailed appraisals made only in those instances when more analytical study is warranted, and (3) appraisals that are individual in nature, made only in the most complex cases. In reading diagnosis, these are called, respectively, general diagnosis, specific diagnosis, and child-study diagnosis.

General diagnosis has three purposes. First, it gives information that is necessary to adjust instruction to meet the needs of groups of children in general. For example, a fifth-grade class as a whole may be found to be relatively weak in reading achievement. If so, the teacher may conclude that more attention should be given to reading instruction than had been given in the past. Second, general diagnosis gives information that is necessary for adjusting instruction to the individual differences in reading found within the class. It can, for example, indicate the range of general reading competence for which the teacher must plan and also indicate specific children that would benefit from instructional modifications. Third, general diagnosis can help find those children who are in need of a more detailed analysis of their reading difficulties.

Specific diagnosis makes two important contributions to the correction of reading difficulties. First, it locates those areas of limitation that need to be examined more fully. Second, it can often indicate instructional adjustments that are required to overcome those limitations.

Child-study diagnosis involves a more detailed, thorough, and time-consuming study than is warranted for children with relatively uncomplicated reading problems. Many children may require only a general study of their educational achievement and intellectual capability to deal with their reading difficulties. Other children may require differential or specific study to locate the exact areas in which they are limited. Some of this latter group of children may have problems that are so elusive or complex, that detailed study is required before a remedial program can be designed for them.

Use of Information from Cumulative Records

The yearly records of the school will give the specialist information about the progress the student has made throughout her school life. They will also indicate the subjects that have been difficult for the student. They will tell, too, about any periods of prolonged absence or changes of school. These records help to establish the grade level at which the student's trouble with reading may have started. The examiner should make a careful study of the school history of the student and should record those circumstances that are related to reading. Such a study often eliminates duplicate testing and gives information that is not available from other sources.

Inclusion of Only Relevant Information

There is a tendency for reading specialists to add tests to their routine diagnostic procedures on an experimental basis. This is as it should be, but when such tests are found to have little diagnostic value, they should be discontinued. The time, energy, and expense involved in obtaining valid diagnostic information is so great, that persons making diagnoses should appraise the measuring instruments being used to make sure that they are efficient and that they add to the understanding of the children's instructional needs. Unnecessary duplication should be avoided.

The child should be given every consideration when diagnostic tests are administered. Indiscriminate testing may set a child against the whole procedure or even may cause him to doubt his ability to learn. The specialist should investigate thoroughly the specific reading pattern of each child who has a reading disability, should obtain a valid estimate of the child's learning ability, and should be satisfied that the child's vision and hearing are normal or have been suitably corrected. The child's classroom behavior should be considered. In addition, any unusual psychological or neurological characteristics should be noted if such information helps provide an understanding of the instructional needs of the child. It is advisable to intersperse reading measures with other activities, since many children who have a serious reading disability become resistant when they have to read. They easily become discouraged or even uncooperative if they are subjected to a long, uninterrupted series of reading tests.

Use of Standardized Procedures

In diagnosing the learning difficulties of a child with reading problems, reading, physical, sensory, behavioral, and environmental factors all must be analyzed. Clearly reading achievement is not the only concern of importance in the life of a child. However, when a child has been identified as having a reading disability and the disability is the child's major problem, it becomes necessary to investigate her reading pattern thoroughly to establish the exact nature of her difficulty. This is always one of the major concerns of the specialist, because without locating the child's specific reading deficiencies, little, if anything, can be done to correct the reading disability.

It may be, for example, that a child with a reading disability is found to be farsighted, and correction is made with glasses. The child is now comfortable visually. She thus stands a more reasonable chance of learning to read, but she still has a reading disability. Accordingly, her reading should be analyzed to locate any faulty learning patterns that may have been caused in part by her visual difficulty, in order to plan instruction to correct the reading disability. No matter what physical, environmental, or behavioral problems caused the child to have difficulty reading, it is necessary to study and correct the reading disability. The other factors associated with the reading disability also need to be studied, so that the correction in reading can be made most efficiently and so that the other conditions can be improved as well.

There are two general types of assessment used in diagnosing reading disabilities. The first involves the application of precise units and numerically expressed norms, such as age or grade norms, percentile norms, or standard score norms requiring measurement by standard procedures. The second is qualitative assessment, for which norms expressed in numerical terms either are not available or are not appropriate. This second kind of assessment is limited in that the procedures used are not systematic and the diagnostician's personal bias may enter into the appraisal. Nonetheless, the procedures gain merit from the fact that they allow the diagnostician to obtain information about things for which no standardized measures are available.

Standardized tests are valuable instruments for analyzing a child's reading strengths and weaknesses. They are also needed to collect facts that are useful in the formulation of a remedial program. Methods of appraisal involving accurate measurement should be used whenever possible. When using standardized tests, it is necessary for the diagnostician to follow precisely the procedures for giving and scoring the instruments, as specified in the accompanying manuals. Any variation from standard procedures may affect the use of the norms supplied.

The results of normative data obtained from standardized tests, of both the survey and diagnostic varieties, must be interpreted carefully. The norms supplied for such tests indicate the performance of typical pupils with respect to typical questions in the field being measured. Therein the standardized tests have their strength and also their weakness. Children with reading disabilities are far from being typical learners. Indeed, they are designated as having a reading disability because they are atypical. Standardized tests allow the diagnostician to compare these children with average learners. This is how strengths and weaknesses can be located with a minimum of bias.

The measurements should be interpreted carefully. A child of sixth-grade age, for example, with a reading expectancy of 6.0 may measure 3.0 in reading. An uninitiated examiner might assume that this child needs the reading materials and methods suitable for the typical third-grade child. This is usually not the case. The sixth-grade child is not a typical third-grade child; she is a sixth-grade child with sixth-grade interests, drives, motives, and friends. She probably is not even a third-grade reader, for further study would very likely indicate that her basic reading skills and abilities, and therefore her instructional needs are closer to those of a second-grade child. Her degree of mental maturity enables her to use her limited basic reading skills better than does the typical child who is a second-grade reader. She has a sixth-grade potential with which to apply her second-grade reading skills. She is able to measure somewhat higher in reading—namely, at the third grade level— because of her greater mental maturity, than the second-grade child with a second-grade reading ability, potential, and chronological age and experience measures. This is but one illustration of the care the reading diagnostician must take. The standardized test is usually, however, the most reliable instrument of measurement. It provides normative data that can be used in reading diagnosis, the accuracy of which is increased through the use of numerical data.

Use of Informal Procedures
The need often arises to study areas for which standardized tests have not been developed. In that case, the diagnostician should explore further, by informal means, any insights into the nature of the particular reading disability that has been discovered during standardized testing. Often, informal assessment procedures supply more insights for planning a remedial program than does standardized testing. Most reading specialists combine formal testing with informal inventories of a child's reading skills, abilities, interests, and attitudes for an optimal understanding of the child's difficulty.

Decisions on the Basis of Patterns of Scores
When information about a child who has reading difficulties has been collected, it must be arranged so that numerical scores can be compared with one another. An adequate diagnosis is made from these comparisons. High as well as low scores must be considered in estimating the instructional needs of the child with reading difficulties. A disability in reading may be the result of overemphasis. One child's sight recognition may be low because she has always been so good at using word analysis techniques that she has found little need to remember words at sight. Another child may have such a compelling need to be accurate in reading that he cannot become a fluent reader. He is always 100-percent accurate, and even if more detail about a passage were required, he would know that, too. These lacks of balance can be detected by making comparisons with standardized norms.

If the diagnostician fails to compare the child's performance in the separate skills with his general reading ability, there will be many mistakes in planning remedial work. For example, when a fifth-grade child has only a third-grade ability in syllabication, the diagnostician may think that his lack of ability to break words into syllables is at the root of the difficulty. But when it is noted that the child's general reading ability is only that of the typical second-grade child, his ability to syllabify becomes a strength rather than a weakness.

After numerical data are compared and judgments are made, decisions should be modified in accordance with the qualitative data gathered from informal approaches. The diagnostician should be careful not to let isolated observations or bits of information alter drastically the judgments she has made from reliable and valid measurements.

Ongoing Diagnosis

Occasionally, a child fails to respond to remedial instruction based upon the original diagnosis. In that case, after 2 or 3 weeks of instruction, the diagnosis should be reevaluated. Additional measurements and other evaluations may be needed. Or perhaps something has been overlooked.

Similarly, it should not be forgotten that when the remedial program is successful, the child's needs change. The original diagnosis indicated the child's needs at the time remedial instruction was undertaken. The remedial program based on it was designed to alter the child's reading profile in ways that would encourage better overall growth in reading. As the child progresses, her needs will have changed, and the remedial program may require modification. Diagnosis must therefore be continuous.

At the start of remedial instruction, a child may have been insecure in reading situations. The diagnostician may have recommended that a chart be kept to show her her progress. After a time, as the child gains security, the chart can be discontinued. Another child may have been relatively poor at using contextual clues to aid word recognition and was depending solely upon word analysis. The remedial instruction may have been directed toward encouraging the use of context. Later, it may be noted that the child is neglecting careful inspection of words and is guessing at their meaning instead. The guesses make sense, but are not correct. Through ongoing diagnosis, the diagnostician can detect when the problem changes and thus maintain a better balance between the two word-recognition techniques.

Analyzing Reading Difficulties

Sometimes, in diagnosing a reading disability, the diagnostician will find other areas that will interfere with the correction of the reading problem. For example, a child's reading disability may be difficult to correct because of a serious behavior problem. It is not the province of this book to describe how to deal with behavior problems. Nevertheless, the reading specialist has to be alert to such problems and should identify related problems needing further study by other specialists. In formulating a remedial program, the specialist must always take into account the presence of conditions that need treatment by other professionals.

The reading specialist needs to find the answers to some specific questions about the child with a reading disability before an effective remedial program can be formulated. Our discussion of the analysis of reading difficulties will be in terms of the following questions:

1. Does the child have a reading disability?
2. What instruction is needed?
3. Who can provide that instruction most effectively?
4. How can improvement be made most effectively?
5. Does the child have any limiting conditions?
6. Are conditions in the child's environment conducive to reading progress?

Does the Child Have a Reading Disability?

Poor reading ability is so interrelated with other characteristics of a child's development that it is often extremely difficult to determine whether a reading disability or some other condition is the basic problem. Not all children who are poor readers have reading disabilities. And some children who do have reading disabilities have a more important problem that should be remedied before correcting their reading. For them, the true nature of the problem must be identified first. Then a decision must be made as to whether the child will profit from remedial instruction in reading or whether some other adjustment is required.

The child who is considered to have a reading disability because he is not as good in reading as other children the same age may be reading as well as could be expected. An example of this is the child with low verbal intelligence. This child cannot be expected to grow as rapidly in reading as can other children. His problem will not be solved by a remedial reading program, but it can be eased by curricular changes, training in language development, and methods better suited to his learning ability. No child should be considered to have a reading disability unless there is a discrepancy between his learning capacity and his reading performance. A classification system for reading disability is given in Figure 7–1.

Physical anomalies may cause a child to be classified as having a reading disability when the real need is to see a doctor, not a reading specialist. For example, children with neurological problems cannot be expected to develop reading capabilities as rapidly as can their equally intelligent, but neurologically sound, contemporaries. Some neurological problems are more difficult for the educational diagnostician to detect and are suspected only after considerable remedial instruction has been given with unsatisfactory results. The diagnostician should be alert to the possibility of neurological limitations, especially in those children high in intelligence and low in other organized skills, such as arithmetical computation. The reading diagnostician and remedial worker must be aware that not all human deficiencies can be corrected by education.

When children have neurological impairments, the reading teacher must often be satisfied with a less than usual rate of progress. The remedial reading program for neurologically impaired children is designed to give the child the individualized help needed. His problem is usually not a misbalanced reading

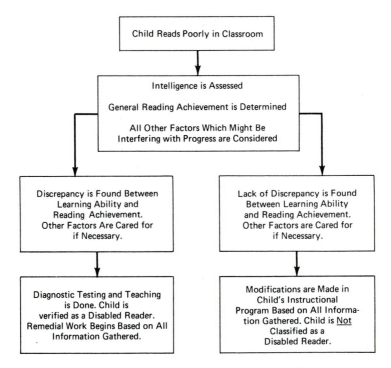

FIGURE 7–1 Classification System for Reading Disability

growth pattern, but rather a restricted overall reading development, produced by the neurological limitation. A more detailed treatment of the visual and perceptual problems encountered in the neurologically impaired child will be given in Chapter 13.

The relationship between reading disabilities and behavior problems often makes it difficult to classify a child's major problem as a reading disability. Sometimes the poor reader is a behaviorally disordered child, and reading achievement suffers along with other school learnings. Or the behavioral disturbance is brought about by the failure to make normal progress in reading. Here, immediate attention to the reading problem will correct the reading problem and improve the behavior problem. Even in those cases in which deep-seated emotional problems are suspected of making the child an inefficient learner, emotional therapy and remedial instruction in reading can be given concurrently, to their mutual benefit.

What Instruction Is Needed?

The instruction a child with a reading disability requires is indicated by the child's reading strengths and weaknesses. Establishing reading competencies and deficiencies is the most important phase of diagnosis for formulating a program of correction. The specialist's main problem is finding just what in the reading pattern of the child is hindering her reading growth. The diagnostic study of what is really wrong with the child's reading—what faulty techniques she is using, what abilities she is overemphasizing, and what abilities she lacks—is essential to formulating a remedial program.

Other limitations in the child's reading patterns also have far-reaching effects. The failure to establish certain skills and abilities and the overemphasis of others, the failure to acquire essential knowledge, or the adoption of faulty approaches may interfere with the child's entire reading development. A lack of flexibility and adaptability may seriously limit the child's ability to adjust her reading skills to the requirements of particular reading material or to certain purposes for reading.

Who Can Provide Instruction Most Effectively?

The regular classroom teacher can and should give remedial instruction to most children with no more than a moderate disability in reading. The size of the class, other responsibilities, and her training limit the teacher to the solution of only the less complicated reading problems. The teacher must always decide just how much attention can be given to one child at the expense of many. In the well-managed classroom, many reading difficulties can be detected early and corrected by the classroom teacher. Even under these circumstances, the teacher frequently needs the help of a reading specialist to aid her in the formulation of a classroom remedial program.

The second place in which remedial work in reading is given is at a reading center or resource room within the school. This center is usually a room that is well stocked with materials for reading and for special practice exercises. Here, a remedial reading teacher works with individual children or groups of children needing more specialized and individual attention than can be given by the classroom teacher.

In general, the smaller the group, the greater are the returns for each child. Remedial teachers working in school reading centers need special training to handle the problems they meet. They should be able to diagnose complex reading problems and offer suggestions for those children who are to be treated by classroom teachers. The teachers in charge of remedial rooms or centers within a school should be successful classroom teachers who have had additional training in reading and in diagnosing and treating reading disabilities. A reading disability is no simple thing to be solved by a novice or by a set of exercises purporting to be suitable for all cases.

To decide where the child with a reading difficulty can be treated most effectively, the diagnostician first needs to decide into which of the general categories described in Chapter 3 the child fits.

Recommendations for General Reading Immaturity

Children who are significantly delayed in reading, but who show no unusual or limiting characteristics in their reading patterns and no personal rejection of reading, can be treated effectively in the regular classroom. They are generally immature in reading, but need no marked reeducation. They do need instruction for their level of achievement, a reading program that promotes motivation, and an opportunity to read a lot.

Some children in this category are better treated in the school reading center. If the child is so low in reading ability that he cannot profit from most of the instruction given in group work in class, he would be taught more productively by the remedial teacher in the school reading center. Most poor readers of secondary school age should be assigned to a remedial reading teacher. It is difficult for the secondary teacher, who works with more than 150 pupils a day, to know any one child well enough to assist the extremely immature reader.

The generally immature reader can usually be discovered by general diagnosis, using achievement tests and nonverbal group mental tests. He may not be isolated until the specific level of diagnosis is reached. The child with simple, general immaturity in reading is one who has a low, but relatively uniform, reading profile and no adverse reactions to his poor reading. He is classed as having a reading disability only because he is not reading as well as he could be expected to read. A study of his reading scores shows that he has normal reading patterns for the typical child of equal reading attainment. There is no interfering habit or faulty attitude present to impede his future growth.

Recommendations for Specific Reading Immaturity

Children with specific reading immaturity are limited severely in one or more areas of reading but have developed the general basic skills and abilities well enough to be able readers in other areas. Practically all of these children can be given the remedial work they need by the classroom teacher. After the skills or abilities in which the child needs further training and experience have been found, the teacher increases emphasis in specific areas in which the child is weak as she participates in the regular developmental reading program. If there are two or three children needing the same amount of emphasis, from time to time the teacher can give them remedial training as a small group. In some instances, children with specific limitations from several classes of about the same grade level can be sent to the school remedial center for group instruction, but for the most part, they should be given training by the classroom teacher. The prognosis for overcoming specific reading immaturity is exceedingly good, even though the degree of disability is sometimes great.

A child with specific immaturity in reading is discovered through reading tests that are more analytical than are those customarily used in general diagnosis. Tests that give scores in various important areas of reading, as well as informal measures, can be used to diagnose the child with specific reading problems. Indications of attainment in the more common types of comprehension and study skills are needed to pinpoint the specific areas of limitation. If a child scores high on some comprehension tests but low on other tests, she is correctly described as a case of specific reading immaturity, and no further diagnosis is needed. The child's high scores indicate that there is no basic limitation in her reading. Her low scores isolate the areas needing attention.

Recommendations for Limiting Reading Disability

The child who has serious deficiencies in basic reading skills and abilities that impede his entire reading growth is best described as having a limiting disability. Such a child is low in all types of reading, because he has acquired interfering habits or has failed to learn one or more essential skills. His reading profile indicates, not the healthy reading growth of the child with simple reading immaturity, but rather, a nonproductive reading pattern.

Most children with a limiting disability should be given remedial work in a school reading center or resource room. A few may be able to be corrected by the classroom teacher, but usually, reeducation takes more time and careful planning than he is able to devote to it.

Recommendations for Complex Reading Disability

Children who are best described as having a complex reading disability include those whose reading problems are subtle and complicated. These children are always severely delayed in reading. They may be bright, capable youngsters who demonstrate antagonism toward reading and who feel embarrassed about their inability to read. They sometimes make a negative adjustment to their lack of success in reading, which spreads to general ineffectiveness in other schoolwork. In many cases, they lack persistence and tend to avoid school in general and reading situations in particular. They are absent from school frequently, and sometimes they become delinquent.

Children with complex reading disabilities include not only those children who have made a faulty adjustment to their reading problems, but also those who have other handicaps. Remedial programs are further complicated when they must be modified to adjust to physiological, emotional, intellectual, environmental, or other atypical conditions.

Many children with complex reading disabilities become blocked and so tense that they are ineffective learners. A child with a complex disability in reading is often found to be anxious and to worry about reading and to have a fear of reading. He tends to be insecure and defeated. Children who are classified in this category need careful, individual attention. A child with a complex reading disability needs a comprehensive diagnosis of his problem, and often the reading diagnostician must enlist the services of other specialists to appraise the child's needs accurately and thoroughly.

The remedial work for such children should be done in the school reading center or resource room, where there is time to give the child the necessary individual help that he requires.

How Can Improvement Be Made Most Effectively?

The answer to the question of how improvement in reading can be achieved most effectively is extremely important, because the corrective program must be efficient in order to develop reading at an accelerated rate. Extensive diagnosis of the nature of the reading problem will have pointed out the type of instruction that is necessary. The specialist must now make several decisions that will increase the efficiency of actual remedial instruction. First, instructional material must be chosen at the optimal level of difficulty. Second, material must be chosen which deals with topics that are interesting to the child, or at least that are as compatible as possible with interests of children of the same age. Third, the specialist suggests the methods by which progress will be demonstrated to the child. Fourth, the specialist must estimate the length of the instructional period. And fifth, the specialist must give the necessary information for planning the independent work that the child needs.

Determining the Proper Level of Difficulty of Material
The specialist must make a careful estimate of the level of difficulty of the material that is to be used at the start of remedial instruction. Usually, the child who has difficulty reading has been having the trouble for some time. It thus becomes vital to select material at the appropriate level of difficulty. This material should be that in which the child can feel competent. The problem of selecting material at the right level of difficulty is complicated by the fact that the child with a reading disability cannot read as well as would be expected of a child of the same age. Some specialists think that the correct approach for estimating the difficulty of material required is to study the results of standardized tests and thus ascertain the child's general reading level. They think that if a child measures, for example, 2.5, he should start remedial instruction in material suitable for the typical child halfway through the second grade. But research and experience have shown that for most children with reading disabilities, this would be an overestimation of the level at which their instruction should start.

Let us suppose that a certain child who obtains a grade-level score of 2.5 on a standardized reading test has a reading expectancy of 5.0. Then the child is really not a typical 2.5 reader. In fact, he may often be a reader with considerably less skill development than a typical 2.5 reader. He is able to bring to the reading scene a much broader background of experience, a keener evaluation of concepts, and a higher level of reasoning ability than can the typical child who is halfway through the second grade. He may measure as much as a year higher in general comprehension than he would in basic reading abilities, such as the ability to recognize words or to phrase them effectively for comprehension.

In judging the level of difficulty for initial remedial instruction, the specialist must consider, in addition to standardized tests, other evidence of the child's level of skill development. An example of such evidence is the ability to read material aloud. In oral reading situations, does the child make more than one error in every 20 running words? What is the child's skill in phrasing? What word-recognition techniques does the child use? What about his facility in retelling a story he has just read or in answering various types of comprehension questions about the material? The level at which the child can read comfortably and effectively can be estimated by trying him out on a series of graded materials and finding the level most suitable for him. The child may be started, for example, in a book at the second-grade level of difficulty. If this book proves difficult, a first-grade book can be tried. If the child reads the second-grade book with great fluency, then the specialist would try a third-grade book. The specialist would sample books until the level was found at which the child could read with reasonable ease. This informal approach gives a rough estimate of the level of difficulty suitable for a given child.

A second consideration in selecting material is the nature of the disability. The specialist must consider the outcomes to be gained from use of the material. For example, if the child's major problem is developing greater speed, the material selected should be easier than that which would normally be used with a child who is at the same general level of reading. If the child can comfortably read material of fourth-grade level, then material that is from a half-year to a year easier should be selected for increasing speed of reading. The material should contain no more than one word that would require analysis in every 100 running words. If the child's problem is developing a knowledge of visual, structural, and phonics elements, she should be given material that is rather difficult—material in which she is likely to meet one word that she needs to analyze in every 20 running words. She may occasionally be given exercises or activities that require phonics analysis for a high percentage of the words. Such exercises would be too difficult for general reading purposes, but, with teacher support, would be suitable to the child's specific problem. It should be noted that in these exercises and activities, the child must have a reasonable chance for success. The selection of materials at the appropriate level of difficulty for a particular child is probably one of the most important decisions the specialist makes.

Selecting Material That Is Suitable in Interest and Format

An important consideration in selecting material to be used in remediation is that it should be suitable to the child in both interest and format. Obtaining this material, however, is often a major problem. Material must be found that will be interesting to the child and that is presented in an appropriate format. The material must be relatively mature in content and format, but must also be at the child's reading level. Published material designed for poor readers may be appropriate, or the teacher may prepare materials. Alternatively, material of special interest that is important to the student may be used, even though the format is somewhat immature. For example, a boy of high school age may be willing to read, in a fourth-grade science book, directions for connecting a battery to a bell in order to make it ring if he is actually allowed to do it.

The task of the specialist is to estimate three things: the level of difficulty at which the child should be expected to read, the areas of interest that seem to be most acceptable to him, and the degree to which he will tolerate an immature format. Estimates of all of these are made on the basis of reading tests, interest inventories, informal appraisals, and work samples with various types of materials.

Selecting a Means of Demonstrating Progress

The teacher should select an appropriate method of demonstrating progress in reading to the child. The teacher should also estimate the amount of emphasis that should be given to demonstrating progress to the child. The method of demonstrating progress is determined by the remedial training to be given. If, for example, the child's problem is oral reading, a tape recording of the child's oral reading could be made at intervals throughout the remedial instruction. Then, from time to time, the child would listen to the tapes and note the growth that is taking place. The amount of time that should be devoted to demonstrating success to the child depends upon the child and her reactions.

Estimating the Length and Frequency of Remedial Lessons
The teacher must estimate the length of time for each training period and also the frequency with which training should be given. These estimates are made from three types of appraisals. First, the results expected from remedial instruction must be considered. If the child needs to increase his speed of reading, the actual lesson should be relatively short and highly motivating. Between lessons, the child may continue independently to emphasize speed of reading.

The second consideration used in judging the length of the remedial sessions is the age and physical stamina of the child. If he tires easily or cannot concentrate for long periods of time, the length of each training period should be short. If he is an older child, physically strong, and able to attend well to the lessons, the training periods can be longer.

Third, any condition, such as poor vision, that limits the child's ability to pay close attention to reading instruction over a period of time will shorten the length of remedial sessions. It is often better to have two short sessions a day than to have one longer one.

A careful inspection of all the information available about the child is necessary to make a reasonable estimate of the length of time for each training period and the frequency of the remedial lessons.

Planning for Independent Work
The child's reading disability will not be corrected in the remedial periods alone. She must extend her remedial reading experiences into her independent work. The level of difficulty of material used for independent work should be considerably easier than that studied during the remedial lessons, and the independent work should be somewhat different from work done in remedial lessons. In planning independent work, the diagnostician must judge how best to motivate the child and what type of exercises would be most beneficial for the child to work on independently. For example, if the child is trying to build a larger sight vocabulary, would it be best for her to have a pack of word cards with which she drills herself, stories containing words in contextual settings, or workbook-type exercises? These decisions are made by the teacher on the basis of the nature of the instruction needed, the characteristics of the child, and the characteristics of her general environment.

Does the Child Have Limiting Conditions?

In formulating a remedial program, the specialist must appraise the causes of reading disability considered in Chapters 4, 5, and 6. Also, the help of other experts must be employed if it is needed. For the reeducation program to be effective, any limitations within the child that might influence his reading growth detrimentally must be located. If the child has poor vision, an examination by an expert is required. Whenever possible, the visual defect should be corrected. For modifications in the remedial program for students with visual limitations, see Chapter 13, which deals with children with disabilities.

If poor hearing is suspected, a hearing specialist should be consulted. Again, the mere correction of the auditory limitation will not improve the child's reading. It will, however, make it more likely that the child will profit from remedial instruction. The child with an auditory disability will need modifications in his instructional program. (See Chapter 13.)

Any factor that causes a reading disability may become a condition that needs to be corrected or a condition to which the program must adjust. Whenever possible, such conditions should be corrected before the start of remedial training. When no correction is possible, the program must be altered to allow for the known limitation. It should be recognized that the correction of a limiting condition does not alter the reading needs of the child. If the child, for example, has third-grade reading skills before the visual correction, he will still have third-grade skills after the visual correction. The correction of a limiting condition does not alter the need for remedial reading instruction. However, it does improve the child's chances of learning to read efficiently and effectively.

Are Conditions in the Child's Environment Conducive to Reading Progress?

The diagnostician must study the child's entire environment, for it may have limitations that could influence the success of the remedial program. Sometimes, in their zeal to help their children, parents create emotional tensions that not only do not help the children read better, but also disturb them greatly. Or parents may try to help their children in ways that are detrimental to the children's reading growth. Parents can contribute much to the success of a remedial program by remembering that they should:

1. Take an interest in independent reading work the child brings home.
2. Give the child a good place in which to work without interruption.
3. Secure materials that will be the child's own, in consultation with the teacher.
4. Hide their anxieties about the child's reading problem.
5. Tell the child a word if she has difficulty with it when reading at home.
6. Read the child's independent material and discuss it with her.
7. Avoid ridiculing the child or making comparisons among siblings.
8. Let the child know that they appreciate her many accomplishments and that they have confidence in her.
9. Recognize that the child's "don't care" attitude toward reading is often a "do care very much" one and that it is wise to let her adopt this apparent attitude as a safety valve.

Not only the home conditions and child-parent relationships, but also the school situation, should be studied. Frequently, improvement in reading is left to the remedial program alone. But the school environment may not be conducive, all by itself, to effective reading development for a child with a reading disability. The child's entire reading environment should be coordinated if she is to progress. Sometimes, a teacher does not fully recognize the seriousness of having a child try to read material that is so difficult that it can be nothing but frustrating to her. At other times, the teacher is not aware that a child's lack of attention may be the result of a hearing loss. The specialist must try to find any problem in the child's environment that might impede her progress in learning to read.

Illustration of an Analysis of Reading Difficulties

The following illustration shows how to diagnose the reading skills of children from a fifth-grade class. The progression is from general diagnosis to specific diagnosis to child-study diagnosis.

General Diagnosis in Reading

The first level of diagnosis may be called *general diagnosis*. It is concerned with appraising all the children's levels of achievement on major indicators of reading growth. To adjust instruction to individual differences, teachers may note each child's facility in oral reading, understanding from silent reading, daily performance on class activities and work sheet exercises, and visible enjoyment, dislike, or avoidance of reading. In addition, progress on unit tests and standardized group achievement tests should be used to assess reading progress.

The teacher can compare each child's progress in reading with his level of progress in nonreading academic areas. The child's general alertness, level of background knowledge brought to the classroom, and level of participation in instruction based on nonreading sources such as film or television should also be compared with his performance on reading tasks.

If the teacher is concerned that the child may have a reading disability, further assessment should be done that includes intelligence testing, based on an individually administered intelligence test, and reading level, based on a standardized individual reading test. At this point, if the child's reading achievement is about the same as his reading expectancy and his success in other fields of learning, he is probably progressing as well in reading as can be expected. This is true even if he reads somewhat more poorly than the other children in his class. This child will need no further diagnosis in reading, even though he may need certain adjustments for the slow learner, to be described in Chapter 13. The classroom teacher should be aware of each child he teaches in the developmental reading program. In regular classwork, the teacher studies every child's reading systematically and in a diagnostic manner.

If a child's achievement in reading is considerably lower than her reading expectancy, or if her achievement is significantly better in nonreading classroom activities than in reading, further diagnosis is needed. General diagnosis helps identify those who are educationally handicapped by ineffective reading, as well as those who need curricular adjustments. Standardized survey tests, achievement tests, intelligence tests, reading series tests, informal teacher-devised tests, and teacher observations are all used in making these judgments.

At the general level of diagnosis, the teacher can study the results of standardized tests, reading tests, and informal observations that indicate the average reading achievement of the entire class. Questions to be asked are "Is the class as a whole progressing at a below-average, average, or above-average rate?" and "Is there any particular aspect of the class's reading, such as knowledge of word meanings or following written directions, that appears to need extra attention?"

From this study of the entire class, the teacher should consider the problem of adjusting materials and methods to individual differences. For example, in a fifth-grade class of 35 children, 13 were found to be instructionally suited to a fifth-grade reader, 10 required simpler material, and 12 were reading at a sixth-grade level or beyond and needed an expanded reading program. Three members of the class who were reading at a middle fourth-grade level or below were assessed further.

Alice was one such child needing further consideration. She was older than most of the children in the class, having repeated a year of school. Alice's reading expectancy was at the middle fourth-grade level, as was her average reading achievement. She did not display negative attitudes toward reading and was making acceptable daily progress. Her achievement in arithmetic computations was at a middle third-grade level. Considering what is reasonable to expect of her, Alice was doing a creditable job of learning to read. She has continued to make progress in developing reading skills, but at a somewhat slower pace than her classmates. Alice needs the type of instruction described in Chapter 13, suitable to a slow-learning child.

Michael, another child needing further assessment, was identified as having a reading disability. He was more than 2 years behind in his reading development, compared with his reading expectancy. He was of average intelligence, so he should have been reading at a beginning fifth-grade level. Michael needs to be studied further in order to plan a remedial program to improve his reading. He is relatively successful in arithmetic, which shows that he is able to achieve in areas other than reading. He shows dislike and avoidance of reading tasks in the classroom.

The third child requiring further assessment, Matt, also has a reading disability, even though he is reading only 2 months below his grade placement. He is one of the youngest members of the class, but he is the most capable intellectually. His reading expectancy, based on a suspected high level of intellectual ability, is probably closer to the seventh-grade level than his current reading grade level of 4.8. His achievement in arithmetic (7.5 grade level) is high and more in keeping with his inferred level of mental ability. From this information, it may be inferred that Matt has a reading disability. A further diagnosis, including an assessment of his level of mental ability, is needed in order to plan appropriate programming for him.

Specific Diagnosis in Reading

Specific diagnosis analyzes reading performance further than general diagnosis does. It enables the diagnostician to detect the specific areas in which a child has difficulty. It shows whether the child's difficulty is in a specific type of comprehension, in word analysis, in reading efficiency, in oral reading, or in basic study skills. A specific diagnosis also might indicate how well the child is able to adapt his reading to the demands of the various fields of study. There are many tests that give the type of information needed for specific diagnosis. Some of the more useful ones are mentioned in Chapter 8.

The general diagnosis revealed that Michael and Matt had reading disabilities and needed further diagnosis. Another child, Barbara, did not show such an overall deficiency, but did show a specific immaturity. Barbara is, in general, a competent reader, but she has great difficulty in one type of reading—reading to follow directions. She is one of the lowest members of the class in this skill, much lower than would be expected of her on the basis of her grade placement, mental ability, and general reading achievement. Her problem is not serious, but it is probable that a short period of emphasis on this type of reading would make Barbara as proficient in reading to follow directions as she is in other comprehension abilities. She thus needs no further diagnosis.

Matt has an uneven profile. His specific diagnosis shows that he is deficient in the more general types of reading comprehension. It also shows that he is considerably better at recognizing words in isolation than he is at recognizing them in context. He is a very slow reader. It is reasonable to suspect that Matt is an overanalytical reader and that he fails to use rapid methods of word recognition. The precise nature of instruction for Matt will have to be determined further through child-study diagnosis.

Michael is slow in all types of reading and must be studied further. The specific diagnosis shows only his reading speed approaching what can be expected of him. Even this, however, cannot be considered good performance, because his reading is so inaccurate. It is apparent, on the basis of the specific diagnosis, that Michael has something basically wrong with his reading. The difficulty appears to be in the word-recognition area, but even this suspicion awaits child-study diagnosis before it can be verified.

Child-Study Diagnosis in Reading

Standardized tests for general and specific diagnosis, individual standardized tests, detailed reading diagnostic tests, and informal study of a child's approaches to the various aspects of reading are used in a thorough child-study diagnosis.

This diagnosis also includes an analysis of the child's strengths and limitations as as an individual—his sensory capacities, emotional reactions, and attitudes toward reading. A child-study diagnosis should also study the child's general school environment, the methods of instruction used in the school, and the home conditions that might be specifically related to reading and that might influence his reading development. In addition, parental attitudes concerning the child's reading problem are important to assess, and parental cooperation is important to enlist. A child-study diagnosis must give answers to the six questions listed on pages 116–117.

The first question, *whether the child is correctly classified as having a reading disability,* is answered frequently by the general diagnosis. In some cases, the child-study approach indicates that a child's major problem is not in fact a disability in reading. The detailed studies of Matt and Michael did not reveal any condition that would lead to a classification other than their having a reading disability. On the other hand, the general diagnosis showed that Alice's problem was one of low intelligence and that she could not be classified as having a reading disability because her reading achievement seemed reasonable for her ability.

The second question, dealing with the *nature of the instruction needed,* was answered for Alice in the general diagnosis. She needed training in reading that was suitable to a slow-learning child. The training needed for Barbara was decided by the specific diagnosis, which showed that she needed training in following exact directions. The child-study diagnosis showed that Matt was indeed an overanalytical reader. He had a high score in knowledge of phonic elements, and he attempted to use this means of word recognition, even with words that he could recognize at sight when they were flashed before him with a speed that allowed him only a single glance at the word. He also demonstrated a tendency to pay great attention to word endings and to neglect somewhat the beginning elements of words. In addition, he was poor at making adequate use of contextual clues. Matt was shown to have a marked limiting disability in word recognition. The remedial work that he needs will be described in Chapter 10.

The training needed by Michael was also indicated by the child-study diagnosis. Michael's problem was complex. He had failed to develop a systematic method of word analysis, had difficulty with reversals, and had rejected reading. In addition, there was evidence that Michael had some visual impairment that had to be corrected before remedial instruction could be undertaken. The necessary remedial work for Michael is discussed in Chapter 12, dealing with left-to-right orientation in reading and word perception, and in Chapter 13, on children with disabilities. He also needed more work on word recognition, as described in Chapters 10 and 11.

The third question, dealing with the problem of *who can give the remedial instruction most effectively,* can sometimes be answered in the general diagnosis and at other times in the specific diagnosis, but frequently must await the completed child study. The general diagnosis showed that Alice's problem could be remedied best by an adjusted program and realistic expectations. Certainly, her basic problem was not a reading disability, nor could it be expected that she would be helped by remedial instruction in reading.

The specific diagnosis showed that Barbara was weak in just one type of reading: She had a specific immaturity in reading that could be handled appropriately by the classroom teacher.

As a result of a thorough child study, it was concluded that Matt would profit from group instruction in remedial reading, while Michael's problem was so complex and charged with rejection of reading, that it was felt that he needed one-to-one remediation in the resource room.

The fourth question that must be answered by the diagnosis deals with *how improvement can be brought about most effectively*. This question could have been answered for Alice in the general diagnosis and for Barbara in the specific diagnosis. Alice should be given material at approximately the middle of the third-grade level. She needs encouragement, success, and many opportunities to use the results of her reading in constructive activities. She needs concrete illustrations of what she is reading. Alice should read for only one well-defined purpose at a time, because she finds it difficult to attend to several purposes at the same time.

For general purposes, Barbara should read material at the middle fifth-grade level of difficulty. Instruction designed to increase her ability to follow exact directions should be started with material somewhat less difficult. The purposes for which Barbara reads should be to organize information, to sense the sequence of ideas, and to follow exact directions. It would be desirable to keep a chart indicating her speed and accuracy in completing these tasks. As her reading increases in accuracy, she can be encouraged to read somewhat more rapidly, and the difficulty of the material can be increased. Barbara can be expected to develop readily the ability to organize and follow exact directions.

Complete child-study diagnoses were necessary to find out how improvement could be brought about most efficiently in the cases of Matt and Michael. Matt should have a time chart indicating the speed at which he reads during exercises designed to increase his speed. He should be given remedial instruction with material about halfway through the fourth grade in difficulty. He should be encouraged to do a lot of independent recreational reading, and the use of contextual clues should be stressed in his reading.

Michael's problem is much more difficult than Matt's. He needs to read material at approximately the second-grade level of difficulty. However, it would be desirable to use material that is as mature in format as possible. The remedial reading teacher must be optimistic and demonstrate to Michael that he is growing in his reading. He should make a card file so that he can see that the number of words he recognizes is increasing. He could dictate some stories of his own, and if his tendency to reverse words persists, it may be necessary to use sound-tracing methods, described in Chapter 12.

The fifth question is concerned with *limiting conditions within a child* that must be considered in formulating the remedial reading program. From a thorough child-study diagnosis, it became clear that Matt had no limiting characteristics the program needed to accommodate or for which there had to be a correction made before remedial instruction could begin. Michael was found to have two limiting conditions. The first was his rejection of reading. This had to be taken into consideration in formulating his remedial reading program. Because his arithmetic score was nearly equal to his reading expectancy, however, it was concluded that in situations not involving reading, Michael was able to apply himself reasonably well. Michael's second limitation was his eyesight. There was some indication that he was farsighted and that he found it difficult to focus on the printed page at a distance that was comfortable for reading. A thorough visual examination was recommended before Michael began remedial instruction.

The sixth question deals with *environmental conditions that might affect the progress of remedial work.* It was found that for three of the children—Matt, Michael, and Alice—instruction would have to make some accommodations to their needs. For Alice, the accommodations would be those expected in adjusting generally to individual differences in any class. It was found, for example, that in science and social studies, the same textbooks were used by all the children in the class. But Alice could not be expected to use this material. A thorough study of Alice's placement will need to be made, but from the information available, a further diagnosis of her reading is not indicated. Matt's overall reading program was found to be appropriate to his needs, but he could not read some subject matter effectively. Somewhat less mature reference material should be made available to him.

The adjustments necessary in instruction for Michael are more complicated than for Matt. Michael should not attempt to read materials in the content fields; rather, he should use his reading time to read materials at his level of achievement. He should be included in classroom discussions and should participate in creative activities.

There were no indications of problems in any of the homes of these children, with the possible exception of Michael. Michael's mother was very concerned about his poor reading. She had attempted to teach him to read using a commercial reading program. After about a month of instruction, she believed not only that Michael was getting worse in reading, but that he was becoming highly upset by her instruction and by his performance. Michael's mother was eager to cooperate with his resource room teacher's suggestions that she provide Michael a special place in his home to read and that she discuss with him the stories he read and pronounce any word he found difficult.

In this example, each child we have discussed from the fifth-grade class was different. Some of the children needed no further study beyond general and specific diagnoses. Two needed detailed child-study diagnoses. It was necessary for the reading specialist to have consultations with both the classroom teacher and the parents of two of the children.

In making the child-study diagnosis of the children, both standardized and informal procedures were used, and in one case the services of an outside expert were needed. Selected reading diagnosis tests that are useful in child-study diagnosis will be described in the next chapter.

Summary

The correction of a reading disability is complicated by the intricate nature of the reading process and by the many differences in children and their environments that influence reading growth. It is little wonder that no two cases of reading disability confront the teacher or specialist with exactly the same problem. It is apparent that any remedial instruction must be based on an adequate diagnosis. More complex instances of reading disability often require more detailed and more analytical study than the classroom teacher has the time or training to give. The services of the reading specialist may be required and perhaps the services of other specialists as well, such as caseworkers, psychologists, or physicians.

The diagnosis of a child with a reading disability must be directed toward improving instruction for that child. Therefore, the therapeutic type of diagnosis is better than the etiological—that is, the one that seeks causes only. The diagnosis is more than an appraisal of reading skills and abilities. It must also assess the mental, physical, sensory, emotional, and environmental factors that could impede the child's progress.

The diagnosis must be efficient and should proceed only as far as is necessary to formulate a remedial reading program. Some children's instructional needs can be found through general diagnosis, others will need a more thorough study by specific means, and still others may need a complete study of their reading disability. Since diagnosing reading disabilities is detailed and time consuming, only pertinent information should be collected, and this by the most efficient means available.

Standardized measurements are essential to diagnosing reading disabilities reliably. Even the results of standardized tests must be interpreted with care, however, because the child with a reading disability has an atypical problem. It is often necessary to use informal procedures to obtain information that cannot be obtained from standardized measurements.

The remedial reading program is planned by first taking into account the numerical information and then modifying it in accordance with whatever other information is obtained. The specialist should treat the data objectively, so that the program can be planned properly. After a reasonable amount of time, if the remedial work proves unsuccessful, a reevaluation should be made to make appropriate changes. Even for successful programs, however, diagnosis should be continuous because reading disability is but one aspect of a dynamic process that changes during remedial instruction and the remedial program must be changed to meet the current needs of the reader.

Decisions must be made in six essential areas:

1. *Classification.* Is the child classified as having a reading disability, or is some other problem of child growth and development the basic difficulty?
2. *Training needed.* What is the nature of the training needed? Identification of the particular character of the reading limitation is the most important part of the diagnosis. The reading pattern of the child must be studied to isolate

the specific faulty learning that is impeding progress in reading. This requires a thorough appraisal of the child's skills and abilities involved in reading.

3. *Setting.* Where can the remedial work be given most effectively? Should the child be reeducated in the classroom, school reading center, or resource room? The answer to this question lies in the nature of the reading problem. Most children with general immaturity and specific immaturity should be given remedial training in the classroom or school reading center. Children with limiting disabilities should be corrected at the school reading center, while complex disabilities, for the most part, should be corrected in the resource room.

4. *Methods.* What are the most efficient methods for improving the child's reading? These include the levels and types of materials to be used, ways of demonstrating progress in reading to the child, and plans for extending the reading instruction that can be accomplished by the child independently.

5. *Limitations.* Are there any conditions within the child that might be detrimental to reading growth? The help of additional experts should be utilized whenever it is needed for diagnosis and correction of these limitations. Modifications in the remedial program must be made to adjust to any limitations.

6. *Learning environment.* Are there any conditions within the child's entire learning environment that might interfere with progress in reading? Cooperation from the home and the school will contribute to the solution of the child's reading problem.

Study Questions

1. Why is therapeutic diagnosis considered more essential than etiological diagnosis in assessing reading difficulties?

2. What are the major purposes of general, specific, and child-study diagnosis? Why are all three needed for some children, while only general diagnosis is needed for others, and only general and specific for still others?

3. Why should standardized test procedures always be used in diagnosing reading difficulties? In which instances are informal procedures most appropriate?

4. Why should one be concerned about whether or not a child is correctly classified as having a reading disability?

5. How do the reading needs of children classified as having the following reading problems differ: simple reading immaturity, specific reading immaturity, limiting reading disability, and complex reading disability? In what ways are they the same?

6. Which would you choose as most important to a child with a reading disability: material of the proper level, of appropriate format, or of suitable interest? Why? How might one compensate for material that is too difficult, too immature in appearance, or of limited interest?

Selected Readings

Harris, A. J., & Sipay, E. R. *How to increase reading ability* (9th ed.) (pp. 181–256). New York: Longman.

McCormick, S. (1987). *Remedial and clinical reading instruction* (pp. 83–163). Columbus, OH: Merrill.

Richek, M. A., List, L. K., & Lerner, J. W. (1989). *Reading problems: Assessment and teaching strategies* (2nd ed.) (pp. 13–24). Englewood Cliffs, NJ: Prentice Hall.

Roswell, F. G., & Natchez, G. (1989). *Reading disability* (4th ed.) (pp. 57–85). New York: Basic Books.

Wilson, R. M., & Cleland, C. J. (1985). *Diagnostic and remedial reading for classroom and clinic* (5th ed.) (pp. 25–38). Columbus, OH: Merrill.

Chapter 8

Use of Specific Assessment Procedures

The preceding chapter discussed six questions that should be answered in any diagnosis of reading disability. In addition, an illustrative analysis was given to show how the sequence of general, specific, and child-study levels of diagnosis helped to answer each question. The question that is the major responsibility of the reading specialist is the one concerned with the instruction needed to correct reading disabilities. The following classification of the more prevalent reading difficulties includes the types of difficulties that must be found if a diagnosis is to indicate clearly the precise kinds of instruction needed:

A. Faulty word identification and recognition

1. Insufficient sight vocabulary
2. Failure to use meaning clues

    a. Weakness in use of prior knowledge
    b. Failure to use contextual clues

3. Ineffective visual-perceptual habits

    a. Faulty visual analysis of words
    b. Excessive word-perception errors
    c. Overanalytical habits

4. Limited knowledge of word elements
5. Lack of fluent oral and visual synthesis
6. Orientational difficulties

B. Deficiencies in basic comprehension

 1. Limited meaning vocabulary
 2. Ineffective use of sentence sense
 3. Insufficient comprehension of longer units

C. Limitations in specific comprehension

 1. Weakness in locating and recalling information read
 2. Difficulty in sensing organization of material
 3. Problems in evaluating what is read
 4. Deficiency in interpretation of content
 5. Inadequate appreciative abilities

D. Insufficient development of basic study skills

 1. Difficulty in locating sources of information
 2. Weakness in use of basic references
 3. Limitations in interpretation of pictorial and tabular materials

E. Deficiencies in reading content

 1. Difficulty adjusting reading procedures to purposes of content
 2. Weakness in specialized vocabulary
 3. Insufficient understanding of complex concepts
 4. Problems with selection, evaluation, and organization of information
 5. Difficulty in using pictures and diagrams
 6. Weakness in following directions
 7. Insufficient knowledge of the meaning of symbols
 8. Difficulty adjusting rate of reading to purposes of content

F. Inefficient rates of comprehension

 1. Overanalysis
 2. Word-by-word reading
 3. Undesirable habits
 4. Faulty eye movements
 5. Excessive vocalization
 6. Inflexibility

G. Ineffective oral reading

 1. Inappropriate eye-voice span
 2. Inadequate phrasing ability
 3. Inappropriate rate and timing
 4. Frustration

These defects in reading patterns that must be appraised in a thorough diagnosis show that a reading disability is not a simple condition that can be corrected by a single approach. Information on a child's strengths and weaknesses in all of the preceding areas is obtained from a variety of evaluative techniques. A competent diagnostician uses both standardized and informal procedures in studying the nature of reading deficiencies, so that appropriate remedial programs can be designed. Detailed procedures for overcoming each of these specific deficiencies will be discussed further, beginning with Chapter 9.

Many testing and evaluation procedures are used in assessing the needs of the child with a reading disability. Usually, the diagnosis starts with the administration of achievement tests, a reading survey test, and an individual intelligence test. It may continue until specific confusions in letter recognition or insecurities with individual important digraphs have been inventoried. A study of strengths and weaknesses should be evaluated in the detail necessary to formulate an appropriate plan of instruction.

In this chapter, a variety of specific approaches to reading diagnosis will be considered. In order to plan appropriately for the child with a reading disability, all relevant information obtainable must be collected and studied.

Tests Used in General Diagnosis in Reading

In general diagnosis, standardized tests of general achievement, achievement in various skill areas, and survey reading are used. General achievement tests are used to measure the relative strengths and weaknesses of students in different areas of the curriculum. They are commonly administered to all of the children in a school. Individual tests of development in several academic skill areas are selectively administered to those children who are experiencing learning difficulties. Reading survey tests are used to obtain an estimate of the students' overall reading achievement and to determine their relative strengths and weaknesses in such attributes as vocabulary, comprehension, word analysis, and reading rate. The teacher can use these results to aid in adjusting instruction to individual differences within the classroom and to help find the areas of reading that need corrective treatment.

General Achievement Tests

A profile of the reader's relative performance in major areas of the curriculum, as measured by general achievement tests, enables the reading specialist to isolate the academic areas in which a student may be experiencing difficulty reading. The specialist can also see whether or not the child with a reading disability scores significantly higher on the nonreading subtests in comparison to the reading section of the test. If so, reading might be a basic problem. A marked variation in the profile might suggest that the student is deficient in a certain specific comprehension ability or in some basic study skill. All of these irregularities would indicate that further diagnosis is needed. Following is a listing of some general achievement tests that are useful in general diagnosis; for additional examples and evaluations, see Conoley and Kramer (1989).

California Achievement Tests. Forms E and F. Grades K.0–K.9, K.6–2.2, 1.6–3.2, 2.6–4.2, 3.6–5.2, 4.6–6.2, 5.6–7.2, 6.6–8.2, 7.6–9.2, 8.6–11.2, 10.6–12.9: reading (vocabulary, comprehension, sound recognition, visual recognition, and word analysis); language (mechanics and expression); spelling; mathematics (computation, concepts, and applications); study skills; science; social studies (CTB/McGraw-Hill, 1986a).

Iowa Tests of Basic Skills. Primary Battery, Multilevel, and Separate Level Editions. Grades K.1–1.5, K.8–1.9, 1.7–2.6, 2.7–3.5, 3, 4, 5, 6, 7, 8–9: listening; word analysis; vocabulary; reading/reading comprehension; language (spelling, capitalization, punctuation, usage, and expression); work study (visual materials and reference materials); mathematics (concepts, problem solving, and computation); social studies; science; listening; writing (Hieronymus et al., 1986).

Metropolitan Achievement Tests (6th edition). Survey Battery. Grades K.0–K.9, K.5–1.9, 1.5–2.9, 2.5–3.9, 3.5–4.9, 5.0–6.9, 7.0–9.9, 10.0–12.9: vocabulary; word-recognition skills; reading comprehension; mathematics (concepts, problem solving, and computation); spelling; language; science; social studies (Prescott, Balow, Hogan, & Farr, 1987).

SRA Achievement Series. Grades K.5–1.5, 1.5–2.5, 2.5–3.5, 3.5–4.5, 4.5–6.5, 6.0–8.5, 8.0–10.5, 9.0–12.9: reading (visual discrimination, auditory discrimination, letters and sounds, listening comprehension, vocabulary, and comprehension); mathematics (concepts, computation, and problem solving); language arts (mechanics and usage); spelling; reference materials; social studies; science (Naslund, Thorpe, & Lefever, 1983, 1984).

Stanford Achievement Test. Grades 1.5–2.9, 2.5–3.9, 3.5–4.9, 4.5–5.9, 5.5–7.9, 7.0–9.9: word study skills; word reading; reading comprehension; vocabulary; listening comprehension; spelling; language/English; concepts of number; mathematics computation; mathematics applications; environment; science; social science (Gardner, Rudmen, Karlsen, & Merwin, 1983a).

Skill Area Achievement Tests

A comparison of the reader's relative performance in overall reading, spelling, and mathematics assists the specialist in determining whether the child's academic difficulties are limited to a reading disability or are more general. Because these tests are administered individually, they also serve to identify the child with satisfactory development in the skill areas, but who performs poorly in group tests. For additional examples and evaluations, see Conoley and Kramer (1989).

Kaufman Test of Educational Achievement, Brief Form. Grades 1–12: reading; mathematics; spelling; battery composite (Kaufman & Kaufman, 1985).

Woodcock-Johnson Psycho-Educational Battery, Revised. Tests of Achievement. Grades K.0–15.9: reading; mathematics; written language; knowledge (Woodcock & Johnson, 1989).

Reading Survey Tests

Reading survey tests provide a general measure of some of the most important components of reading, such as power of comprehension, word recognition, and speed of reading. The performance of a child on a reading survey test suggests how the child might perform in a real-life reading situation. The information gained can be used to confirm or disconfirm the existence of a reading difficulty.

The complex nature of a child's reading development requires that no single type of test be used as the sole criterion of the child's reading achievement. Each subtest of a survey test is in itself a measure of an important reading outcome. The score of each subtest can be compared with the average reading score of the survey test to see whether the child is weak in power of comprehension, word recognition, speed, or accuracy. If a given score were significantly lower than the child's average reading score, an area of reading needing further study would be identified.

The following tests are examples of suitable reading survey tests for general diagnosis. They also have some analytical value. (For more examples and an evaluation of these tests, see Conoley & Kramer, 1989.)

California Achievement Tests, Reading. Forms E and F. Grades K.0–K.9, K.6–2.2, 1.6–3.2, 2.6–4.2, 3.6–7.2, 6.6–12.9: vocabulary; comprehension; sound recognition; visual recognition; word analysis (CTB/McGraw-Hill, 1986b).

Gates-MacGinitie Reading Tests. Grades 1.0–1.9, 1.5–1.9, 2, 3, 4–6, 7–9, 10–12: vocabulary; comprehension (MacGinitie, Kamons, Kowalski, MacGinitie, Mackay, T., 1978).

Nelson-Denny Reading Test. Forms E and F. Grades 9–12 and adults: vocabulary; comprehension; total; rate (Brown, Bennett, & Hanna, 1981).

Stanford Achievement Test, Reading Tests. Grades 1.5–2.9, 2.5–3.9: reading (word, comprehension, word plus comprehension); word study skills; total; vocabulary; Grades 3.5–4.9, 4.5–5.9, 5.5–7.9: comprehension; word study skills; total; vocabulary; Grades 7.0–9.9: vocabulary; comprehension; total (Gardner, Rudmen, Karlsen, & Merwin, 1983b).

Tests Used in Specific Diagnosis in Reading

Specific diagnosis explores systematically particular areas of reading weakness. It can indicate that a child's problem is, for example, a deficiency in the area of basic comprehension abilities, but it will not isolate the exact limitations involved. Or it might indicate the instruction needed for general or specific reading immaturity. The tests used in specific diagnosis do not go into enough detail to plan remedial instruction for those children classified as having a limiting or complex reading disability.

Many standardized tests are available that can systematically analyze the various areas of reading growth. Some reading problems can be identified clearly enough to enable the diagnostician or the classroom teacher to develop an individual remedial plan to overcome the specific difficulty. Other problems indicated by the specific diagnosis will need further study, using child-study techniques, before a suitable remedial plan can be formulated.

If the diagnosis requires a child-study approach, the diagnostician will need to include all of the information acquired in the general and specific levels of diagnosis, as well as any other data required to complete the case study. The reading specialist will need to make comparisons among the various measures of reading proficiency. The chronological age and I.Q. of the student will also need to be taken into consideration.

Following is a listing of a few tests for specific diagnosis. For more examples and critical evaluations, see Conoley and Kramer (1989).

Decoding Skills Test. Grades 1.0–5.8+: basal vocabulary (instructional level, frustration level); phonic patterns (monosyllabic, polysyllabic [long vowel, short vowel, vowel diagraph, single consonant, consonant blend on real and nonsensical words]) (Richardson & DiBenedetto, 1985).

Metropolitan Achievement Test (6th edition). Reading Diagnostic Tests. Grades K.5–1.9: visual discrimination, letter recognition, auditory discrimination, sight vocabulary, phoneme/grapheme consonants, vocabulary in context, reading comprehension, total; Grades 1.5–2.9: auditory discrimination, sight vocabulary, phoneme/grapheme (consonants and vowels), vocabulary in context, word part clues, reading comprehension, total; Grades 2.5–3.9: sight vocabulary, phoneme/grapheme (consonants and vowels), vocabulary in context, word part clues, reading comprehension, total; Grades 3.5–4.9: phoneme/grapheme (consonants and vowels), vocabulary in context, word part clues, rate of comprehension, reading comprehension, total; Grades 5.0–6.9: phoneme/grapheme (consonants and vowels), vocabulary in context, word part clues, rate of comprehension, skimming and scanning, reading comprehension, total; Grades 7.0–9.9: vocabulary in context, rate of comprehension, skimming and scanning, reading comprehension, total (Prescott et al., 1987).

Stanford Diagnostic Reading Test. Grades 1.5–12 (four levels: red, green, brown, blue): word reading; reading comprehension; auditory discrimination; phonetic analysis; structural analysis; auditory vocabulary; vocabulary; word parts; reading rate; scanning and skimming (Karlsen, Madden, & Gardner, 1984).

Woodcock Reading Mastery Test, Revised. Forms G and H. Grades K–14 and adult: visual auditory learning; letter identification; word identification; word attack; word comprehension (antonyms, synonyms, and analogies); passage comprehension (Woodcock, 1986).

Tests Used in Child-Study Diagnosis in Reading

The tests used in the general and specific levels of diagnosis form the basis of the child-study diagnosis. For some children with reading disabilities, these tests give the diagnostician sufficient information to develop an appropriate individual plan of remediation, and further diagnosis is not needed. For those students who have not yet been diagnosed adequately, a study of their test results usually indicates the areas of reading limitation that should be explored further. The techniques used are confined mostly to individual testing procedures that require special training and some supervised clinical experience to yield valid results. The specific standardized tests used at three levels of diagnosis in reading are summarized in Figure 8–1.

The techniques of individual diagnosis in Figure 8–1 are representative, but by no means inclusive, of all the tests discussed in the literature. The reader should bear in mind that each of these techniques (and others not described) has had successful use in the field.

The descriptions in this chapter are designed to give a general impression of the main characteristics of the diagnostic tests. Actual use of any particular test is based upon the detailed directions accompanying it. (For further information, see Conoley & Kramer, 1989.)

Diagnostic Reading Scales. Grades 1–7: word recognition lists (word list 1, word list 2, word list 3); reading selections (two sets of graded paragraphs); word analysis and phonics tests (initial consonants, final consonants, consonant digraphs, consonant blends, initial consonant substitution, initial consonant sounds recognized auditorily, auditory discrimination, short and long vowel sounds, vowels with the letter *r*, vowel diphthongs and digraphs, common syllables or phonograms, blending) (Spache, 1981).

Durrell Analysis of Reading Difficulty (3rd edition). Grades K–6: oral reading; silent reading; listening comprehension; listening vocabulary; word recognition/word analysis; spelling; auditory analysis of words and word elements; pronunciation of word elements; visual memory of words; prereading phonics abilities (Durrell & Catterson, 1980).

Gates-McKillop-Horowitz Reading Diagnostic Test (2nd edition). Grades 1–6: oral reading (omissions, additions, repetitions, directional errors, wrong beginning, wrong middle, wrong ending, wrong in several parts, and accent errors); reading sentences; words (flash and untimed); word attack

General Diagnosis in Reading

General Achievement Tests. Measure relative strengths and weaknesses in various areas of the curriculum (group testing).

> *California Achievement Tests*
> *Iowa Tests of Basic Skills*
> *Metropolitan Achievement Tests* (6th edition)
> *SRA Achievement Series*
> *Stanford Achievement Test*

Skill Area Achievement Tests. Measure relative strengths and weaknesses in various academic skill areas (individual testing).

> *Kaufman Test of Educational Achievement, Brief Form*
> *Woodcock-Johnson Psycho-Educational Battery, Revised*

Reading Survey Tests. Measure overall reading achievement, relative strengths and weaknesses in major aspects of reading (group testing).

> *California Achievement Tests, Reading*
> *Gates-MacGinitie Reading Tests*
> *Nelson-Denny Reading Test*
> *Stanford Achievement Test, Reading Tests*

Specific Diagnosis in Reading

Decoding Skills Test
Metropolitan Achievement Test, Reading Diagnostic Tests
Stanford Diagnostic Reading Test
Woodcock Reading Mastery Test, Revised

Child-Study Diagnosis in Reading

Diagnostic Reading Scales
Durrell Analysis of Reading Difficulty
Gates-McKillop-Horowitz Reading Diagnostic Tests

FIGURE 8–1   Sample Standardized Tests Used in Reading Diagnosis

(syllabication, recognizing and blending common parts of words, reading words, giving letter sounds, naming capital letters, and naming lowercase letters); recognizing the visual form of vowels; auditory tests (auditory blending and auditory discrimination); written expression (spelling and informal writing sample) (Gates, McKillop, & Horowitz, 1981).

Informal Diagnosis

The diagnosis of reading abilities and deficiencies is best achieved through quantitative information from standardized tests and procedures such as those just described. In planning a program for the child with reading difficulties, however, it is also wise to gather qualitative information by less formal procedures such as analyzing the child's classroom reading and using informal reading inventories.

Analysis of Classroom Reading

Classroom teachers have the opportunity to make extensive informal analyses of the reading achievement of their students. During each school day, the teacher may unobtrusively observe every child's overall performance on a variety of daily reading and writing tasks. The child's response to reading instruction and proficiency in oral and silent reading may be noted. Qualitative consideration may be given to a child's oral reading performance, to questions he generates about the content of his reading, and to his contributions to class discussions and to small-group projects. The child's performance on worksheets and on reading and writing activities may be evaluated informally, as well as by the classroom teacher. Such analyses are valuable because they are based on many observations, are taken over an extended period of time, and cover many aspects of reading under natural, nonthreatening conditions.

The astute teacher, through day-by-day observation, is able to judge when a child requires an adjustment in reading instruction. Through focused discussion, a teacher may assess the child's background knowledge prior to his reading a selection. She may note, using a simple record-keeping procedure, the nature of the child's word-recognition or comprehension difficulties. By having the child retell a selection after reading it (testing unaided recall), she may monitor his understanding of what he reads, sense of structure, and use of oral language. By analyzing the child's writing, the teacher may evaluate the child's use of language and functional knowledge of letter-sound associations. In addition, the classroom teacher has the opportunity to observe, throughout the school year and on a daily basis, each child's attitude toward reading, ability to apply knowledge gained through reading, efficiency in extended reading, and skill in reading a wide variety of materials.

It is usually the classroom teacher who first recognizes that a child is experiencing reading difficulties. It is often the classroom teacher who, solely on the basis of classroom diagnosis, makes special adaptations to assist a child in overcoming minor reading problems. It is generally the classroom teacher who brings a child's emergent reading difficulties to the attention of the reading specialist and others who can provide remedial services. It is the classroom teacher who works with specialists in coordinating special reading programs with the ongoing classroom routine. The classroom teacher helps support the progress of children receiving special help by fostering their improving competence in applying reading skills in the classroom and by encouraging their more favorable attitudes toward reading.

Although reading specialists provide the more time-consuming and systematic analyses of reading problems necessary to plan special instruction for the child with serious reading difficulties, it is the ongoing observation and analysis of the child and the constant modifications to the program made by all persons who teach the child that make instruction successful. In the classroom, teachers use observational analysis and instructional adaptation on a continuing basis to promote optimal reading growth for all children.

Informal Reading Inventories

The use of informal reading inventories allows the teacher to make a qualitative evaluation of the child's word-recognition and comprehension strengths and weaknesses. In addition, informal reading inventories allow for instructional adjustments based on an estimate of three reading levels the child attains (Betts, 1957):

1. The child's *independent reading level* is ascertained from the book in which he can read with no more than one error in word recognition (pronunciation) in each 100 words and has a comprehension score of at least 90 percent. At this level, the child must read aloud in a natural conversational tone. The reading should be rhythmical and well phrased. At the same time, the child is free from tension and has good reading posture. His silent reading will be faster than his oral reading and free from vocalizations. This is the level at which the child should do extensive supplementary reading for enjoyment or for information in line with his interests. At this level, the child has complete control of experience (concepts), vocabulary, construction, and organization. He has, therefore, the maximum opportunity for doing the thinking that is required for a full understanding of what he is reading.

2. The child's *instructional reading level* is determined from the level of the book in which he can read with no more than one word-recognition error in each 20 words and with a comprehension score of at least 75 percent. This is the level at which a pupil is able to make successful progress in reading *under a teacher's guidance*. In the classroom, oral reading after silent study is performed without tension, in a conversational tone, and with rhythm and proper phrasing. Silent reading is faster than oral, except at the beginning levels. The child is able properly to use word-recognition clues and techniques with the use of challenging materials at this level, and with purposeful reading directed by the teacher, the result should be maximum progress in acquiring reading abilities.

3. The child's *frustration reading level* is marked by the book in which he bogs down when he tries to read. At this level, the child reads orally without rhythm and in an unnatural voice. Errors and refusals are numerous and tensions are obvious. The child comprehends less than half of what he is trying to read. The test should be stopped as soon as it is clear that the child is at his frustration level.

Estimating Reading Levels
The child's reading levels can be estimated by using carefully graded materials similar to those available for instruction. These materials should not have been

used previously with the child. Selections of from 100 to 150 words should be chosen from each successive difficulty level. A few questions involving both fact, inference, and vocabulary may be constructed for each selection. After the child, starting at a relatively easy level, has read each selection aloud to the teacher or specialist, he then answers the comprehension questions based upon its content. If the child has great difficulty with the first reading selection, he is moved back to an easier level. When the child reads with ease, he is asked to read successively more difficult selections until his three reading levels are determined.

No child should be asked to go on reading at the frustration level when being taught or in any other situation. The teacher, however, should recognize that such a level exists. Too frequently, children are found to be working at their frustration levels in classes in which instruction is not satisfactorily adjusted to individual differences.

Commercial Informal Reading Inventories

A variety of well-constructed and convenient informal reading inventories have been produced for general reading evaluation. Among these are the following:

Analytical Reading Inventory (3rd edition). Grades primer–9: Forms A, B, and C; graded word lists (primer–Grade 6) and graded passages (primer–Grade 9). Used to determine general level of word recognition, strengths and weaknesses in word-recognition skills, performance in oral or silent reading, comprehension strategies, independent reading level, instructional reading level, frustration reading level, and reading capacity or listening level (Woods & Moe, 1985).

Bader Reading and Language Inventory. Children, adolescents, and adults: graded reading passages, word-recognition lists, phonics, word analysis, spelling, cloze tests, visual discrimination, auditory discrimination, unfinished sentences, evaluation of language abilities (Bader, 1983).

Qualitative Reading Inventory. Grades primer, 1–2 passages, 3–junior high passages: independent reading level, instructional reading level, frustration reading level, level variety, oral reading, silent reading, word identification ability (in isolation and in context), miscue analysis, comprehension ability, prior knowledge (Leslie & Caldwell, 1990).

Informal Diagnosis of Word-Recognition Difficulties

Word-recognition difficulties are diagnosed effectively by evaluating oral reading behavior. Many of the standardized individual diagnostic tests described in this chapter use quantitative measures of oral reading performance to find strengths and weaknesses in the student's reading. Often, additional insights into reading problems can be obtained by informal qualitative appraisals of the child's oral reading habits and errors.

After the child's reading levels have been determined, the specialist selects material more advanced than the child's instructional level, so as to get a good sample of her reading errors, but still below the level of frustration, so that meaningful reading is possible. The child should read the selection aloud without any help. She should also be told to guess any of the words she does not know, and she should be told that she will be asked about the story when she finishes it. Every error should be recorded so that it can be classified according to type. A tape recording of the oral reading sample might be helpful in making a careful study of the errors.

We have found that three types of classifications are necessary to obtain a complete understanding of word-recognition problems that children with reading disabilities have. First, we classify the errors to indicate the child's phonic and structural decoding strengths and weaknesses. The error classification we use are:

Vowel errors. Mispronunciations that alter one or more vowel sounds, as *dig* read *dug.*

Consonant errors. Alteration of one or more consonant sounds, as *send* read *sent.*

Addition of sounds. Insertion of one or more sounds in a word, as *tack* read *track.*

Omission of sounds. Mispronunciations that involve omission of one or more sounds in a word, as *blind* read *bind.*

Substitution of words. Substitution of a word unrelated in form or sound to the word to be read, as *lived* read *was.*

Repetition of words. Words repeated, whether read correctly or incorrectly, are counted as repetition, as *"a boy a boy had a dog"* (one repetition).

Addition of words. Insertion of words into the text as when *once there was* is read *once upon a time there was* (three word additions).

Omission of words. Omissions of words from the text, as *a little pig* read *a pig.*

Refusals and words aided. Refusal of a child to attempt a word or when a word is supplied by the specialist after a delay of 15 seconds.

Suggestions for helping children overcome such word-recognition problems are discussed in Chapters 11 and 12.

Next, we study possible faulty perceptual habits, such as a tendency to reverse letters or words. We also look for error patterns involving primarily specific parts of words, such as wrong beginnings, wrong middles, or wrong endings, and words that are wrong in several parts. Suggestions for helping children overcome such perceptual errors are discussed in Chapters 11 and 12.

The third type of diagnosis of oral reading behavior deals with limitations in the use of meaning clues to word recognition. We have found helpful a somewhat modified use of the linguistic classification of oral reading miscues suggested by

Goodman, Watson, and Burke (1987). We are interested especially in word mis-cues that indicate (1) the ineffective use of clues gained from the reader's prior knowledge (for example, a child might fail to recognize a word, such as *rhinoceros,* even though she was reading about a trip to the zoo, where she has been many times); (2) miscues that indicate little use of syntactic aids derived from a knowl-edge of language structure (for example, "They all were happy" read as "They all where happy"); (3) miscues that indicate a lack of use of semantic aids gained from an ongoing understanding of the content presented (for example, "The girl was riding a horse" read as "The girl was riding a house").

We assess the reader's limitations in the use of meaning clues in anticipating the next word or words to be read. Skill in using meaning clues facilitates any perceptual skills. We also diagnose the reader's difficulties in using meaning clues to check the accuracy of decoded, unknown words. These last two limita-tions are identified by the number of repetitions made, the compatibility of the errors made with the ongoing content, and the omissions or additions of words that alter the meaning of the passage being read.

A more complete analysis of miscues, developed by Goodman et al. (1987) involves classifying each miscue according to:

1. Syntactic acceptability—that is, how structurally acceptable is the miscue?
2. Semantic acceptability—that is, how acceptable is the meaning of the miscue?
3. Meaning change—that is, how much does the miscue result in a change of meaning?
4. Correction—that is, how successful is any attempt to correct the miscue?
5. Graphic similarity—that is, how much does the miscue look like the text?
6. Sound similarity—that is, how much does the miscue sound like the expected response?

Having the child pronounce words from word lists provides additional infor-mation about her word-recognition skills. The words should be selected to be at the child's instructional level. Errors are recorded and analyzed. Then we have the child try again to pronounce the missed or refused words to discover her identification patterns. After this, the missed words are presented orally to the child for her to use in oral sentences. In this way, we can ascertain whether they are part of her meaning vocabulary.

The remedial methods suggested throughout this book emphasize the use of meaning clues, because all skills are taught in meaningful reading situations rather than in isolated drills. The remedial methods suggested in Chapter 10 are specifically designed to correct deficiencies in meaning clues to word recognition.

Informal Diagnosis of Comprehension Difficulties

Most of the standardized diagnostic tests mentioned in this chapter provide quantitative measures of silent reading comprehension. Further diagnostic infor-mation may be gained by appraising a child's comprehension informally. Both oral and silent reading comprehension may be evaluated. Listening to a child answer questions about, or tell about, a passage he has just read can reveal a good deal about the quality of his comprehension.

Following each passage read, a child may be asked several questions. Summary, factual, inferential, and vocabulary questions are commonly used. An analysis can be made of the child's total responses to all passages, to determine his patterns of strength and weakness. Oral reading comprehension can be compared with silent reading comprehension, recall of major ideas can be compared with recall of facts, strength of inferential comprehension can be compared with strength of factual comprehension, and development of vocabulary knowledge can be assessed and compared with development of overall comprehension. An alternative procedure some teachers might prefer for assessing a child's comprehension of narrative text involves asking questions based on the setting, theme, plot, and resolution of the story and analyzing the results.

Retelling (free recall of a story) can also be used in analyzing reading comprehension. Teachers who use this procedure ask a child the content of a passage he has read to retell as if he were telling it to a friend. The child's performance in recalling the major ideas and facts presented in the passage, in comprehending inferences and facts, in sequencing, in gaining a sense of the structure of the story, and in using language can be evaluated.

Construction of an Informal Reading Inventory

Preferable to published informal inventories are inventories constructed by reading specialists or teachers using materials that are available for instruction. These inventories are superior because they give information that is useful for making instructional decisions for a specific child. The inventory can be made in the form of a booklet with representative passages selected from various grade levels of reading material. Oral reading passages may be affixed to the left-hand page of the booklet, with a comparable selection for silent reading affixed to the right-hand page.

After the reading selections, five comprehension questions for each passage should be listed in the following order: a summary question, followed by two factual questions, then an inferential question, and then a vocabulary question if possible. As an alternative, for assessing comprehension of narrative text, questions based on setting, theme, plot, and resolution may be used. On the fourth page, a list of words selected from the same book from which the oral and silent reading passages were taken should be typed on the page for use as a vocabulary test. The words should be selected from the entire book and should be representative of the book in its entirety.

The same four-page arrangement is repeated at half-yearly intervals for material at first- through third-grade level and at yearly intervals for material at more advanced grade levels. Tabs indicating the grade levels should be used for quick selection of passages. (For more detailed suggestions, the specialist should refer to Johnson, Kress, and Pikulski, 1987.)

Specialists who prefer to assess comprehension through retelling a passage should make a vertical sequential list of the phrases in the passage on a sheet of paper. To the right of each phrase, they then draw two lines. During retelling, they use the left-hand column of lines and number each phrase in the order in which its meaning was recalled. They then encourage the student to tell them anything else she can remember. In the right-hand column of lines, they should similarly number any additional phrases whose meanings were recalled. In this manner, the specialist can analyze the child's responses for recall of main ideas and details, ability to sequence, use of inference, sense of structure, and use of language, as well as evaluate the overall quality of the child's response.

The use of commercially produced informal reading inventories saves the time needed to make the booklet described. However, self-created informal inventories can be constructed so that they are more suited than commercially produced inventories to a given diagnostic situation.

Suggestions for the Reading Specialist

A specialist collecting information from informal sources should follow certain procedures that will enable the data obtained to be as accurate as possible. The following suggestions may be helpful for collecting evaluative data:

1. *Isolate specific outcomes or characteristics to be evaluated.* If, for example, information is needed on the method of attack a child uses on words in isolation when working orally, the observer should be alert to all of the approaches that might be used by the child.
2. *Define the observable results or characteristics in exact terms.* The specialist should have, for example, a checklist of possible methods that the child might use when orally solving a word-recognition problem.
3. *Plan the informal situation so that reading results or characteristics will be easily observable.* The child whose methods of word study are to be observed should be given a list of words of increasing difficulty and should be requested to work out the unknown words aloud so that the specialist can note which word-recognition approaches the child is using.
4. *Classify information in uniform and useful ways.* The specialist studying word recognition may wish to classify the errors made by a child as to both their location within the word (beginning, middle, ending, or reversal errors) and their phonetic type (vowel, consonant blend, digraph, addition of sounds, omission of sounds, or transposition of sounds). The specialist should classify the analytical attack under categories such as spelling, letter-by-letter sounding, phonic, structural, syllabic, or a combination of these forms of attacks on words. The specialist should also notice whether the child tries to recognize each word as a sight word, without any otherwise discernible form of attack.
5. *Make a record of the findings, with illustrative samples of the performance on the basis of which judgments were made.* Using the methods of word study just described, the specialist may find that the child is attempting a phonic approach to the problem, but his knowledge of word elements is weak. Sample words should be listed to show (1) visual separation of the words, (2) ele-

ments miscalled, (3) any difficulty in synthesis that results, and (4) the final pronunciation of the word. In addition, a summary of the specialist's opinion at the time should be recorded.

6. *Evaluate the significance of the observed behavior or characteristic.* The specialist should indicate the importance of the information to the understanding of the instructional needs of the child.

The usefulness of information obtained through informal procedures depends on the experience of the observer, the number of observations, the degree to which the observations are unbiased, and the relevance of the information to the understanding of the child's reading difficulties. Many elements in reading diagnosis must be determined by informal procedures.

The information acquired by informal approaches should be gathered as systematically as possible, and it must be interpreted and used with caution. Misjudgments will occur even on normative data if the personal biases of the specialist are allowed to influence diagnostic judgments. Misjudgments are more prevalent when the data are collected informally. For example, suppose a specialist has a particular interest in reversals. Then, when a child makes a few, as many children do, they may be overemphasized by the specialist. As a result, remediation may dwell unnecessarily on reversals, rather than on the child's true difficulty.

Informal procedures have merit when they allow the specialist to explore further some characteristic suspected from more standardized measurements. Many times, when administering a standardized diagnostic reading test, the specialist notices a possible reading difficulty that should be studied further. The specialist will complete the test as designed so as not to invalidate it, but then may informally explore items to follow a hunch. For example, the specialist may be giving a standardized list of isolated words to find out how well a child can work out the pronunciations in an untimed situation. The test is administered and scored properly. The specialist may have noted, however, that the child seemed to have trouble separating the words visually into usable elements. The examiner then may wish to go back to some of the words missed and, by covering up parts of the words, show the child the correct way to analyze them. The specialist might then see whether the child could have recognized the words had her visual analysis been correct. This information would be recorded, but would not affect the application of the normative data. The informal diagnostic inventory in Figure 8–2 has been organized to facilitate recording data obtained during informal diagnosis.

Informal observation of the child's oral reading when she is confronted with selections of increasing difficulty often provides insights into her reading problems. The specialist should especially note the child's word-by-word reading, failure to use contextual clues, inability to group words into thought units or language patterns, and limited sense of sentences, as well as any other indication of a basic comprehension problem. Many of these basic abilities are most easily detected by the way in which the child reads a passage aloud that is somewhat

Name _____ Sex ____ School _____ Age ____
Intelligence Test Results _____ Reading Exectancy Grade _____ Date _____

Standardized Group Reading Tests:

1. _____ R.G. _____ Date _____
2. _____ R.G. _____ Date _____
3. _____ R.G. _____ Date _____

Reading Levels

1. Independent _____ 2. Instructional _____ 3. Frustration _____

Oral Reading

1. Slow Rate _____
2. Overfast Rate _____
3. Faulty Enunciation _____
4. Inappropriate Phrasing _____
5. Faulty Expression _____
6. Word by Word _____
7. Comprehension _____
8. Signs of Tension _____
9. Unusual Posture _____
10. Pointing _____

Word Recognition Difficulties

1. Omissions _____
2. Additions _____
3. Repetitions _____
4. Reversals _____
5. Wrong Beginnings _____
6. Wrong Middles _____
7. Wrong Endings _____
8. Wrong in Several Parts _____
9. Limited Self-correction _____
10. Refusals _____
11. Semantic Miscues _____
12. Syntactic Miscues _____
13. Limited Prior Knowledge _____
14. Other _____

Silent Reading

1. Rate: Words per Minute _____
2. Literal Comprehension _____
3. Inferential Comprehension _____
4. Lip Movements _____
5. Audible Speech _____
6. Finger Pointing _____
7. Head Movements _____
8. Signs of Tension _____
9. Distractibility _____
10. Other _____

Word Pronunciation

1. Strategy
   a. Whole Word _____
   b. Structural _____
   c. Syllabic _____
   d. Phonics _____
   e. Letter by Letter _____
   f. Spelling _____
2. Errors
   a. Faulty Consonants _____
   b. Faulty Vowels _____
   c. Omission of Sounds _____
   d. Addition of Sounds _____
   e. Reversals _____
   f. Substitution of Words _____
   g. Faulty Visual Analysis _____
   h. Faulty Blending _____
   i. Words Refused _____
   j. Other _____

Other Information

1. Vision _____
2. Hearing _____
3. Handedness _____
4. Use of Language _____
5. Physical Difficulties _____
6. Concentration _____
7. Persistence _____
8. Other _____
9. Emotional Reactions (confident, shy, overaggressive, negative, cheerful, etc.) _____
_____
10. Attitudes toward (school, teacher, reading) _____
_____
11. Home Environment _____
12. Other Observations _____
Preliminary Diagnosis _____
Trial Appropriate Remedial Plan _____

(Permission for duplication and use of the *Informal Diagnostic Inventory* is hereby granted.)

FIGURE 8–2 Informal Diagnostic Inventory

difficult for her. Specific suggestions for correcting difficulties in these abilities will be given in Chapter 14.

Use of Standardized Reading Diagnostic Tests in Combination with Informal Procedures

In clinical diagnosis at the child-study level, a combination of standardized diagnostic tests and brief informal procedures can be used. In this way, the specialist has the advantages of the impartial standardized procedures and the freedom to design her own reading and learning tasks, using whatever materials seem most appropriate.

For example, after considering referral information, intelligence testing results, and results of standardized group reading tests, a clinician might choose to administer the word list and paragraph sections of the Spache Diagnostic Reading Scales. From such limited use of a standardized reading diagnostic test, the clinician would have adequate information to judge the student's relative strengths in reading comprehension, rate of comprehension, and general word recognition.

If the student's word recognition and reading comprehension appeared to be strengths, but the rate of comprehension was noticeably slow, the clinician could proceed directly to refinement and verification of the diagnosis. Using materials at the reading level indicated by the diagnostic test just administered, the clinician could set specific purposes for rapid reading, to appraise whether the slow rate indicated inefficient word recognition, overconcern with detailed comprehension, or simply a habitual response to all reading tasks.

Similarly, in the area of comprehension, a child-study diagnostic finding could be sharpened. For example, a student who was not accurate in recall of factual detail could be given a suitable selection and asked several questions requiring such recall. The specialist could then ask the student to explain how he arrived at his answers. In this way, misunderstandings of word meanings in contextual reading or insufficient attention to syntactic clues to precise understanding often are uncovered. The diagnostician should review *all* answers and should not indicate whether any answer is considered good or bad. It is diagnostically important to know how the child arrived at his answers and the exact nature of his understandings and misunderstandings. The child should also be directed to find where the relevant information is in the passage. It is important to determine how efficiently this is accomplished and whether, in the review process, the student is able to clear up spontaneously any of his own confusions.

Similar diagnostic procedures can be used in most areas of comprehension difficulty. It is important to assess how the child approaches comprehension tasks, the nature of his misunderstandings, and his ability to correct his own errors when his attention is specifically focused on a single aspect of reading comprehension.

When the diagnostic concern is centered on word-recognition difficulties, the diagnostician must make, refine, and verify judgments about its various aspects. Using referral information and a child's performance on the word list and paragraph sections of the standardized diagnostic test, a clinician might decide that the child's weakness included a lack of instant recognition of common words he should know by sight at his level of reading development. This judgment could be verified and refined by additional testing, using word lists from the child's own reading series or from other instructional materials. A trial lesson might be taught by the clinician to determine whether any special methodologies, such as a word-tracing method, would enhance learning in the child.

When word-recognition difficulties appear to result from inadequate analytic techniques, diagnostic information obtained from word lists and paragraph sections of standardized diagnostic tests is often found to be insufficient to enable the specialist to turn directly to informal diagnostic methods. For a standardized picture of word-recognition techniques as used in silent reading, a diagnostic instrument such as the Stanford Diagnostic Reading Test should be used. From a comparison of results obtained from this instrument, along with diagnostic insights from referral information and oral word lists and paragraph reading, the specialist will be able to evaluate the relative strengths and weaknesses within the broader general area of word recognition. Informal procedures then can be used to refine and verify the diagnosis.

For example, if a student appeared to be ineffective in using meaning clues as an aid to word recognition, the specialist could have the student complete some simple, informal cloze passages to analyze the nature of the difficulty further. Some short paragraphs could be prepared or selected, and the student could be asked to fill in the blanks. For diagnosis, a paragraph of the following form could be used:

Filling in blanks demands _____ background knowledge, language competence, and reading _____ , to supply a meaningful _____ when all graphic clues are _____ .

From the nature of the errors and from a discussion of the errors with the student, the specialist will be able to refine and verify the diagnosis. Two cautions are important. First, the specialist should select or prepare cloze passages at a distinctly easy reading level for the student, because all graphic clues to the recognition of certain words have been eliminated. Second, the student should have developed sufficiently good reading and writing skills to be able to complete the task independently. For information on the use of the cloze procedure to judge readability, see Bormuth (1976).

Similarly, if the student demonstrated difficulty with word beginnings and with beginning sounds, the specialist might want to check more thoroughly the exact nature of the student's confusion by having him read aloud a list of common words beginning with the essential beginning blends and digraphs. A few sample exercises and activities might also be tried in order to help the clinician decide how the child might be helped most effectively to gain a functional knowledge of common word beginnings.

When the major diagnostic concern involves word-recognition techniques used in oral reading, the specialist should first obtain a complete, unified, and standardized picture of the child's oral word recognition by means of an oral-reading diagnostic instrument such as the Gates-McKillop-Horowitz Reading Diagnostic Tests. When using this instrument, the diagnostician should administer the following subtests: (1) oral reading; (2) words: flash; (3) words: untimed; and (4) knowledge of word parts: word attack (starting with syllabication, recognizing and blending common parts, or reading words—whichever seems most appropriate). Other information pertinent to the child study can be obtained through judicious use of additional subtests useful to a more complete understanding of a child's word-recognition difficulties. Appropriate comparisons of results obtained from these subtests, together with referral information and other standardized and informal diagnostic assessment, will suggest weaknesses that can and should be understood even more completely through informal testing procedures.

For the child with a reading disability, standardized tests serve best to put into perspective major areas of reading competence or areas of concern. Informal methods are best, once an area of concern has been established, to clarify what exactly should be taught and how learning can be enhanced.

Summary

A classification of reading difficulties shows that both standardized and informal procedures are needed to diagnose the needs of children with reading disabilities. The diagnosis is a series of screenings going as far as is needed, from general diagnosis to specific diagnosis to child-study diagnosis, until all the information necessary to develop an appropriate individual plan of remediation is gathered. Representative standardized procedures appropriate for each level of diagnosis are presented.

Suggested informal procedures are described, including classroom analysis and specialist-constructed informal reading inventories. Systematic informal data collection methods are presented. A sample informal diagnostic inventory is offered.

Whenever a detailed diagnosis of a child's reading difficulty is called for, the most appropriate evaluative techniques must be chosen from both standardized and informal procedures. Skill in choosing the proper techniques in testing and in interpreting the results of tests comes from both effort and experience.

Study Questions

1. Differentiate between general, specific, and child-study diagnosis.
2. Why is an analysis of a child's classroom reading an essential part of a complete reading assessment?

3. Describe the reading behavior of a child at the *independent, instructional,* and *frustration* levels of reading.
4. What three types of classifications are said to be necessary to obtain a complete understanding of the word-recognition problems of a child with a reading disability?
5. What is the diagnostic importance of understanding how a student has arrived at her answers?
6. What is meant by "using informal procedures to verify and refine the results of standardized testing"?

Selected Readings

Cooter, R. B. (1990). *The teacher's guide to reading tests.* Scottsdale, AZ: Gorsuch Scarisbrick.

Gillet, J. W., & Temple, C. (1990). *Understanding reading problems: Assessment and instruction* (3rd ed.) (pp. 128–213). Glenview, IL: Scott Foresman.

Glazer, S. M., Searfoss, L. W., & Gentile, L. M. (Eds.). (1988). *Reexamining reading diagnosis.* Newark, DE: International Reading Association.

Harris, A. J., & Sipay, E. R. (1990). *How to increase reading ability* (9th ed.) (pp. 181–256). New York: Longman.

Maggart, Z. R., & Zintz, M. V. (1990). *Corrective reading* (6th ed.) (pp. 102–196). Dubuque, IA: Wm. C. Brown.

Roswell, F. G., & Natchez, G. (1989). *Reading disability* (4th ed.) (pp. 57–76). New York: Basic Books.

Taylor, B., Harris, L. A., & Pearson, P. D. (1988). *Reading difficulties: Instruction and assessment* (pp. 173–199, 235–253, 277–291). New York: Random House.

Chapter 9

Planning Appropriate Remediation

The specialist or reading teacher studies the diagnostic findings pertaining to a child with reading difficulties and then arranges learning conditions to facilitate the child's maximum growth in reading. In making an appropriate educational plan of remediation, it is necessary to identify the specific limitations in the child's reading profile that are impeding her reading growth. Methods, motivation, and materials are considered in designing the educational plan most suited to the child's remedial program.

The remedial program must be based on more than an understanding of the child's reading needs, however. It must also be based on the child's characteristics. The child who is hearing impaired needs an approach to reading different from that for her counterpart with normal hearing. The child with poor vision needs adjustment in methods and, if her limitation is severe enough, in materials also. The child who is a slow learner needs modified methods, and so does the child who has a behavioral disorder. The modifications required of instructional techniques for such children will be discussed in a later chapter.

As each child is different, there can be no "bag of tricks." Nor can there be a universal approach that will solve all problems. Many times, remedial training suited to one child would be detrimental to another. If, for example, a remedial program has been planned to develop more adequate phrasing, a child might be required to do considerable prepared oral reading in order to help her read in thought units. This same approach might be harmful to a child who is already overvocalizing in his silent reading. It could exaggerate the faulty habit he has acquired and increase his reading difficulty. To sum up, every remedial program must be planned on the basis of a thorough appraisal of the child's instructional needs, strengths, and weaknesses, as well as of the environment in which correction is to take place.

The remedial plan should be in written form, indicating in some detail what is recommended for each child. This must be done because it is too difficult to remember each child's needs, levels of attainment, and limitations with the exactness that is necessary for an effective correctional program. The written remedial plan should indicate the nature of the reading difficulty and the approach recommended to correct it. It should also identify the level of material to be used. The plan should state any of the child's physical or sensory characteristics that need to be corrected or for which the program needs to be modified. The child's interests, hobbies, and attitudes should become part of the written record. Most important, the plan should include a description of the remedial program recommended and the types of material to be used.

The original individual remedial plan is not to be considered permanent. It needs to be modified from time to time as the child progresses in reading. Often, a child with reading difficulties changes rapidly in her instructional needs. The better the diagnosis and the more successful the remedial plan, the more rapidly her needs will change. One child with reading difficulties, for example, may have failed to acquire sufficient word analysis techniques and depends on sight recognition and contextual analysis to recognize new words. She would be given remedial work designed to teach her word analysis. After some time, she may develop considerable skill in this area, but may not make a corresponding gain in rate of reading. Her problem would then no longer be one of developing word analysis. In fact, continued emphasis on this phase of the program might become detrimental to her future reading growth. Instead, the use of more rapid word-recognition techniques would be advisable. As the problem changes, so must the plan of remediation, in order to meet new reading needs.

Because the child's instructional needs change rapidly, it is unwise to put her into a remedial program that resembles a factory production line. Such a program assumes that once a given child's level of reading performance is identified, all that is needed is to put her through a set of materials that are uniform for all children. The child with reading difficulties whose needs change rapidly as her limitations are corrected is in dire need of a program that adjusts readily to every change in her reading pattern. To achieve success, a remedial program must be based on a continuous diagnosis, and the original plan must be modified somewhat as instructional needs change.

In some instances, the original plan of remediation does not result in improvement. When this occurs, a reevaluation of the diagnosis is needed, and perhaps additional appraisals should be made. A somewhat altered approach to instruction may then be necessary for success.

To achieve success in remedial programs, the teacher must (1) individualize the remedial plan, (2) encourage the reader, (3) choose appropriate materials, (4) use effective teaching procedures, and (5) enlist the cooperation of others, including the child.

Individualizing the Remedial Plan

The child with reading difficulties is one who has failed to respond to reading programs designed to meet the instructional needs and characteristics of the majority of children. The onset of reading difficulties is usually gradual. The child who develops serious reading difficulties gets into a moderate amount of trouble reading, misses some instruction, and falls behind or gets confused. As the class progresses, he is left further and further behind. Soon the child is bewildered, may develop an aversion to reading, and is quite likely to develop poor reading habits. All of these things accumulate, until it is apparent to the teacher that the child is having difficulty reading. He has not learned to be an effective reader at his level of advancement. Faulty habits of reading have become established, and he is developing or has already developed a dislike of and antagonism toward reading. As time goes on, his sense of defeat mounts increasingly higher.

A plan designed to treat reading difficulties is based on the assumption that children learn differently and need programs that meet their individual requirements. Such programs must be based on recognizing a particular child's physical and mental characteristics and must be individually designed to be efficient in overcoming his difficulties.

Study the Child's Characteristics

The expected results of instruction and the methods used must reflect the child's characteristics. If the child is below average in general intelligence, she cannot be expected to reach the goals in reading expected of children of greater mental ability. Nor can she be expected to progress as rapidly as these children do. The remedial reading teacher should modify the goals of the program accordingly. In addition to being flexible in the results he expects, the remedial reading teacher should modify his methods of instruction to meet the child's needs. Children who are below average in intelligence need more concrete experiences, more carefully given directions, and more repetition and drill than do children of higher intelligence.

If the child has poor vision or poor hearing, modifications in methods need to be made. Such limitations make learning to read more difficult, but do not preclude the child from achieving at a satisfactory level. Even children with serious visual and auditory impairments have been taught to read. The child with reading difficulties who experiences lesser sensory handicaps can be taught more efficiently if her limitations are known and modifications in methods of instruction are made. Adjustments in methods that have proved helpful will be discussed in Chapter 13.

Be Specific

The remedial reading teacher should focus instruction upon the child's specific reading needs. Usually, the diagnosis has indicated that there is something specifically wrong with the child's pattern of reading. One child, for example, may have learned to read with speed, but falls short of the accuracy required in certain situations. This child should read material with factual content and should read for purposes that demand exact recall of those facts. Another child may be so overconcerned with detail that he reads excessively slowly, looking for more facts than the author wrote. He becomes so concerned with detail that he cannot understand the author's overall intent. The teacher should endeavor to make him less compulsive, so that his rate of reading and the results he achieves can be compatible with his purposes for reading.

The principle that remedial reading instruction should be specific and not general means that the remedial reading teacher should emphasize those aspects of reading development that will correct the child's limitations. It does not mean either that just one type of reading activity should be used, or that a specific skill should be isolated and the child receive drill in that skill. For a child with a reading disability whose knowledge of the larger visual and structural elements used in word recognition is insufficient, the teacher would be in error if she used a method that consisted exclusively of isolated drill on word elements.

A better procedure would be to emphasize reading interesting material that challenged the child to use his knowledge of larger word elements. The child would read for several purposes, but when he encountered a word that required analysis, the teacher would help him by emphasizing the larger elements in the word. When exercises for developing basic skills were studied, the remedial reading teacher would have him do those that gave him experience in using the larger visual and structural parts of words. The teacher could find or construct additional exercises and activities that would provide experiences with larger elements in words he had encountered in his reading, so that he could learn to use these larger word elements in recognizing new words.

Use Varied Techniques

There is an unfortunate tendency, once remedial instruction has been prescribed, to stick to one specific method to overcome a known deficiency. However, basing a remedial reading program on a diagnosis does not imply that only one method must be used until the child's reading difficulty is overcome. There are many ways to develop competence in reading. An effective remedial reading plan includes a variety of teaching techniques and instructional procedures.

Many sources describing teaching techniques are available to the remedial reading teacher. Professional books and journals give suggestions for correcting specific types of reading difficulties. Manuals and workbooks accompanying basal reading programs are also sources of teaching techniques. The exercises suggested for teaching skills and abilities when they are first introduced in such manuals and workbooks may prove beneficial in remedial reading programs. As he examines the teaching techniques suggested in various materials, the remedial reading teacher can accumulate a variety of activities for each of the important types of disabilities listed in Chapter 8. He can keep the program appealing to the child by using a variety of techniques and at the same time be assured that the instruction emphasizes the reading deficiencies indicated in the individual educational plan of remediation.

In using a variety of teaching methods and techniques, care must be taken that the teaching approaches do not confuse the child. Directions should be simple, and teaching techniques should not be changed too often. Instruction should emphasize genuine reading as much as possible. The child should not have to spend time learning complicated procedures or directions. Enough variety should be introduced, however, to keep the program stimulating.

Engage Active Learning

Growth in reading presupposes an energetic learner. Of course, the child must learn to read by reading. She must interact with the printed page intensely and frequently if she is to succeed. A fatigued child cannot be expected to make gains during the remedial session. Therefore, the length of the session for remedial instruction should be such that concentrated work is possible. The child with reading difficulties frequently finds it difficult to read for a considerable length of time. Her lack of attention may be due to a variety of causes: lack of physical stamina, not enough sleep at night, or emotional reactions to reading that diminish her vitality. Her inattention or lack of vigor may be a reaction to an unsuccessful situation. Whatever the cause, most children, if properly motivated, can apply themselves to reading at least for a short amount of time. Obviously, if lack of attention and vigor result from a condition that can be corrected, the correction should be made. In any case, the length of the remedial reading session should be adjusted so that energetic participation can be maintained.

Frequently, it is necessary to divide remedial sessions into short periods. The child may work with the remedial reading teacher for 45 minutes. At the start of remediation, it may be necessary to read to her, or to have her read for only 10 minutes for specific purposes and then have her use the results of her reading in some creative activity, such as drawing. Then she might work on some activity or exercise that emphasizes the training she needs. These activities or exercises might require rereading the material she read during the first part of the session, or they might require the further study of words from the material read. Finally, the child might dictate to the teacher a story of her own suggested by the reading she did. As she gains in reading growth, the length of concentrated reading time should be increased. Soon, the child who has no physical limitations will be reading longer without interruption.

Encouraging the Reader

Most children with reading difficulties are discouraged about their failure to learn to read. They frequently think that they cannot learn. This lack of confidence in their ability to learn is detrimental to their reading improvement. The effective learner is a confident and purposeful learner, one who has a desire to learn and finds pleasure in doing so. In order for a child with reading difficulties to progress rapidly in reading, it is necessary for him to know that he can learn and to see that he is advancing satisfactorily.

Frequently, the child with reading difficulties is anxious or insecure. He has had no real opportunity to gain confidence in himself because most of his school day is spent reading and for some time he has been ineffective in many areas of schoolwork. Such a child may become submissive or demanding, aggressive or withdrawn, or may show his basic insecurity in a variety of ways. He may develop attitudes of indifference toward or dislike or rejection of reading. He may resist help, display few interests, or be antagonistic toward reading instruction. Remedial reading programs must overcome these attitudes and related behavior problems.

One of the first responsibilities of the remedial reading teacher is to develop a need for learning to read in the child. Another is to gain his confidence to such a degree that he will know that she has taken a personal interest in him and that she will solve his reading problem. A direct attack on the reading problem by a businesslike, considerate adult will do much to overcome stress and reading-avoidance attitudes. When a child recognizes that an interest is taken in him and his reading problem, it increases his sense of personal worth and confidence in himself.

Emphasize Success

In order for the remedial reading program to be encouraging to the child, her success rather than her mistakes should be emphasized. Teachers have a tendency to point out errors to children with reading difficulties, rather than to make them feel that, for the most part, they are doing well. A child with reading difficulties who is reminded continually of her errors may become overwhelmed by a sense of defeat. A wise teacher will start this child in a remedial reading program that is somewhat easy for her, so that her successful performance will be immediately apparent. As she gains confidence, the program will gradually be made more challenging. The teacher should always be quick to recognize when the child has put forth real effort and done something well. Many times—particularly at the start of the program—recognition will have to be given to activities related to the reading, rather than to the reading itself. Gradually, the teacher will find more opportunities to give praise for actual reading accomplishments. It should always be remembered that the effectiveness of remedial instruction depends to a large extent upon the child's gain in confidence. This is brought about through success-ful experiences with reading, which in the past had caused so much difficulty.

Emphasis upon success does not mean that errors are to be overlooked. A child's faulty reading, of course, must be brought to her attention. Errors in word recognition must be pointed out. Faulty habits in reading that limit the child's speed must be recognized by her before they can be corrected. Sometimes, it is necessary to demand greater exactness in reading. While it is true that the teacher must point out mistakes, he should first praise what the child has done well. He should also indicate that the child is improving and that, for the most part, her reading is good. If, for example, a child calls the word *house, horse* in the sentence "The dog ran up to the house," the teacher should point out to her that the sentence was almost perfect, but to be perfect, she should look at the last word more carefully. As a matter of fact, the child did recognize most of the words in the sentence correctly. And the error she made indicated good use of context. The sentence made sense: the words *house* and *horse* do look very much alike.

When answering a comprehension question, the child may give the wrong answer. Instead of saying that the answer is wrong, it would be far better for the teacher to say, "Let's see what the book says about this" and then find out why the child made the error. It will be frequently found that she did not understand the meaning of a word, or that she failed to notice a key word such as *not*, or that she had not grouped the words into proper thought units. Whatever the cause, it should be found, and the child should be shown the correct way to read the passage. The attitude of the teacher should be one not of pointing out errors, but of helping the child learn to read.

An effective remedial program must satisfy the child, make her feel that she is getting along well, and keep at a minimum any anxiety that she feels about her reading level. The teacher's responsibility in encouraging the child to read energetically is great. He should neither hurry her unduly nor allow her to dawdle; he should be sure she is working hard and yet avoid putting pressure on her. Practically all children can be expected to work intently on improving their reading. This is especially true if the reading materials are at an appropriate level of difficulty, if they are interesting to the child, and if she is reading for purposes that are real to her. There should always be a friendly atmosphere, but one that has as its first priority that the child is there to learn to read.

Demonstrate Reading Growth

The child with reading difficulties needs to have his reading growth demonstrated to him. There are many ways to do this. The choice will depend on the nature of the child's reading problem. If, for example, the child is trying to develop a sight vocabulary, he could make a picture dictionary of the words he has learned. As the dictionary becomes larger, he recognizes that he has increased his sight vocabulary. The child who is working on accuracy of comprehension could develop a chart (Figure 9–1) in which he indicates his percent of accuracy from week to week. If he fails to improve over the period of a week, the teacher simplifies the material or asks more general questions, so that accuracy increases. Then, as the child gains confidence, the difficulty of the material is again increased gradually. It is good for the child to go back, from time to time, and reread something that he has read previously. If he does so, he will usually discover that material that was difficult for him a short while ago is now relatively easy for

Jerry's Accuracy Chart

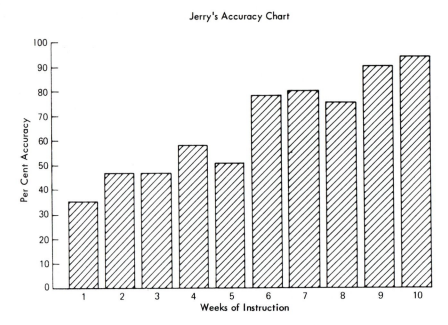

FIGURE 9–1   **A Bar Chart Showing Accuracy in Reading**

him to read. This will be especially true if the teacher takes time to prepare him to read it. Tape recordings of former and improved oral readings of the same passages are especially effective, as the child clearly hears the improvement for himself.

Whatever the nature of the difficulty, it is important for the remedial reading program to be organized in such a a manner as to demonstrate to the child that he is progressing toward his goal of reading better. The child who has had reading difficulties for a long time needs whatever encouragement can be given. He needs not only to be in a comfortable learning situation, but also to see that he is making effective advancement in reading.

Avoid Interfering with Enjoyable Activities

The remedial reading teacher must organize instructional sessions so that children are not required to take part in them at times at which other, competing activities of great importance to them take place. For example, sometimes children are given extra help after school. This is a bad time for a child who enjoys outdoor sports with friends and who finds it the only time that outdoor games are played in her neighborhood. Similarly, in scheduling summer reading programs, it is wise to delay their start until a week or so after school is out and the children have found that they have time they do not know what to do with. Even then, the better scheduling time for classes is probably in the morning, because the majority of things that the child likes to do, such as going swimming or playing baseball, are done in the afternoon.

The busy classroom teacher often finds it difficult to give a child the attention she needs when the class is in session. He may select recess time or the time other children have art or music activities for helping a child with her reading. Such a practice is understandable, but it is not good for the correction of a reading problem. A better time would be to work with the children needing reeducation in reading while the rest of the class is busily engaged in studying or reading independently. Whatever time is used for giving remedial help, it is important that it not conflict with activities that are important to the child.

Choosing Appropriate Materials

The selection of appropriate material for remedial work in reading is one of the main problems the remedial reading teacher has to solve. Some teachers believe that the most important element is that the material be interesting. Others regard the level of difficulty to be of even more importance. Still others consider having material that is compatible with the nature of the remedial instruction to be of paramount importance. In fact, all three of these elements enter into the selection. Without trying to decide among them, we may conclude that the more important considerations in selecting materials are that the materials must be (1) suitable in level of difficulty, (2) of the proper type, (3) appropriate in interest and format, and (4) abundant.

Choose Materials That Are Suitable in Level of Difficulty

A child grows in reading by reading; therefore, the material that is used for remedial instruction should be of a level of difficulty that enables the child to read comfortably and with enjoyment. The diagnosis will have disclosed the level at which the child with reading difficulties could be expected to read. The remedial reading teacher should pick out materials at a suitable level to accommodate the findings. The difficulty of material can be judged in many ways. Readability formulas, such as the Dale-Chall (Dale & Chall, 1948) and the Spache (1953) formulas, are useful in estimating the child's reading level. Comprehensive book lists that include information on level of difficulty, such as those provided by Spache (1975, 1978) and Maggart and Zintz (1990, appendix B), are helpful. The extensive listing of easy-to-read, high-interest, content-area books offered by McCormick (1987, appendix D), which includes information on level of difficulty, should also be of value.

The difficulty level of ungraded materials can be estimated by a formula or by using a reading series as a standard for comparison. The difficulty of an ungraded library book, for example, may be judged by comparing it with books in a reading series that are on various grade levels. The book can be compared with a third-grade reader, and if it is judged to be harder, it then can be compared with a fourth-grade reader, and so forth, until the approximate level of difficulty can be estimated. In making a judgment, the teacher should consider the number of unusual words, the length of the sentences, the number of prepositional phrases, the number of unusual word orders, and the complexity of the ideas that are in the book. In selecting books, it is important that the remedial reading teacher remember that the results of standardized tests tend to overestimate the reading development of a child with reading difficulties. Therefore, it is usually wise to start remedial instruction with material that is somewhat lower than the child's general reading score indicated by standardized tests.

The difficulty of the material appropriate for remedial instruction will vary somewhat with the nature of the child's reading difficulty. The teacher should modify the level of difficulty according to the goals of instruction. For example, if the child's major problem is one of developing sight recognition, the material should be relatively easy, with few new words. Whatever new words are present should be used often in the material. For this child, a relatively easy level would be desirable. By contrast, for the child who needs help in analyzing words effectively, a higher concentration of new words would be desirable. This child could meet a new word approximately every 20 running words. This ratio would give him an opportunity to use the techniques of word analysis that he needs to develop, and at the same time, it would enable him to maintain the thought of the passage, so that meaning clues could enable him to monitor his accuracy in word recognition.

A child who is trying to increase his speed of comprehension should use material that is easy for him—material that contains few, if any, word-recognition problems. The child who is trying to increase his *power* of comprehension, on the other hand, should use material that challenges him; but he must have a reasonable chance of comprehending the material successfully.

Choose Materials That Are of the Proper Type

It is truly said that any kind of material suitable for a child to read is suitable for remedial instruction. It is important, however, to recognize also that progress in reading will be maximized when the material that is selected meets the reader's instructional needs. The type of material that is best for one kind of reading difficulty is not necessarily appropriate for another. If the major instructional problem is to increase a child's speed of reading, the best material would be short stories with fast-moving plots. Not only should the material be easy to read, but the content should also encourage the child to read the material to gain a general impression of it or to understand its general significance. If the reading problem is in the word-recognition area, a basal reader, along with exercises selected to address the specific word-recognition problem, would be an excellent choice. If the problem is in comprehension, and increased accuracy in reading is sought, an expository text might be used. In every instance, the material should be at an appropriate level of difficulty and suitable for meeting the specific reading needs of the child.

Choose Materials That Are Appropriate in Interest and Format

A relatively mature, intelligent 12-year-old will usually not find first- and second-grade material interesting. Nor will she find the format of such material very attractive. But when she has a second-grade reading ability, she must nevertheless use material that she can read. The problem facing the remedial reading teacher in this respect is great. Second-grade books are designed for children 7 or 8 years of age. The pictures are of small children, and the print looks large and juvenile. The topics are for a 7- or 8-year-old and not for a 12-year-old. Many books that might be used for remedial reading instruction lose some of their value to a particular child because they are uninteresting and have an immature format for that child. The problem is how to find material that is both at a suitable level for and as appealing as possible to a child who is older, but reads at a second-grade level.

An increasing number of books are being developed for remedial readers. Books designed primarily for the less capable reader include the Action and Double Action Libraries (Scholastic Book Services). Material designed for use with readers who require selective skill development include the Reading Comprehension Series (Bowmar/Noble Publishers), Dolch First Reading Books (DLM Teaching Resources), and Specific Skills Series (Barnell Loft, Ltd.). Phonetically consistent materials that are useful for readers who are weak in the phonic aspects of word recognition include series such as Corrective Reading: Decoding (Science Research Associates, Inc). These materials prove helpful when used according to individual student needs.

The skill books that accompany basal readers can also be used selectively to provide practice in specific skills. It is fortunate that these books often appear to be on a more mature level than the readers they accompany. In many instances, the drills they contain give no indications of the maturity level they expect of the child who is to use them.

Choose an Abundance of Materials

In selecting materials for remedial reading, one should make sure that there is a wide variety of material that meets many interests and that is at various levels of difficulty. For any one child, there should be ample material for him to read. There should be material for his remedial instruction and also for his independent reading. Independent reading materials should be considerably easier than those used in remedial instruction and should be on many topics, because the children have a wide variety of interests.

The Use of Computers

Recently, there has been increasing interest in the use of computers in remedial reading instruction. To assess the instructional value of computers, one must judge both the value of the computer as a means of presenting reading materials and the worth of the computer-based materials themselves. As instructional materials, computer programs should be evaluated by the same criteria that are applied to other materials used for reading improvement.

An advantage of using computers in remedial reading instruction is the enthusiasm children with reading problems show toward working with computers, even when these same children resist other forms of reading. Another advantage is the opportunity computers afford children to take risks, and even make mistakes, in private with no other person looking on. Computers respond consistently, appropriately, and predictably when children use them. They provide immediate feedback, so that the children know whether they are right or wrong, and they provide sufficient repetition so that children learn completely. Computers invite children to learn actively and to respond frequently. They free the teacher to work with others. Among the disadvantages of using computers in remedial reading instruction are their cost and the inadequacy of some of their programs. Inadequate programs are those that are instructionally deficient or difficult for the child to operate; they should not be used at all.

Many attractive computer programs are available as instructional materials at all levels of difficulty. In fact, some programs with voice synthesizers make it possible for the child to receive all instructions through listening. Many types of programs are currently available, including drill programs for various phases of word attack and comprehension, programs to teach students the mechanics of writing, and programs for the development of vocabulary. In addition, programs are available that provide students with simulations, interactive fiction, and problem-solving opportunities. (For more information, see Blanchard, Mason, & Daniel, 1987, or Strickland, Feeley, & Wepner, 1987.)

Computer programs are interesting to many children and are available in a variety of formats. They can present visual hints that help children attend to passages, words, or parts of words by illuminating these as appropriate or by providing selective color cues. By using voice synthesis, computers can present words visually and auditorily at one and the same time. The format of computer programs is usually inviting to children and does not appear immature to them. Educational programs are now numerous and are becoming increasingly more abundant.

The use of computers for remedial reading instruction appeals to most students, serves to free teachers, and offers an abundance of specialized learning materials. At present, however, most computer materials are designed to provide drill and therefore do not relieve the teacher from the responsibility of introducing and teaching new skills. In addition, computer materials will not lead to improvement in reading, unless they are specifically selected to match each student's learning needs. Computer materials add to the material resources of the teacher, but they need to be managed with careful judgment.

Using Effective Teaching Procedures

Earlier, it was mentioned that remedial reading instruction requires sound teaching procedures directed toward the specific needs of the child. The most essential differences between remedial and developmental reading instruction are in the amount of individualization and in the extent of study of the child, rather than in the uniqueness of the methods or materials used in instruction. We consider the reading of text to be at the core of any remedial reading plan. The plan for a child with reading difficulties should include the reading of text, taught in much the same way as it is in a developmental reading program. In teaching this kind of reading, the following series of steps will foster growth:

1. Build readiness
2. Introduce difficult words
3. Set purposes for reading
4. Guide silent reading
5. Discuss the content read
6. Reread when desirable
7. Develop specific skills and abilities
8. Extend reading to related material
9. Use the results of reading

Unfortunately, some of these steps are not always followed in remedial work. Readiness should be built carefully for every topic and every selection to be read by the child with reading difficulties. Building readiness includes creating interest in, developing the background for, and introducing new words for each selection the child reads. The child who has difficulty reading, just as the child who does not, should understand the purposes for reading, before it is done.

Developing specific skills and abilities is of great importance for remedial instruction. Having children with reading problems merely read and discuss a selection does not itself develop the skills and abilities necessary for orderly growth in reading proficiency. The most essential phases of instruction take place in the preparatory activities, during which background knowledge is provided, new vocabulary is introduced, and purposes are set, and in follow-up skill development. A teacher demonstrates her teaching skill when she shows the child with reading difficulties how to read and when she provides him with the experiences necessary for establishing the specific skills and abilities that make for mature reading.

Children with many types of reading difficulty need repetition beyond that amount required for students with normal reading development. In Chapters 10, 11, 14, 15, and 16, on remedial instruction for specific reading problems, sample types of supplementary reinforcing activities are presented.

Like other children, the child with reading difficulties should use the results of reading in a creative way. If, for example, she has read a selection about flood control to find out what techniques are used, it would be as important for her to make a diagram of a riverbed illustrating what she had learned as it would be for children in the developmental reading program. Using the results of their reading is a good procedure for all children. It is *essential*—though often neglected—for those who are receiving remedial instruction. The results of reading may be used in a discussion, a picture (or series of pictures) drawn, a chart developed, or a map made. There need be only a small amount of time given over to these things, but above all, the creative work should be the child's own.

The remedial reading teacher will find it helpful to keep a cumulative account of the child's progress. The record should include books read, types of exercises and activities used and the success of each, charts used to demonstrate progress to the child, and the results of periodic tests. Indications of interests and anecdotal accounts of the child's reactions to the remedial program should be included. By reviewing this record, the teacher can gain insight into the strengths and weaknesses of various approaches used with a given child. A study of past records will recall those approaches that were successful with other children with similar reading problems. The teacher can assemble a file of folders, arranged according to specific reading problems.

Make Reading Meaningful

One reason children have difficulty reading is that they do not understand the processes involved in being a good reader. The remedial reading teacher has the responsibility not only for teaching the child what to do, but also for showing him how to proceed. Certainly, the teacher should teach the child to use context clues in word recognition, but she should also demonstrate to him how useful this is when he is reading. The teacher should not just tell the child to try to remember what he has read, but should also show him how to organize the material he reads for effective retention. She should show him why a suggested procedure is effective. The child should understand why certain material is read carefully and with attention to detail, while other material is read rapidly to understand its general ideas. If the remedial reading teacher expects the child to retain knowledge of word elements, it is important for her to show him how much they will help him to recognize new words.

Some remedial reading teachers feel that if a child is simply encouraged to read, he will automatically develop needed skills of which he is unaware. A more reasonable supposition is that children should be *shown* how to read. In addition, they should be shown how to use each added skill they achieve. Suppose, for example, that a child has learned to pronounce a list of isolated prefixes by rote. How much better it would have been to point out to him the prefixes in words and show him how they change the meanings of the root words! The remedial reading teacher will find that demonstrating the processes of reading to the learner helps to solve his reading confusions. Drilling the child on isolated parts of words is not an effective approach to reading, because it lacks meaning for him.

Use Remedial Procedures That Resemble Real Reading

Although many devices and mechanical aids are available for remedial instruction, most reading growth comes from training allied with reading itself and from much opportunity to read. Most expensive equipment is unnecessary and often wastes time that could be used for authentic reading activities. In establishing a reading center, priority should be given to obtaining varied reading materials. These include books, pamphlets, and skill-development materials of a wide range of reading difficulty. The resources of the school library should be used as well. A computer and printer are also useful to the remedial reading teacher in constructing materials to meet student needs.

When exercises are used to develop specific skills, ways should be found to use these skills in meaningful reading for content. For example, even in a simple exercise for developing rapid sight recognition of words, it is better to have the child read the word flashed before her, and at the same time tell whether it names an animal or is an action verb than just to have her identify the words without giving any thought to their meaning. In reading, the child not only must pronounce a word, but also must associate meaning with it. Exercises and activities that place skill development in context rather than in isolation are superior to those that do not. The suggestions made in the chapters that follow illustrate this principle of remedial reading instruction.

The more that exercises and activities used for building skills and abilities approximate real reading, the more likely it is that those skills and abilities will be transferred to reading. For example, if a child is shown phonic patterns upon recognizing words, she will be more likely to use phonics in identifying new words when she is reading a book than she would be if the same elements had been taught by the use of isolated drills. Not only will she be more likely to transfer what she has learned to new situations, but she will also establish the habit of noting the phonic patterns within troublesome words and thereby become more independent in word recognition.

Be Optimistic

A teacher helping a child overcome reading difficulties should be a buoyant, energetic person. She must make the child sense her confidence in him. The problems in correcting a complex reading problem may seem to be almost insurmountable. Nevertheless, the teacher must show each child with reading difficulties that she knows he will learn to read. This attitude comes from a sound diagnosis leading to a thorough understanding of the child's instructional needs and to a clear set of remedial objectives. The teacher gains immediate confidence through knowing exactly what is going to be done during each remedial lesson. A well-prepared teacher who knows precisely where each session is going will instill confidence in the child. With preparation, there usually will be progress in reading.

The teacher can be optimistic because most children with reading difficulties do make immediate gains with remedial instruction. If a child's reading problem and personal characteristics have been evaluated carefully, and if the program is based upon an appropriate individual remedial plan, success is practically assured. Of course, the teacher's confidence may sometimes be shaken: There are periods during the corrective treatment of practically every poor reader when there is little evidence of new growth. But all the same, confidence in the child's ultimate success must remain, even when things do not appear to be going well. Under some circumstances, the remedial reading plan should be restudied and the diagnosis reviewed, but this need not diminish confidence in the child's ultimate success.

Provide for Group and Individual Work

The child with reading difficulties needs to share her experiences with other children just as much as, or even more than, the child whose growth in reading is normal. Not only should her classroom work be organized so that she can participate in some of the important activities of the class, but she should also see that other children have problems reading. It is recommended that children with reading difficulties be given remedial instruction in groups, not individually, whenever possible. Much can be gained by seeing other children with similar difficulties who are making progress in overcoming them. It is often assumed that remedial reading instruction is a formal procedure in which the child is separated from other children and drilled until her disability is corrected. Such instruction is unwise. It is a boost to the child to know that there are other children learning to read who are able to use their newly gained proficiencies in reading.

Enlisting the Cooperation of Others

Although implementation of the remedial plan may be the direct responsibility of the remedial reading teacher, many other people should be involved in formulating and helping to implement the plan. Among these are other professionals, classroom teachers, and parents, as well as the remedial reader himself.

Involve Other Professionals

It would be rather unusual for such professionals as the school principal, the school psychologist, the school social worker, a physician, a media expert, a speech and language pathologist, and the school nurse to be in any way involved in direct remediation. Nevertheless, the insights of one or more of these professionals may prove invaluable to the formulation of an appropriate individual remedial plan. Knowledge of a student's reading difficulties and remedial plan helps other professionals coordinate their efforts. Some children receive not only remedial reading services, but also the services of a social worker or a speech pathologist. It is important for the remedial reading teacher and such other professionals to share information, insights, and concerns on a regular basis.

Involve Classroom Teachers

In most people's minds, including those of most children with reading difficulties and their parents, success or failure in reading is measured not in the school reading center or resource room, but in the regular classroom. That is where the child spends the greater part of her day, and that is where she must establish social relationships with her peers. If a child is really to find success in school, she must find it in the classroom. For this reason, it is imperative that classroom teachers cooperate and become closely involved in initial planning and that they maintain their involvement, in order to coordinate their efforts with those of the reading specialist. Collaboration between the remedial reading teacher and the classroom teacher enables them both to plan activities that benefit the child directly in the classroom. For example, if students in the classroom have been told that they may make an optional, brief oral report on a book that they think others in the class might enjoy, the remedial reading teacher can aid the child in the selection of a book that she can read successfully, but that will also appeal to her classmates. He can give her an opportunity to practice her presentation privately, in order to gain the confidence she needs to speak effectively to the class. In collaboration with the remedial reading teacher, the classroom teacher can adapt and adjust classroom expectations to ensure that when the child with reading difficulties exerts an honest effort, she will be successful. Although a student may be making real and rapid progress in reading in the reading center or resource room, she will be denied a true sense of accomplishment if the rest of her day is filled with reading demands that are far beyond her. She will lose the opportunity to practice her newly acquired reading skills in the regular classroom, she will lose the opportunity to view herself and have her classmates view her as a reader, she will lose the positive attitudes she may have acquired about reading, and she will lose that sense of confidence that is so necessary to learning.

Involve Parents

Parental cooperation is beneficial to successful remediation for two reasons. First, parents can make a unique contribution to a teacher's understanding of their child. Parents are concerned with their children's behavior in nonschool settings and therefore are often aware of certain attributes that teachers are less likely to see. For example, it is often parents who alert teachers to signs of tension or frustration that a child hides when in school. And it is parents who are the first to sense that positive change of attitude that characterizes a child's response to successful remediation. The second reason parental cooperation is so beneficial is because parents are very important people in a child's life. When his parents understand the remedial plan and support it, a child receives a form of encouragement that helps him overcome his reading difficulty.

Furthermore, parents are concerned about their children's difficulties—sometimes, extremely concerned. A complete understanding of the remedial plan and the remedial program's outcomes helps to relieve the extreme anxiety some parents feel when their children have reading problems. Some parents of children with reading difficulties become interested in aiding their children directly in reading. Parents can do much to help their children with reading, but their efforts are most valuable when they receive guidance from the remedial reading teacher and when they enhance and support the remedial program.

Involve the Child

The true focus of every successful remedial plan is the child herself. It is the child, after all, who has to learn. If the child is not enthusiastic about the plan or does not believe in it, the efforts of teachers, parents, and others will have little effect. The child should assist as much as possible in formulating the plan; indeed, older students often have valuable insights into the nature of their reading problems. At the secondary level, many wise remedial reading teachers have found that enlisting students' cooperation in planning activities, choosing materials, and setting goals is a necessary first step in provoking their interest in reading improvement. Discussing a child's feelings and attitudes about reading and about plans for reading improvement is an essential beginning to helping him develop more positive feelings and attitudes about reading, about learning, and even about himself. It is important for every one concerned—not least of all the child—to understand the remedial program, to support it, and to cooperate with it.

Summary

In making an appropriate educational plan of remediation, it is necessary to identify the specific limitations hindering a child's reading growth. Although remedial work for each child with reading difficulties must be different in certain respects, there are some common elements among all corrective programs. All remedial programs must be designed to meet the child's instructional needs as shown by the diagnosis, and therefore, there can be no universal approach to all cases. The remedial program for each child with reading difficulties must be planned carefully and written down. It is necessary to modify the program from time to time to keep abreast of the child's changing instructional needs. Even though the program is planned to emphasize overcoming a specific difficulty, a variety of remedial techniques should be used. The remedial reading teacher will find manuals and instruction booklets for commercial materials a good source of teaching techniques.

Remedial reading programs must be individualized and must be designed in keeping with the child's instructional needs and characteristics. It is necessary to modify the approaches to reading in order to adjust to limitations such as poor hearing or poor vision. Remedial instruction should not emphasize one specific skill or ability in isolation, but should provide new experiences in whatever skills are needed in connection with purposeful reading. The length of remedial reading sessions should be planned so that the child will not become fatigued or inattentive.

Reading instruction for the child with reading difficulties must be well organized, so that reading improvement can progress smoothly, with no undue burden on the child, with little chance for overemphasis, and without omission of essential skills. The teacher should help the child understand the processes that are involved in being a good reader.

The remedial reading program must encourage the child, since much of his trouble was probably caused by loss of confidence in his ability to learn. The teacher should be optimistic, the child's successes should be emphasized, and his progress should be demonstrated to him. Materials must be geared to the child's reading abilities and instructional needs. They should be at the appropriate level of difficulty, consist of the proper content, be as near as possible to the child's interests, and look "mature" to him. Computer materials provide attractive supplements to the remedial program and have great appeal to many children with reading disabilities. The materials used for remedial instruction must be at a level of difficulty that the child can deal with and must be so interesting that he will be motivated to read them. There can be no compromise with the level of difficulty of the material, because the child will not be interested in reading material he cannot read, no matter how attractive the subject matter. In all remedial work, sound teaching procedures should be used, and artificial devices and isolated drills should be avoided.

Involved professionals, the classroom teacher, the child's parents, and, most of all, the child himself should have an active part in formulating the individual plan of remediation.

Study Questions

1. Why must the remedial reading plan be based on more than just an understanding of the child's reading needs?
2. Why is it necessary to give a child with reading difficulties successful reading experiences? How can the teacher help such a child see success?
3. What features would you include in an individual reading program for a fifth-grade student who tested at a beginning third-grade level on a standardized test? The student loves sports and outdoor activities. She hates to read. Her word analysis is extremely poor. She has frequently been embarrassed in oral reading situations in the classroom. Be sure to consider motivation and demonstration of progress, as well as levels and kinds of appropriate reading materials you would initially consider using with this student.
4. Why must a child be prepared for reading in remedial instruction by building readiness, developing a background, introducing new words, and setting immediate purposes?

5. Is one-to-one remedial instruction always best? Why or why not?
6. What are the advantages of involving a child in remedial planning? To what extent should the child receiving remedial help be involved in such planning?

Selected Readings

Harris, A. J., & Sipay, E. R. (1990). *How to increase reading ability* (9th ed.) (pp. 390–430). New York: Longman.

McCormick, S. (1987). *Remedial and clinical reading instruction* (pp. 186–201). Columbus, OH: Merrill.

Richek, M. A., List, L. K., & Lerner, J. W. (1989). *Reading problems: Assessment and teaching strategies* (2nd ed.) (pp. 144–164). Englewood Cliffs, NJ: Prentice Hall.

Wilson, R. M., & Cleland, C. J. (1985). *Diagnostic and remedial reading for classroom and clinic* (5th ed.) (pp. 183–200). Columbus, OH: Merrill.

Chapter 10

Correcting Insufficient Attention to Meaning in Word Recognition

Skill in word recognition is fundamental to successful reading at any level. As children mature in reading, the materials and methods used to teach them gradually require increasing independence in word recognition. The child who has failed to establish effective means of identifying and recognizing words for his level of advancement is disadvantaged in all other aspects of reading as well.

Current approaches to teaching word recognition are based upon integration of the nature of reading growth, as analyzed by reading researchers, with oral communication, as described by linguistic researchers. The first-grade reading studies sponsored by the United States Office of Education gave some insight into the development of word-recognition skills. The major conclusions reached by Bond and Dykstra (1967) from their analyses of the combined data compiled from 27 individual studies offer some definitive evidence of the importance of word-study skills to reading success. They found that, regardless of the approach to reading instruction used in the first grade, word-recognition skills must be emphasized. A 2nd-year follow-up study indicated that this was true for the second grade as well.

The combined analyses also showed that much of the variation in success in reading during the first 2 years of reading instruction could be accounted for by attributes the children brought to the learning situation. Capabilities such as auditory and visual discrimination and an awareness of books and print prior to entering first grade were substantially related to success in learning to read, whatever approach to initial instruction was used.

The joint data from these extensive studies show further that combinations of methods, including the use of such components as basal readers, phonics and linguistic training, and child-centered reading activities, are superior to any of these approaches used alone. The programs that were especially effective in developing word-recognition skills were not as successful in the comprehension areas. Conversely, the programs that emphasized meaning needed to be augmented by the addition of training in word recognition.

The studies indicated that initial reading programs should strive for an effective balance between phonetically regular words, as emphasized by some linguists, and high-utility words, as emphasized in many basal readers. The use of vocabularies selected largely on the basis of frequency of use or utility alone can generate word-recognition problems. Conversely, the exclusive use of words spelled in a phonetically regular way can make meaningful reading difficult. The analysis also showed that encouraging children to write words as they learned to read them and to associate words with sounds and meanings was helpful in developing their word-recognition skills.

How to correct difficulties in the *word-perceptual* skills, necessary in recognizing the printed symbols that make up words, will be the concern of the next two chapters. These skills must be taught so as to encourage a child to attempt *rapid recognition* of known or partially familiar words, so that he will be able to group them into thought units. At the same time, training in *word identification* must be given, so that the learner can develop the skill of decoding the printed forms of words that printed symbols represent when he first sees them in their written forms. All of these skills are not easily developed, and it is not surprising that some children run into difficulties before they acquire them. In fact, most children with severe reading disabilities have weaknesses in the word-recognition area.

Word study involves two types of goals. The first is expanding the child's meaning vocabulary and word-recognition techniques so that meanings accompany the identification of the symbols. The child must learn to associate meaning with printed symbols. The meaning he invests those symbols with must be clear and precise if he is to comprehend the material he is reading. He must also be able to select, among all the meanings of a word, the one that is correct for the particular context in which the word is used. For example, the word *run*, which is one of the first words many children learn to read, has 56 different definitions, even in a dictionary used in the elementary grades. The child must learn to use context as he recognizes the printed symbols, to help him select the correct meaning. For instance, the meaning of *run* can be derived from the context in the statements, "He was tired after the long run" and "All will turn out well in the long run." Often, however, the sentence alone will not give the meaning of a word; only the sense of the passage it is embedded in will. Thus, the precise meaning of *run* cannot be obtained from the sentence, "She was out of breath after she made the run." In order to understand the word *run* here, the reader must know not only that the girl was playing baseball, but also that she scored rather than chased a fly ball. The development of the skill of recognizing meanings of words will be discussed in detail in Chapter 14; but it is important to teach word-recognition techniques in such a way that words are recognized rapidly and the proper meanings are associated with them.

The second goal of instruction in word study is the development of competencies that enable the child to recognize words he already knows and to identify new words with speed and understanding. *Word identification* and *word recognition* are closely related features of word perception. The child's first contact with a new word calls for identification of the printed symbol in terms of its sound and meaning. Subsequent contacts develop recognition of the word. In this text, the development of word recognition implies identification as the first step in the process. Until a printed symbol is grasped at a glance—until it has become what we term a *sight word*—recognition requires some degree of identification. Instruction in word recognition is designed to enable the child to perform three interrelated tasks. First, the child must be able to recognize known words rapidly, with a minimum of analysis. For example, if he knows the word *think* as a sight word, he should not analyze it into *th-ink*, pronouncing each part and then blending it into the word *think*. Indeed, to do so repeatedly would be detrimental to his reading. There are children who have difficulty reading for just this reason. Second, the child should be skilled in recognizing partially known words with little analysis. Thus, if the child knows the word *think*, he should be adept at identifying it in all of its variant forms. Applying syntactic skills, he should need but a glance at the word to enable him to recognize and know the meanings of *think, thinks, thinking,* and, as he gains maturity, unthinkable. In such words, the child should learn to identify the root word, recognize the modified form rapidly, and understand the changed meaning. Third, the child must develop adaptable approaches that enable him to identify new words by himself. As he matures in reading, he must be able not only to pronounce new words, but also be so skilled that he can recognize them silently, without interrupting the thought of the passage he is reading.

Instruction in word identification is complex. It is understandable why reading instruction has progressed through a series of methods, from a spelling approach to a whole-word approach, to systems that emphasize phonics, to an emphasis on sentence or context, to the current combined approach using contextual, whole-word, phonics, and structural analysis as aids to word identification. The major problem in the combined approach is teaching the various procedures needed in such a manner that none will be omitted or over- or underemphasized and that the more analytical and time-consuming aids to recognition will be used only when needed. To teach the child the word-recognition techniques necessary for her to recognize known words and to identify the new ones visually or by the use of phonics, at least five sorts of balance must be maintained.

First, a balance between the establishment of *word-recognition techniques* and the development of *meaning vocabulary* is desirable for reading growth. If there is too much isolated drill on word parts, the child may become a capable word caller, but she may not understand what she is reading. The child may be able to make a fairly accurate attempt at pronouncing new words, but unless what she pronounces is associated with meaning, the results of reading will be unsatisfactory. Even when a child's early reading deals with very common words, the teacher who neglects to introduce the words in context may encourage an over-emphasis on analytical techniques at the expense of word meaning. Conversely, the teacher who neglects to teach identification skills may cause the child to make disorganized attempts at pronouncing words, saying any word that comes to mind, or may make the child too dependent on him for answers. In sum, word-recognition skills must be taught and learned as part of a coordinated reading program.

Second, a balance between the acquisition of a *sight vocabulary*—words the child knows at a glance—and the establishment of *word recognition* is essential. The child must learn to recognize, at sight, an ever-increasing number of words, because it is on these that her fluency as a reader depends. These words also provide much of her ability to derive meaning from printed matter. If the child is led to place too much emphasis on either one of these skills at the expense of the other, the results will be unsatisfactory. The teacher may place so much emphasis upon building a sight vocabulary, that the child fails to establish the needed word-recognition techniques. Such a child may seem to progress well at the start, but she will soon experience reading difficulties. She will lack independence, since she will be unable to identify new words by herself. On the other hand, a reading program that stresses word-recognition skills and neglects to build a sight vocabulary encourages the child to become a slow, laborious, and overanalytical reader. The child needs to build both an ever-increasing sight vocabulary and an increasingly diversified array of word-recognition techniques. If she underuses one in favor of the other, she will encounter reading problems (Vellutino & Scanlon, 1986). This is one of the most difficult balances to achieve. As a result, there are many children who proceed to use analysis on words that they really know at sight, and there are other children who are at a loss to work out the pronunciation of new words independently because they are weak at word identification.

Third, there must be a balance between the *meaning clues* and the *analytical aids* to word recognition. The child who depends too much on meaning clues to recognize words will make many errors that have little relationship to the appearance of the word she miscalls. These errors involve substituting words that make sense although they are not the words of the author, nor do they evoke his meaning. For example, a child might read the sentence "The ship sailed over the equator" as "The ship sailed over the seas." Such a reader is often inaccurate and becomes confused in comprehension. On the other hand, the child who depends too much upon analytical aids to the exclusion of meaning makes errors that often reflect reasonable letter-sound associations, but do not make any real sense in what is read. For example, the sentence "The Scottish girl's dress was plaid" might be read "The Scottish girl's dress was played." In either case, little or no understanding results. The child must develop both abilities, and when she has done so, she can use them to reinforce one another. If she lacks the analytical techniques, she is handicapped because exact recognition is often impossible from context alone. If she depends too much upon word analysis, she will be unable to use context to speed her recognition of words and to check the accuracy of her recognition through the sense it makes.

Fourth, a balance between *phonic* and *structural* techniques must be maintained. If the teacher places too much emphasis on phonics training, the child may fail to develop the ability to use larger structural elements in recognizing words. The result may be an element-by-element, sound-blending approach, which is ineffective as a major means of word recognition. Too much of an emphasis on phonics may teach the child to separate words to such an extent that synthesizing or blending sounds into one word becomes impossible. But if, by contrast, the emphasis on larger structural and visual elements is too great, the child's skill in using smaller elements or letter sounds may not be sufficiently developed for her to recognize certain words, such as unusual names, that require sounding. Many children with reading difficulties have failed to establish this balance and hence have become either overanalytical or have not attained sufficient knowledge of phonics.

Fifth, there must be a balance between the emphasis placed on *knowledge of word parts* and that placed on the *orderly inspection of words along the line of print*, from left to right and from the beginning of the word to the end. If too much stress is placed, for example, on word families, such as the *at* family in *cat, sat, fat*, and *hat*, the child may neglect the beginning elements of words and thus make an unreasonable number of errors in them. Another child overusing this technique may develop reversal problems because she has the habit of looking at the end of words to pick up her clues to recognizing them. When a child makes an excessive number of errors in any specific location within words, it usually indicates that, in her case, knowledge of word parts has been emphasized at the expense of orderly inspection from the beginning to the end of a word. And as regards the latter, another balance is required: The child must develop flexibility in her visual analysis of the word she is trying to recognize. For example, suppose the word is *frighten*, and the child selects *fri* as the first element she recognizes. Then, unless she rejects this result of her analysis rather quickly, she will be unable to work out the rest of the word, because *ght* will not be helpful to her. She may try to sound each letter, *g—h—t*, and then get into marked confusion. A child who was more flexible in the visual analysis of words would reject the first separation of the word and break it into more suitable parts, such as *fr—ight—en*. Then, applying her knowledge of the elements, she would be able to pronounce the word with little difficulty.

Word recognition is much more complex than is assumed in programs emphasizing a single set of skills or in instruction placing the child in a stimulating reading environment and expecting her to discover all the needed skills and to maintain the balances among them. Word recognition entails the use of too many interrelated learned skills to allow the program to be narrow or incidental.

The major source of a child's difficulty in recognizing words is usually the child's failure to establish one or more of these basic skills or in her overdependence on any of them. Word-recognition problems are often found to be at the root of the difficulty those readers have who fall into the categories of having a *limiting* and *complex* reading disability. The more prevalent meaning-clue disabilities are failure to associate meaning with printed symbols, having an insufficient sight vocabulary, and failure to use meaning clues. Each will be discussed next, along with methods of correction that have been found helpful.

Failure to Associate Meaning with Printed Symbols

The goal of word recognition is to enable the child to identify words and associate the correct meanings with them. Often, however, word-recognition programs emphasize oral word study and pronunciation so strongly that the child fails to establish the habit, or to sense the importance, of understanding the meaning of printed symbols. When reading, the child may give fairly close approximations to the pronunciation of the words he studies, but he may not have identified the word as one he knows in his listening or speaking vocabulary. Sometimes, the teacher can detect a mispronunciation or an insecurity that indicates that the word was almost, but not quite, recognized. At other times, it is necessary to ask the child what the word means in order to detect whether he is having this basic difficulty. Of course, a relatively low level of performance by a child on oral vocabulary or meaning vocabulary tests, in the presence of a higher score on tests of word-recognition techniques, such as knowledge of word elements and visual analysis of words, indicates this type of difficulty.

To correct the deficiency, remedial work should emphasize the basic comprehension abilities and reading for meaning that will be described in Chapter 14. In all word-recognition exercises, the meanings of the words should be emphasized. Drills on isolated word elements should be rejected for children with this difficulty. Whenever possible, word-identification exercises should be in contextual settings, so that there is the need to recognize not only the word, but also its meaning, to complete the tasks successfully.

In reading for content or entertainment, there are methods that help the child develop the habit and ability of associating meanings with word symbols. For example, the child may be requested to draw illustrations for a story he is reading—even stick-figure drawings will do. To comply with the request, it is necessary for him to attend to the meaning of descriptive words. If the child is expected to retell a story in his own words, rather than just to repeat the words in the book, he will learn to interpret the meaning of the word symbols. Any comprehension exercise that requires the child to paraphrase and not merely repeat words encourages the association of meaning with the words read.

Besides emphasizing word meanings whenever he is reading, the child must be encouraged to develop his word-recognition techniques if he is to associate precise ideas with the printed symbols. The child who needs to strengthen this ability may profit from exercises of the following types:

1. Exercises to develop clear sensory impressions.

   a. What did you hear:
      when a stone hit the water?
      splash   crack

   b. An animal with stripes on it is a (an):
      elephant   horse   zebra

   c. Match the words with the phrase that tells the same thing. Put the number of the word before the phrase.

      1. lagged   _____ flowed with force
      2. gushed   _____ moved slowly
      3. gurgled   _____ made a noise as it flowed
      4. rushed   _____ moved rapidly along

   d. Put *J* before each word that would tell about a jolly person.

      _____ merry   _____ laughing   _____ joyful
      _____ beaming   _____ bitter   _____ dreary

2. Exercises to develop precise meanings.

   a. In each line, find two words that have an opposite meaning.

good	tired	sad	bad
right	bad	wrong	trouble
wet	dry	damp	moist

   b. Find the words that have a similar meaning.

glow	bright	shine	spark
rushed	walked	ran	hurried
replied	said	answered	wrote

   c. Complete the sentence with the best word from those listed after the sentence.

      When the boy saw the people far away, he _____ to them.
      said   shouted   whispered   muttered.

3. Exercises to develop extensiveness of meaning.

   a. Tell the difference in the meaning of *roll* in the following sentences.

      (1) We ate a *roll* for lunch.
      (2) We watched the big waves *roll* along the beach.

(3) Get a *roll* of paper.
(4) Please *roll* the ball to Jim.
(5) The dog could *roll* over.
(6) The teacher called the *roll.*
(7) We could see the *roll* of the hills.
(8) We could hear the *roll* of the drums.

b. Put the number of the right definition in front of each sentence.

trunk   (1) The main stem of a tree   _____ He picked up the
                                            peanut with his trunk.

           (2) A box used to carry clothes _____ The trunk of the
                                            oak was rough.

           (3) Part of an elephant   _____ He put the trunk
                                            on the train.

Semantic mapping allows children to learn the meanings of words through observing relationships between the words. In an application suggested by Heimlich and Pittelman (1986) for sixth-grade poor readers, semantic mapping is used in pre- and postreading activities surrounding a story about rattlesnakes. Figure 10–1 shows a semantic map developed by the group of poor readers concerning rattlesnakes.

Computer programs such as *Tiger's Tales* (Hermann, 1987) feature the presentation of new words in association with pictures. When the child matches a word to a picture correctly, he is rewarded with a short animated sequence. If the child matches the two incorrectly, the wrong words are crossed out and disappear, leaving only the correct word and picture. Provisions are included in the program to ensure ample review. Interactive, child-determined stories emphasize the meanings of the words in a contextual setting.

Further suggestions, which will be made in Chapter 14, aid in building the habit of attending to word meanings and also develop skill in associating meaning with word symbols. Many times, a child makes a close approximation to a word by the use of phonics and other word-recognition techniques, but unless he keeps the context in mind, the word remains unidentified. In addition to other means, the promotion of extensive reading wherein the child attends to the expressive use of words will help him associate meaning with printed symbols.

When children listen carefully to their teacher's expressive reading of a well-written story, they learn to associate meaning with print. When they engage in creative writing, they associate their own words with printed symbols. Expressive writing, illustrating stories, dramatizing stories, creating puppet shows, and other such activities emphasize the meaning carried by words. Since, in order to read, children must derive meaning from printed symbols, all word-recognition activities should demand not only the identification of words, but also an understanding of their meanings.

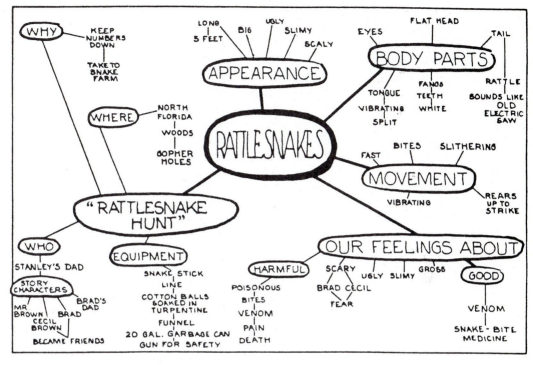

FIGURE 10–1 Group Map for *Rattlesnakes*

Source: From *Semantic Mapping: Classroom Applications* by Joan E. Heimlich and Susan D. Pittelman, eds., 1986, p. 28. Newark, DE: International Reading Association. Reprinted with permission of Joan E. Heimlich and the International Reading Association.

Insufficient Sight Vocabulary

The importance of forming the habit of recognizing known words rapidly, rather than studying each word encountered as though it never had been seen before, cannot be emphasized too strongly. The child who fails to build a large sight vocabulary and who does not have the habit of recognizing these words at a glance cannot hope to become an able reader. Not only will she be limited in her ability to group words into thought units, necessary for comprehension and fluency, but also, she will be seriously handicapped in identifying new words. This latter limitation comes about in two ways. First, the child will be unable to use contextual clues effectively, because her vocabulary load of unknown words will be too great. Second, she will be inefficient in the more mature methods of word study. Words affixed with prefixes, for example, will be difficult for her to recognize because she does not know the root word, since it is not in her sight vocabulary. Compound words will also present her with a tough problem, since she has not developed the habit of sight recognition of the two smaller words from which the compound word is made. The child who does not have a substantial sight vocabulary and who does not recognize words automatically and rapidly will find learning to read a bewildering undertaking. For these reasons, it is beneficial to build the sight vocabulary from the start.

Children who rely too completely on working out words analytically may fail to acquire a sufficient sight vocabulary. In the early grades, the teacher may find it difficult to detect that these children are not acquiring a sufficient sight vocabulary. Eventually, however, persistence in analysis of too many words will prove detrimental to their reading growth. Detailed study of so many words will have to be rejected and a sight vocabulary built, or severe disability will occur.

With other children, a limited sight vocabulary is easily detected. They may be word-by-word readers, making phonetic errors with words they should know at sight, or they may fail to phrase well in what they read orally. Another indication is the tendency for the child to make about an equal number of errors, regardless of the difficulty of the material she is reading. If a child, for example, makes about the same percentage of errors in reading material at a second-grade level as she makes in material at a fourth-grade level, she is likely to be limited in her development of a sight vocabulary. If she tends to make more mistakes on small, common words than she does on polysyllabic words, she is probably limited in her sight vocabulary.

The teacher can easily measure sight vocabulary by rapid-exposure techniques. For example, she can quickly flash words printed on cards. The child who cannot automatically and rapidly identify common words at a glance has failed to develop a sufficient sight vocabulary. When reading from flash cards, if the child makes a considerably greater number of errors than she does when looking at the same words for an unlimited time, she can be assumed to have an insufficient sight vocabulary. These indications of a limited ability in recognizing words at a glance mandate remedial work in building a larger sight vocabulary.

Remedial training for increasing the sight vocabulary of a child with a reading disability is done best by using material that is somewhat easy for the child to read. Tasks that require rapid reading to locate a specific statement or to understand the general significance of a passage should be emphasized for a child who is trying to increase her sight vocabulary. She should be given tasks that require new words to be read as whole words, and tasks that require words to be analyzed should be avoided. Extended practice reading easy material is desirable, so that automatic and rapid recognition of words is encouraged (Samuels, 1988).

In addition, the following types of exercises have proven effective as additional reinforcement of the habit of reading words at a glance. These exercises use the basic vocabulary that is being developed and emphasize meaning, categorization, and classification:

1. Exercises in which the word is so much expected that recognition is rapid.

   In winter, there is _____ .
   snow   house   well

2. Exercises in which a child finds the correct word in a list on the chalkboard as the teacher gives the clue.
Find the word in this list that tells us where we:

Clue	Words
buy food	farm
go swimming	table
find cows	store
eat dinner	beach

3. Exercises that require meaningful scanning of a list. See how fast you can draw a line under all the things that can run.

horse	house	girl	pig
tree	dog	road	man
cat	boy	store	window

4. Various word games that call for immediate responses and require sight recognition of words and their meanings.

   a. Cards with names of animals printed on them can be used. Two children can play together. One child can flash the cards, and the other can respond. Words such as the following can be used:

chicken	elephant	bird	goose
dog	duck	pony	donkey
horse	goat	wren	fish

   One child may tell the name of an animal with four feet as the cards are flashed. Then the other may tell which can fly.

   b. Another set of cards could be made of verbs, and the child could tell which words on the cards indicate movement. The types of words that might be used are:

afraid	listen	march	walk
jump	roll	sleep	feel
think	skip	ride	guess
flew	know	slide	was

   c. A fish-pond game is played in which words are attached to paper clips and the child uses a pole with a magnet on the end of the line. If the child can read at a glance the word that she fishes out of the pond, it is caught. If she has to study the word, that "fish" gets away, but she may be able to catch it another time. Any words that caused the child trouble in her reader could be used in this game, as well as other words that she knows well.

   d. A game similar to Authors can be played with words. The words are grouped in sets of four similar things, such as clothes, animals, trees, time, food, toys, people, and colors. Four children may play together. Each child gets eight cards, and the remaining cards are place in a pile in the center. The children take turns drawing one card from the center pile and then discarding one. The child who gets two complete sets of four similar words first wins the game. The set of word cards for this game might be these:

Clothes	Animals	TreesTime	
coat	lion	oak	afternoon
hat	elephant	maple	spring
shoe	donkey	fir	tomorrow
dress	horse	willow	morning

Food	Toys	People	Colors
bread	doll	aunt	yellow
pudding	wagon	father	green
peanuts	football	uncle	blue
carrots	balloon	mother	brown

Furniture	Flowers	Places	Meals
chair	rose	farm	breakfast
table	tulip	beach	dinner
bed	daisy	city	lunch
desk	poppy	zoo	supper

e. Many other games, such as Wordo (like Bingo), Old Maid, Spin the Wheel, Climb the Ladder, Dominoes with words, and Grab Bag, can be played. All of the preceding exercises and activities can be developed using phrases, too.

5. One of the best exercises involves the rapid recognition of groups of high-utility words. These words are typed on flash cards and are presented rapidly.

a. *Directions.* The child demonstrates understanding through action.

jump up	point to me
sit down	open the book
come here	look at the door
raise your hand	go to the window

b. *Classification.* The child demonstrates recognition by indicating whether the words tell about something one would find in a home or at a zoo.

table and chairs	barking seal
lion and tiger	iron cage
set of dishes	baby elephant
pretty picture	pots and pans
big red rug	little brown monkey

Computer programs, such as *Trickster Coyote* (Prentice Associates, 1986), provide practice in reading words quickly and matching them with definitions. Presented in an exciting game format, this program can be played by up to four players. Students are given an opportunity to study any words they miss. Teachers may reprogram the game to include any words they choose. As is true for many computer games, some students will require assistance from the teacher in learning how to play the game at the onset.

Any exercises or activities used in building a child's sight vocabulary should encourage the child to inspect the words rapidly, rather than resort to a detailed study of them. The words should be presented in contexts that require understanding of their meanings.

The child should be reading material that introduces new words gradually and repeats them at well-spaced intervals. If the child is motivated to read a selection, if the new words are introduced before the selection is read, and if the purposes require rapid reading, the child should be able to increase her sight vocabulary. When this instruction is reinforced with exercises like those previously described using the words being emphasized, the gains should be even greater. In all reading and drill, recognizing the meaning of the words should be required. What the child with an insufficient sight vocabulary needs is experience in recognizing the word and its meaning at a glance.

Failure to Use Meaning Clues

Meaning clues are among the most powerful aids to recognizing words. The effective adult reader uses these clues in all of his word identification and recognition. Meaning clues enable the reader to anticipate new or unfamiliar words before he actually sees them. No matter what other aids to recognition are used, the proficient reader invariably uses some form of meaning clue to assist him. Either he may predict words he might expect from prior knowledge of a given topic, or he may use context to gain the meaning of a passage (*semantic clues*) or sense the structure of a sentence (*syntactic clues*).

We agree with Goodman (1973) that word recognition is, in a sense, "a psycholinguistic guessing game." In recognizing words, the child anticipates them through prior knowledge and contextual clues. He then applies word-recognition skills, such as perceptual skills, for instant recognition or decoding skills for more intensive identification if necessary. Simultaneously, he checks the content. He sometimes resorts to rereading if he doubts his accuracy or if his guess does not gibe with the content immediately following.

Many children with reading disabilities do not use meaning clues effectively, and as a consequence, they are inept in recognizing words. The failure to use meaning clues precludes the acquisition of such mature reading skills as grouping words into thought units. It also limits the development of accuracy in using the other word-recognition techniques. The ineffective use of meaning clues forces the child to analyze carefully many words that should be identified with a minimum of inspection.

Meaning clues can be divided into two types. The first is prior knowledge, which enables the student to anticipate the sorts of words and concepts that he is likely to encounter when reading about a given topic. If, for example, a mature reader is reading about soil conservation, he might expect to meet such words as *erosion, soil depletion, levee, irrigation, crop rotation*, and *drainage*. This anticipation would make recognition or identification of these words more rapid than if they appeared unexpectedly in prose on some other subject. The second type of meaning clue is the contextual clue. The use of contextual clues is a rapid recognition technique in which a word or phrase is so completely anticipated from the meaning of the sentence or paragraph, that the merest flick of a glance is all that is needed to confirm that it is that expected word or phrase. Even if the word is unfamiliar, the context plus a minimum of inspection are all that is needed for its identification.

Weakness in Use of Prior Knowledge

The child who does not anticipate words that she is likely to meet when reading about a specific topic or within a specific field is to some degree handicapped in recognizing words. There are many children, and even some adult readers, who fail to use their knowledge of a subject to aid them in identifying and recognizing words. Many adult readers, for example, skip a graphic presentation of facts discussed in the accompanying text when a brief study of the table, chart, or graph would enable them to anticipate the content of and the words within the passage. The reader who uses pictorial aids effectively becomes a more fluent reader and understands a passage better, partly because she is prepared for the words in the passage. She can identify them with ease and devote herself to the meaning of what is read, rather than to the mere recognition of words. For the younger reader, picture clues operate in much the same way. A well-illustrated book builds prior knowledge, which helps a child succeed with the text. The child, however, must be taught to use such pictures effectively. Many reading materials use pictures as a means of building the habit of anticipating words and concepts. There is, however, a possible danger in overusing pictures. If the pictures tell too much of the story, or if all of the concepts in the text are illustrated, there is little for the child to discover by reading. The preparatory activities preceding reading about a topic, which include planning, developing a background, and introducing new words, are a form of building prior knowledge for the youngsters. These activities are necessary in both the general classroom and the resource room. Teaching that neglects such essentials of reading instruction predisposes the child to be weak in using the prior knowledge she has and in gaining the prior knowledge she needs.

Lack of or ineffective use of prior knowledge in word recognition can be detected by noting whether a child has unusual difficulty recognizing words related specifically to a topic. If, for example, the child is asked to tell what words might be used in a story about a rabbit, and if she did not mention some such words as *jump, carrot, run, hop, long ears, cottontail*, and *burrow*, she probably lacks prior knowledge. If she has such knowledge, but does not use it to recognize these words, then she is ineffective in applying her knowledge to word recognition.

The approach to remediation for this child would be, for the most part, to place a greater emphasis on preparing the child for reading about a topic. Preteaching essential vocabulary and concepts should be stressed. A discussion of pictures that are germane to the topic and the development of semantic maps would be advantageous. During reading, the child could be reminded to use her knowledge; the pictures should be reviewed and the semantic maps expanded.

Failure to Use Contextual Clues

The child who has failed to develop the ability to use contextual clues as an aid to word recognition is missing an essential means of recognizing words. The use of context is a rapid technique that enables the reader to identify a word immediately. For example, in the sentence, "The man put his hat on his _____ ," it is not difficult for the child to know the missing word from the context. In effect, the context narrows the number of choices dramatically from the 800,000 words that would be possible if context were irrelevant. In addition, the use of contextual clues makes the selection of the correct *meaning* of the word possible. Thus, in the sentence cited, the meaning of the word *head* could not have been that of *head* in the *head of a stream* or in *a head of steam.*

The reader who uses context is more likely to recognize a new word correctly than if he did not use context. Often, he can make an approximation of the pronunciation of a word from his analytical techniques. Contextual clues then enable him to identify the word completely. Such clues usually work in combination with other word-recognition techniques. The use of context clues makes analysis much more rapid and accurate.

An equally, if not more, important use of contextual clues is to check on the application of all the other recognition techniques. Just as in subtraction it pays to add afterward to check the answer, so in reading it pays to check the meaning of the sentence to see whether a problem in word recognition has been solved correctly. When the child has figured out a word, he must be aware of whether it makes sense in the context in which it is found. If it does, he has probably found the correct solution. If it does not, he should reinspect the word, because, undoubtedly, he has made a mistake. Without at least a fair degree of skill in the use of contextual clues, the child will be slow and inaccurate in recognizing words. With this skill, he can be a good reader if he also has other well-developed word-recognition techniques. Similarly, a child who depends on contextual clues alone also will be inaccurate in recognizing words. It is important to know that many children who are thought to have difficulty reading because of limited analytical skills or because they have insufficient knowledge of phonic, structural, or visual elements are really having difficulty because they are not using contextual clues well.

The child who is limited in the use of contextual clues is spotted easily. If he makes as many errors reading words in context as he does reading a list of words, then he is not making sufficient use of the meaning of sentences or paragraphs as an aid to recognition. If the child's errors do not fit the meaning of the text and are senseless, he is not using contextual clues. For example, if the child reads the word *cat* as *sat* in the sentence "The dog ran after the cat," he is not using context, because *sat* makes no sense at all. If, however, he reads *cat* as *car*, he is probably using context, because *car* does make sense.

Remedial training in the use of contextual clues involves having the child read materials at a level of difficulty in which he encounters about 1 new word in every 40 running words. He should be reading for purposes that demand a thorough understanding of the content. If his problem is severe, a separate and immediate purpose for each paragraph, or even each sentence, should be stated. This emphasizes reading for meaning and enables the child to recognize known words at a glance and use contextual clues in combination with other techniques in the identification of unfamiliar words. The teacher may need to ask the child from time to time what he thinks the word might be. Or, more generally, she might ask, "Does that make sense?" On occasion, the child may use the context plus the initial sound to help him identify or recognize a difficult word.

In addition to the preceding suggestions, the following more formal exercises encourage the child to use contextual clues:

1. Exercises in which the meaning of the sentence indicates the word to be recognized.

    a. The boys rode over the snow on it. What was it?
       boat   store   sled

    b. Mother put a candle on the cake for Bob's _____ .
       football   birthday   bedroom

2. Exercises in which the child reads a paragraph and fills in the missing words, using the initial elements given. He does not need to write them, but reads the sentences to himself. Comprehension questions can be asked.

    Billy caught the ball.
    Then he th_____ the ball to his father.
    Father c_____ the ball, too.
    Billy and his father were pl_____ catch.
    A dog came to play.
    He j_____ up and got the ball.
    Then he ran a_____ with it.

3. Exercises in which the context plus initial elements are used as aids to word recognition.

    a. We will get some apples at the st_____ .
       store   steep   farm
    b. The car went down the str_____ .
       strong   road   street

4. Riddles in which the context gives the answer.

> It lives in a zoo.
> It hops about.
> It carries a baby in its pouch.
> It is a(n) _____ .
> elephant   crocodile   kangaroo

5. Closure-type exercises using syntax clues and initial-element clues.

   a. They went sw_____ at the beach.
   b. Tom l_____ candy.
   c. Mary likes h_____ new doll.
   d. The boys w_____ to play, but they d_____ not have a ball.

6. Pure cloze exercises in which the student must fill in the blank from the meaning of a sentence or paragraph.

> Mary and John went to the _____ to buy some candy.
> On their way home, they meet their _____ Tom.
> Tom was riding his _____ bicycle.

In this type of exercise, it is imperative that the reading be at an easy level for the student. For this use of the cloze technique, any word that fits the meaning and the structure of the sentence will do.

7. Deletions of nonsensical additions. Exercises in which the child reads a paragraph and deletes the words that do not belong because they do not make sense.

> Mary and John went dog to the store to barn buy some candy. On their zoo way home, they met their friend Tom. Tom was kangaroo riding his new bicycle.

Case Study of a Primary Grade Student Who Had Difficulty Relating Meaning to Printed Symbols

Steven, a third-grade student, was referred to the school reading center by his classroom teacher toward the middle of the school year. The teacher was concerned because he did not seem to understand what he read, he did not participate in class discussions relating to materials read, and, although his oral reading was accurate in terms of word pronunciation, his phrasing was poor and he ignored punctuation.

School History. Steven had attended the same school all of his primary school years. He had no record of previous academic problems in school, and he had not previously received special help in reading.

School Behavior. During his third-grade year, Steven became increasingly reticent about participating in classroom discussion and activities. He had difficulty completing independent work. However, when his classroom teacher worked individually with Steven, he paid attention to what was expected and tried hard.

Abilities. According to the Wechsler Intelligence Scale for Children, Revised, Steven's inability to learn was low average, with a full-scale I.Q. of 90. His performance I.Q. was 96 and his verbal I.Q. was 85. This would place his reading expectancy at the 3.3 level, based on his full-scale I.Q.

Reading Achievement Testing. In the fall of Steven's third-grade year, he was given the Metropolitan Achievement Test along with the rest of the third grade. His grade scores and percentile ranks in reading and spelling were as follows:

Name of Subtest	Grade Equivalent	Percentile Rank
Word Knowledge	2.7	36
Word Analysis	3.2	56
Reading Comprehension	2.7	34
(Total Reading)	(2.7)	(36)
Spelling	3.0	44

In order to determine the exact nature and severity of Steven's reading problem, the reading center diagnostician administered the Woodcock Reading Mastery Tests, Revised. Steven's scores on these tests were as follows:

Name of Subtest	Grade Equivalent	Percentile Rank	Standard Score
Word Identification	3.7	52	101
Word Attack	4.2	56	102
Basic Skills	3.8	57	103
Word Comprehension	1.9	3	72
Passage Comprehension	2.6	14	84
Comprehension Skill	2.2	6	77
Total Reading	2.9	20	90

Steven was also given the Diagnostic Reading Scales. On the Word Recognition subtest, he achieved at a satisfactory level for his grade. His pronunciations were phonetically very close to the correct word (e.g., "triumpant" for "triumphant" and "standidize" for "standardize"). During oral reading, he pronounced most words correctly, but often accented the wrong syllable of multisyllabic words, and he failed to note punctuation. Errors in comprehension indicated poor understanding of what he read. His comprehension of silent reading was poor, and his reading rate was slow. His reading potential, as measured by listening to selections read aloud to him and answering questions about them, was satisfactory for his grade level.

Observation of Behavior. Steven was cooperative during individual testing. His responses were slow and careful; he spoke with a soft voice and put his head on the desk at times. He often complained that the tests were too long and that he was tired.

Interpretation of Test Results. Steven is a third-grade child of low average ability to learn. General, specific, and child-study diagnostic testing revealed that he was making adequate general progress in reading at his grade level. However, all measures suggested that his word-identification skills surpassed his word-knowledge and comprehension skills. His performance indicated that he had difficulty working flexibly with word meanings. Case study testing revealed that he had great difficulty understanding the meaning of selections he read aloud and greater difficulty with selections he read silently. However, when listening, Steven was able to understand material at a reasonable level of difficulty for a third-grade child.

Informal testing was conducted during which Steven pronounced difficult words and told what they meant and then listened to the diagnostician pronounce them and then told what they meant. Although Steven's ability to pronounce the words was good (18/20), his ability to define words or use them in a sentence was much poorer (12/20). After hearing the diagnostician pronounce the words, Steven was able to define or use 16 of the 20 words correctly.

In the child-study meeting, it was decided that although Steven's progress in reading was generally satisfactory for his grade level and mental ability, he was having a specific problem associating meaning with printed words. Word pronunciation was a strength for Steven, and his ability to associate meaning with spoken words was satisfactory. It was decided that he should have small-group work with the reading specialist for a limited amount of time for direct assistance with his problem. Difficulties with nonparticipation, incomplete assignments, and fatigue were judged to be a result of his specific reading problems, not a cause.

It is also useful, in considering remediation for Steven, to answer the diagnostic questions posed in Chapter 7.

1. *Is Steven correctly classified as a child with a reading disability?* Steven is an example of a child with a limiting reading disability. Although his word-pronunciation skills are satisfactorily advanced for his grade placement, he has unusual difficulty associating printed words with their meanings.
2. *What is the nature of the training needed?* The remedial plan for Steven included (1) a variety of highly interesting children's books on a wide range of topics; (2) specific vocabulary development drills; (3) oral reading of plays, poems, and exercises designed for expressive reading; (4) tape recordings of oral reading so that he could monitor his expression and note his progress; (5) games used to stress multiple word meanings and precise word meanings; and (6) developing a word bank of words he wanted to save from his favorite stories. Since Steven's remedial work took place in a small-group setting, many of his oral reading activities and word-meaning games were participated in by the entire group.
3. *Who can give the remedial work most effectively?* Steven received 3 months of small-group instruction on a daily basis. Although he could have received corrective instruction in his classroom, it was felt that it was best to give him

remedial instruction for a limited time in the reading center because of his reticence to speak. In the reading center, he would be able to use techniques involving a great deal of oral reading and taping. At the beginning of the fourth-grade year, Steven returned to the regular classroom on a full-time basis.

4. *How can improvement be made most efficiently?* Since oral reading and listening were relative strengths for Steven, they were emphasized in developing associations between printed words and meanings. Enjoyable activities were chosen for Steven; the reading selections were often humorous. Not only formal methods, but also less structured group activities, were used, which seemed to help Steven express himself more freely.

5. *Does the child have any limiting conditions that must be considered?* In the regular classroom, Steven had given little evidence of interest or desire to participate in class activities. Although he worked hard on assignments given by his teacher, he had difficulty completing them and rarely joined spontaneously with the other children in less structured activities. In a small-group situation, with much adult encouragement and materials handpicked to delight him, Steven developed the need to know what the words meant and responded with increasing enthusiasm.

6. *Are there any environmental conditions that might interfere with the child's progress in reading?* Both Steven's parents and the classroom teacher supported his reading program entirely.

Results. In the beginning of the fourth-grade year, Steven returned full time to the regular classroom. He seemed enthusiastic and confident in the classroom and appeared to understand what he read. When group standardized tests were administered during his fourth-grade year, gains in comprehension of both words and passages were evident.

Summary

It is important for all readers to develop skills in word recognition. Word study involves two major goals: (1) to develop a word-meaning vocabulary and word-recognition techniques in such a way that the identification of symbols is accompanied by meaning and (2) to develop flexibility in applying word-recognition techniques. It is necessary to maintain five balances among such techniques: (1) balance between the formation of word-recognition skills and the acquisition of meaning vocabulary; (2) balance between the development of word-recognition skills and that of sight vocabulary; (3) balance between the development of meaning clues in word recognition and the use of word analysis; (4) balance between the use of phonic techniques and the use of structural techniques; and (5) balance in emphasis between knowledge of word parts and the orderly, left-to-right inspection of words.

Meaning clues are helpful to word recognition in three ways. First, they enable the reader to anticipate the words he is to read. This makes recognition of known words rapid and accurate and allows the reader to work out the identification of unfamiliar words with a minimum of study. Second, meaning clues are essential in checking the accuracy of recognition of words. If the word recognized does not make sense, the reader should study further the word missed. Third, the application of other word-recognition techniques frequently gives the child an approximation of the word; and then the meaning clues enable him to recognize the word correctly.

Certain reading behaviors suggest a child's failure to associate meaning with printed symbols, an insufficient sight vocabulary, or an ineffective use of meaning clues. Various techniques and exercises aid the child in overcoming each type of problem.

Study Questions

1. Why is the development of reading skills alone not enough for a child who is being taught to read? Why must a reasonable balance of skills be maintained?
2. What clues should alert a teacher that a child is not associating meaning (or correct meaning) with the words read?
3. List three characteristics of good exercises, games, or activities designed to increase sight recognition of common words.
4. What should be done to assist a youngster who has little or no prior knowledge of a general topic to be covered in a reading selection?
5. Why is the successful use of contextual clues considered more essential than some of the other word-recognition skills?

Selected Readings

Ekwall, E. E. (1986). *Teacher's handbook on diagnosis and remediation in reading* (2nd ed.) (pp. 23–46). Boston: Allyn and Bacon.

Maggart, Z. R., & Zintz, M. V. (1990). *Corrective reading* (pp. 256–275). Dubuque, IA: Wm. C. Brown.

McCormick, S. (1987). *Remedial and clinical reading instruction* (pp. 230–250, 280–301). Columbus, OH: Merrill.

Richek, M. A., List, L. K., & Lerner, J. W. (1989). *Reading problems: Assessment and teaching strategies* (2nd ed.) (pp. 166–184). Englewood Cliffs, NJ: Prentice Hall.

Rubin, D. (1991). *Diagnosis and correction in reading instruction* (2nd ed.) (pp. 306–319). Boston: Allyn and Bacon.

Rupley, W. H. & Blair, T. R. (1989). *Reading diagnosis and remediation* (3rd ed.) (pp. 147–168). Columbus, OH: Merrill.

Chapter 11

Correcting Ineffective Perceptual and Decoding Skills in Word Recognition

Proficiency in both the use of meaning clues and the application of analytical word-recognition techniques is required if the reader is to associate concepts with printed symbols. Meaning clues alone are not enough for good reading at any level; they must be accompanied by the use of flexible word-recognition skills. It is through the interaction of all the word-study skills that a competent reader improves her reading capability.

Three types of interrelated skills are needed to support meaning clues in word recognition: (1) flexible visual-perceptual habits, (2) knowledge of phonics and structural word elements, and (3) fluent oral and visual synthesis of word parts. Weakness in any one, or any combination, of these precludes adequate growth in reading. Readers who are deficient in word-recognition skills are classified as having a limiting or complex disability. This chapter treats basic problems associated with the faulty study of words. Included are suggestions for corrective instruction in word recognition, as well as an examination of ineffective visual-perceptual skills, a consideration of children with limited knowledge of word elements, and a discussion of children who lack fluent oral and visual synthesis.

Suggestions for Corrective Instruction in Word Recognition

To correct limitations in how a child studies words, instructional procedures must be planned carefully, according to the findings of a thorough diagnosis. There are certain suggestions, however, that strengthen the remedial teaching of children with all types of word-recognition difficulties:

1. Any material a child reads can be used in teaching word recognition. To be most useful, however, it must be at the reader's instructional level. Thus, select material that does not have too many new words. If the child with a reading difficulty is to use the meanings of printed words and contextual clues to aid in word recognition, a sufficient number of sight words must be known. It is especially important that new words not be too numerous in the initial lessons.

2. Teach word recognition when it is important to the child to recognize a word. If the purpose of reading is genuine to the child, and if he is pursuing that purpose, he will energetically attempt to recognize difficult words that prevent him from reaching his goal. He will persist in recognizing words, even when doing so entails careful analysis.

3. Always teach word recognition with meaningful material. Because the objective of all word-recognition techniques is to recognize words, it is better to develop those techniques with material whose content is meaningful to the child. This allows the child to use not only the analytical techniques taught him, but also various meaning clues that exist in the material. It teaches him to interpret a word in the context in which he finds it. Word recognition is not word calling, but recognition of the correct meaning of a word in a given situation. Teaching word recognition in context encourages a balance between the development of meaning vocabulary and that of the word-recognition techniques.

4. Undertake the more analytical types of word-recognition techniques only after the child is aware of the meaningful nature of reading, has established the habit of recognizing whole words, and has built a supportive sight vocabulary. This enables the reader to use meaning clues, and it also encourages him to use more rapid recognition techniques.

5. Be sure that the child knows the meanings of the words he is trying to identify or has the background necessary to derive their meaning. Using identification clues is difficult for him even when meaning is present; if meaning is absent, he may never find out whether or not he has recognized the word correctly.

6. Teach the child to segment unknown words visually before attempting to sound them. Visual analysis must always precede sounding, because it is through visual analysis that the reader isolates usable word elements to be sounded. A major aspect of effective decoding of words is the ability to locate usable elements in those words. The flexible study of words is essential, because a faulty start will have to be rejected quickly if words are to be recognized by analytical means.

7. Teach the child to notice similarities and differences among words. Through many comparisons, careful and rapid inspection of words will become habitual. The child who attends to similarities and differences among words can build his own families of words and notice similarities in the meaning and configurations of words with the same roots. This habit encourages building a large sight-recognition vocabulary and discourages overanalysis.

8. Teach the child to locate a new word-recognition element in known words before applying knowledge of that element to identify new words. By this means, the child is led to discover, for example, the initial-letter sound in the known words *run, ride,* and *rat* before he uses this knowledge in identifying the new word *rabbit.*

9. Help the child establish the routine of inspecting words rapidly, thoroughly, and systematically from left to right. Many of the difficulties in word recognition result from a failure to study the whole word from left to right. The child who fails to inspect words from left to right may recognize a word like *stop* as *pots* at one time and *tops* at another. Although the parts are recognized adequately, their order is confused, causing difficulty. Reversal problems may be caused by the failure to establish a systematic, left-to-right inspection of words. Neglect of any part of the word during inspection can cause difficulty.

10. Adjust instruction in word-recognition techniques to the individual. In developing these techniques, it should be kept in mind that there are some children with reading difficulties who do not profit from certain types of instruction. For example, for a child with an auditory impairment, it would be unwise to emphasize phonic approaches; indeed, sometimes these approaches may have to be omitted entirely with such a child. Similarly, in developing independence in word recognition for a child with visual impairment, more dependence should be placed on large word elements, such as syllables, than would be necessary for the child with unimpaired vision.

11. Avoid drilling the child on isolated word elements, and avoid using contrived teaching devices. Whenever possible, the child should recognize words as sight words. Drilling him on isolated elements could cause him to analyze words that he otherwise might have recognized easily on sight. Excessive analysis, if transferred to actual reading, may interfere with the child's reading fluency and understanding of meaning.

12. Discuss with the child exactly what remedial instruction is designed to accomplish, and let him aid in formulating his individual remedial plan. The child will be more motivated to participate actively in remediation if he is working toward known goals. Awareness of the plan allows him to be a more effective learner and enables him to assist his teacher in making some instructional decisions. The child will feel a greater sense of accomplishment when he achieves reading goals that have become his own, not just his teacher's.

Ineffective Visual-Perceptual Habits

The ability to read depends upon a group of visual-perceptual skills that are essential to decoding the printed symbols. These skills must be highly coordinated and flexible if a reader is to read in thought units at speeds that far exceed the rate at which she can listen. The thought units are made up of words that are perceived so quickly that they can be grouped together and recognized at a single glance. The child with a reading disability is often in major difficulty because her perceptual habits when reading preclude such rapid recognition of words. Her problem may be in any one, or in any combination, of the following interrelated perceptual defects:

1. Faulty visual analysis of words
2. Excessive word-perception errors
3. Overanalytical habits

Faulty Visual Analysis of Words

Visual analysis of an unfamiliar word (also known as *visual segmentation*) must always precede the application of symbol-sound association (also known as knowledge of word parts). Both of these, however, come before the final synthesis of the parts into recognition of the word. For example, a child who is unfamiliar with the word *something* might separate the word visually into *so—met—hing*. She might then associate sounds orally with the perceived symbol groups. Then she would try to blend the outcome, whereupon she would find that she had failed in her attempt because her original visual separation of the word was unproductive. She would then have to reject her first visual analysis and try another one. This time, she might see the first of the two words from which the word *something* is made and separate the word into *some—th—ing*. Then, by applying symbol-sound association orally and synthesizing the results, she would recognize the word. Of course, this approach to recognizing the word *something* is rather immature. A more advanced reader would analyze the word visually into the largest known elements, *some* and *thing*. She would recognize these parts visually and then synthesize them. Aided by contextual clues, she would not have to speak and blend the separate parts, but would recognize the whole word *something* at a glance. Nonetheless, even with this sophisticated approach, she would have analyzed the word visually, applied symbol-sound associations, and synthesized the parts mentally, all with great rapidity.

To become an able reader, the child must develop great skill and flexibility in the visual analysis of words. She must be able to segment words into useful elements at a glance. An element that is useful in one word may not be so in another. For example, the element *on* in the word *upon* is useful, but separating *on* out of the word *portion* would be detrimental to recognizing the whole word. The child must be adaptable, so that when one approach does not work, she can quickly reinspect the word and reanalyze it visually. She must analyze a word only when she does not know it as a sight word, and even then, she should select the largest usable elements in the word, rather than resort to unsystematic analysis.

The child who has difficulty with analyzing words visually can be identified by the classroom teacher in two ways: First, when pronouncing words aloud, she selects inappropriate elements to sound out and then often tries again and again to use the same analysis even when it does not work; second, when the teacher shows her how to analyze the word by covering up parts of it, she is able to recognize it. Accordingly, remedial training for a child with this kind of reading difficulty must focus on two results: First, it should give the child assistance in finding the most useful structural, visual, and phonic elements in words; second, it must develop a flexible strategy for segmentating words visually, teaching the child to use the larger elements first and to change quickly from an analysis that does not work to one that does.

The most effective remedial measures are similar to those used by the classroom teacher when first developing visual analytic ability in children without reading disabilities. When introducing unfamiliar words in preparation for reading, the teacher should work carefully to demonstrate how to analyze new words visually. During subsequent instruction, visual analysis should be emphasized. Such training as finding similarities in known words like *fight* and *sight* or *three* and *throw* gives the child experience in visual analysis. The material for this kind of instruction should be at a level of difficulty wherein the child needs to segment words visually. Help in finding parts of compound words or in isolating roots in words with affixes gives excellent experience in visual analysis. Syllabifying words is also useful. Maintenance exercises like the following, first using known words and then having the child find similar elements in unknown words, should be used abundantly with a child who has serious difficulty analyzing words visually:

1. Exercises in finding the root word in words with variant ending forms.

    a. Find the root words from which these words are made:

        (1) looks   looking   looked
        (2) worker   worked   working

    b. Find the root words in words having variant endings, such as *want* in *wanting, wait* in *waited,* and *swim* in *swimming.*

2. Exercises having the child use syntactical clues in choosing between variant forms, such as

    a. The bear   wanting   the honey
                 wanted

    b. The man was   talk   to them.
              talking
              talked

3. Exercises that require finding similar blends.

    You see the picture of the clown; say *clown.* Look at the words here, and circle the ones that begin like *clown* and that tell something we can do:

    clap   clean   clocks
    come   clothes   play
    climb   cook   clam

4. Exercises that emphasize seeing similar parts of words.
   Draw a line under the right word.

   a. The sun cannot be seen at _____ .
      fight   night   right   sight

   b. The train runs on a _____ .
      sack   black   track   tack

5. Exercises in syllabication.
   Mark the syllables in these words, for example, dif/fer/ent.

ahead	forgotten	furniture
yellow	interested	tomorrow
after	moment	electricity

6. Exercises that emphasize seeing both parts of compound words.

   a. Find the two small words in each compound word, and tell how they help us know what it means.

fireplace	baseball	sailboat
fireside	football	rowboat
firefly	basketball	ferryboat

   b. Take one of the two words from each compound word below the sentence, and make a new compound word to fill in the blank.

      (1) We were seated by the _____ to get warm.
          firehouse   inside

      (2) The wind makes the _____ go fast.
          sailfish   steamboat

7. Exercises that develop skills in analyzing words with affixes.

   a. Draw a line around the part of the word that means *again.*

relive	remake	retell
rework	replay	relearn

   b. Draw a line around the root word, that is, the word from which the larger word is made. Tell how the prefix and suffix change the meaning of the root word.

unfriendly	unthankful	distrustful
unkindly	unlikely	dishonesty
disagreeable	repayable	unkindness

Information a child gains from exercises to improve her visual analysis of words must be applied to actual reading. This sort of drill should be used, not in isolation, but as a part of a broader program of word recognition. The words used in exercises should be familiar to the child or should be words that will soon be met in reading.

Flexibility and the habit of dividing words into the largest usable elements should be stressed. The program should teach the child to avoid faulty approaches to word recognition, such as letter-by-letter spelling or sounding. Sounding of individual letters, for example, may help a child to recognize a small word, such as *cat*, but would be unnecessarily confusing in recognizing a longer or more complicated word, such as *caterpillar*. Yet some children try letter-by-letter sounding for all unfamiliar words.

Many children have difficulty recognizing words because they are too dependent on one technique or because they do not use the most efficient techniques. For example, they may have the habit of searching for known little words in larger words. This technique is helpful in identifying compound words or words with affixes, but it is detrimental to recognizing many other words. For example, finding *ear* in *bear* is of doubtful help, as is finding *to—get—her* in the word *together*. Instruction must encourage a diversified and flexible attack on words. It must also emphasize orderly progression through the word, from its beginning element to its end.

Excessive Word-Perception Errors

Some children's word-perception difficulties are different from those just discussed. Their mispronunciations tend to form a consistent pattern that can be readily diagnosed. The errors exemplified in this pattern are classified in many ways by various professionals in the reading field, but are best thought of as word-perception errors. In general, the classifications are based on where the errors are located in the words in which they occur. For example, a child may make an excessive number of errors in the initial part of words, such as calling *house mouse*. Another child might cluster his errors around the middle of words, calling *house horse*, for example. A third child may make an unusually high percentage of errors at the end of words. Such a child might call *house hour*.

For a given child, these errors tend to be most frequent in a specific part of the word because his word perception consistently neglects that part of the word. Roughly, these perceptual errors can be classified as "initial errors," "middle errors," and "ending errors." In addition, the child can confuse the order of word parts and make "orientation errors."

Locational errors can be diagnosed by classifying a sample of errors made in word pronunciation. This method is used in the Gates-McKillop-Horowitz Reading Diagnostic Tests. The diagnostician may also collect a sample of errors to classify informally. The disadvantage of this technique is that she cannot know the number of possibilities present in the sample she takes and she cannot judge how frequently a certain type of error typically occurs.

Initial errors indicate that as he inspects words, the child neglects to notice the beginnings of words closely enough. He makes errors such as calling *his this* or *the he*. Another type of initial error is calling the word *tall fall* or *when then*.

The remedial procedures used for correcting initial errors are similar to those used for fostering better visual analysis of words and knowledge of initial elements. The difference is emphasis. For the child who, even though he knows initial elements, makes an undue number of errors in the initial part of words, attention must be focused more directly and systematically on the beginnings of words. During word study, the teacher should help by asking, "How does the word begin?" Building a picture dictionary causes the child to look systematically at words. Alphabetizing words helps him pay greater attention to word beginnings. Sorting labeled pictures for filing also helps. The child should be shown the nature of his errors and the difference between the word he pronounced and the way it appeared in print. For example, if he calls *cat eat*, he should be told, "close," but that he must pay even closer attention to the beginning of the word. This sort of encouragement should be maintained throughout instruction. Teaching initial consonant blends and digraphs helps to overcome a child's tendency to neglect the beginnings of words. The following exercises are also good:

1. Multiple-choice questions in which the child is asked to differentiate among initial elements.

                        boat.
    The man put on his goat.
                        coat.

2. Classification exercises that emphasize initial sounds and word meanings.
    Find every word that starts like *crack* and is something we can eat.

crab	candy	cranberries
apple	crown	cradle
cracker	bread	crumbs

3. Multiple-choice exercises in which the initial blend is given.

    The car went down the str_____ .   strange   road   street

Middle errors result from two major causes: First, the child may hurry his inspection of unfamiliar words to such an extent that he neglects the middles of words; second, he may have limited knowledge of vowel sounds. Instruction in letter-sound associations for vowels and in useful rules for vowels is helpful. Encouraging the child to inspect words in an orderly, left-to-right manner helps correct any tendency to neglect the middles of words. During word study, the teacher should encourage the child to "look at the word all the way through, especially the middle." Copying words that cause special difficulty may help, as does tracing these words. Using context as a check on accuracy encourages the child to reinspect words that don't make sense. A child using contextual clues, for example, could not very well call *cat cot* in the sentence, "The cat climbed the tree," without rereading to find out what was wrong. He should be told why he needs to make a closer inspection of the middles of words and shown the difference between the error made and the printed word. Multiple-choice exercises such as the following are helpful in correcting this difficulty because the child must visually differentiate the middle parts of words:

pen.
1. The pig was in the pan.
                pin.

                      children.
2. The egg was laid by the citizen.
                      chicken.

Ending errors are made frequently. Even good readers, when they do make errors, tend to make ending errors more frequently than other locational errors. An overemphasis on word endings can cause neglect of the very important initial elements and may also promote reversals and other orientation confusions. The mature reader starts at the beginning of an unfamiliar word and works systematically through it from left to right, until it is completely inspected. All instruction designed to increase the child's knowledge of variant endings, word families, and suffixes helps him avoid making errors in the final elements of words. During word study, the teacher should help by guiding the child to "look at the word all the way through to the end." The teacher should avoid overreacting to ending errors made in oral reading by children who have perfect understanding, but whose mispronunciations simply reflect dialectal differences. All exercises given to encourage careful inspection of word endings should be in context, so that attention is called to the final element in the word while maintaining a systematic inspection of the entire word. Some exercises that may be used safely are the following:

1. Finish the word. It should rhyme with *call.*
   The boy was playing with a b____ .
   tall   back   ball

2. Find the word that ends like *coat* which you would like to play with.
   goat   doll   float
   gloat   boat   clock

Orientation confusions are among the most troublesome perceptual errors made by children with reading difficulties. Orientation problems will be discussed in the next chapter, which deals with the child with extreme reading difficulties.

Overanalytical Habits

The overanalytical reader is the child who either fails to build an adequate sight vocabulary and therefore must analyze many words she meets or who acquires the habit of analyzing all words, even those known at sight. Habitual overanalysis takes two forms. In the first variety, the child may analyze words she knows at sight. Not only is this technique slow, but it obstructs thoughtful reading and can lead the child to make excessive errors in word recognition. Some children have established the habit of analyzing known words so thoroughly that they make more errors when allowed unlimited time to pronounce a list of words than they do when the same list of words is flashed before them on cards, requiring them to read the words at sight. Recall that word-recognition techniques should be so ingrained that the child will identify known words without detailed study and that she will rapidly recognize the words she knows in any of their variant forms. Indeed, she will resort to time-consuming, analytical procedures only when she is working out words she has not met previously. A good reader inspects a word in only as much detail as is required for its recognition. The overanalytical reader reverses this process. She approaches most words as unfamiliar, she studies them in detail, isolates elements within them, applies her knowledge of word elements, and then synthesizes the elements back into a word, only to find that it is familiar. This pattern is harmful both to reading fluency and to comprehension. The child is so concerned with analyzing known words that she has no time to understand the content of what she is reading. It takes her so long to recognize each word that she cannot group them into thought units. Both her comprehension and her speed of reading of connected text suffer.

The second type of overanalytical reader is the one who breaks words into too many parts. Instead of using large elements that are already known to her, she resorts too early and too often to a study of individual letter sounds. This habit of recognizing words is exceedingly inefficient and often confusing. For many words, letter-by-letter sounding precludes recognition of them. Take the words in the previous sentence, for example, and try to sound each letter in the words and then blend them into words. Not all of the words could be recognized in this way, and even for those that could, it would be a time-consuming and inefficient method. It is foolish, for example, for a child who knows the word *talk* to resort to a letter-by-letter sounding of the word *talking*. Yet many overanalytical readers do this. It would be equally foolish and completely ineffective for the child who knew the suffix *tion* in *action* to try a letter-by-letter sounding of that element. Care must be taken to maintain proper balance in word recognition.

Some children who are overanalytical go to the extreme of a "spelling analysis" of words. They try to remember each new word by spelling it out. For example, they encounter the unknown word *donkey* and try to learn it by naming each letter. It is impossible for a child to remember all of the words she is expected to learn by trying to recall the sequence of letters through spelling. There are children who, when asked to work out an unknown word aloud, name each letter in turn and sometimes, after calling the letters, can say the word. For example, a child will see the word *horse,* which she doesn't identify. When asked to try to pronounce it, she will say, "*h—o—r—s—e,* horse." This type of word recognition is detrimental to reading growth.

The overanalytic reader can be detected by studying her relative effectiveness on timed and untimed word-recognition tests. She can also be identified by asking her to work aloud on words when she gets into difficulty. A third way of detecting this type of reader is to note children who rank relatively high on tests of word elements, but who are low on tests of word recognition. These children also tend to be slow readers with poor comprehension.

The remedial treatment for children who tend to analyze words that are already known by sight is to give more instruction in sight vocabulary, associating words with meanings, and using contextual clues effectively. Flash cards are useful, too. The instruction should be consistent with the child's other reading experiences. Reading material with few, if any, word difficulties should be used. The purposes for reading should include reading to comprehend the general significance of a passage, scanning to find a specific bit of information, and reading to predict outcomes.

The overanalytical reader who breaks words up into too many parts is corrected by emphasizing structural analysis and knowledge of the larger elements of words. Stress on syllabication, rather than on sounding each letter, is desirable. Noting root words, prefixes, suffixes, and variant endings gives the child the habit of analyzing words into their larger elements. Instruction in word recognition should encourage her to select as large elements as she can when she is analyzing words not known by sight. In remedial work, weight should be put on exercises for developing effective visual analysis that teach the child to isolate the larger structural and visual elements within words. In addition, it should be stressed that wide reading of relatively easy material helps the child who tends to resort to haphazard observation of words.

Limited Knowledge of Word Elements

The child who is to become a capable, fluent, and independent reader must develop an extensive knowledge of word elements. There is no point to the child's being skillful in analyzing words visually, unless he can associate the parts of the words with sounds. It does not help, for example, for the child to separate visually the word *spring* into *spr—ing*, unless he recalls how the initial blend *spr* and the ending *ing* sound. The child needs to learn a vast number of word parts. The larger the elements he can use in recognizing words, the more fluent and effortless his reading will be. The more he uses contextual and meaning clues, the less he needs to analyze words. It is often necessary for a child to break a word into small parts in order to recognize it. But this does not aid him if he does not associate the small elements with their sounds. The child must master the knowledge of many phonic, structural, and visual elements in words.

The diagnostician has several ways of detecting when a child has limited knowledge of word parts. Most diagnostic reading tests sample the more useful phonic, structural, and visual elements. Any weakness on these tests, in comparison with the child's general reading capability, indicates that he may be limited in the number of elements with which he is familiar. Another indication of this kind of weakness is difficulty associating sounds with word elements when the child is working out the pronunciation of words orally. If the child analyzes a word visually but does not know letter sounds, common phonograms, or visual elements, he is limited in his knowledge of word parts. If he seems to be able to segment a word into syllables, but cannot pronounce many of them, he is limited in his knowledge of important word parts and should be given remedial training.

When the teacher points out to a child the similarity between a new word and other words he knows, the child is receiving instruction in knowledge of word elements. In presenting new words, the teacher should not only make their meanings clear, but also show the child the most efficient visual analysis of each word and compare the words, when necessary, with known words which contain the element that might cause the child difficulty. If, for example, the new word is *trouble,* the teacher might say that it begins like *train* and ends like *double* as she writes the three words on the chalkboard. The teacher might also say that it is something we would rather not have. In this example, the teacher has provided the symbol-sound association of the word part *tr* and the word part *ouble*.

Manuals of most reading series give suggestions for instructing children in knowledge of word parts. Used at an appropriate level of difficulty, reading series can provide good material for children who need extra instruction and practice in knowledge of word parts because of the systematic introduction of word parts and the vocabulary control maintained by the authors. An emphasis on the introduction of new vocabulary and on word study is essential. Word-recognition exercises in skill books accompanying readers are also suitable.

If the teacher chooses to use materials other than reading series, she should select words to be met in reading that might cause difficulty or that illustrate an important word element. These words should be studied employing the principles described in the section titled "Using Effective Teaching Procedures" in Chapter 9.

Some remedial reading teachers report success in using a linguistically regular approach, as described by Fries (1963) and Bloomfield and Barnhart (1961). Programmed materials with a linguistically regular vocabulary, such as *The Programmed Reading Series* (Sullivan Associates, 1973), have proven effective in training children who are seriously confused in distinguishing the letter-sound relationships described by linguists.

All the exercises suggested in the preceding section for improving the child's visual analysis of words aid in teaching knowledge of visual, structural, and phonic elements. Additional exercises such as the following are beneficial to the child who is limited in knowledge of word parts. The words used should be familiar or should be words soon to be learned.

1. Exercises to teach initial consonant sounds.

    a. Say the words *can* and *come*. Put *C* before all the words that start like *can* and *come* and that also name an animal.

_____ cat	_____ cookies	_____ chicken
_____ duck	_____ elephant	_____ cake
_____ eel	_____ calf	_____ cub

b. Write the first part of the word in the space. It starts like one of the words below the sentence.

(1) The dog ran __ome.
son   hope   cone

(2) The cat wanted some __ilk.
pig   like   mill

2. Exercises to teach initial blend sounds.

a. Write in the blank the word that begins with the same blend as the word underlined.

(1) The <u>branch</u> soon _____ .
bring   fell   broke

(2) The <u>block</u> was painted _____ .
brown   blue   green

b. Draw a line under the right word. It must start with the same blend as the key word.

(1) *clown*   (2) *smile*

	feet.		brown.
The cat has	claws.	The puppy was	small.
	close.		smoke.

A child who is limited in this area of knowledge of word parts may be taught other important blends such as *cr, dr, fl, gl, pl, scr, sk, sl, sn, sp,* and *st,* in exercises such as those just presented.

3. Exercises to reinforce knowledge of digraph sounds.

a. Finish the words. They begin like one of the words below the sentences. The first one is done for you.

(1) <u>Th</u>at cat can run.
Boy   This   Sing

(2) __ere will we go?
What   Hear   Play

(3) The __est was full of gold.
toy   boy   chair

(4) We get wool from __eep.
ducks   ships   sleds

(5) His brother was only __ee.
where   thread   see

b. Draw a line around the right word. It must start with the same digraph as the key word.

(1) *church*

                                        chimney.

We make butter in a   pail.

                                          churn.

(2) *ship*

                                          coat.

She put on her new   shoes.

                                          sharp.

4. Exercise to teach vowel sounds.

a. The vowels *a, e, i, o,* and *u* say their names in many words. This is their long sound. Write the vowel that is long following each word. Then use the word in a sentence.

age ____	dine ____	vase ____
like ____	cave ____	use ____
alone ____	home ____	rope ____

Call attention to the fact that each word has one consonant between the vowel and the final *e* that usually signals that the first vowel has a long sound. Some exceptions may be given, as in

give	love	come	where
some	live	whose	were

b. Write the vowel that is *long* following each word. Then use the word in a sentence.

peach ____	snail ____	heel ____
reach ____	road ____	keep ____
tease ____	bead ____	leaf ____
plains ____	boat ____	mean ____

Call attention to the fact that many times, when two vowels come together, the first vowel takes the long sound and the second vowel is silent. Some exceptions may be given, as

bread	heavy	meant
break	great	house
chief	head	piece

c. Put in the right word. It must have a short vowel.

The boy ran after the ____ .

boat   game   cat

Other exercises, using contextual clues can be used, because these clues can help the child decide whether a vowel is long or short.

5. Exercises to teach hard and soft consonant sounds.

   a. When *C* has the sound of *S*, it has a soft sound. When it sounds like *K*, it has a hard sound. Put *S* following the sentences in which *C* is soft and *H* when it is hard. The first one is done for you.

      (1) We went to camp. <u>H</u>
      (2) I saw his face. ____
      (3) We rode on a camel. ____
      (4) It sold for ten cents. ____
      (5) The calf was brown. ____

   b. Similar exercises can be used to teach the other hard and soft consonant sounds.

6. Exercises using syntactical clues to teach variant endings.

   a. Draw a line under the right word.

      (1) The cat   drink / drinks   her milk.

      (2) Now she   wanted / wanting   to run away.

7. Exercises using contextual clues to teach common word elements.

   a. Put in the right word. It must end like the key word.

      (1) *talk*
          We had a brisk ____ .
          chalk   walk   run

      (2) *light*
          It was a dark ____ .
          right   room   night

   b. See how many words you can make that rhyme with the following words. Use each of them in a sentence.

      bat   street   bright
      ball   rake   sand

Any exercises or activities employed to increase the child's knowledge of visual, structural, or phonic elements as often as possible should be used in contextual settings. This is desirable because, many times, the true sound of an element can be known only from its use in context. For example, the vowel sound in *read* cannot be known out of context. Context also stimulates more rapid recognition of the parts being taught, and it offers an immediate and independent check on the accuracy of the association of the printed symbols with the pronunciation of the word read. There are certain drilling techniques that are used to increase the child's knowledge of word parts. They should be used sparingly, and the words drilled should be read in context, so that the elements learned have a reasonable chance of being transferred into actual reading. Among these devices are word wheels, word slips, word tachistoscopes, and certain computer programs.

Word wheels are constructed by cutting two disks. One should be about 5 inches in diameter and the other slightly smaller. On the larger disk, words are printed with the initial element missing. These words should all start at the same distance from the center (about 1 inch) and progress toward the outer edge like the spokes of a wheel. Only words that begin with the same word element should be used on one disk. The initial element should be omitted. For example, if the initial blend *str* is to be taught, words such as *strap, strong, straw, string, strip, stream*, and *strange* should be used. Only the word endings are printed on the larger disk (see Figure 11–1). On the smaller disk, a radial slit of the proper size and position is cut to expose one word ending at a time. The initial blend *str* is printed just to the left of the slit (see Figure 11–1). The two disks are fastened together at the center with a paper fastener (A), with the smaller disk on top. As the lower disk is rotated, the *str* on the smaller disk makes a word as it combines with each ending on the larger disk.

Other word parts can be taught this way. With word endings, such as *ing, ake*, and *alk*, the word wheel needs to be changed so that the ending is printed at the right of the slit cut in the smaller disk and the word beginnings are printed on the larger disk (see Figure 11–2).

Word slips can be constructed to practice the various word parts. They have an advantage over word wheels because they are easier to make. A manila folder

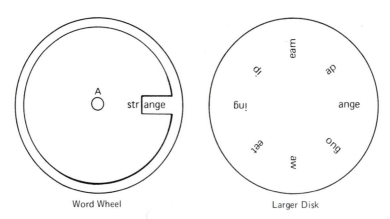

Word Wheel   Larger Disk

FIGURE 11–1   **"str" word wheel**

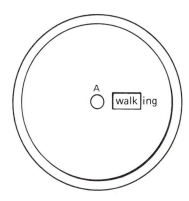

FIGURE 11–2 **"ing" word wheel**

can be used to make the removable faces and slips. Figure 11–3 illustrates the use of a word slip. The removable faces and slips can be varied to drill the child on any particular word part. The word slips and faces are made by typing the word part to be drilled at the appropriate place on the face (see Figure 11–3, faces, 1, 2, and 3). The remaining parts of the words can be typed or printed at intervals on the slip. A permanent posterboard back can be used for all exercises, since the face is removable.

Word beginnings that could be typed on word slips to use with the *ing* ending on removable face 2 are *th, s, br, r, str, wr,* and *k.* The following words could also be used with this face: *walk, talk, sing, jump, build, play, say, feed, hear,* etc.

Slips and faces, such as face 1, could be made for all the important initial consonants, blends, and digraphs. Number 2 faces and slips could be made for all the important variant endings and phonograms. Number 3 faces and slips could be made to teach long and short vowels and vowel combinations. The words used in these exercises should be those taught in the basal readers or taken from lists of common words as compiled by Dolch (1960) and Harris and Jacobson (1972).

The word-slip devices can be used as a tachistoscope by moving a small card up and down to expose quickly each new word to be studied. This is sometimes advisable for the child who has a tendency to dawdle or to break words into too many parts. The device can also be used for drilling on sight words if another face, with just an exposure slit without any letters, is made. In this case, the words on the typed slip should be spaced farther apart, with a heavy black line between them. The teacher shows the black line, says "ready," exposes the word for an instant, and then moves the word slip to the next black line while the child responds.

Computer programs such as *Word Munchers* (Minnesota Educational Computing Corporation, 1985) also review phonic elements in words, using a motivational, gamelike format. These programs are useful for review only; they serve to supplement, rather than to replace, systematic, teacher-directed instruction.

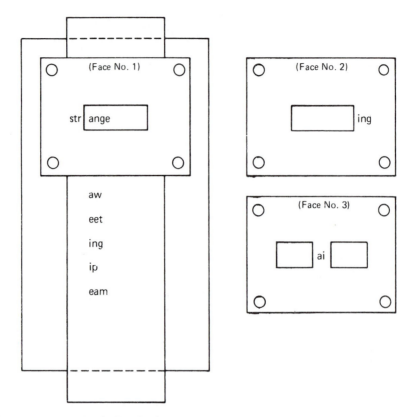

FIGURE 11–3   Word-slip device

More detailed ways of teaching children to relate word elements to sounds will be discussed in the next chapter. These methods are individualized and time consuming, but they do help the child who is severely limited in knowledge of word parts. Sound-tracing methods will also be discussed in the next chapter.

Difficulty in Oral and Visual Synthesis

The child must be able to reassemble a word after she has separated it visually into parts that she recognizes. Effective and rapid synthesis of the parts into the whole word (also called blending) is essential to word recognition. Many children have difficulty with their reading because they lack ability in synthesizing. Although immature readers commonly sound parts aloud and synthesize them using auditory blending, mature readers rarely resort to such a technique. Rather, they usually perceive the larger elements within a word visually and then synthesize them without resorting to oral pronunciation at all. In the word *anytime*, for example, the more experienced reader sees the words *any* and *time* in the larger word. She neither pronounces these parts nor pronounces the word as a whole, but immediately sees that it is a compound word made up of two well-known words. That is, the more experienced reader identifies the word *anytime* by visually synthesizing the known parts into the known compound word. This form of visual analysis, perception, and synthesis takes place so rapidly that the mature reader is rarely aware of such perceptual acts. To her, she senses the meaning of the printed symbol immediately, without reflecting on the symbol itself.

While reading silently, the mature reader does not even sound the parts of a broken word at the end of a line of print. She just looks at the part of the word on the line and then glances quickly down to the remainder of the word on the next line. She identifies the word and its meaning immediately. No oral pronunciation or auditory blending takes place at all.

The child who is beginning to learn to read, or the child who has a disability synthesizing words cannot so readily synthesize words visually. Indeed, he often finds it difficult to blend a word auditorily once he has pronounced it part by part. In early reading instruction, a child may be required to sound out words part by part and then blend the sound elements together. Some children make too great a separation of the parts when sounding the word out, and cannot reassemble it auditorily.

Some children have difficulty synthesizing words because they lack the capacity to blend sounds orally. They are, for example, unable to tell what word the teacher is saying if she pronounces the word part by part. If she says the word *drink* as *dr—ink,* with about a second of time between the parts, the child cannot tell what the word is. In some cases, the child cannot even tell that the teacher is saying *drink* if she pronounces it normally a second time after dissociating it. Bond (1935) has shown that a child who is limited in this ability is much more likely to incur a disability if he is taught by methods requiring him to use auditory blending than he would be if visual recognition and synthesis were emphasized.

Many children have difficulty in blending when word parts are learned in isolation rather than in words or when they are taught too often with drill exercises rather than in contextual settings. In such circumstances, the child may learn to depend too much on oral pronunciation and auditory blending of word parts. The pronunciation of words, part by part, can lead the child to pause between each part, making blending much more difficult. Frequently, the child who resorts to letter-by-letter sounding has forgotten the beginning of the word before she has completed sounding the letters. This does not necessarily indicate that the child has a synthesis difficulty; rather, it suggests an ineffective technique of word recognition that should be corrected.

The diagnosis of inability to synthesize words is somewhat complex. Three judgments must be made: (1) Is the child's problem really one of poor synthesis, or is it the result of ineffective visual analysis? (2) Is the child's problem one of poor auditory blending, or is it poor visual synthesis? (3) Is the child's difficulty the result of faulty learning, or does he have an auditory handicap? These questions can be answered by studying the results of reading diagnostic tests. In the Gates-McKillop-Horowitz Reading Diagnostic Tests (described in Chapter 8), the results of the tests of syllabication, recognizing and blending common word parts, and auditory blending will indicate whether the child has a real deficiency in visual or auditory synthesis (Gates, McKillop, & Horowitz, 1981).

The diagnostician or teacher can also observe the child's ability to reassemble words that have been analyzed and pronounced correctly, part by part. If the child is unable to blend words she has analyzed, she lacks ability in auditory blending. If the diagnostician or teacher pronounces some words, part by part, it can be determined whether the child can blend the sounds she hears. If the child is able to blend words and recognize them comparably to other children of her age and grade, the child's difficulty is not due to an auditory problem.

For the child who lacks ability in auditory blending, any sounding out of words should be done in a smooth, rather than an interrupted, fashion. This child should have much experience in blending two-syllable words, and she should have training in oral blending. The teacher could pronounce words with the syllables only slightly separated, and the child could say the parts and blend them. It would be best to start with two-syllable words and build up gradually to longer words. Then, single-syllable words could be separated and blended. For children who have difficulty blending, because they have learned to separate the words so distinctly that they are unable to synthesize them, there should be more instruction to develop their sight vocabulary, to associate meanings with words, and to use contextual clues. Children with this type of difficulty should read relatively easy material abundantly.

The remedial work that should be given to a child who is poor in the visual synthesis of words is to have her recognize words presented to her by rapid-exposure techniques. A spaced slip of words correctly analyzed into syllables could be exposed in the word-slip tachistoscope, and the child could classify each word. For example, the following list could be used, and the child could tell if the word named an animal or a food:

ba boon	chip munk
but ter	don key
buf fa lo	choc o late
ce re al	cook ies
bumb ble bee	lem on ade
car rot	let tuce
mon key	rob in

Any of the word-slip exercises developed for teaching the child with limited knowledge of word elements could also be used for rapid-exposure exercises to improve the child's visual synthesis. The tachistoscopic type of rapid exposure is also helpful in overcoming the overanalytical reader's problems. In addition, it is useful as a quick-exposure technique for developing rapid recognition of sight words.

Whenever a child who is weak in blending words analyzes an unknown word visually, the teacher can encourage her to work silently. Exercises with many words broken at the ends of the lines read under timed conditions also help in developing rapid visual synthesis of words.

Case Study of an Upper Elementary Grade Student with Difficulty in Word Recognition

When Andy was referred to the Psycho-Educational Clinic for study, he was an attractive boy from a fourth-grade classroom. He was large for a boy 10 years and 6 months of age. His teacher was concerned about Andy's reading progress. She described his discussions in class and his expression of his ideas as very good. In certain class activities he was an eager participant, while in others he tended to withdraw. His teacher was well aware that there was a relationship between Andy's tendency to lose interest in an activity and the amount of reading involved with it. She also noticed that he had to gather most of his information from class discussion, but once he had sufficient information, his reasoning and judgment about what he had just learned were mature. She had watched the difficulties he experienced whenever he was asked to read aloud. She knew that Andy had a reading disability.

From an examination of Andy's cumulative records and recent test scores, his teacher had made the general diagnosis that his reading disability called for more detailed study. These records showed that Andy had a reading score of 2.5. His arithmetic grade score was 3.5 for problem solving and 5.2 for computation. His score on a group intelligence test indicated that he had an I.Q. of 98. His previous school records showed that Andy had repeated the third grade and that during the second year in that grade, less reading growth took place than in the previous year.

Andy's teacher did not think that the 98 I.Q. represented his true intelligence, even though it was in keeping with the level of his general school achievement. She based this judgment on the quality of his discussions of a topic he knew something about and on his score in the computation section of the arithmetic test. She had also noticed that when problems were read to him, his arithmetical reasoning seemed competent. From all of this information, she felt that a thorough study of Andy's educational problem was required.

At the clinic, a more specific diagnosis was made, as the first step in studying Andy's problem. This phase of the diagnosis consisted of giving Andy the Wechsler Intelligence Scale for Children, Revised, and the Stanford Diagnostic Reading Test, Green Level. The intelligence test indicated that he had a full-scale I.Q. of 124, a verbal I.Q. of 126, and a performance I.Q. of 123 and that he should be expected to read at $(4.2 \times 1.24) + 1.0$, or about the sixth-grade level. (The grade expectancy was computed by the formula explained in Chapter 3.) A comparison between the scores obtained thus far showed that Andy was a bright boy who should be reading at about the sixth-grade level of difficulty. His arithmetic scores of 3.5 for problem solving (written problems) and 5.2 for computations (no reading involved) showed that he was doing reasonably well in an area not directly related to reading. Scores from the Stanford Diagnostic Reading Test, Green Level (Fall Norms), showed the following:

Auditory Vocabulary	5.8
Auditory Discrimination	3.6
Phonetic Analysis	3.2
Structural Analysis	1.3
Reading Comprehension	
Literal	2.7
Inferential	2.5
Total Reading Comprehension	2.5
TOTAL READING	2.7

Andy's average reading achievement of only 2.7 showed that he was seriously disabled in reading. His auditory abilities and skill in phonetic analysis appeared to be strengths, in comparison to his ability to recognize words and to answer literal and inferential questions about passages he read. His skill in structural analysis seemed to be a major weakness. The pattern of scores in the areas of reading measured indicated that his problem was a basic one. A study of the comprehension subtest revealed accurate performance on the items he attempted, but such slow speed that he completed only about two-thirds of the test, even though the time limits are ample for the ordinary child.

Andy was also tested using an informal reading inventory constructed by the reading specialist. It was found that he could comfortably read material no higher than beginning second-grade level and that he was frustrated by material beyond halfway through the second-grade level. An analysis of his errors revealed that when he was asked to read material that was difficult for him, he started to leave out words, and his frequency of errors increased as he continued to read. Although his use of context appeared to be adequate when he read easy material, when reading became difficult for him, he started to leave out words, his frequency of errors increased as he continued to read, and he was not able to use context effectively to predict words, to correct errors, or to anticipate sentence structure. Andy tended to make errors involving word beginnings. Although his knowledge of letter-sound associations appeared to be good, he had difficulty identifying larger word parts such as phonograms, syllables, prefixes, and suffixes. When large word parts were isolated for him, he had difficulty pronouncing them. He read slowly both silently and orally.

It was felt, from the information thus far obtained, that Andy should be classified as a child with a *limiting disability in reading* and that his area of difficulty was in word recognition. A thorough case study was made.

We must now answer the questions raised in Chapter 7:

1. Is Andy correctly classified as a child with a reading disability? The case study showed that he indeed had a reading disability and that there was no indication of any physical, mental, or neurological condition to alter his classification to anything other than that. Even when Andy was tense and nonfluent when reading aloud, there was no evidence of any basic emotional problem. There seemed, however, to be an emotional involvement with respect to his reading and some accompanying avoidance of reading activities.

2. What is the training needed? This is the essential question in reeducating a child who has been classified correctly as having a reading disability. Andy's performance on the Stanford Diagnostic Reading Test and on the informal reading inventory showed his pattern of reading limitations. He could not be expected to become a good reader until his basic word-recognition problems were corrected. Andy's pattern of responses suggested that the remedial emphasis should be placed on:

   a. Word recognition skills: (1) attention to word beginnings, (2) visual analysis of large word parts, and (3) recognition of large word parts.
   b. Use of context: (1) to predict words, (2) to correct errors, and (3) to anticipate sentence structure.
   c. Reading fluency.

Parts of the Gates-McKillop-Horowitz Reading Diagnostic Tests were also given to Andy. A study of the tabulated results of his responses indicated that this test verified some of the conclusions obtained from previous testing. Specifically, Andy made a disproportionate number of errors in the beginnings of words, his knowledge of large word parts was inadequate for his general reading level, and he was ineffective in the use of context as an aid to word recognition. The test added the information that Andy had a relatively good sight vocabulary compared with his overall functioning in reading and also that when he was given more time to study words, his performance deteriorated.

3. Who can give the most effective remedial work? From recommendations made after the diagnosis was completed, it was decided that Andy would be given help best by the reading specialist in the school reading center, since his limiting disability needed only focused instruction and minor emotional support.

4. How can improvement be made most efficiently? Andy was given remedial work in the school reading center for an hour each day with material at the beginning second-grade level of difficulty. Exercises and activities designed to improve his visual awareness of beginning elements, analysis, and recognition of large word parts, and use of context were emphasized. Games, word wheels, and computer programs suitable for practicing these skills were also used, for review and because Andy enjoyed them. Short selections were used for practice in rapid reading.

5. Does the child have any limiting conditions that must be considered? Andy had no visual or hearing difficulties, and no other limiting condition was identified.

6. Are there any environmental conditions that might interfere with the child's progress in reading? Andy's parents were very concerned about his reading, as well they might be. His mother had tried to help him at home, but didn't feel that he was making any progress, and so she discontinued working with him. His mother thought that there was something wrong with Andy's memory, because the words they worked on one day were forgotten the next. She was eager to cooperate and accepted the suggestion of helping him by showing approval of his reading, discussing it with him in a relaxed manner, and telling him words he didn't know. The technical teaching was left to the reading specialist.

Andy's classroom teacher was also informed of the results of his reading assessment. She already knew that he was a slow reader and an ineffective one. She was interested in the findings of the complete diagnosis and was pleased to make adjustments to his level of reading in the regular classroom.

At the end of 6 months of instruction in the reading center, Andy was measured again. His reading achievement, as tested by the Stanford Diagnostic Reading Test, Green Level (Spring Norms), showed gratifying results:

Auditory Vocabulary	5.9
Auditory Discrimination	3.9
Phonetic Analysis	4.5
Structural Analysis	3.6
Reading Comprehension	
Literal	3.8
Inferential	3.5
Total Reading Comprehension	3.3
TOTAL READING	4.6

Andy continued to work in the reading center for the remainder of his fourth-grade year. At the beginning of his fifth-grade year, he discontinued work in the reading center. He still had a reading disability, but he had overcome much of his basic difficulty. His cooperative fifth-grade teacher was able to give him the additional instruction and experience he needed.

Summary

Word recognition is difficult and complex to learn. It requires a highly integrated and flexible set of skills and abilities. To avoid some of the more serious types of word-recognition difficulties, well-organized instruction must be given. The child must be started by teaching her the habit of trying to recognize words as words. Early training includes the use of contextual clues, picture clues, and teachers' questions. The child is taught to note similarities in initial elements and gradually to acquire the whole hierarchy of word-recognition skills, abilities, and techniques. These are classified into five general types: (1) the ability to recognize many words at sight and to associate meanings with printed symbols; (2) skill in using context and other meaning clues to anticipate the words to be recognized and to check on the accuracy of recognition; (3) skill in using flexible and efficient perceptual techniques in analyzing words visually into usable elements for recognizing words; (4) knowledge of a wide variety of visual, structural, and phonic elements; (5) skill in the auditory and visual synthesis of word parts into complete words.

The major sources of difficulty in word recognition involve the failure to establish these basic skills and techniques and the failure to maintain a balance among them. The best method of correction is to have the child develop them in the course of meaningful reading. The remedial reading teacher should take great care in the methods he uses to introduce new words, so that the child's strengths can be utilized and any limitations in recognition can be corrected while the proper balances are maintained. Instruction stressing the skills needed by the child should be emphasized.

Worksheet and supplementary exercises are helpful in correcting limitations in word recognition. They should be used with caution, however, and should be recognized as drill devices, rather than as a complete solution to word-recognition problems. The child who has difficulty recognizing words needs more than the usual amount of practice in those areas in which he has failed to learn sufficiently to maintain a balance among the word-recognition skills.

Study Questions

1. What is visual analysis? Why does it precede the application of knowledge of word parts? How can a teacher identify faulty visual analysis using informal techniques?
2. What is the danger of informal analysis, compared with standardized test analysis of locational errors? Why is it more difficult to construct useful exercises for ending errors than for beginning errors?
3. How can overanalytical readers who tend to analyze words they already know and those who tend to analyze unknown words into too many parts be helped?
4. When should drill be used to enhance knowledge of word elements? Why must exercises designed to increase knowledge of visual, structural, and phonic elements be put in contextual settings?
5. What diagnostic judgments should be made when a child appears to have unusual difficulty synthesizing words?

Selected Readings

Ekwall, E. E. (1986). *Teacher's handbook on diagnosis and remediation in reading* (2nd ed.) (pp. 48–66). Boston: Allyn and Bacon.

Maggart, Z. R., & Zintz, M. V. (1990). *Corrective reading* (6th ed.) (pp. 75–87). Dubuque, IA: Wm. C. Brown.

McCormick, S. (1987). *Remedial and clinical reading instruction* (pp. 254–277). Columbus, OH: Merrill.

Rubin, D. (1991). *Diagnosis and correction in reading instruction* (2nd ed.) (pp. 275–306). Boston: Allyn and Bacon.

Rupley, W. H., & Blair, T. R. (1989). *Reading diagnosis and remediation* (3rd ed.) (pp. 147–168). Columbus, OH: Merrill.

Taylor, B., Harris, L. A., & Pearson, P. D. (1988). *Reading difficulties: Instruction and assessment* (pp. 138–152, 157–164). New York: Random House.

Chapter 12

Treating Students with Extreme Reading Disability

Reading disabilities vary in degree. Some children have learned practically nothing, while others read poorly, but at a level barely below what is reasonable to predict for them based on their reading expectancy. Children with extreme disabilities in reading, sometimes called nonreaders or dyslexics, are at the low end of the range. They have the most obstinate cases of disability and have failed to learn even after reasonably extended instruction. They are not all alike. Students with extreme reading disabilities differ in backgrounds, attitudes, perceptual competencies, special difficulties, and other respects. It is necessary to recognize individual differences among these students when organizing effective remedial instruction. No single method or formula of remediation can possibly work for all such students.

Methods of Treatment

Skill in teaching is very important for helping those with extreme reading disabilities. Besides understanding the reading process, the teacher should be familiar with a variety of diagnostic and remedial procedures. She must be versatile in adapting these, both for accurate diagnosis of difficulties and for planning appropriate instruction, to each student. Patience, sympathetic understanding of the child's difficulties, and skillful guidance and encouragement throughout the instructional program are important for managing these extreme cases.

Certain methods of remedial instruction have been notably successful in teaching students with extreme reading disabilities to read. Three of these general approaches are outlined briefly in the following sections.

Methods with a Kinesthetic-Auditory-Visual Emphasis

The Fernald method, described in detail by Fernald (1971), was originally designed for and used successfully with students with extreme reading disabilities. The features of the technique are to teach the child to write words correctly, to motivate him to do this, to have him read the printed copy of what he has written, and to move on eventually to extensive reading of materials other than his own. The program consists of four stages.

Stage 1

The essence of this first stage is to have the child learn words through finger tracing of written copy while pronouncing each part of the word. This is repeated until the child *can write the word without looking at the copy.* Clinical experience shows that it is best if the words are written in large letters. They may be written for the child with crayon on paper or with chalk on the chalkboard. Some teachers even have the child trace in the air with his eyes closed after having traced on paper or chalkboard. Cursive writing is preferred, but many teachers feel that it is best to use manuscript writing with young children. Words learned through tracing may be used in stories a child wishes to write and may be filed in alphabetical order. Points stressed in this first stage are that finger contact is important in tracing, pronunciation of words must coincide with tracing them, words must be written without looking at the copy, words should always be written as units, and words should always be used in context. This means that the child must use the words in meaningful groups in sentences.

Duration of tracing period. The length of the tracing period varies greatly from child to child, depending on the individual need for tracing to retain the word. Usually, the tracing period continues for about 1 to 2 months.

Material used. In the Fernald method, materials are not simplified in either vocabulary or subject matter. Any word or sentence the child is capable of using properly in oral language can be learned so that it can be written and read. Clinical experience shows that when children learn using tracing methods, longer words are often retained better than are shorter ones.

Stage 2

This is similar to stage 1, except that the child no longer needs to trace. Rather, he is able to learn a new word by looking at it, saying it to himself as he looks at it, and then writing it without looking at the copy. With multisyllabic words, he says each part of the word as he writes it, stressing the syllables. Using new words for writing activities and filing them are continued. In all activities, pronouncing words as whole, unbroken units is emphasized.

Stage 3

This stage dispenses with the use of specially prepared copy. The child now learns directly from standard printed words. He must still look at a printed word, say it to himself, and then write it. He may read from ordinary books, with the teacher telling him words he does not know. Upon conclusion of reading, the words the teacher has helped him with are learned by the child, following the look-say-write method described previously. Many teachers select the books children read in this stage, so as to minimize the number of unknown words a child will encounter.

Stage 4

The child is able to recognize some new words from their resemblance to words or word parts he remembers and on the basis of contextual clues. As in the previous stage, the teacher tells the child all the words he cannot recognize. Difficult words are looked at, said, and then written from memory. Retention of words learned in this way is reported to be 80% to 95%.

During remedial instruction, the child is not required to sound out any word when he is reading, nor is any word sounded out for him by the teacher. Nevertheless, children taught by this method do acquire phonic skills through the tracing-sounding and writing-sounding training. Although Fernald's children were weak in phonics at the beginning of instruction and were given no formal training in phonics, they were able, at the end of the instruction, to pass phonics tests at their age level. For a much more complete description of the Fernald method, see Fernald (1971, Chapter 5).

Many teachers have reported great success in having children trace troublesome words in the air with their eyes closed while pronouncing the words. This modification emphasizes kinesthetic and auditory clues to word recognition while reducing the role of vision. For some children with severe visual-perceptual problems, tracing in the air with closed eyes seems to enable them to acquire an organized percept of the word, which eludes them when vision is involved.

When teaching a group of children, a kinesthetic-auditory-visual emphasis can be achieved to some extent by inviting the children to listen carefully to the word pronounced, to look carefully at the word in print, to say the word softly, and to write the word.

Evaluation

When used by experienced clinicians, the Fernald method is undoubtedly successful. In the early stages, it tends to be time consuming. In an extreme case, tracing may continue for 8 months, although the average is only 2 months. But other methods also require long periods of instruction when dealing with extreme disabilities. So the time factors can hardly be termed a drawback. When instruction is given properly, the pupils can be as well motivated as by any other method.

It is worthwhile inquiring into why this method is successful. Fernald considers the *kinesthesis*, coupled with enthusiastic and efficient teaching, the key to its success. It should be noted that in addition to kinesthesis, other important features are included in proper teaching of this method: (1) The child learns effectively the left-to-right sequences of perception by his simultaneous tracing-sounding and writing-sounding of words. (2) The visual structure of the word is associated with sounding the pronounceable units of the word. (3) Skill in phonics is learned without being taught formally. As part of his sounding, the child learns what is equivalent to substitution of consonants in recognizing new words. After recognizing a familiar element in a word, the child attaches the proper beginning or ending sound. Meanings supplied by the verbal context are used to choose the proper ending or to begin to recognize the new word. In the sentence, "Mary *took* the kitten home," the element *ook* may be associated with or recognized as part of the familiar word *book* or *look*. The context then helps to give the proper word *took*. Also, through tracing-writing-sounding, many initial and final elements become familiar to the child, so that he makes substitutions readily. (4) The very nature of the program leads to skill in syllabication. The Fernald method teaches left-to-right direction of word perception, the visual form of words, skill in phonics (including syllabication and the equivalent of substitution of consonants), and the use of contextual clues for identifying and recognizing words. (5) Added to all this is the fact that the child is strongly motivated by working with materials that are interesting to him. Although the kinesthetic aspects of this method may be very important for certain visually handicapped and neurologically impaired children and for certain children with visual-perceptual or visual-processing difficulties, it should be noted that the emphasis on left-to-right perception, the visual structure of words, skill in phonics, skill in syllabication, and the use of context are inherent to the method when it is properly taught. It is doubtful that kinesthesis alone is responsible for the success of the method, but rather, kinesthesis in combination with a sound, well-balanced program for teaching word perception in remedial instruction seems to be the key. Besides word recognition, the Fernald method stresses the development of vocabulary, concepts, and comprehension.

Methods with an Auditory (Sound-Blending) Emphasis

A strong phonic analysis approach has been incorporated into a number of remedial procedures. Among the comprehensive programs that have been successful in teaching students with extreme reading disabilities are those developed by Monroe (1932) and by Gillingham and Stillman (1960). To use any phonics-based remedial approach, it is imperative that the teacher be familiar with the details of the program. Teachers using such an approach should be familiar with the two sources just mentioned.

Successful phonics-based techniques emphasize patient, repetitive drill work, but include sufficient variety to retain the learner's interest without sacrificing the fundamental purposes of the drill. Such remedial programs must be prescribed by the teacher for each child. Known phonic elements should be passed over very lightly, and unknown elements should receive heavy emphasis, to ensure maximum benefit to each child.

Monroe's Method

In extreme cases, faulty pronunciation of vowels and consonants is a major source of difficulty. Although exact remedial needs differ from child to child, many who have a severe disability need instruction in discriminating specific speech sounds, in associating visual symbols with letter sounds, and in coordinating the temporal sequence of sounds with the left-to-right sequence of letters in a word.

One of the first steps is to strengthen the ability to discriminate speech sounds. Pictures of several objects beginning with the same consonant or containing the same vowel are mounted on cards. The pictures may be obtained from magazines or old books. Examples of typical initial consonants used are

b as in boy, book	*m* as in man, moon
c as in coat, cat	*t* as in tiger, table

As far as possible, words that contain a vowel immediately after the initial consonant are chosen for this early drill. Single consonant sounds are learned more readily than consonant blends. Thus, the *s* sound is learned more easily in *seed* than in *store*.

Cards with pictures are arranged similarly for the vowels, such as

a as in man, cat	*o* as in box, top
e as in pen, hen	*i* as in fire, kite

To develop discrimination, the instruction is started with unlike sounds, for example, *m* compared with *s*. The cards for *m* and *s* are arranged in a row in mixed order, thus:

men   soap   moon   seed

The child is instructed to sound the *m* and then name the object in the picture. After she succeeds with unlike sounds, the more difficult discriminations are taught, such as *s* and *sh* in *seed* and *shell*, respectively. These drills are varied by asking the child to give words beginning with a certain sound. A similar procedure is followed in the drills on vowels.

The next step is associating the letters with their most frequent sounds. Tracing is introduced as a reinforcement when necessary. The child traces a letter written by the teacher. She then sounds it as she traces. This is repeated until she can look at the letter and sound it correctly without tracing. Ordinarily, five or six consonant sounds can be learned at one sitting. After learning several consonant and vowel sounds, the child is taught blending letter sounds into words. The sounding-tracing method is an important aid in this. The sounding becomes a slow, distinct articulation of the word as a unit while it is being traced. Recall is tested by presenting the words printed on cards. With this, the child is encouraged to articulate the separate letter sounds and blend them. The phonics skills the child acquires give her a feeling of mastery in word recognition.

Next, the child progresses to reading specially prepared phonetic stories. Soon, she is able to handle stories in ordinary primers and first readers. Nonphonetic words are learned by tracing-sounding. As the child gains vocabulary and reading ability, the nonphonetic words are identified from context.

Monroe (1932) found it necessary to give the child a definite motor cue to the correct direction for left-to-right sequencing in perceiving words. This is accomplished by tracing-sounding similar to that practiced by Fernald (1971).

Failure to discriminate consonant blends and failure to discriminate word forms accurately frequently lead to adding sounds. The sounds more frequently added are *r* and *l*. When this tendency persists, drills are given on lists of words that are alike, except for the presence of *r* or *l*. Examples include *fog-frog* and *pan-plan.*

Errors of omission, addition, subtraction, or repetition are usually the result of a failure to recognize words accurately or an overemphasis on speed. Reading aloud by the teacher and child together helps, as does more emphasis on developing better word-analysis skills and going back to easier reading materials. If any of these errors remain, the teacher should call them to the attention of the child so that she may try to avoid them. A tape recorder can be useful as a check on accuracy. Emphasis on contextual clues is also helpful.

The Gillingham-Stillman Method

Another phonics approach, advanced by Gillingham and Stillman (1960), has been used widely with children experiencing serious reading difficulties. In contrast to methods we generally advocate, which deal with letters and sounds found in words, the Gillingham-Stillman method teaches the sounds of the letters and then builds these letters into words. Letter-sound correspondence is established by forming close associations between visual, auditory, and kinesthetic elements.

First, the child is taught the name of each letter. This is done by showing a letter card and teaching the child to say the name. Second, sounds are taught. If the child's production of sounds is faulty, the teacher produces the sound and the child imitates it. Such drill is given only when needed and for no longer than necessary.

Third, a practice drill is given. The teacher says the names of various letters, and the child responds with the related sound she has learned. Fourth, practice is given as necessary in tracing, copying, and writing from memory to dictation. In all instances, the child says the name of the letter as she writes it.

The procedure progresses through the teaching of letters, elements, and syllables, to work with words. Lessons are highly structured, and reading, spelling, and handwriting are all taught in a unified program. Special materials with a high degree of phonic consistency are employed. The student learning by this method is required to do no reading or spelling, except with the remedial reading teacher.

DISTAR

The program, Reading Mastery: DISTAR Reading I (Englemann & Bruner, 1983), has also been used to provide remedial work for students with extreme reading disabilities. DISTAR incorporates a heavy emphasis on blending sounds, but is a more complete program that uses scripted teaching instructions, instructional reading, and a behavioral management system, in addition to isolated drills.

Evaluation

Both the Monroe and the Gillingham-Stillman methods are definite, rigid drill programs requiring much time. They progress from letter sounds to words in sentences. Both methods use kinesthesis as an aid to associating letters with their sounds. They delay reading of words longer than the Fernald method. However, teaching reading to students with severe reading disabilities takes time, whatever the method used. When successful, the Monroe technique enables the child to use reading skills in a variety of ordinary reading materials more quickly than does the Gillingham-Stillman method, which stresses keeping the child on a restricted set of reading materials during her training. The view taken in this book is that, although these techniques are necessary for some students with severe reading disabilities, generally, other methods achieve quicker results. The Gillingham-Stillman method in particular is exceptionally rigid and restrictive and is recommended only for students with the most severe reading disabilities who have failed to establish a fundamental knowledge of phonics. Englemann and Bruner's DISTAR reading program shares the auditory-emphasis approach just described, but is a more complete, faster-paced reading method that lacks the depth and the individual focus of the Monroe and the Gillingham-Stillman procedures.

Methods with a Visual-Structural Emphasis

Visual-structural approaches are similar to approaches used in good classroom teaching, but are more intensified. The child is encouraged to recognize words as entities and, in studying them, to inspect each word carefully, part by part, from left to right. At the same time, the child notes similarities and differences, including minimal differences, among words, with an early emphasis on word beginnings and a later emphasis on the overall structure of the words. In this way, the child establishes a knowledge of word elements in the actual process of contextual reading. Knowledge of phonic and structural elements is not neglected, but is taught so closely with actual reading that the transfer of the skills into total word-recognition capabilities is accomplished. When successful, this method helps to produce fluent, thoughtful readers. Of course, some children will need more diversified programs, with added intensive drill on the word elements themselves.

Remedial instruction for children with extreme reading disabilities is like that for students without reading disabilities, except that the program of instruction is managed more precisely. Its adjustment to individual needs and use of individual instruction are emphasized. The teacher has to spend more time and exercise more care explaining and demonstrating each technique explicitly. Additional explanations, demonstrations, and suggestions are given as needed. The teacher ensures that the student moves ahead at a suitable pace. When a method does not appear to help, the teacher shifts to some other form of assistance.

If individualized teaching of commonly used procedures is not successful, the teacher may resort to some of the more specialized techniques. First, the customary methods of observing words, using contextual clues, analyzing words visually and through sounds, and developing an appropriate left-to-right orientation in word perception are given adequate time to function. If the child's responses then reveal inadequate progress in learning to read, the teacher may resort, for example, to a tracing technique. Even in this case, however, the specialized technique is not continued for weeks and months. Rather, it is used merely as a means of getting the child started, so that he will consistently maintain the left-to-right progression in reading words. Once the child has begun to make headway in the tracing technique, he should be shifted back to a program that covers the full range of reading activities for a child without reading disabilities.

Evaluation

Methods with a visual-structural emphasis have certain advantages over other methods: (1) They tend to be flexible, with provisions for shifting temporarily to more specialized techniques when needed. (2) Many, but not all, children with severe reading disabilities achieve overall reading improvement sooner with visual-structural methods than with the more specialized techniques. (3) Often, it is desirable to start a student with a severe reading disability with a visual-structural program. Then, if, after a fair trial, the student's progress is not satisfactory, the teacher can turn to one of the other techniques. Programs that emphasize the tracing and writing of words seem to benefit most the child who has difficulty forming an organized percept of whole words, and auditory (sound-blending) methods seem to help most the child who is notably stronger in auditory than in other learning abilities. After some progress is made with specialized fixed procedures, a gradual transition can be made toward the broader and less mechanical instruction used with children without reading disabilities.

Almost any competent remedial reading teacher can teach many of her students with extreme reading disabilities to read through the use of any of the methods discussed here. To be really expert, the teacher should be able to use each of the methods effectively and, after a thorough analysis of a child's reading needs, apply the method most suitable for that particular child. There is no single surefire method for teaching every student who has extreme reading disabilities, and the same is true for less extreme cases.

Probably, the reason for the success of the highly specialized methods used with students with extreme reading disabilities is that a high percentage of these students have basic problems with word recognition, which is the aspect of reading these methods stress. It should be also noted that, although each method is successful in general, any of them could prove detrimental to a specific individual. Accordingly, the best approach to extreme reading disability appears to lie in making an exact diagnosis and then applying the indicated remedial work, which in some instances might well be a tracing-writing or a phonic drill program. In most cases, however, a more balanced approach, as described in Chapters 10 and 11, should be used.

Treating Orientational Difficulties

Word-orientation confusions are among the most troublesome errors made by children with extreme reading disabilities. Full reversals, part reversals, axial rotations of letters, and other orientational confusions in word recognition interfere with the child's reading development. Any child who makes an excessive number of such errors has a limiting condition that must be corrected before continued advancement in reading can be expected.

The term *reversals* is used to describe several different kinds of errors in orientation: perceiving letters in reverse orientation, for example, *d* for *b* when reading *dig* for *big*, and perceiving letters in reverse order or partial reverse order. An example of a complete reversal is reading *saw* for *was* or *no* for *on*. A partial reversal is illustrated in a student's reading *own* for *now* or *ate* for *tea*. Also, there may be a reversal of the order of words in a sentence, as in "The rat caught a cat" for "The cat caught a rat."

During the preschool years, children learn to recognize people, places, animals, and objects, both from firsthand visual experience and from viewing television or pictures. In either case, the direction of the perceptual sequences, as revealed by the child's eye movements, is neither orderly nor oriented to a specific direction. Rather, they are a series of brief glances, while the eyes move in an irregular pattern of fixations over the object or picture. The direction of the movements is just as likely to be from right to left as left to right, or upward as downward, or obliquely in any direction. As children look over an object, noting features of interest or searching for familiar details, the direction of the eye movements is not only irregular, but also unpredictable to a large degree. These habits of perception are established before children enter school. Unless systematic instruction is given by the time a child begins to read words and sentences, she is likely to continue the habit of examining words by means of irregular directional sequences. To be efficient, the child must read words in a sentence, one after another, from left to right. Unless a word is recognized at a glance, the child must proceed along the word from left to right to identify it correctly.

The development of proper directional habits in reading requires two related learned skills. The first is the left-to-right sequence of eye movements along a line of print. This is a somewhat gross orientation that, nonetheless, must be learned. The second habit is the left-to-right direction of analysis required to identify and recognize words proficiently. This is a more precise and difficult facility. Contrary to one's first impression, these two aspects of sequential orientation in reading are related only roughly. True enough, both involve beginning at the left and progressing toward the right. But a child may have learned to begin at the left end of a line of print and, in general, move her eyes toward the right, without having mastered proper directional orientation within particular words. Extensive, continual training is needed for the latter.

Word Perception

Because reversals result from an incorrect orientation in perceiving words, both diagnosis and remedial instruction are necessarily more complicated for reversals than for directional habits in reading lines of print. The most exact diagnosis of reversal tendencies is obtained through the use of standardized tests such as the Gates-McKillop-Horowitz test, described in Chapter 8.

It has already been noted that it is normal for beginning readers to make some reversals and that these are gradually eliminated by most children as they progress in reading. For each student with a reading problem, therefore, it must be determined whether the reversals are excessive enough to cause trouble, rather than being merely occasional incidents in otherwise adequate reading. In other words, it is necessary to decide whether the frequency of reversals is merely a sign of immature reading or is a genuine reading handicap.

As soon as children begin to read words and lines of print, proper directional orientation must be stressed. Effective reading is achieved only when perceptual sequences, guided largely by eye movements, move from left to right. Except for sight words—those which are recognized at a glance—children must be instructed to examine a word from left to right in attempting to recognize it. It is necessary for the teacher to demonstrate repeatedly the proper directional orientation in perceiving words. She should be sure, before using the terms *left* and *right*, that all the children know their meaning.

The left-to-right habit is by no means confined to beginning instruction in reading. This orientational training is continued, more or less, throughout instruction designed to develop the word-recognition techniques. Such training is constructive only when done correctly and systematically. Working out word identification through attention to initial consonants, substitution of consonants, phonetic analysis, structural analysis, syllabication, and use of the dictionary requires constant attention to left-to-right orientation. Some students with proper directional habits in the early stages of reading abandon these habits at later stages, unless additional instruction is given.

Remedial Procedures

In general, substantial problems in reversing the order of letters in words occur more frequently among those readers who have the most disabilities (DeHirsh, Jansky, & Langford, 1966). This is not surprising when one refers back to the causes of reversals in word perception discussed previously. The child who has severe eye defects, who has received inadequate training in left-to-right orientation, who has been taught to emphasize word endings rather than beginnings, or who has been exposed to an improper program of phonics training, not only develops reversals but also seldom progresses far in learning to read. Any analysis of the methods used successfully to instruct nonreaders or readers with severe reading disabilities reveals that much emphasis is given to orderly, left-to-right inspection of words, with stress on developing a suitable perception of words as entities and with instruction in the proper blending of letter sounds into complete words.

Nevertheless, the remedial reading teacher must not assume that correction of reversal tendencies is the entire instructional program for any child with reversal difficulties. Ordinarily, other difficulties are also present and must be remedied. But when reversals exist in significant numbers, as is found in about 10 percent of cases of children with severe reading disabilities, they are crucial and require carefully organized and sometimes prolonged treatment.

At first, the teacher should explain the necessity of viewing words from left to right. She should accompany this explanation with a demonstration. After writing a word on the chalkboard or on paper, she should move a pointer or her finger along the word as she pronounces it slowly. To emphasize this process when restudy is needed, she should move her finger quickly back to the very beginning of the word and progress to the right again as she reads it a second time. This time, the teacher should stress the desirability of grasping the word as a unit after the difficult part is worked out. Next, the method of recognizing an unfamiliar word found in the context of a sentence is explained and demonstrated by the teacher in a similar manner. Her finger underlines the words as they are read. After a slight pause on reaching the unfamiliar word, the teacher moves her finger slowly along the word, pronouncing it as she did with the isolated word. The explanations and demonstrations are repeated as often as necessary while the student is practicing the left-to-right orientation in perceiving words. It is desirable for the student to practice with words in sentences as soon as possible, so that he may use contextual clues as much as possible in word recognition. In practicing sentences, he will become accustomed to using left-to-right progression along lines of print and to identifying unknown words in actual reading situations. Guided practice is transferred to sentences and paragraphs in book materials as soon as possible. It is important for the teacher to make sure that the child's skill in proper perceptual orientation in reading isolated words and words in isolated sentences does transfer to book reading. For some children, this transfer is difficult and they need much directed practice.

Although a child may be encouraged at first to use his finger or a manilla marker to guide his perception along the lines of print and along the successive letters in an unknown word, certain precautions are necessary. This technique is definitely a crutch and should be eliminated gradually when it is no longer needed. Some teachers feel that the use of a marker is better because it is easier to eliminate than is finger pointing. Whether the child uses his finger or a marker, the teacher should instruct him so that the perceptual aid is used properly; that is, the child should not point at one word after another with stops, but should use a consistent and *continuous* sliding movement from left to right to guide sequences of perception. Otherwise, the finger or marker may be used only to keep place, rather than to promote left-to-right progression. It accomplishes nothing if the finger or marker is moved forward and backward along a line or a word or if it is held in one place while the reader examines a word in random order. Using the finger or marker as a pointer produces proper directional movements in reading and corrects reversal tendencies only when it is carefully supervised by the teacher.

Other Systematic Approaches

The approach with a kinesthetic-auditory-visual emphasis, described earlier, is one of the most effective methods to use with children who experience persistent reversal difficulties. A modification of an approach with a phonics emphasis using sounding and tracing is also effective. The procedure is illustrated by the following example. The word *man* is written in large, cursive writing on a piece of paper. The teacher directs the child's attention to the word and its pronunciation. The child is asked to say *man* as slowly as possible, as demonstrated by the teacher. She then traces over the word while saying *man* slowly. She is encouraged to trace quickly and speak slowly, so as to come out even. The aim of this is to pronounce the word distinctly and slowly enough that its sequence of sounds becomes evident. Further training teaches the knack of sliding the voice from one sound to the next so that the word is pronounced as a unit.

A sound-dictation method has been substituted as a variation of the tracing method. Here, the child writes words as the teacher dictates their sounds slowly. First, the child is told that she will hear the separate sounds and is asked to say them slowly as she writes the letters for each sound. Thus, the teacher pronounces *man*, first having asked the child both to say and to write whatever word she says. For *man*, the child determines that the *a* is short by hearing the teacher sound it that way. In this method, the child must have learned the letters that correspond to the letter sounds and know how to write them. Children achieving at the second- and third-grade levels usually do well on such drills. According to Monroe (1932), writing from dictation with these directions is as helpful as tracing, and some children prefer to write. Both the tracing-sounding and the writing-sounding techniques encourage the discrimination of sound sequences in words and the coordination of these with visual sequences.

Writing Words
Many children with reversal problems have already had some experience writing. The remedial reading teacher can make good use of writing to promote a correct orientation in dealing with words. When writing, it is necessary to begin at the left and move to the right. When writing is used to develop a left-to-right orientation, it should be performed free rather than by copying material from a chalkboard, a chart, or a book. The latter tends to become a piecemeal operation instead of a continuous sequence. The training can be started with simple words and sentences. Some polysyllabic words should be used as soon as the child can

handle them. She should be encouraged to observe and pronounce each word aloud to herself as she writes it. This calls attention to the sequence of the word elements needed for correct perception. If writing is to be effective in correcting reversals, the child must observe the correct order of letters and letter sounds in the words she is writing. Whether the writing used is cursive or manuscript, the same approach should be used.

If the child has any tendency to use mirror writing (writing from right to left), it will immediately be obvious. Ordinarily, this reverse writing can be corrected by explaining to the child the need to move from left to right and by having her start writing words at the extreme left of the paper or chalkboard. She will then move readily in the only direction possible, which is to the right. In extreme cases, the child may be told, when writing sentences, to write the separate words underneath each other, each word starting at the left margin of the paper. Or the teacher may make a short vertical line at which the first letter of each succeeding word in a sentence is to begin. This special procedure should be eliminated as soon as possible.

Keyboarding

Keyboarding has been suggested as a technique for developing correct orientation in word perception. Presumably, the child will observe the correct sequence of letters in words as she enters them. It is true that she will get some practice in noting the beginnings of words on the copy as she enters the first letter, then the second, then the third, and so on through the word. But if she is just learning to keyboard, she is merely entering a series of letters that happen to be in groups. She will be so engrossed in selecting and pressing each key that she will be unable to use the correct techniques of word perception, either on the copy or in what she enters. Studies of keyboarding reveal that words are entered as units only after a good deal of skill has been attained. This certainly would not be the case with most young children. Furthermore, if the child is at the beginning stage of keyboarding, she likely has little understanding of what is being entered. The beginner's attention is devoted to the mechanics of keyboarding letters, not to word units and meanings. Moreover, it is possible to enter words and not recognize them. Left-to-right progression along a word must be combined with identification of the word in order to be effective in developing correct orientation in word perception. The teacher will find it very difficult to teach proper orientation for word perception through keyboarding; other methods are better and less cumbersome.

Other Techniques

There are several other techniques for encouraging the correct directional orientation in perceiving words. Of primary concern is developing the habit of initial attention to beginnings of words. Familiarity with and proper use of *initial consonants and consonant blends*, as explained in the previous chapter, are extremely important. Many children with reversal problems do not have this familiarity.

While remedial work is being done on deficiencies in knowledge of initial consonants, the teacher may employ a variety of exercises for teaching the child to notice word beginnings first of all. The following are examples:

1. To direct attention to the initial sound of words and, at the same time, to ensure that the whole word is read, sentences are arranged with one word missing. The child is instructed to read each sentence, to notice the beginning sound that is underlined in one word in each sentence, and then to draw a circle around the word below the sentence that begins with the same sound and makes sense in the sentence. To choose correctly, the child must note both the beginning sound and the meaning of the right word:

John wet his feet in the _____ .
  wall   lake   water

Mary's kitten likes to drink _____ .
  milk   make   cream

2. Training in substitution of consonants may be used to emphasize word beginnings:

    a. Using words in context, show the child a sentence such as "He came to see the new game." Ask the child to read the sentence and find two words that look alike, except for the first letter. Pronounce *came,* and have the child point to the letter that stands for the first sound. Do the same for *game.* Next, write the letters *t, s, n, g, c,* and have the child give the sounds of the letters. Then write the word *came.* After the beginning letter is located correctly, erase *c* and substitute *t.* Pronounce the new word. Continue with the word *game.* Interchange the initial consonants *s, n,* and *c* again, emphasizing the function of the initial letter and its sound in pronouncing the words.

    b. Present a word such as *may* or *last* or *pig* to the child. Then ask the child to tell you a word that looks and sounds like *may,* except at the beginning. When he mentions a word like *day,* erase the *m* in *may* while he watches, and substitute the initial consonant of the word mentioned. Ask the child to pronounce the new word, and note how changing just the first letter makes a new word.

When using substitution of consonants to emphasize attention to word beginnings, remember to stress initial letters and sounds.

3. Various games may be played for informal training in using initial consonants to direct attention to word beginnings. Consonant Lotto and the first part of the Group Sounding Game in the Dolch materials (The Garrard Press, Champaign, Illinois) are designed for this purpose.

Word wheels and the other devices described in the previous chapter may be made for drilling the child on initial consonants in emphasizing word beginnings. In using a word wheel, words having the same ending are used, such as *throat, coat, goat, boat, float,* and *gloat.* On the bottom disk, only the word beginnings are typed or printed, and they are placed so that they show through an opening in the top disk, on which the ending *-oat* is printed to the right of the opening. The two disks may be rotated so that the child can see that, by changing the initial elements, new words are made. This causes the child to pay attention to the word beginnings in order to recognize the words shown.

In a similar manner, a column of initial elements of words having the same ending can be typed or printed, using triple spacing, on a slip cut from a manilla folder. Then an exposure card can be made by cutting a slit in a piece of manilla folder. The word ending should be typed or printed just to the right of the slit. (See the word-slip device in Chapter 11.) When the slip is moved into position, the various initial elements are exposed, one after another, for the child to use in making the words. He will notice the changing elements, since they determine what the words will be.

In all this work, the teacher should present the exercise so that the child always sees the initial consonant as the word is exposed. This is done by going at a leisurely pace, by pointing to the initial consonant, and by having the child sound the consonant and blend it with the word ending. If this technique is not used, the child may remember the initial sound and look first at the ending. The purpose is to teach the child always to notice first the beginning of the word. Noticing the beginning of a word first must become an ingrained habit.

4. It has been suggested that a demonstration of reversal errors is valuable in discussing directional orientation in word perception. The purpose of this is to show a child what happens when he starts reading at the end or the middle of a word, rather than at the beginning. For instance, the teacher writes *war* and *raw* one above the other. She then points out that the same letters are in both words, but they are different words, so that he should always start at the left end of a word in reading it. Similarly, she calls attention to *left* and *felt* or other partial or complete reversals.

5. Alphabetizing and dictionary exercises promote left-to-right orientation in perceiving words. For early practice in alphabetizing, the child should have a file box or folder with the alphabet marked on the dividing cards. A single word that has been learned is written on a slip of paper. The word is then filed by its initial letter. When the order of the alphabet has been learned, several words beginning with the same letter can be filed, according to the sequence of letters within the word. All this develops the habit of looking first at the beginnings of words and then progressing from left to right. Information on developing skills in alphabetizing and using the dictionary are given in teachers' manuals accompanying basic reading series.

A picture dictionary can be made for more immature readers. Picture dictionaries show a child how the alphabet is used for classification. Also, when the child writes a word for the dictionary, it gives him practice in progressing through a word from left to right.

Other temporary ways to support a student who is having difficulty with reversals include teaching the child to cover confusing words with a card and to move it from left to right to uncover the letters in sequence, drilling the child with flash cards of words he persistently reverses, or underlining with a green marker the first letters of words to be read.

Preventing Reversals

It is desirable to teach beginning reading so that reversal tendencies are averted. From the start, proper orientation in word study should be stressed, as discussed in the initial parts of this chapter and in the previous chapter. This becomes particularly important in teaching aspects of word analysis such as observing initial consonants and phonograms and blending letter sounds into correct sequences. The first letter or letter group in a word should be sounded first, followed by an orderly progression to the right. A well-organized program of teaching word analysis (see the preceding chapter), with attention to individual needs, should help to establish the customary left-to-right progression needed to prevent reversals.

Summary

The child with an extreme reading disability is the child who has learned little or no reading during several or more years in school. Three types of remedial methods have proved to be especially successful in teaching these children to read. A tracing-sounding-writing method, such as was suggested originally by Fernald, has been effective in developing a left-to-right orientation in word perception, in directing attention to the visual characteristics of words, in developing skill in phonics and syllabication, and in the use of context in recognizing words. This method also emphasizes developing vocabulary, concepts, and comprehension, but it is detailed and time consuming and must be done on an individual basis. The approach is often successful with students with extreme reading disabilities, but it requires an unusually great amount of time on the part of the teacher.

Phonic (sound-blending) methods, such as those developed by Monroe (1932) and Gillingham and Stillman (1960), have been successful for some children with extreme reading disabilities. These methods emphasize patient repetition of necessary drill. Tracing-sounding is employed when necessary. The Reading Mastery: DISTAR Program (Englemann & Bruner, 1983) also stresses sound blending heavily, in a more complete reading program. Although phonic methods are useful for many children, they should not be used with those who are already overanalytical.

Another method embodies all the procedures and techniques used to teach children without reading disabilities in good classroom programs. This method works with children who have reading disabilities when they receive intensive instruction based on an accurate understanding of their individual needs.

The expert remedial teacher should be familiar with all these methods so that she will use the most appropriate procedure for each child. A careful diagnosis can usually specify the area of difficulty and suggest the type of instruction needed. Such a diagnosis shows which approach or combination of approaches would be best in a particular case.

A special problem that most beginning readers experience and soon overcome, but that remains a genuine reading handicap for a few, is difficulty with left-to-right word perception. Many methods to eliminate reversal tendencies in word perception have been described. The more important ones include (1) explanation and demonstration of the left-to-right progression in studying unknown words, (2) the Fernald tracing-sounding-writing method, (3) the combined phonic and sounding-tracing method, (4) writing words, (5) instruction in substitution of consonants, and (6) practice in alphabetizing and the use of the dictionary.

Remedial instruction for reversals includes methods that direct the pupil's attention to the beginning of a word and that lead to a consistent left-to-right progression in studying a word. These twin techniques encourage the habit of noticing the beginnings of words, followed by visually surveying the word elements from left to right, followed by sounding and blending these elements into whole words. The particular methods used will depend upon the nature and severity of a child's reading difficulties, as revealed by diagnosis.

Study Questions

1. Describe the stages used in teaching a student to read new words with the Fernald approach. What cautions are indicated when using this method?
2. What essential similarities and differences were there between the phonic approaches discussed in this chapter?
3. What can teachers do to help students with orientational difficulties?

Selected Readings

Crawley, S. J., & Merritt, K. (1991). *Remediating reading difficulties* (pp. 44–46). Dubuque IA: Wm. C. Brown.

Fernald, G. M. (1971). *Remedial techniques in basic school subjects*. New York: McGraw-Hill.

Gillingham, A., & Stillman, B. W. (1960). *Remedial training for children with specific disability in reading, spelling, and penmanship*. Cambridge, MA: Educators Publishing Service.

Kirk, S. A., Kliebhan, J. M., & Lerner, J. W. (1978). *Teaching reading to slow and disabled learners* (pp. 136–153). Boston: Houghton Mifflin.

Monroe, M. (1932). *Children who cannot read*. Chicago: University of Chicago Press.

Richek, M. A., List, L. K., & Lerner, J. W. (1989). *Reading problems: Assessment and teaching strategies* (2nd ed.) (pp. 286–313). Englewood Cliffs, NJ: Prentice Hall.

Chapter 13

Adapting Instruction for Children with Disabilities

Teachers must be aware that some children with reading difficulties also have special learning disabilities. Children with complex reading disabilities not only need expert remedial reading instruction, but must also have instruction modified according the characteristics of their specific disabilities.

Many children with disabilities find complex learning, such as reading, confusing and frustrating. Others learn to read exceedingly well despite their disabilities. For example, many children with a mild hearing impairment derive great satisfaction from reading. If their reading skills become well developed, these children may become such avid readers that they eventually demonstrate better-than-average reading achievement. But if a child with another disability also becomes disabled in reading, her problem becomes more complex. Disabling conditions that may contribute to and complicate the correction of reading difficulties include poor vision, imperfect hearing, speech defects, emotional problems, and neurological limitations. The diagnostic and remedial methods described in previous chapters are, by themselves, insufficient to solve the learning problems of children with these disabilities.

In some instances, the educational program for any specific group of children with disabilities may be conducted in special classes using methods and equipment designed to meet the children's particular instructional needs. More commonly, these children are taught in the mainstream classroom and perhaps in the resource room, with procedures adapted as needed to enable them to progress effectively. Appropriate educational adjustments are treated in books dealing with the psychology and education of exceptional children and youth. In this chapter, we discuss the special modifications of remedial procedures that are needed for dealing with the added complications a separate disability causes in conjunction with reading difficulties.

Throughout this book, the emphasis has been on adapting instruction to the requirements of the individual, as ascertained by a careful diagnosis. When dealing with reading difficulties complicated by other disabilities, there is need for even more exacting individual adaptation. Much depends upon skillful guidance. The fullest measure of success is achieved when an alert teacher senses every aspect of a student's difficulty and has at her command the exact procedures, demonstrations, materials, and instructional techniques to overcome or at least alleviate the difficulty. She must know just what materials and procedures to select for that difficulty and when to shift from one procedure to another in order to help the student continue to improve in reading. In other words, the teacher must be flexible in organizing his remedial programs, in beginning at the right point, and in introducing new materials and techniques to promote continuous progress toward learning to read better.

Especially relevant is the personality of the teacher, who must be willing to work patiently to gain and maintain good rapport with the child. For even the prospect of success, the child must like his teacher and expect that he is going to help her. Only when there is a secure, positive relationship between the child and the teacher is it possible for the teacher to provide the incentives that will maintain the motivation necessary to achieve lasting improvement in reading. Besides being well trained, the teacher must like children and be enthusiastic about his work. It is not too much to say that success in teaching children with disabilities depends mostly on the teacher.

It is inconceivable that any single, narrow, or limited approach to reading will be found adequate for helping children with complex reading disabilities become effective readers. The very nature of the learning adjustments these children must make to read successfully varies from one type of disability to another. Programs for such children have to be devised to foster the adjustments they must make in order to be effective learners.

Children with both reading and other disabilities especially need to feel successful in the remedial reading venture. Teachers must remember that the basic task in teaching these children is to modify the teaching procedures that are used to correct the reading problem in light of the unique adjustments that must be made to overcome the additional learning problems the children have because of their other disabilities. Among these disabilities are visual impairment, auditory impairment, neurological impairment, emotional maladjustment, mental deficits, and speech impairment.

The Child with Visual Impairment

Many visual defects, such as ordinary myopia, hyperopia, astigmatism, and muscular imbalance, can be remedied by properly fitted glasses, contact lenses, or other medical means. Children with fully corrected vision suffer no visual difficulties when they learn to read.

Every child should have visual screening and adequate follow-up when needed, before he receives instruction in reading. Any necessary treatment or correction must be provided. There should be periodic visual examinations throughout the school years to identify and correct any significant defects that may develop. Methods for diagnosing visual impairments were discussed in Chapter 4.

A small number of children have visual impairments that cannot be corrected completely. Accompanied by consultation with a competent eye specialist, educational adaptations are necessary for children with low visual acuity. In teaching these children, the length of the lesson, typography, and illumination must be considered. Reading periods should be brief, and the instructional conditions should make the visual task as effortless as possible. There is ample evidence that both children without visual impairment and children with visual impairment find that words in large type sizes are easier to perceive correctly. Children of elementary school age express a preference for large type, as do children with low visual acuity (Wiess, 1982). It is also advisable to use material printed on a line of about 24 to 27 picas (4 to $4\frac{1}{2}$ inches), with ample leading or space between lines, for children with visual acuity problems. Supplementary material can be prepared for these children, using typewriters with primer-size type. Children with visual impairment should have an ample amount and variety of reading material.

Also necessary is abundant illumination. This means at least 50 foot-candles of light in any area where visually demanding activities, such as reading, art and craft work, chalkboard work, or writing, are performed. Felt-tipped pens and pencils that produce thick black lines should be used.

Reading should be coordinated with other means of learning. Learning through listening and discussing should be emphasized, and creative activities, such as dramatics, are beneficial. The teacher must assume responsibility for encouraging learning through listening and doing. This entails much discussion, reading aloud, storytelling, guidance of group discussion, and supervision of creative activities on the part of the teacher. Audiovisual instruction, employing audiotapes, sound motion pictures, tape and slide presentations, videotapes, and television, is also valuable.

Children with visual impairment are usually not at a disadvantage in phonological awareness. As a consequence, an emphasis on phonics in beginning reading instruction can be helpful for many of them. Care must be taken, however, not to overemphasize letter-sound associations and, as soon as possible, to direct the children's attention to whole-word recognition and to perceiving the larger pronounceable units of words, such as syllables, word roots, prefixes, and suffixes. Doing this enhances effective visual perception and minimizes the need for a minute examination of the details of letters in working out words. Contextual clues should be stressed as an aid to word recognition and to recognizing words in thought units. Any procedure that leads to perceiving groups of words, whole words, and larger parts of words in word analysis helps reduce the detailed visual work in reading.

Children with only a mild degree of visual impairment can participate in the standard reading program. The teacher should select recreational reading materials with clear print, see that there is adequate illumination in the classroom, and encourage these students to rest their eyes occasionally. Some children with mild visual impairment benefit from being taught to use paper or tagboard markers to isolate the line of print they are reading, in order to minimize visual distraction. Reading speed should be deemphasized, and accurate word recognition and close attention to meaning should be stressed.

The Child with Auditory Impairment

Adaptations for children with hearing impairments differ, since they are impaired to varying degrees. The deaf are those whose hearing loss is so severe and is acquired so young that it precludes the normal development of spoken language. Other children are classified as partially hearing. They are able to use spoken language, but their auditory handicap limits their learning and use of language. Auditory limitations range from slight to profound.

The sooner the hearing loss is detected, the better off the child is, because appropriate help in the early years enables children to use their hearing as effectively as possible and acquire language as fully as possible. All children should be given an adequate hearing screening before entering school. The measurement of hearing has been discussed in Chapter 4.

Slight Hearing Impairment

Moderate educational adaptations help the child with a slight hearing impairment to succeed in the mainstream classroom. Such a student should be given a favorable seat close to where the teacher usually talks to the class. Words should always be enunciated clearly whenever a child with hearing impairment is the listener. The child will be able to follow oral discussion more accurately if she watches the lips of the person speaking. Some training in speech reading is also helpful. To avoid embarrassing the child, discussion groups should be arranged so that she can watch the lips of each speaker without obviously turning her head. Seating the children in a circle, in a semicircle, or around a table does this nicely.

The child with a hearing impairment is likely to have some degree of difficulty in auditory discrimination. Because of this, the teaching of word perception should emphasize a visual approach to word identification and recognition, rather than an auditory approach. This does not imply that letter sounds should not be taught; the child with a hearing impairment needs a great deal of emphasis on letter sounds as an aid to both speech and reading. However, depending upon the specific nature of the auditory deficit, the child will not be able to use phonics as an aid to word recognition as successfully as a child with normal hearing. For this reason, more attention than usual should be paid to the visual characteristics of words and to the use of visual analysis, along with contextual clues, for recognizing words previously met and for identifying unfamiliar words. The extent of the emphasis on visual and de-emphasis of auditory identification and recognition techniques depends upon how much difficulty the child has with auditory discrimination. If the teacher is sensitive to her auditory limitations, the child with a relatively slight hearing defect should be able to make normal progress in learning to read.

Slight to Moderate Hearing Impairment

Children with slight to moderate hearing impairment are under a severe handicap if they learn to read in classes in which oral reading and phonics are stressed. They need more emphasis upon silent reading and a visual approach to word recognition. It is important that they be given many opportunities to show what they know through performance. Work sheet activities are helpful. Language difficulties may preclude a clear understanding of words read, unless the teacher provides many opportunities for the child to demonstrate her understanding. These children should receive special speech-reading and language instruction.

The child with a hearing impairment may experience adjustment difficulties unless special care is taken. Such a child can easily feel alienated from her peers. Every effort should be made in her classwork and play activities to make the child feel that she belongs to the group.

Severe to Extreme Hearing Impairment

It is very difficult to teach reading to children with severe to extreme hearing impairments, especially those children who have not developed language concepts. Visual materials are used for such children. Words are introduced in a variety of ways, usually through presenting actual objects with accompanying demonstrations. Extensive use is made of pictures in association with words and of picture dictionary material. Mastery of each step is required before going on to the next. Progress from words to phrases to sentences to paragraphs is achieved by successful learners.

Teaching children with serious auditory impairments to read is a highly specialized task that the ordinary remedial reading teacher will not encounter. Those who teach these children should consult such references as Hart (1976).

The Child with Neurological Impairment

There are a limited number of children with reading disabilities who, after carefully planned and thoroughly implemented programs of reeducation, fail to show the desired progress. Some of these children may have neurological impairments. Of course, this conclusion should never be assumed unless it is supported by expert medical evidence. Whatever can be done medically to improve the learning ability of such children should precede or accompany any attempt at reading-improvement programs.

Remedial reading programs for children who have a neurological problem should take into account the behavioral characteristics of each child. Response patterns that suggest neurological impairment include visual perception and synthesis problems, auditory discrimination and blending difficulties, symbol-sound or symbol-meaning association problems, and motor-coordination limitations. These difficulties necessitate two types of modifications in remedial reading instruction: training to improve the child's visual, auditory, associative, or motor skills and adaptations in the methods of remedial instruction so as to use the child's strengths and avoid his weaknesses in reading tasks.

Visual Perception and Synthesis Problems

The ability to perceive differences in word configurations and to note the fine distinctions within the printed symbols is necessary for effective word recognition and for success in learning to read. The child who cannot visually distinguish rapidly between word patterns such as *fall* and *fell, learn* and *lean,* or *stop* and *tops* will have trouble acquiring even beginning reading skill. Many children start learning to read with just such limitations. For the neurologically impaired, these problems of visual perception may be even more troublesome.

Direct training in noting likenesses and differences may be given to children with visual perception and synthesis problems in much the same way it is given to prereading children. The teacher who instructs a child with this type of neurological impairment will find that materials developed for prereading children who are immature in visual perception and synthesis, but who have no other disabilities, are effective. For all but those with the most severe disabilities, exercises that deal with similarities and differences in real printed symbols are more useful than exercises using geometric shapes or designs. Matching activities involving individual stimulus cards prompt close visual attention and reduce distractions. Tracing activities benefit greatly some children with neurological impairment, especially if they are encouraged to trace large figures or symbols. During the school day, these children should be encouraged to participate fully in appropriate art, craft, and physical education activities. Although children with poor visual perception often have difficulty with activities of this nature, with sensible adaptations, such pursuits help strengthen their visual perceptual abilities. In dealing with the child who has both a reading disability and a visual-neurological impairment, the paramount remedial reading task is to teach her to attend to word patterns as effectively as her limited perceptual capacity will allow. Caution should be exercised in the length of practice periods used for such training; these periods should not be extended to the point of fatigue. Also, this kind of training can continue along with standard remedial teaching that is designed to improve word recognition. Much of the child's ability to discriminate words visually is developed in the actual process of learning word-recognition techniques.

In teaching the child with limited visual perception to read, the remedial reading program should rely strongly upon methods that emphasize auditory sound-blending approaches. For children who still do not make progress, kinesthetic-auditory-visual training may be needed. Periods of demanding visual effort should be of short duration and well spaced. Sometimes it is necessary to break the reading material into single sentences or short paragraphs. These are read and discussed one at a time, thus giving the child frequent intervals of visual relaxation. As she matures in reading and perceptual skills, the segments of reading can be lengthened. Even then, the child should be encouraged to look up from the print, to relax and to think about what she has read. The use of contextual clues should be developed as an aid to word recognition.

Auditory Discrimination and Blending Difficulties

Children who cannot detect the differences in spoken words that sound somewhat alike, who are not able to select which of two words completes a rhyme, or who cannot discriminate well enough to select which of a group of words starts with the same sound as a given spoken word do not have the auditory capabilities necessary to learn to read by certain methods of instruction. Such word-discrimination skills must exist in order to profit from oral word study and training in phonics. The ability to blend letter sounds or phonemes into whole words when presented orally is required for oral-phonic training methods to succeed.

Auditory skills can be developed by having the child learn to listen more carefully to the sound patterns of words. Materials for instruction are as extensive as the rhymes and words found in children's literature and in the spoken language of the children being taught. As with visual skills, the remedial reading teacher can find many good ideas in prereading materials and in oral games used in kindergarten. These sources will provide the teacher with models of activities that she can develop. The child with neurological limitations who has auditory discrimination and blending deficiencies needs a more extensive program of training than does the child without these limitations and deficiencies. Auditory training might well start with distinguishing between gross sounds such as crumpling paper, running water, shutting doors, and pounding with a hammer. Then it might progress to noting which two out of four orally presented words sound the same; first using words that have markedly contrasting patterns, such as *make, want, make, have,* and then progressing to finer discriminations, such as in *roam, room, ram, roam.* The child should be able to make these auditory discriminations with his eyes closed or when his teacher's face is not in view, to ensure that he has heard the differences, rather than read his teacher's lips. Auditory training periods should be short, both to ensure attention and because such training tends to be tiring. Children with auditory discrimination and blending limitations like visual clues. They may enjoy using picture cards to perform such tasks as naming the pictures and then sorting the cards according to the beginning sounds of the names. Occasionally, they may need practice recalling the names of common objects pictured. For training in auditory discrimination to help a child read, the ability to distinguish sounds in words based on the child's, as well as other people's, pronunciations must be present or must be developed. To enhance sound-blending skill specifically, the teacher can ask the child to hand her the picture of the *c—ar* or of the *b—oa—t*. Many exercises designed to develop auditory skills are included in reading-readiness materials.

Symbol Association Problems

The abilities needed to make instant and accurate associations between printed symbols and spoken sounds, and between printed symbols and meaningful words, are necessary for effective reading. The child who cannot make these associations instantly will be a faltering reader, and the child who cannot make them accurately will be unable to make much progress at all. For most children, these difficulties signal that the pace of reading instruction has been too fast and that they have not been given enough opportunity for review. For children with neurological impairments, symbol association problems may be much more severe.

Direct training in symbol-sound and symbol-meaning associations may have to be given in a manner similar to that used in beginning reading instruction. Some children with neurological impairments require so much practice that the remedial reading teacher may have to find or design supplementary materials to maintain their interest. Gamelike activities can make repetitive practice seem more enjoyable. Sorting word cards into categories by meaning gives good practice in symbol-meaning associations.

The teacher of children with neurological impairments must be able to judge when to practice further and when to move on. Enough practice is essential, but too much only causes the child to fall farther behind. The issue is complicated further by the great variability in associative abilities that some children with neurological impairments demonstrate from one day to the next. The willingness to make appropriate instructional adjustments and emphasize at all times what the child has done well maximizes instructional effectiveness for these children.

Motor Coordination Limitations

The major area of limited motor coordination related to reading is oculomotor coordination. The child with an oculomotor control problem has difficulty focusing on the printed page and coordinating her eyes when reading. She also has trouble following the line of print rhythmically as she progresses along it. Kephart (1971) gives suggestions for improving oculomotor coordination.

It is enough to state here that methods using markers as aids to maintaining one's location on the line, sweeping below the line of print with a marker, and emphasizing left-to-right progression are helpful. The discussion of orientational problems in word recognition presented in Chapter 12 suggests methods that should help the child overcome oculomotor problems in reading. Kinesthetic methods are often suggested to augment inadequate oculomotor control in reading. Clinical workers giving remedial training to children with severe oculomotor disabilities may find the methods suggested by Fernald (1971) helpful.

Correcting the reading disabilities of children with neurological impairments is difficult and usually time consuming. But if training is given and adjustments are made, these children can develop a reading capability. Additional suggestions for teaching children with learning disorders associated with neurological impairment are described by Cruickshank (1971), Kephart (1971), Myers and Hammill (1976), and Westman (1990).

Teachers and clinicians working with children who have reading disabilities should be aware that these children may show many symptoms of neurological impairment and that a child should not be assumed to have a neurological problem unless it is confirmed by a medical examination. Children who have no neurological impairments, but who do have perceptual and motor problems, should have training similar to that described in this section. However, the training need not be as intense, and progress should be expected to be more rapid than would be the case for the child with a neurological impairment.

The Child with Behavioral Problems

In Chapter 6, it was noted that most children with reading problems also display some behavior problems. Some children exhibit behavior problems when they first arrive at school. Others develop such problems when they are frustrated in their attempts to learn to read. Whatever the origin of the trouble, it is certain that, to some extent, behavior problems are a concern of many remedial reading teachers.

Children who experience reading difficulties are often characterized by a variety of behaviors, ranging from inattentiveness, anxiety, or submissiveness to overdemanding behavior, anger, or hostility. These behaviors also range from just noticeable to very obvious.

Gentile and McMillan (1987) believe that some behavioral problems can be understood as flight-or-fight reactions to the stress associated with reading difficulties. If a student's behavior is understood as a flight reaction, the teacher should focus on interaction with the student and drawing the student out. The student should be moved toward participation in the reading task and toward a meaningful relationship with the teacher. The teacher should attempt to build motivation and should provide helpful prompting as necessary. If a student's behavior is understood as a fight reaction, the teacher must severely limit interaction with the student—especially confrontational interaction—and move the student back to the reading task. The teacher must be concise and consistent and should keep verbal interaction to a minimum.

Hewett and Taylor (1980) have stressed the importance of helping children with behavior and learning problems to behave as learners. This is necessary because certain specific behaviors interfere with reading progress. These behaviors include inattention to reading tasks, lack of active response to reading, and inability to complete work.

To help children attend to reading, the teacher should consider the physical environment first of all. It should be free from distraction. Many children can attend better to their reading when allowed to work in a carrel or study booth. For others, it is helpful to remove all unnecessary materials from work surfaces, as these materials are often distracting. Short, definite units of work are an aid to the child who has difficulty attending to his reading. Tokens for paying attention, such as plastic chips, colorful stickers, or simple check marks can be awarded to a child for attentive behavior. Charts or other records of progress often help children learn to increase their attention to reading.

In the clinic, teachers have noticed that jewelry, such as dangling beads or brightly colored pins, distracts certain students. Teachers have also observed that a soft voice and short, simple, direct instructions help children who have difficulty attending to a reading task. Gamelike supplementary reading activities often help children attend to such tasks because of the added incentive of wanting to win. Very few children will attend to reading when they have no purpose for reading, when the reading is uninteresting to them, or when it is too difficult for them.

Children with complex disabilities may refuse to read at all or may respond only minimally to reading tasks. These children read orally so slowly and hesitantly and in such a muffled tone that they cannot be heard, or they stop at every difficult word and refuse to try to read it, or they rush rapidly through all their reading with little thought of the meaning, thinking only of finishing. Other children spend their reading time trying to converse with the teacher about any conceivable subject, rather than proceeding with their reading, and others are perpetually late and frequently absent. To help such children respond to reading, teachers can reduce the level and amount of reading the child must do, until he can see that he can accomplish the task easily. Reading instructions for these children should be specific, not vague and open ended, because vague and open-ended reading tasks appear to them to be without end. The teacher should guarantee the child success by having him compete against himself, not against others. As an example, she might have him see whether he can do better today than he did yesterday. Charts of the child's work are helpful for comparison. Well-written reading selections closely tied to the child's interests help to kindle enthusiasm for reading.

Children having difficulty completing reading tasks can be helped if the teacher prepares and organizes their work carefully. Often, teachers find that they must plan in stages what must be done to finish a work sheet or reading selection and then help the student through these same stages to finish the work. Some children who have difficulty completing their work are not aware of time. Therefore, they must be given reminders of the time. It is also important to reward and praise them for completing their reading.

When remediation is successful, the usual result is that as the child gains power in reading, his stress is reduced, his confusions diminish, his interest expands, his behavior problems decrease, and he appears to be a happier, better adjusted person. His confidence has been reestablished. Other evidences of personal and social well-being also become apparent.

The Child with a Mental Disability

Children with below-average intelligence are commonly classified into the following groups, according to Kirk, Kliebhan, and Lerner (1978): (1) slow learners (I.Q. 68–85), (2) mildly mentally retarded (I.Q. 52–67), (3) moderately mentally retarded (I.Q. 36–51), (4) severely mentally retarded (I.Q. 20–35), and (5) profoundly mentally retarded (I.Q. 19 and below). People with I.Q.s in the moderately mentally retarded range can learn to read on a word-by-word basis when given intensive instruction and massive review. For those with I.Q.s of about 50 to about 70, progress in reading is extremely slow. With superior extended reading instruction, the expected reading grade of a child with an I.Q. of 70 is 5.2 at age 16. Ordinarily, children with I.Q.s of about 50 to 70 receive reading instruction in a special education class or resource room. Children with I.Q.s above 70 are usually able to achieve more and, if given excellent instruction, may be expected to achieve reading grades at the 6.0 to 7.5 grade level by the age of 16.

Slow Learners

Slow learners are children with I.Q.s between 68 and 85 who are taught to read in mainstream classes. In general, with proper instruction, slow learners can make progress up to the grade level corresponding to their mental age. As noted by Kirk, Kliebhan, and Lerner (1978), slow learners differ from other children in learning to read because they cannot be expected to begin learning to read at the chronological age of 6, and even thereafter they naturally learn at a slower rate. They become discouraged in the mainstream classroom because of continued failure.

On entering school, slow learners lag behind the typical child in the abilities and skills that form the basis for success in beginning reading. According to Savage and Mooney (1979), the readiness program for slow learners should be more intense and prolonged than usual, so as to reduce the difficulty of the learning the new skills required when the child actually begins to read. Some general aspects of reading readiness have been discussed in earlier chapters; details of such programs may be found in Durkin (1987), Jewell and Zintz (1986), and Heilman, Blair, and Rupley (1986).

During prereading instruction, when the child's mental age is between 5 and 6, she is able to learn to recognize her name and a few words used as labels and signs. Before the child reaches at least 6 years of mental age, systematic reading instruction, as is ordinarily given, results only in a tremendous waste of time and energy on the part of the teacher, because so little is learned from it. Nevertheless, if special instructional methods (described later) are employed, these children can be given worthwhile reading instruction before 6 years of mental age. Without these methods, some of them would not begin to read until 8 or 9 years old.

The child with a mental disability differs from the child without a mental disability in her reading progress—mainly by being slower to learn. She is ready to begin formal lessons at a somewhat later chronological age, and she progresses at a slower rate. This means that at each succeeding level in the developmental program, she should have more materials and more individualized guidance than the child who does not have a mental disability. The slow learner needs many repetitions of a word in the context of reading before she can learn the word. The best reading materials to use are those which have proved satisfactory with other students. But there needs to be more of the materials, and the instruction needs to be more individual and more intensive. Repetition, explanations, demonstrations, experiences, and the amount of recreational reading should be extensive.

Reading Difficulties
When classroom reading instruction and materials are not adjusted to the slow learner, he may experience reading difficulties. That is, his reading achievement may come to be less than what is reasonable to expect for him. According to evidence cited by Kirk (1940), between 5 and 10 percent of mentally retarded children experience reading difficulties, but can benefit from remedial instruction. Coincidentally, this is about the frequency of reading difficulty found among children with average and above average intelligence. A precise diagnosis of the extent and nature of reading difficulties among children with mental disabilities rests on the use of techniques described in earlier chapters.

Remedial Instruction
Results cited by Kirk (1940) and by Featherstone (1951) demonstrate that slow learners who incur reading disabilities benefit significantly from remedial instruction. For instance, in a group of 10 children with a mean age of 12 years and 9 months and a mean I.Q. of 75, an average grade-equivalent gain of 1.2 grades was achieved by 68 standard lessons, each 30 minutes long, over a period of about 5 months. This rate of progress was five times that of 100 children of similar age and mental ability who did not receive such remedial instruction. Furthermore, 5 months after the remedial training ended, the children continued to progress in the mainstream classroom at a rate twice that of the 100 children who had not been given the remedial instruction. It was concluded that significant and satisfying results can be obtained from remedial instruction with slow-learning children who experience reading difficulties.

The Hegge-Kirk remedial method (Hegge, Kirk, & Kirk, 1945) was devised primarily for children with mental disabilities. In its initial stage, the method is primarily phonic. However, it is more complete than most phonic systems. There is much drill and an emphasis on such principles of learning as the use of concrete associative aids to help the child learn a new sound. Retention is aided by having the child say the sound, write the letter, and then blend the sound with other sounds into words. Reading sentences and stories and the teaching of words are introduced at appropriate places as the child progresses. Any teacher who plans to use this method should consult Kirk (1940).

The following are suggestions for adapting teaching to slow-learning children:

1. Instruction in reading should begin later than is customary. Initial instruction should be delayed until the child is prepared to be successful in reading.
2. Slow-learning children develop reading ability in much the same way as their classmates, but at a somewhat slower pace. This is true for both word recognition and vocabulary. Any necessary modifications in instruction are more a matter of changed emphasis and pacing than a drastically different program.
3. A large amount of material must be used with slow learners. To make new words a permanent part of the child's sight vocabulary, they must be introduced more carefully and practiced more often. That is, the development of a reading vocabulary is more gradual.
4. Slow learners require more review. This is achieved by the use and reuse of materials and by rereading a selection several times for different purposes.
5. The slow-learning child has to be given more step-by-step and more simplified instruction. Frequently, she finds the directions in standard reading materials difficult to grasp. The teacher must be sure that the child always understands what is expected of her.
6. The slow-learning child needs more concrete examples of the things about which she is reading. She should be given every opportunity to come into direct contact with these things.
7. Reading goals should be relatively short range, that is, reached quickly. The slow learner cannot work effectively on projects of long duration.
8. The slow learner requires more rereading before she can thoroughly comprehend what she reads, but she does not mind rereading, because it helps her get a more complete understanding of the material.
9. There should be more experience and more guidance in the slow learner's study of the visual and auditory characteristics of words. Slow learners benefit from additional drill in analyzing words and in learning the sounds of various word elements. Since rapid reading is not essential to slow learners, a moderate degree of overanalysis is of little consequence, provided that it does not interfere with comprehension.
10. It is advisable to use more oral reading and oral prestudy in instructing slow-learning children. Many of them need to vocalize what they are reading before they can comprehend it well. Although vocalization slows their reading rate, comprehension is more important.
11. Slow-learning children should be given more tasks such as building models or cutting out pictures in connection with their reading than is common.
12. Finally, slow-learning children benefit from remaining in the mainstream classroom, provided that some instructional accommodations are made. Al-

though the slow learner may not be able to read much above her level of expectancy, in most other respects her learning experiences should be similar to those of other children.

The Child with Speech Impairment

Occasionally, children with reading difficulties also have speech impairments. Inability to enunciate words clearly is often associated with inadequate auditory discrimination. In this case, some difficulty with word recognition is probable. Children who have difficulty because of inadequate auditory discrimination benefit less from the use of phonics as a primary aid to word recognition than do children who discriminate sounds well. They progress better when emphasis is placed on the visual characteristics of words, especially during beginning reading. Also, silent rather than oral reading should be stressed.

Some children with speech defects are embarrassed when asked to read aloud or take part in discussion. In consideration of the child's sensitivities, the teacher should be supportive and tactful. But it is not wise to excuse the child altogether from oral work. The problem of balancing oral and silent work is difficult.

A first step is to give the child proper training with a speech therapist. As the child progresses toward smoother and more fluent speech, he gains self-confidence. One way of correcting speech difficulties is reading aloud. At first, the child should read some well-prepared selection aloud to his teacher in private. As the speech difficulty is overcome, the child will be ready and perhaps eager to do some oral reading in class. The teacher should encourage, but not force, the child to do this. In addition, as the child becomes more sure of himself, remedial measures for correcting specific reading difficulties may be undertaken.

Case Study of an Upper Elementary Grade Student with a Basic Word-Recognition Problem and an Auditory Limitation

Paul, a fifth-grade student, was referred to the achievement center for help in reading during an 8-week summer period. He came from the achievement center service area, where he had attended school during the previous school year. Before that he had attended a school in a district approximately 100 miles away.

School history.   When Paul was admitted to the center, he was 11 years and 5 months old. His school referral form showed that he had had a slight hearing impairment, which was first diagnosed in the first grade. He had received no type of special services before his fifth-grade year. He was referred for resource room services by his fifth-grade teacher, who also requested achievement center services because of her concern for his reading difficulties.

School behavior. According to the referral information, Paul was described as having an excellent attitude toward school, peers, and teachers. His classroom behavior was characterized by his fifth-grade classroom teacher as normal in all ways, except that he "always seemed unusually attentive." The classroom teacher's interpretation was that the child was straining to listen due to his auditory impairment.

Abilities. According to the Wechsler Intelligence Scale for Children (Revised), Paul's ability to learn was above average, with a full-scale I.Q. of 114. The difference between his verbal I.Q. and performance I.Q., however, was large: 98 versus 130. This would place his reading expectancy at Grade 6.6. However, in view of the 32-point discrepancy between his verbal and performance I.Q.s, the clinician noted that had his reading expectancy been based on his verbal I.Q. alone, it would have been 4.8, and had it been based on his performance I.Q. alone, it would have been 7.4. The clinician felt that under the circumstances, it was difficult to conclude definitely what was reasonable to expect of this child in reading, but chose 6.6 as the best of the three alternatives.

Paul was given the Peabody Individual Achievement Test. His grade scores were as follows:

Name of Subtest	Grade Equivalent	Standard Score
Mathematics	6.4	103
Reading Recognition	3.9	85
Reading Comprehension	5.3	97
Spelling	4.2	89
General Information	5.8	100
Total Test	5.0	97

Observation of behavior during testing. Paul was cooperative during testing. He showed some signs of nervousness on the reading subtests, running his fingers through his hair and glancing around the room frequently.

Interpretation of test results. Paul scored below his estimated potential in all areas tested except mathematics. His mathematics vocabulary and reasoning appeared to be adequate.

The clinician decided to test him further in reading and spelling to determine his strengths and weaknesses in those academic subjects, but noted that his mathematical computational ability was not adequately screened by the diagnostic instrument. The clinician noted that Paul's spelling was at a grade level of 4.2 on a test that required him to pick the correctly spelled word from four visual presentations. To prevent a superficial diagnosis, the clinician administered the spelling subtest of the Wide Range Achievement Test. Paul achieved a grade equivalent of 2.9, with a standard score of 77 and a percentile rank of 6. The discrepancy was sufficient to cause suspicion that it was due to the different tasks that the child was expected to perform. Although the Peabody Individual Achievement Test required a highly visual form of spelling, the Wide Range Achievement Test required Paul to spell words from dictation.

Diagnostic Achievement Tests

Paul was given the Durrell Analysis of Reading Difficulty Test (selected sections) and achieved the following results:

Name of Subtest	Grade Equivalent	Comprehension
Oral Reading	4 Low	Good
Silent Reading	4 Low	Fair
Listening Comprehension	3	—
Flash Words	3 High	—
Word Analysis	4 High	—

Observation of behavior. Paul appeared to be nervous during testing. He moved a great deal in his chair and ran his fingers through his hair. He appeared to be trying very hard to do well.

Interpretation of test results. On this test, Paul's oral and silent reading scores were at the same grade level and well below his estimated reading potential. The low scores appeared to be due to slow reading time. His comprehension was better in oral reading, compared with silent reading. Both his flash words and word analysis scores were below his estimated level, with the flash words score being significantly lower. From the results of these four subtests, it appeared that Paul had difficulty in immediate recognition of words, which seemed to result in accurate but slow and inefficient reading at a fourth-grade level. Paul's score on the listening comprehension subtest showed that skill to be one of significant weakness for him. A very important skill necessary for school success, it would require remediation.

Paul's scores on the Silent Reading Diagnostic Test were as follows:

Name of Subtest	Grade Equivalent
Word Recognition Skills	
Total	3.6
Words in Isolation	3.8
Words in Context	3.1
Recognition Techniques	
Total	6.2
Visual Structureal Analysis	6.8
Syllabication	6.0
Word Synthesis	4.5

Phonic Knowledge

Total	3.9
Beginning Sounds	4.0
Ending Sounds	4.0
Vowel and Consonant Sounds	3.0

Observation of behavior. Paul appeared to try very hard. He showed some signs of nervousness: tapping his pencil on the table, running his fingers through his hair, and asking when the test would be over.

Interpretations of test results. Paul's weaknesses on the Silent Reading Diagnostic Test were in the areas of word recognition skills and phonic knowledge. He showed strength in the recognition techniques, mostly in visual analysis, and weakness in his knowledge of phonics, especially in isolated single-letter sounds. His error pattern showed strength in proper left-to-right visual inspection of words, with freedom from reversals and orientation difficulties.

Further informal testing in phonics knowledge revealed that Paul had a secure knowledge of consonant-vowel-consonant (CVC) words and common vowel teams in reading, was insecure in applying his phonics knowledge to spelling, and had great difficulty giving the sounds of isolated letters, especially short vowel sounds and *r*-controlled vowel sounds.

The answers to the diagnostic questions presented in Chapter 7 are:

1. Is Paul correctly classified as a child with a reading disability? Yes; although he possessed some well-developed skills in the visual analysis of words, his overall level of functioning in reading was well below what was reasonable to expect of him. He had a limiting condition complicated by a slight hearing impairment.

2. What is the nature of the training needed? The remedial plan for Paul included five items. (1) Paul was given phonic work-sheet activities stressing visual associations among word elements, larger word parts, and their sounds. He completed them silently. (2) He was taught games using word and phrase cards designed to exemplify various generalizations in phonics to which he was required to respond orally. (3) He was also taught to make visual-mental pictures to aid himself with certain difficult sounds. For example, he chose to think of a view of a city to help himself with the soft sound of *c*. (4) During reading instruction time, and especially at home, Paul was encouraged to read from several high-interest, easy-reading books that were chosen to be at a recreational reading level. He also did some prepared oral reading. (5) Paul was given exercises in which he listened to short, simple stories about subjects that were interesting to him and then paraphrased the stories, answered questions about them, or drew illustrations of them. He also followed increasingly complex oral directions.

3. Who can give the remedial work most effectively? Paul received 40 hours of direct one-to-one instruction during the summer and returned to his school in the fall, where he received daily, small-group instruction. Diagnostic findings were shared with the classroom teacher.

4. How can improvement be made most efficiently? Aside from encouraging Paul to do a lot of recreational reading, the rest of the educational program emphasized overcoming auditory difficulties by using visual means and emphasizing work-sheet activities and games. Although much of his work was done silently, Paul did respond orally in gamelike situations, in prepared reading situations, and in response to short stories read to him.

5. Does the child have any limiting conditions that must be considered? Paul was a friendly, likable, well-mannered boy. But because he was hearing impaired, he was uneasy and insecure in situations in which he had to listen carefully. In teaching him, it seemed to be important to use visual examples and to help him see what was wanted. Once he knew what was expected, he worked well. He enjoyed activities in which he could express himself through drawing, and he was able to draw fairly well.

6. Are there any environmental conditions that might interfere with progress in reading? Paul's parents were completely supportive of him and of the reading program. They were interested in the books he brought home for reading and showed obvious delight in his progress.

Results.   After the summer instruction period, Paul demonstrated mastery of all letter sounds in reading. His silent and oral reading speed became more typical of a fifth- than of a fourth-grade student. His listening improved to the point where he could obey a series of five complex commands with 100-percent accuracy. As Paul progressed in the program, it was noted that he became less tense when he read. His mother also remarked that at home she noticed he was beginning to enjoy reading. Paul continued to make gains in subsequent small-group instruction during his sixth-grade year. Then the instructional emphasis was changed, and letter-sound associations were no longer stressed. Rather, instruction was directed toward helping Paul develop his knowledge of word meanings, increase his fund of sight words, utilize contextual clues, and rely heavily on his visual abilities in reading. Although during his sixth-grade year Paul had not as yet reached his expectancy level in reading, his classroom work reflected improvement in reading and was comparable to that of his classmates.

Summary

In this chapter, we have considered the modifications of remedial instruction that are necessary for correcting reading disabilities that are made more complex because of limiting conditions within the child. Children who have reading problems as well as other disabilities are encountered by every remedial teacher. Frequently, the overall education of these children is directed by specialists who have been trained to teach children with the various disabilities discussed in this chapter. The remedial reading teacher can obtain many helpful suggestions and insights into the particular adjustments needed for a specific child by discussing the child's problems with the special-education teacher. The responsibility of the remedial teacher is to diagnose the reading problem, locate the nature of the confusions in reading, and suggest modifications in reading methods needed for correcting the disability. The classroom teacher, working cooperatively with the remedial reading teacher, should be aware of the child's reading program, so that other phases of her education may be coordinated with the reading-improvement program. What these children need most is an adequate diagnosis of the nature of their reading disabilities and a well-planned program of remedial instruction, modified to take into account their learning disabilities.

Among the children with complex reading disabilities are those who are visually impaired, auditorily impaired, neurologically impaired, emotionally maladjusted, mentally handicapped, or speech impaired. Individualized treatment is necessary for any child with a complex reading disability. The teacher is especially important for these children. He must be patient, understanding, skilled, and versatile in remedial reading because one approach will not fit all children.

Children with moderate visual impairments should be taught by methods that emphasize auditory approaches. Those with more severe visual impairments require, in addition, bright light, large print, and short reading periods. Learning activities that do not require close visual work should be stressed.

Children with mild hearing impairments get along well in normal classroom activities that emphasize visual approaches to reading. Overreliance on phonics should be avoided in teaching hearing-impaired children. For them, visual techniques of word recognition should be stressed. Children with severe and extreme hearing impairments should be taught to read by specialists in deaf education. Emphasis should be upon sight words, the visual characteristics of words, and silent reading.

The few children with reading disabilities who also have neurological impairments constitute some of the most complex cases of remediation. These children require carefully arranged training programs, designed to develop their impaired perceptual and motor skills to the fullest extent possible. They also require remedial reading instruction that is modified to use their areas of strength and to avoid their weak perceptual and motor skills.

Most children with reading disabilities show some symptoms of emotional maladjustment or behavioral disorder. A variety of behaviors are common. Certain students need to be drawn out, while others need to be instructed with a minimum of teacher interaction. Children with behavioral disorders benefit from close management coupled with reasonable goals.

Children with mental disability can also have reading disabilities. In fact, the proportion of reading disabilities in this group is about the same as among children with average and above-average intelligence. With proper instruction, many of those with mental disabilities can learn to read and to maintain their reading competence at a reasonable level. A modified phonics approach stressing drill had been used successfully in remedial work with slow-learning children.

The Hegge-Kirk method, which provides a gradual introduction of skills, much repetition, and a great deal of phonics drill, is a method that has worked well with many educable children with mental disabilities. A broader method, similar to good developmental reading instruction, but highly individualized, seems appropriate for regular reading instruction for children with mental disabilities.

Children with speech difficulties should have corrective work done by a speech specialist. As their speech becomes better and more fluent, they may be reintroduced to regular methods of remedial instruction.

Study Questions

1. What educational adaptations should be considered for children with poor vision?
2. How do educational adaptations for the child with a slight hearing impairment, with a slight to moderate hearing impairment, and with a severe to extreme hearing impairment differ?
3. Why do teachers of children with neurological impairments have to adjust instruction on a daily basis for some of their students?
4. How can children be helped to attend to their reading, to work actively, and to complete their work?
5. What simple educational adaptations benefit slow learners most?

Selected Readings

Gentile, L. M., & McMillan, M. M. (1987). *Stress and reading difficulties: Research, assessment, intervention*. Newark, DE: International Reading Association.

Hallahan, D. P., & Kauffman, J. M. (1991). *Exceptional children* (5th ed.) (pp. 77–341). Englewood Cliffs, NJ: Prentice Hall.

Hardman, M. L., Drew, C. J., Egan, W., & Wolf, B. (1990). *Human exceptionality: Society, school, and family* (3rd ed.) (pp. 87–341). Boston: Allyn and Bacon.

Hart, B. O. (1976). *Teaching reading to deaf children*. New York: Alexander Graham Bell Association for the Deaf.

Hewett, F. M., & Taylor, F. D. (1980). *The emotionally disturbed child in the classroom: The orchestration of success* (2nd ed.) (pp. 176–240, 274–287). Boston: Allyn and Bacon.

Kirk, S. A., & Gallagher, J. J. (1989). *Educating exceptional children* (6th ed.) (pp. 130–447). Boston: Houghton Mifflin.

Moores, D. F. (1982). *Educating the deaf: Psychology, principles, and practices* (2nd ed.) (pp. 286–299). Boston: Houghton Mifflin.

Snowling, M. (1987). *Dyslexia: A cognitive developmental perspective*. New York: Basil Blackwell.

Westman, J. C. (1990). *Handbook of learning disabilities: A multisystem approach* (pp. 643–679). Boston: Allyn and Bacon.

Chapter 14

Correcting Basic Comprehension Deficiencies

At all grade levels, reading instruction must serve to develop comprehension. The fundamental aim of reading instruction is to enable readers to comprehend those printed materials that will serve their goals, be they simple or complex. The acquisition of a sight vocabulary, skill in recognizing words, and linguistic skill in general are all directed at achieving an adequate understanding and interpretation of the meanings embodied in printed symbols. The extent to which these meanings are clearly and accurately understood and interpreted by the reader characterizes the degree to which he has become a good reader.

Comprehension depends on the background knowledge the reader brings to the reading, his vocabulary development, and his ability to translate the author's words into concepts. Through constant attention to words and their use, the child builds a listening vocabulary. He attends to words, phrases, and sentence structure because he finds them valuable in relating to his environment. There is diversity in the vocabulary, use of sentence structure clues (*syntax clues*), and use of essential meaning clues (*semantic clues*) that children bring to reading. The language of children is diversified because of differences in their preschool learning environments, and their language patterns may be quite different one from another.

It has been emphasized that true reading is reading with understanding—that is, comprehension. A person's level of comprehension depends on his facility in using concepts or meanings evolved through experience. To be of use in reading, the concepts acquired through experience must be associated with words or groups of words that are symbols representing the meanings of the concepts. These words become a part of the reader's listening and speaking vocabulary. Then, when the reader recognizes a word or group of words, his perception of the printed symbol stimulates him to recollect or construct meanings for which the symbol stands. The meanings recalled are those possessed by the reader and must have evolved through experience. The meaning of a word may be derived directly from those experiences, or it may consist of a newly constructed meaning that results from combining and reorganizing meanings the reader already possesses. The author brings known ideas together in such a way that the reader senses a new relationship and therefore gains a new idea, concept, or sensory impression. Take, for instance, the meanings aroused when a fourth-grade urban child reads the sentence, "The tired rider drooped in his saddle as his spotted horse walked along the mountain trail." Since the reader has not seen such a rider, he may organize the meaning of the sentence from a variety of remembered visual experiences, such as (1) his father napping with his head bent forward as he rests in an easy chair, (2) a hiking path, (3) a mounted police officer sitting erect on a black horse, (4) a spotted black and white dog, and (5) the scenery during a trip through hilly country. By combining these concepts, the child may achieve an approximation of the meaning intended by the writer of the sentence. So one reads primarily with one's own experiences, which are based upon sensory impressions such as hearing, seeing, tasting, smelling, and touching. Also involved is one's manner of adjusting to all kinds of situations, including the accompanying emotional reactions, and imagination.

The development of concepts that carry meanings begins early in a child's life. Performing activities at home, hearing the talk of parents and other children and adults, listening to radio and viewing television, and taking journeys around the neighborhood and, occasionally, more extended trips are all involved in developing a listening vocabulary. Concepts are acquired as the child begins to use words and, later, sentences suitably. The use of precise oral language is acquired gradually. For application to reading, a meaning must be associated with a word, for in reading, it is only by the use of words that meanings can be recalled. If the meanings that are recalled are to be precise, the words that stand for those meanings have to be in the usage vocabulary of the reader. The degree to which he is able to use a word in his language and thinking determines, to a large extent, how effectively he will be able to use that word in reading.

In normal development, a child's experiences lead him to use sentences for verbal communication. Sentences are groups of words organized into meaningful relationships. Nearly all reading matter is in the form of sentences. How well a reader understands sentences and how skillful he is in using sentence forms determine how well he will be able to read print organized into sentences. The precise meanings of certain words in a sentence are comprehended from the context of the sentence.

The comprehension of sentences is facilitated when reading is done by thought units. A thought unit is a group of words that make up a meaningful sequence in a sentence. For instance, in the sentence, "One of the girls / saw the bricks / start to fall," there are three thought units, indicated by the spacings. Verbal facility in oral communication leads to phrasing into thought units. Improvement in reading sentences by thought units, however, is relatively slow, because it is dependent on increased efficiency in recognizing single words. Only when the child has developed an adequate sight vocabulary, can she group words into thought units. Typically, some grouping (into two-word units) occurs during the latter part of Grade 1. Improvement continues slowly through Grade 3, after which progress becomes more rapid. The average reader is fairly proficient in reading by thought units by the time she reaches the sixth grade.

The child with good verbal facility is able to organize her ideas into thought units, reflected in her spoken sentences. A similar trend is found in reading. The child who is a word-by-word reader has difficulty grasping the meaning of a sentence as a whole. But when a child reads by thought units, the resulting organization of the material aids comprehension. That is, proficiency in perceiving printed material in terms of thought units is usually accompanied by understanding of the material being read.

Attention must also be directed to the comprehension of paragraphs and longer units of discourse. To comprehend the material in a paragraph requires an understanding of the relationships among the sentences in that paragraph. This in turn involves identifying the topic sentence containing the key idea of the paragraph and understanding its relationship to the explanatory or amplifying sentences.

We must also note the relationships among paragraphs in longer selections. In a well-written piece of fiction or nonfiction, the paragraphs are arranged in an orderly manner. Usually, the introductory paragraphs briefly present the plan, central theme, or intended purpose of the piece. Succeeding paragraphs, arranged in logical sequence, carry the narrative through its principal points and on to the ending. In expository material, the paragraphs follow one another in an orderly sequence, providing the details to explain the event, process, or activity outlined in the introduction. To comprehend longer units of discourse, the student needs to understand this relationship between the prefatory and succeeding paragraphs.

Essentially the same processes are involved in comprehending printed material as are involved in understanding spoken words. In both, the perception of words provokes recall of meanings, which leads to comprehension. The meanings provoked by the perceived words depend mainly on two factors: the learner's or reader's entire background of experience and her facility in using language for purposes of communication. Children show marked differences in the length and complexity of selections that they can comprehend.

During the primary grades, when children are in the process of mastering the mechanics of reading, listening comprehension tends to be superior to reading comprehension. It must be kept in mind that when a child begins Grade 1, there is a 6-year lag between her listening comprehension and her reading comprehension. From birth on, the child has been developing listening comprehension. Furthermore, at the first-grade level, a child normally hears more running words in 2 days than she reads in the entire first grade. With increasing maturity and improved reading proficiency through the upper grades, her reading comprehension becomes superior to her listening comprehension. This is because she can stop and reflect on, evaluate or debate, or reread parts of printed material.

The implication of these trends for instruction to improve reading comprehension seems clear: Although word-recognition techniques and other mechanics should be emphasized in the early grades, so that they may become as automatic as possible, comprehension should not be neglected. With mastery of the mechanics, the major portion of the student's attention during reading can be devoted to comprehension. With the teacher's guidance, reading comprehension will become more and more skilled. Thus, a well-balanced program of instruction through all the grades is essential to developing a student's reading comprehension to a level that is as good as or better than his listening comprehension. Of course, such a program will also give appropriate emphasis to oral language and usage and to written expression, both of which play an important role in improving reading.

Essential to mature reading comprehension is the development of the child's *metacognition,* or awareness and control of his own thought processes. Examples of metacognitive abilities are setting one's own reading goals, determining one's own methods for reaching them, deciding for oneself what strategies to pursue if difficulties are encountered, and confirming for oneself when the reading goals are attained. There is also a distinct need for improving the child's ability to comprehend a wide variety of materials for many purposes. Different abilities are used when one is reading to decide which of two items is a better buy, compared with reading to enjoy a book of poetry.

Overcoming specific comprehension defects will be discussed in the next chapter. The reader who does poorly in all types of comprehension is limited either in suitable word-recognition skills, discussed in Chapters 10 and 11, or in one or more of the basic comprehension abilities. This chapter is devoted to a discussion of remedial teaching of the basic comprehension abilities to those with any combination of limited meaning vocabulary, ineffective use of sentence sense, and insufficient comprehension of longer units.

Limited Meaning Vocabulary

Acquisition of the meanings of words is fundamental to all comprehension in reading. When word meanings are ample, precise, and rich, and when semantic variations are understood, children possess the linguistic basis needed for effective reading. Without understanding word meanings satisfactorily, comprehension of either spoken or printed language is impossible.

There are four classifications of vocabulary: listening, speaking, reading, and writing. When a child enters school, her listening vocabulary far exceeds the other three. While estimates of the size of the listening vocabularies of first-grade children vary considerably, the consensus is that the average is nearly 20,000 words. Whatever the actual number, authorities agree that the listening vocabularies of first-grade children are extensive.

Entering first-grade, children's average speaking vocabularies are about 6,000 words. Their reading and writing vocabularies are usually little more than their own names. Within a few years, the typical child's reading vocabulary exceeds her speaking vocabulary, and for some, their reading vocabulary surpasses even their listening vocabulary. Other children, however, will not have developed meaning vocabularies large enough to read and understand materials above the level of the primary grades. These children should be classified as limited in their meaning vocabulary.

There are two tasks in the remediation of a limited meaning vocabulary. First, the meaning vocabulary must be increased, and second, the habit of paying attention to words and their meanings must be established. It must also be recognized that meanings have several aspects, which are not discrete, but overlap in both their importance and their development. The teaching of vocabulary entails more than merely teaching the child to recognize words; it involves, in addition, enriching and extending the meanings of those words.

The meaning of a word has several properties:

1. *Extensiveness,* depending upon the number and kinds of situations in which the word has been met.
2. *Accuracy,* depending upon the skill with which the reader relates her understanding of the meaning to her previous background.
3. *Vividness,* depending upon the emotions, interest, and motivation of the reader.
4. *Retainability,* depending upon the usefulness of the word to the reader.

General Remedial Approaches to Vocabulary Development

Certain general approaches to vocabulary development, used by the classroom teacher from kindergarten on, should be emphasized further for the child who has shown limited growth in learning word meanings and who has failed to establish the habit of attending to them. These approaches include building background knowledge and concepts through the use of both direct and vicarious experiences.

Direct experiences offer many opportunities for building understanding of words and for acquiring the habit of learning their meanings. Children with reading difficulties are frequently lacking in those experiences which furnish a supply of word meanings sufficient to ensure reading with understanding. The remedial reading teacher should therefore provide the needed experiences as much as possible. The procedures are essentially the same as in any good instructional program; the only difference is that the instruction is more individualized. Part of the time, the teacher will be concerned with a single child. At other times, she may deal with a small group of children with similar deficiencies. Furnishing the desired experiences should be integrated with the rest of a well-coordinated program of remedial instruction.

Although teachers often plan field trips to provide direct experiences, many valuable firsthand experiences do not involve elaborate field trips. McCormick

(1987) suggests taking students outside to examine details of the school building or walking to nearby sites. Highlights of the trip can be videotaped for later use in language development. An alternative is to make use of real experiences that students have had outside of school. For example, an athletic event a student has attended can be the basis of vocabulary-building activities. Firsthand experiences within the classroom, as, for example, when a child brings in a model airplane to show the class, when a science experiment is performed, when a presentation is made by a parent or community member, or when children engage in activities such as collecting insects, cooking, or constructing a mural, can form the basis for vocabulary development for a small group of remedial readers. Reutzel (1985) has proposed that, on occasion, enrichment activities suggested as the concluding part of a basal reader lesson can be introduced first, to build experiential background and introduce essential vocabulary.

To gain the most from an experience, careful planning is necessary. As noted by Dolch (1951), experience alone does not educate. Since the meanings a child learns from reading are determined by the nature and clearness of his concepts, direct experiences should yield as varied and accurate concepts as possible. Children should be prepared beforehand, so that they may look for and understand as many aspects of an experience as possible. They should know what to look for and what questions they would like to have answered.

If experiences are to be beneficial, the child must think about them, seek out their meanings, and make use of them in subsequent speaking, listening, reading, and writing. To achieve this end, the child should have the opportunity, both before and after an experience, to discuss it, guided, of course, by the teacher. During this exchange of ideas and answering of questions, there will be the opportunity to define purposes, extend information, clear up misconceptions, and clarify and enrich meanings. The preparation for an experience and the discussion following it tend to be highly worthwhile, whatever the nature of the experience. The development of word meanings and concepts is also promoted by the exchange of experiences in informal discussion. Children should be encouraged to seek meaning in everything they encounter and to ask for additional explanations and further clarification of whatever they do not understand.

Vicarious experiences, such as extensive reading, provide another way in which word meanings and the habit of attending to them is built. Many remedial reading teachers select a book that is highly interesting to a child with reading difficulties and read it aloud to her as a motivating device. In this way, they demonstrate to the child some of the rewards that come from being able to read. These teachers also use the content of the book to teach word meanings and the habit of studying them. The teacher discusses the story with the child, pointing out the well-chosen words and picturesque connotations the author has used. He also shows the child ways in which the content defines the meaning of words and how the author defines words for the reader. Not only the teacher, but also the child, should be aware that she needs to build her vocabulary. The child should be shown how a mature reader uses reading itself to build a vocabulary. This suggestion is applicable as well to the intermediate-grade child and, even more so, to the high school student or adult with a reading disability. Indeed, it is at the last two levels that a vocabulary that has not grown becomes most evident.

The child with reading difficulties should be encouraged to note, by himself, words that are interesting to him, that have unusual meanings, or that are especially descriptive. In this way, he will develop the habit of attending to word meanings and achieve vocabulary-building skills. The child with reading difficulties who is limited in vocabulary should also do extensive independent reading, both in school and at home.

Remedial reading teachers can have interesting, easy-to-read materials available for students and can ask the students to check them out for home reading. Parents can provide a short block of time in the home, free of distractions, when children are expected to read. Classroom teachers can encourage all children, including those who experience reading difficulties, to read more widely by providing short blocks of class time for the children to read books of their own choosing.

Extending and enriching word meanings is aided by abundant reading of interesting and relatively easy materials. For such reading, not more than one unfamiliar word should appear in 100 to 200 running words. Ordinarily, each new book, story, or article a child reads includes both words that are new to him and words that he has previously encountered. The use of old words in a variety of contexts broadens and clarifies their meanings. The more essential new words are seen enough to acquire more and more meaning. It is unrealistic to expect that a clear meaning for every new word will be learned right away, but this does not mean that unfamiliar words should be ignored. It is particularly important that the reader pay attention to any unfamiliar words he meets in context. Eventually, many of these words will become familiar. Motivation is maintained by guiding children to material that catches their interest and is of appropriate difficulty, so that the context will yield the most intelligible clues to the meanings of any new words.

If extensive reading is to help a child develop new concepts and learn new words, the proper use of context is essential. The remedial reading teacher, therefore, needs to evaluate the child's proficiency in the use of context and word structure and to give whatever instruction is necessary. For the best results, monitoring of and training in the use of context must be a continuing process with each child, since this skill is ordinarily slow to develop.

The child with reading difficulties should be encouraged to discuss his independent reading with his remedial reading teacher. The discussion should include new words he has found useful, and further instruction should include using them in his own speech and writing. He should also indicate how he discovered the new word meanings. This should be done because the child must become aware of how he is improving his vocabulary, so that he can continue to do so independently.

Other types of vicarious experiences can be used to build clear, precise, and extensive meanings of words. It is not feasible, and frequently not possible, to develop word meanings by direct experience alone. Much worthwhile experience can be provided students through supplemental media. Among these are models, pictures, exhibits of materials related to a new topic, motion pictures, filmstrips, chalkboard sketches, charts, maps, slides, videotapes, and computer programs.

In using supplemental media to help build word meanings, the remedial reading teacher should recognize that vocabularies are built to the extent that the media are used appropriately. It is inefficient merely to present experiences afforded by these media without first preparing the students for them and without following the presentation with discussion. The preparation should set the purposes for viewing or listening, one of which should be the idea that vocabulary growth is one outcome of the experience. The preparation should indicate the way in which the media may best be studied. During the discussion following the presentation, the students should be encouraged to use the new vocabulary and even to explain the meanings of the terms used. The fundamental steps in teaching a reading selection, discussed in Chapter 9, could well be used with supplemental media. Of course, it is essential that the teacher preview the material before using it in the classroom.

Formal Methods of Enriching Word Meanings

The teaching of word meanings is valuable only when it is done properly. We have emphasized that direct, systematic, well-planned practice reading and otherwise using words in context increases one's vocabulary, but that teaching of words in isolation is usually wasteful and ineffective. This is because the exact meaning of a word frequently depends on its context. Often, familiar words are used in an unfamiliar sense. Teaching these new meanings of old words and the association of a particular meaning with a particular context is a considerable part of vocabulary training.

It is the authors' view that word study is useful in developing meanings only when it consists of using each word in various contexts, associating it with concrete experiences, and giving it a sufficient number of oral and written repetitions in a varied program of extensive reading. The process goes as follows: First of all, new words are studied as they are met in context. That way, learning a word's meaning fulfills the child's immediate concern, namely, her desire to understand the passage she is reading. Then, the child uses the word she has learned in discussion and in writing. Finally, she reads materials in which the word occurs frequently.

Since many words have several meanings or shades of meaning, the initial contact with a new word in context can provide it with only a limited meaning. To extend and enrich the meaning of a new word, the word should also be presented in various contexts that bring out and emphasize some of its different shades of meaning or different meanings. It is also helpful if the remedial reading teacher introduces activities that apply meanings of the word to such concrete situations as demonstrations, giving titles to pictures or drawings, or writing letters. These concrete activities are useful techniques for extending and enriching the meaning of a word through tasks that are not strictly limited to talking and reading. Also, more formal reading practices, such as building a sight vocabulary, using contextual clues and authors' definitions, analyzing word structure, and availing oneself of the dictionary, are helpful in overcoming vocabulary limitations.

Building a Sight Vocabulary

As stated many times throughout this work, a child can make little progress in reading without a basic sight vocabulary. This becomes especially important for the child with reading difficulties. The Dolch Basic Sight Vocabulary (1945) of 220 service words contains about 60 percent of all the words that appear on the pages children read in the elementary grades. With normal progress, a child will have mastered these 220 words during his third year in school.

Many students with reading difficulties are particularly deficient in recognizing and understanding the proper use of the service words. When recognition of these words is being taught, emphasis should be placed on developing an understanding of their meanings in context. One way to do this is to present exercises such as the following:

Directions: Read the sentence on the left, and then underline the word at the right that gives the idea or meaning of the word underlined in the sentence.

1. He sat <u>*under*</u> the tree.	(a) when	(b) where	(c) how	(d) why
2. He left <u>*on*</u> July 6.	(a) when	(b) where	(c) how	(d) why
3. He ran <u>*because*</u> he was late.	(a) when	(b) where	(c) how	(d) why
4. Jack has a <u>*brown*</u> coat.	(a) color	(b) wood	(c) cloth	(d) straw
5. Ann has the <u>*right*</u> box.	(a) odd	(b) wooden	(c) correct	(d) small

The meanings of some of the service words can be taught best in terms of their use in context, rather than by defining them. For instance, in the sentence

When John and Bill came home, mother gave *them* some cookies.

children are taught that *them* means the persons, animals, or things talked or written about.

A variety of sentences to illustrate this meaning should be presented to the child. The meaning of the word should also be discussed with the child and noted in the child's writings. A similar treatment should be given to the meanings of such words as *they, could,* and *what.*

Many of these basic sight words are particularly difficult for children with reading difficulties to learn and retain. It is a cardinal principle that those words which carry the most meaning are remembered best. Without the teacher's guidance, such words as *where, their, by, myself,* and *which* do not have much meaning to many children with reading disabilities.

Using Contextual Clues and Authors' Definitions

The meaning of a new word can frequently be derived from its context. To do this, a child needs to comprehend the rest of the words in the sentence or passage.

Many children with reading problems make ineffective use of context in trying to discover the meanings of unfamiliar words. They should be taught to read the rest of the sentence or passage and then look back and try to decide what the unknown word probably means. For instance, consider the sentence:

The Indians at the powwow were from a *reservation*, the land set aside for Indians who still lived in the northern part of the state.

Here, the word *reservation* acquires meaning from the context that follows it in the rest of the sentence. This type of contextual clue can be called a "forward clue," because the child must read forward to discover the meaning of the word. Another example of the context providing a forward clue is the sentence

Although Mary was surprised when Jack *glared* at her, she was not disturbed by his angry look.

Sometimes, if a sentence is part of a story, other sentences may amplify and clarify the meaning of some of the words in it. Although some meanings derived this way may be incorrect, such training usually builds considerable skill in deriving meaning from context.

Frequently, contextual clues to word meanings come from the author's definitions. Such a definition may be an explanation given in the rest of the sentence, or it may come from another word or phrase in the sentence. Sometimes, it is even in a separate sentence. An example of each of these follows:

1. When Mother did not like the *retort* DiAnn made, she asked her to *answer* more politely.
2. The boys were delighted with the summer *cruise—a voyage by steamship* on the Great Lakes.
3. Just after we got on the train, the *conductor* gave the engineer the signal to start. In addition to *directing the engineer*, the conductor *collects the passengers' tickets.*

Another difficulty children with reading difficulties have is choosing the correct meaning of a word that has multiple meanings. For instance, the correct meaning of *paid* in the sentence, "Jack paid dearly for his mistake" depends on the context given by the entire sentence. In fact, the correct meaning of such words is sensed *only* in terms of the context.

Analyzing Word Structure
Direct, systematic, well-organized practice on words is valuable for the child who has difficulty with word meanings when this practice is on words in context or is related to words used in context. When the remedial reading teacher instills sufficient motivation in the child to lead to a general interest in words, she will find it useful to devote some study to the meanings suggested by common

prefixes, suffixes, and word roots and to synonyms and antonyms. This approach to word study should be used when a word that lends itself to analysis is met in the child's ongoing reading. The following examples are illustrative:

1. The sailors sailed *aboard* the ship (prefix and word root).
2. He has a *kingly* appearance (word root and suffix).
3. The army was *undefeated* (prefix, root, suffix).

In addition to associating root words and affixes with their meanings, the teacher can explore the possibility of creating additional words by adding other prefixes or suffixes to appropriate words. The meanings of the more common word roots, prefixes, and suffixes may be worked out in this manner. The child will be helped by the following types of exercises in identifying and understanding word roots, prefixes, and suffixes.

1. Draw a line under the root word in each of the following, and tell what the root word means:
   worker   untie   kindly
2. Draw a line under the prefix in each of the following, and tell how the prefix changes the meaning of the root word:
   unlike   return   displace
3. Draw a line under the suffix in each of the following, and tell how the suffix changes the meaning of the root word:
   slowly   kindness   doubtful

After roots, prefixes, and suffixes have been identified, their uses in developing meanings should be established through discussion and supplementary activities. One way of doing this is to rewrite sentences. The child is given a sentence containing a word with a prefix. He is asked to identify the word with the prefix and then to rewrite the sentence with a new word or phrase that replaces the prefix, but does not change the meaning of the sentence. An example of a result of this technique is the following:

Your bicycle is unlike mine.
Your bicycle is different from mine.

Training in structural aids to meaning should be given in context, as illustrated in the following exercises:

The prefix *un* can mean (a) not, (b) opposite action, or (c) something was removed. Show which meaning is implied by putting the appropriate letter before each sentence.

_____ 1. The boy untied the horse.
_____ 2. The man was unkind to the horse.
_____ 3. The rider was unhorsed.

Complete the following sentences:

1. A snowball is a ball made of _____ .
2. A steamboat is a boat run by _____ .
3. A flowerpot is a pot for a _____ .
4. A fireplace is a place to have a _____ .

Using the Dictionary

Proper use of a suitable dictionary can be an important aid to the child who is having difficulty developing word meanings. Few children acquire the habit of consulting a dictionary or know the wealth of fascinating information that can be found in a dictionary. Development of the habit depends upon a systematic program of instruction carried out by a skilled and enthusiastic remedial reading teacher. No child will enjoy using a dictionary to get word meanings until she has become skillful in finding a desired word quickly. After finding the word, the child must know how to select, from the several meanings listed, the one that fits the context from which the word came. This means that she must grasp the meaning of the rest of the sentence or paragraph in which the unknown word occurs. Considerable training is required to develop skill in choosing correct dictionary meanings. Activities of the following type are easily found or constructed:

Directions: Several numbered definitions are given for the word in heavy black type. Read the word and its definitions. Next, read the sentences below the definitions. Write the number of the definition in front of the sentence in which the meaning of the word is used.

grate: (1) grind off in small pieces, (2) rub with a harsh sound, (3) have any annoying or unpleasant effect.

_____ Please *grate* the cheese to put on the salad.
_____ Mary's manners always *grate* on me.

In addition to developing skill in using the dictionary to find word meanings, this type of exercise provides further training in deriving meanings from contextual clues and in noting different meanings for the same word. Similarly, experiences with synonyms and antonyms enrich word meanings when the words are studied in context.

Informal Methods of Enriching Word Meanings

There are many informal approaches to enriching and expanding the meanings of the words found in the reading vocabularies of children. These approaches also develop the word-study habits necessary for continuing growth in the reading vocabularies of intermediate-level, high school, and adult readers. The following activity is merely one of many possible suggestions:

As the horse approached his stable, he _____ ahead, but his rider _____ _____ in the saddle.

The student is to think of as many groups of words as he can to complete the sentence in order to change the picture the sentence paints. The student might think of groups such as

> galloped, slumped over
> trudged, sat erect
> walked, felt insecure
> stumbled, sat confidently

The cloze procedure, often used in testing comprehension, can also be used in an imaginative application to the study of word meanings.

The child with reading difficulties might help his remedial reading teacher by writing similar sentences for younger readers. Multiple-choice exercises using antonyms, synonyms, or semantic variations could be constructed. A dictionary could be used to find the choices. This would be both an appealing and a useful dictionary activity. Another dictionary activity that would be both interesting and instructive would be for the child with a limited meaning vocabulary to make his own dictionary of new words he has found interesting. He would see his list of words grow, and he would discover new meanings for many of the words.

Encouraging the child to write is invariably helpful. He should be prompted to use the new words he has learned. Experience charts are an especially effective activity for building vocabulary when groups of children work together. The group should discuss the choice of words while making the experience chart and decide why one word expresses an idea better than another.

Ineffective Use of Sentence Sense

Besides knowing the meanings of words, other basic comprehension skills are needed to understand sentences. Among them are reading in thought units, using punctuation as an aid to meaning, interpreting connectives, identifying pronoun-antecedent relationships, and adjusting to varied sentence structures.

Grouping Words into Thought Units

Many children with reading difficulties either are word-by-word readers or are inclined to group words inappropriately, so that it is impossible for them to gain a clear comprehension of an entire sentence. At the start of instruction in reading, a child must recognize each word separately. In the beginning, she is required by her inexperience to study each word closely in order to identify it at all, so there is only a slight chance that she will be able to group several words together for recognition as a thought unit. As the child becomes more adept at word identification, and as she builds a stock of words that she can recognize at sight, she is able to group some of them together.

The first grouping by thought units rather than by individual words is two-word combinations, such as "the cat," "Daddy said," or "to ride." This simple grouping of words takes place only after the child is very familiar with each of the words and only when they are set off together by the typography. For example, in the sentence, "Daddy said, 'We can stop,' " the punctuation makes the grouping of "Daddy said" easy to detect. Later, when the child is expected to read two-line sentences, additional help is given to help the child learn to read in thought units. For example, in the two-line sentence

> Meg said, "Put the duck
> in the water."

the child is almost forced by the format to read by thought units. Still later, she is expected to be able to analyze a sentence into thought units rapidly, as she progresses along the line of print. This is a mature type of reading that is predicated on recognizing the words and phrases at sight.

Inability to read in thought units can be diagnosed in several ways. The simplest method is to listen to the child read easy material orally. If she reads in a word-by-word manner, or if she clusters words in meaningless groups, she is probably ineffective in recognizing thought units in her silent reading, and she is certainly not reading orally by thought units. Another method of diagnosing this inability is to flash phrases before the child for recognition. If she reads the phrases noticeably less well than does a child with generally equal reading ability, it is safe to assume that she has limited ability in recognizing thought units in isolation. It is then probable that she cannot recognize thought units in a sentence either.

Remedial methods must be based on the premise that ultimately the child will have to learn to recognize meaningful groups of words as she silently reads consecutive sentences. She will then be reading sentences, not isolated thought units. But skill in reading by groups of words is dependent in part on the ability to segment sentences into reasonable units. Also, it is necessary for the child to convert the groups of words she separates into single ideas. Remedial instruction must teach the child to recognize thought units of several words rapidly and also to locate such groups of words in the sentences she reads. Many readers who are limited in recognizing thought units are able to recognize isolated thought units flashed before them, but are incapable of reading whole sentences silently or aloud by thought units. Since they cannot readily divide a sentence into proper clusters of words, they must read each word separately.

Remedial instruction designed to enable a child to read in thought units either should be done in context, or the phrases learned in isolation should be read immediately in complete sentences. Following are some suggestions for instruction and practice in reading by thought units:

1. Whenever the remedial reading teacher introduces new words from a selection, the words should be read in the phrases in which they will appear in the selection.
2. After a selection has been read, the child can reread it to locate certain expressive phrases suggested by the teacher.
3. Having the child prepare material to read orally provides excellent experience in reading by thought units. The teacher should stress that the selection should be read "like talking."
4. Multiple-choice exercises in which phrases appear as answers and distractors may be used.

   a. Draw a line under the correct phrase to complete the sentence.

   over the fence.

   (1) The ball sailed down under the hole.
   under the water.

   flew away

   (2) The dog talked softly.
   ran fast.

   b. On the pages given, quickly find the phrases at the right and answer these questions.

Question	Phrase
Where was the rooster?	(near the barn)
Who was happy?	(the white bear)
When did the boys swim?	(one summer day)

   c. Mark off the thought units in the following sentences, and tell the *who, what, did what, where,* or *why* questions they answer.

   1. The large truck went slowly down the street.
   2. Billy and Frank quickly made a snow fort to hide behind.

   d. Draw a line from the phrase to the word that has a similar meaning.

a big meal	stroke
to rub softly	feast
to cut down	chop

   e. Find these phrases in your book on the page I give, and tell what they mean.

answer the knock	with a splash
bright as stars	cry for help
break the horse	fine fishing country

   f. On the pages I tell you, find a phrase that makes you:

hear something	(the screaming gulls)
feel something	(the cool breeze)

see something	(colored autumn leaves)
smell something	(sweet-scented flowers)
taste something	(a sour apple)

5. The use of rapid-exposure techniques, described in Chapter 11, will aid in teaching children with reading disabilities to recognize a phrase or thought unit with one eye fixation. For group work, an opaque projector can be used. A piece of cardboard is placed before the lens and moved up and down to expose thought units for about a half second. The phrases for this work should be in the form of sentences, such as the following:

A brown beaver
was at work
near the island.
He was making
a tunnel
at the bottom
of the pond.

6. Sentences may be separated into thought units to be read by the children:

| The old man | with the angry face | was happy now. |
| He had found | the one thing | he liked. |

Using Punctuation

Ineffective interpretation of punctuation or ignoring it altogether may also hinder sentence comprehension. Possibly the most common problem with punctuation among children with reading difficulties is the failure to learn the more common uses of the comma—that is, to separate words and groups of words written as a series in a sentence, to set off an appositive, or to set off a parenthetical expression in a sentence.

Informal procedures must be used to find out whether a child is using punctuation properly. For instance, commas that are used properly should aid in grouping words into thought units. Much is learned about a child's use of commas by having him read sentences aloud. If the child does not use commas to guide inflection and emphasis in phrasing, it is likely that he does not understand the function of the punctuation marks in what he reads. If this is so, he will have difficulty comprehending the full meaning of sentences. To illustrate the use of commas, sentences such as the following may be taken from books the child is reading:

1. Deer, too, were there.
2. They stood still, heads up, listening.
3. Mary said, "Now we can go home."
4. After dark, when all was quiet, he walked slowly down the street.

A few children will need supervision to recognize that a capital letter is a clue to the beginning of a sentence and that a period or question mark signals the end of a sentence.

Remedial training in the use of punctuation to facilitate comprehension involves at least two aspects: (1) Through discussion, the student is made aware that the punctuation within a sentence indicates the relationship between what has just been read and what follows; and (2) the student is given ample practice with sentences from his own reading. Training should start with relatively simple sentences and progress gradually to more complex ones. In all cases, the sentences should be made of words the child knows and can pronounce. In general, direct explanation and supervised practice lead to improvement.

In a similar manner, as the child progresses in his reading, he may need help interpreting semicolons, colons, and dashes. Training in this aspect of reading is necessary for full sentence comprehension and for reading aloud. In fact, interpretive oral reading helps to develop this skill.

Interpreting Connectives

The child who is weak in sentence comprehension must be taught how a sentence is constructed. Remedial teaching should begin with direct sentences whose parts are easily found. Then, more complex sentences should be introduced. Finally, the child should be taught the importance of learning connectives. She should be shown that they can change the anticipated flow of the thought or qualify it in some way. This problem is often encountered in social studies material. Teaching the function of connectives should start with relatively simple illustrations. Then some examples, perhaps taken from the student's social studies textbook, should be provided. A sentence similar to the following might be used:

We were going swimming, but a thunderstorm began, so we decided to watch television instead.

After the sentence is read, the child can be asked whether the people went swimming, what words show that they did not go, and why they changed their minds.

Identifying Pronoun-Antecedent Relationships

Sometimes, difficulties arise when the person or object referred to by a pronoun is not readily grasped. Children who have difficulty with basic comprehension often have this problem. To deal with it, examples can be discussed from books a child is reading, or the following type of exercises can be used for remedial instruction:

Directions: In the following sentences, the underlined word is used in place of the name of a person or thing mentioned earlier or later in the sentence. Draw a circle around the word or words that tell who or what is meant by the underlined word.

1. After <u>he</u> arrived home from school, Jack shoveled the snow off the walk.
2. As the horses were freed, <u>they</u> galloped across the field.
3. Bill looked on with interest as <u>his</u> sister, Jane, rode toward <u>him</u> on <u>her</u> new bicycle.

Using Syntax

Understanding word order within a sentence is vital to understanding the sentence. For example, the sentence, *Only Tom went to the store,* has a meaning different from *Tom went to the only store.* The child who cannot use syntax to grasp meaning while reading often will not comprehend what he has read. The child should be encouraged to note relationships among the various words in a sentence, such as the actor, the action, and the object of the action. Exercises designed to bring together knowledge of spoken language and reading comprehension are also helpful in this regard.

1. Read this sentence:
   The big gray elephants at the zoo wanted more roasted peanuts.

   a. Put "C" before the three most important words in the sentence, in order.
      _____ zoo peanuts
      _____ peanuts wanted elephants
      _____ elephants wanted peanuts
   b. Put "C" before the words that show that the elephants had already had some peanuts.
      _____ wanted zoo peanuts
      _____ wanted roasted peanuts
      _____ wanted more peanuts
      _____ elephants roasted peanuts

2. Read this sentence:
   The boys ran to the circus to see the clowns do funny tricks.

   a. Who did tricks?
      _____ the boys   _____ the clowns   _____ the circus
   b. Why did the boys run to the circus?
      _____ to see the clowns   _____ to do some tricks
   c. Where did the boys run?
      _____ to see the clowns   _____ to the circus
   d. What was funny?
      _____the tricks   _____ the boys   _____ the circus

Adjusting to Varied Sentence Structures

The inability of readers to sort out and properly relate the meanings of different parts of a sentence is sometimes complicated by sentence structure. For instance, difficulties may arise when the subject is last or when it is between two parts of the predicate, rather than at the beginning. Informal methods for diagnosing such difficulties and for remedial instruction are similar to those described previously for developing sentence comprehension. For example, the child could be asked what word answers the question "Who?" in each of the following sentences: "Hearing the low, rumbling sound again, Anita suddenly remembered something" and "Then, into the cool water dove Margo."

Writers themselves can hinder sentence comprehension. When sentences are excessively long and too complex, they prevent the reader from understanding them clearly. Sometimes, sentences are just written poorly. Nevertheless, the reader must learn to adjust if he wishes to read them.

The teacher can help the reader develop flexibility through analyzing of sentences. For example, the student can be asked to tell whether a phrase signifies when, why, how, what, or where, as in the following example:

The large farm belongs to father.
   "The large farm" tells us when, why, how, what, or where?

Because Annemarie was ill, she did not go to school.
   "Because Annemarie was ill" tells us when, why, how, what, or where?
   "to school" tells us when, why, how, what, or where?

A variation of the preceding example is to find and copy the word or words that answer the question "who?" or "where?" After the pupil is informed that the sentences answer the questions "who?" and "where?" she is directed to write, below the sentences, the word or words that answer the questions.

1. The boy went to the chalkboard to write the word.
2. "From school to the park is only one-half mile," explained the teacher.

	Words that tell	
Sentence Number	Who?	Where?
1	⸻	⸻
2	⸻	⸻

The responses may be made by having the child draw a line under the words that answer the question "where?" and the like.

Activities and exercises similar to the foregoing may be constructed directly from any books the children are currently reading. Sample items may be found in Mueser (1981).

Insufficient Comprehension of Longer Units

Frequently, children with basic comprehension problems are unable to understand the meaning of a paragraph. These children are apt to consider each sentence as a separate unit, unrelated to the other sentences in the paragraph. It is possible for them to read and understand words, thought units, and sentences and yet not comprehend fully the connected material in a paragraph. Similarly, some children are unable to sense the relationships among paragraphs in various narrative and expository materials. Each of these is a separate difficulty and must be dealt with in its own way.

Knowledge of Organization within a Paragraph

Comprehension of a paragraph requires an understanding of the relationships among the sentences of the paragraph. Many readers who have difficulty with comprehension need guidance in identifying the topic sentence of the paragraph and in relating it to other, explanatory or amplifying sentences within the paragraph.

Remedial teaching in regard to the organization of the sentences in the paragraph centers on helping the child understand the interrelationships among those sentences. Activities requiring the child to find which one of several statements best represents the general meaning of a given paragraph are effective. Calling attention to various types of organization in paragraphs is even more important in increasing comprehension. This instruction should start with the commonest type of paragraph, that in which the topic sentence is presented first and the sentences that follow it expand the main idea. A second type of paragraph presents a series of related facts and concepts, and the topic sentence comes last in the form of a generalization. This type of paragraph is used frequently in scientific writing. Finally, the child should be taught to recognize a third type of paragraph organization, one in which introductory concepts are presented initially, a summary topic sentence follows, and the paragraph is concluded with sentences that modify or limit the general idea. This type of paragraph is often found in social studies materials.

To develop skill in finding the topic sentence, the child is given demonstrations and explanations, using a variety of paragraphs. Then he is asked to indicate the topic sentence in other paragraphs. Besides this, the child should learn how the other sentences in the paragraph develop the idea presented in the topic sentence—by details, by emphasis, by explanations, by contrast, and by repetition of the same idea in other words. One technique for teaching this skill is to number the sentences in a paragraph, and then, through questions and analysis, the role of each sentence in relation to the others is determined.

A well-written paragraph is concerned with one central idea. The child can be trained to grasp this idea in various ways. (1) A paragraph is given, followed by three phrases, one of which best expresses the topic of the paragraph. The child indicates which one is best. (2) The child is asked to write a "title" for a paragraph or to express what the paragraph is about in his own words. (3) The child is given a topic sentence and asked to write a short paragraph with supporting and amplifying sentences. (4) The child is given a paragraph that is correct, except for one sentence which has been added. He is asked to underline the topic sentence and then to cross out the sentence that does not belong.

Although comprehending paragraphs is important in all reading, it is *essential* for a clear understanding of the content fields. Some training in understanding the unity of a paragraph is usually introduced when a third-grade reading ability is reached. More formal training to develop the child's comprehension of paragraphs becomes a regular part of reading instruction at the intermediate grade levels.

Relating the Parts of a Long Selection

For full comprehension of longer units, the child should be taught to sense the relationships among the paragraphs that make up the selection (Hoskins, 1986). Usually, in good expository writing, the introductory paragraphs state what is to be described or explained or set forth the reasons for writing about it. The paragraphs that follow then give the details or the explanation in logical sequence. Finally, the last paragraph or two state the outcome or conclusion, or they summarize what has been said.

In well-written narratives, the text is organized around important elements in the story and the relationships among them (Temple & Mowery, 1985). For example, stories commonly comprise three parts: (1) the beginning, which gives the setting (the time or the place of the story, or both) and sometimes also the characters; (2) the body of the story, which includes the plot and the actions and reactions of the protagonist and others, and (3) the final paragraphs, which relate the resolution of the problem or the conclusion of the events. Kent (1984) cautions that teachers need to be aware of the differences between the expository and the narrative text structure in order to teach useful strategies for comprehending each.

The remedial reading teacher assists the child who is having difficulty comprehending longer units by teaching her text structure so that she understands the relationships among paragraphs better and is able to identify the main parts of stories and expository materials. Idol (1987) emphasizes the importance of the teacher demonstrating and modeling correct responses explicitly. Some computer programs guide students in writing well-organized narrative or expository text.

In teaching textual structure, a teacher might try one of the following techniques: (1) Explain the main parts and elements of a story, and then demonstrate how to find these parts with examples. Ask questions about each part that are designed to show its content. (2) Discuss the transitional expressions that often start a paragraph. Demonstrate that these expressions precede the main idea or topic of many of the paragraphs from a selection, using examples such as (a) *But something else has happened. . .* , (b) *Then he turned to Jesse . . .* , (c) *When this was done, she began. . . .* (3) Have the child write one sentence to express the main idea in each paragraph of a story. Then have her join the sentences together in a coordinated pattern of thought, using transitional words or phrases as needed. (4) Help the child discover the pattern or grammar of a story, and help her compose an original story following the same pattern. With expository materials, it is useful to have the student make an outline of the main and subordinate ideas.

According to research by Smith and Friend (1986), direct instruction in textual structure improves comprehension, even for older students who are experiencing severe difficulty in reading comprehension.

Summary

To read means to read with understanding. To accomplish this, the student must comprehend words, thought units, sentences, paragraphs, and longer units. Instruction for developing comprehension coordinates all of these.

Listening comprehension develops ahead of reading comprehension in the early grades. As the mechanics of reading are mastered, reading comprehension catches up with and soon equals listening comprehension. With still further progress in reading, reading comprehension becomes superior.

Comprehension depends upon concepts or meanings evolved through experience. Any deficiencies that are discovered should be remedied as much as possible. Direct experience is best, supplemented by vicarious experience. The aim of either is to form concepts associated with words, which can be used by the student in thinking, speaking, listening, writing, and reading.

Instructional techniques for teaching word meanings include demonstrating the use of contextual clues, ensuring that the student reads extensively, encouraging the attitude of insisting that words read be understood, encouraging the attitude of noting authors' definitions, and developing the student's word study and dictionary skills. For these techniques to be effective, all words studied must be used in context.

To comprehend sentences, the child must understand the words in them and the relationships among those words. He must also be able to read by thought units, interpret punctuation, and understand figures of speech, symbolic expressions, and semantic variations. Remedial instruction for sentence comprehension is based on informal activities involving books the child is currently reading.

The comprehension of paragraphs depends on the comprehension of the sentences in them and of the relationships among those sentences. Similarly, the comprehension of longer units is based upon the comprehension of paragraphs and of the relationships among them.

Study Questions

1. For the successful reader, what is the relationship between listening comprehension and reading comprehension through the grades? What part does the mechanics of reading play in this relationship?

2. If experiences alone do not educate a student, what can a teacher do to ensure that they do?
3. Why do some students who have adequate word recognition in reading experience difficulty comprehending sentences?
4. What are some specific techniques to help a child who can read and understand words and sentences, but who is unable to understand the meaning of a paragraph?
5. How do the writing activities suggested for correcting basic comprehension deficiencies help a child read better?

Selected Readings

Durkin, D. (1987). *Teaching young children to read* (4th ed.) (pp. 376–411). Boston: Allyn and Bacon.

Harris, A. J., & Sipay, E. R. (1990). *How to increase reading ability* (9th ed.) (pp. 510–598). New York: Longman.

Heilman, A. W., Blair, T. R., & Rupley, W. H. (1986). *Principles and practices of teaching reading* (6th ed.) (pp. 183–225). Columbus, OH: Merrill.

Jewell, M. G., & Zintz, M. V. (1986). *Learning to read naturally* (pp. 130–159). Dubuque, IA: Kendall/Hunt.

Maggart, Z. R., & Zintz, M. V. (1990). *Corrective reading* (6th ed.) (pp. 298–333). Dubuque, IA: Wm. C. Brown.

Robinson, H. A., Faraone, V., Hittleman, D. R., & Unruh, E. (1990). *Reading comprehension instruction 1783–1987: A review of trends and research.* Newark, DE: International Reading Association.

Rubin, D. (1991). *Diagnosis and correction in reading instruction* (2nd ed.) (pp. 322–381). Boston: Allyn and Bacon.

Rupley, W. H., & Blair, T. R. (1989). *Reading diagnosis and remediation* (3rd ed.) (pp. 201–268). Columbus, OH: Merrill.

Spache, G. D., & Spache, E. B. (1986). *Reading in the elementary school* (5th ed.) (pp. 544–563). Boston: Allyn and Bacon.

Taylor, B., Harris, L. A., & Pearson, P. D. (1988). *Reading difficulties: Instruction and assessment* (pp. 200–234). New York: Random House.

Vacca, J. A., Vacca, R. T., & Gove, M. K. (1987). *Reading and learning to read* (pp. 142–203). Boston: Little, Brown.

Chapter 15

Overcoming Specific Comprehension Limitations

The preceding chapters of this book have considered those limitations in reading abilities that affect the child's entire reading achievement. Deficiencies in basic comprehension and in word recognition prevent the effective reading of all types of materials and, unless corrected, preclude future reading progress. The children so far discussed are those classified as having *limiting* or *complex* reading problems. Often, they have difficulties in reading that are so severe or so complicated by various handicaps that they require extensive remedial adjustments.

This chapter and the next will consider students who are experiencing reading difficulties because of a *specific immaturity*. These students need corrections in reading patterns that must be made if maturity in reading and satisfactory communication between author and reader are to be achieved. Basically, they are competent readers, but they have specific problems that must be corrected if their full reading potential is to be realized. The reader with a specific immaturity can and should receive corrective training.

The kind of remedial teaching discussed in this chapter is of special importance in the intermediate grades, high school, and adult education programs. Students with difficulties in the areas at which such teaching is directed are often unable to progress as well as they should in their general education, besides their reading advancement. Three types of difficulties are seen most frequently: limitations in specific comprehension abilities, insufficient development of basic study skills, and deficiencies in reading the content of various fields of study.

Limitations in Specific Comprehension Abilities

Although the basic comprehension abilities discussed in the preceding chapter underlie the communicative act of reading, they alone are not sufficient to make a child a good reader. Rather, the child needs a group of diversified comprehension abilities and needs to use them flexibly. Unfortunately, there are many adults whose reading programs did not give them flexibility in the use of specific comprehension abilities. Some people read all material as though each illustrative detail were to be retained forever. They have not developed such higher order comprehension abilities as the ability to organize facts so that generalizations can be made, the ability to evaluate what they are reading, or the ability to reflect upon what they are reading. Other people read primarily for enjoyment and retain little of the content in material that should be read for more specific purposes.

Location and Recall of Information Read

To locate and recall information one has read requires exact, careful reading. It involves identifying and recalling specific items of information, noting details within a passage, retaining fundamental concepts, using facts to answer specific questions, and finding statements to confirm an assertion or answer a general question. These specific comprehension abilities begin developing as a part of the child's early reading experiences and increase as long as systematic training is given. Many children, however, fail to become effective at locating and retaining factual information. On the other hand, numerous other children are found to be overly exact at these tasks. These latter should be encouraged to read relatively uncomplicated material for the purpose of enjoyment. They should read to predict what is going to happen next or to get a general impression of a story or passage.

Children who are not demanding enough in their reading or who cannot remember details within a passage when it is necessary to do so should be given reading that requires the accumulation of factual information with close attention to detail and that requires that this factual information be used. For these purposes, expository material is better than narrative. Material that is not overly challenging, but that contains an abundance of facts, is most useful in developing the ability to read for informational purposes.

The following are a few samples of exercises that give the child experience in reading to locate and retain factual information:

1. Read a selection about animals to find all the things a beaver uses in making its home.
2. Reread the selection to find additional facts to add to your list about the animals discussed.
3. Find and read sentences to prove or disprove these statements:
   a. A big sea lion weighs about 600 pounds.
   b. A big elephant may be 8 feet high.

    c. A baby kangaroo sleeps in its mother's pouch.
    d. A full-grown kangaroo weighs more that a sea lion.
    e. Baboons like to swim.

In addition to providing appropriate materials and purposes for reading to locate and recall information, teachers should instruct students directly and model for them how to answer questions through reading. Armbruster (1992) suggests that there are three steps in answering questions through reading: interpreting the question, locating the required information, and formulating the answer. Teachers can model these steps by (1) thinking aloud about what a question means, rephrasing the question, and inviting students to put the question in their own words or to try to say the question in a different way, (2) demonstrating how to find the answer to a question, and (3) modeling how to formulate a well-constructed answer. In thinking aloud about their answers, teachers can review the entire process, including how they decided what information to retain and what to omit. Cooperative discussion of the processes by which the student obtained the answers and of the appropriateness of the answers will provide a nonintimidating form of practice.

In mature reading, however, it is the reader who must set the purposes for and ask the questions about what is read. Students can be directly taught how to do these through demonstration and modeling—for example, by means of the active comprehension strategy described by Nolte and Singer (1985). To teach this strategy, the teacher models questions at pertinent points in a story and then gradually invites the students to ask questions as well. Eventually, the teacher's questions are phased out and the students' questions are phased in. In this way, self-questioning is not something done before reading, after reading, or as an aid to reading; but rather, it becomes a part of reading. Our own research suggests that self-questioning enhances children's recall of material they have read.

Among the ways students can use information obtained through reading are incorporating the information into their writing, exchanging it with others in group discussion, contributing it to group projects, and creating a graphic representation of the information, such as by the use of semantic webs.

Sense of Organization of Material

Effectiveness in sensing the order or relationship among facts read includes abilities such as classifying and listing facts in a sensible manner, establishing a sequence of events, following a series of related directions, sensing relationships, and distinguishing between major ideas and related facts. These are exacting requirements, but they are important. Reading to organize information begins in children's prereading activities, when, for example, they classify pictures of animals into those they would see on a farm and those they would see in a forest or when they arrange a series of pictures in an orderly sequence of events. Some children fail to become effective in sensing the organization and relationship among the ideas they are reading. These children need remedial work to become proficient in this area of comprehension.

Material for developing skill in organizing and sensing relationships among facts must contain an abundance of facts. Science and social studies materials at an appropriate level of difficulty can be used for the purpose. The remedial reading teacher must provide reasons for requiring the child to organize reading material, and she should monitor the child's effectiveness in organizing the material. The following are some specific purposes for sensing the organization of ideas and information in what one is reading:

1. Read about animals to make a summary chart showing where they live, what they eat, how to recognize them, how they protect themselves, who their enemies are, and how they get ready for winter.
2. Read to make a list of (a) the kinds of damage done by floods and (b) means that are used to prevent such damage.
3. Read to map the information given about petroleum under the following headings: how petroleum was formed, how oil wells are located, how oil is obtained from below the ground, the uses of petroleum, and how we can conserve our petroleum resources.
4. Read to find and list, in order, the steps taken by Charles Hall in his experiments to find a quick and inexpensive way of changing alumina into aluminum.
5. Read to find out in what ways the life of a child who lives by the sea in Brittany is the same as and how it is different from that of a child who lives in Bora Bora.

Other ways students learn to sense an author's organization include making an outline of the main ideas and important details from their reading, making a visual representation of the organization of their reading through the use of semantic maps or webs, and writing notes from their reading in their own words. Students can also complete study guides that emphasize the organization of a passage and write passages patterned after these guides (Miller & George, 1992).

Evaluation of What Is Read

Evaluating what is read involves not only reading and understanding what the author said, but reflecting on the material so that critical judgments can be made. It includes such specific types of comprehension as differentiating between fancy, fact, and opinion; judging the reasonableness and relevancy of ideas presented; sensing implied meanings; establishing cause-and-effect relationships; making comparisons; judging the authenticity of material read; and critically appraising the validity of the author's presentation. Like all other comprehension abilities, these have their start in early reading instruction and develop as long as growth in reading continues. For example, it is appropriate, even at the prereading level, to ask a child whether a fanciful tale really could have happened. Reading for evaluation is one of the most important types of reading. The person who is taught to read, but not to reflect on what she has read, is in danger of coming to faulty conclusions when she reads. The child who is unable to read critically and to judge the reasonableness of material at her level of advancement should be given remedial instruction to overcome this deficiency. Reading for evaluation develops gradually and should not be left to chance.

The best material for learning how to evaluate what one reads is material (1) that is written to influence people, (2) in which ideas are implied rather than directly stated, (3) in which there are cause-and-effect relationships, or (4) in which statements of fact and opinion can be compared. Any material that is at the child's general reading level may be used to increase her ability to evaluate what she reads, including newspaper and magazine articles, stories, and advertisements. Comprehension activities that improve one's ability in this regard often require the child to reread material in order to evaluate it in a variety of ways. The following exercises illustrate material that teaches the child to judge, reflect on, and evaluate what she has read:

1. Have the child read a somewhat fanciful story about animals and then reread it to distinguish between the realistic and fanciful statements.
2. Have the child decide from the titles of stories whether they are likely to be real or fanciful.
3. Have the child discuss whether a story read could have happened and give reasons for her opinion.
4. Have the child find and read aloud just the part that proves a point and no more.
5. Have the child find facts that are relevant to a topic.
6. Have the child read to find statements which characters make that the child knows to be true and those that are opinions.

Interpretation of Content

The ability to interpret content involves extending the understanding of the selection beyond the statements of the author. It differs from organizing what is read in that it requires a child to derive new ideas from what he reads. Reading to interpret includes understanding the significance of a selection read, drawing an inference or conclusion that is not expressly stated, predicting the outcome of given events, forming one's own opinions, and inferring time and measurement relationships. These comprehension abilities require the reorganization of information and ideas expressed so that new relationships can be understood. Some children with good general reading ability find it difficult to interpret what they read.

The ability to interpret is best developed in material that requires careful, considered judgments. It is also encouraged by setting purposes for reading that necessitate reflecting upon what is read. The child must learn to take the facts and ideas presented, reorganize them, and recognize relationships among them that he did not at first find apparent. Social studies and science lend themselves to these sorts of reasoning, but well-written narratives and essays are also useful in developing the ability to interpret.

The main requirement of remedial instruction for the reader who has difficulty interpreting, but who is otherwise a capable reader, is to have him read for purposes that cause him to reflect upon what he reads. The following exercises illustrate the nature of assignments that encourage interpretive reading:

1. Have the children predict the ending of a story.
2. Have the children read to find out why the signing of the Magna Carta is important to them.
3. Have the children form conclusions about how climatic conditions have affected the ways in which people live.

In addition, the teacher should directly instruct the child in how to interpret content. For example, she might explain why it is important to understand the significance of a passage and describe how to do it. She should also demonstrate the process of interpretation, thinking aloud, for instance, to model how she reasons beyond specific facts to come to a conclusion about a passage. Finally, providing materials and setting purposes that suit a student's prior knowledge and interests facilitates successful interpretation, as does the pleasant discussion of a passage with the teacher or with a congenial small group.

Appreciative Abilities

Appreciative abilities are somewhat different from the other abilities discussed in this chapter. The ability to appreciate centers on the aesthetic qualities of reading. Abilities such as discerning the mood expressed by the author; understanding the plot, humor, and action of a story; forming various sensory impressions from the story; and recognizing the distinctive qualities of the characters one reads about are essential for appreciating what is read. The reading program and the guided literature program are designed to build these abilities.

The child who cannot visualize the scene described in her reading, or sense the feeling of aloneness experienced by an early explorer, or appreciate the humor of an absurd situation has a reading difficulty, even though she may be able to understand, organize, evaluate, and interpret factual content satisfactorily. The best materials for developing the appreciative abilities in regard to reading are works of literature, short stories, and anthologies. The child must read for reasons that encourage appreciation. It would be unfortunate to force the factual type of reading, required for other comprehension abilities, on a child who is reading material that should be read for personal development, appreciation, or its own beauty.

To cultivate reading appreciation, the teacher first must find material that is worthy of being read, that is appropriate for the child's age, and that will be interesting to her. The student should be given enough time to read the entire piece and should be encouraged to discuss it (Samway et al., 1991). Although guiding children to read and discuss quality materials is essential to improving their reading appreciation, there are certain other things that can be done to encourage it as well. The following instructions indicate the kinds of purposes that improve one's reading appreciation skills:

1. Read a story so that you can act the part of one of the characters.
2. Read several stories, and select one that you think would make a good play.
3. Discuss how you think the character felt.
4. Locate some descriptive words within a poem.
5. Read a story to enjoy it.

Among the focuses of discussion that improve reading appreciation are the following:

1. Which of the characters do you think is most like you? Why?
2. If this story were going to be on television, but only some parts could be used, which parts would you choose?
3. How did you feel when you finished reading this poem?

Insufficient Development of Basic Study Skills

A child can be an excellent reader in general and yet be unable to locate sources of information, use basic references, or interpret pictorial and tabular materials. A child who is limited in any of these skills has a specific difficulty in reading that should be corrected if he is to use the printed page effectively.

Each of the categories of basic study skills listed in this section is composed of many parts. The teacher must know just where a child's difficulty lies if remedial treatment is to be effective and not waste time on elements already mastered. It would be wasteful to spend time teaching a child who is weak in locating sources of information to alphabetize a list of names he has read if he already knows how to do so. It would be equally undesirable to spend time and effort teaching him guide words when his real difficulty is that he does not know in which type of book he can find the information he wants.

It is essential to sample the reader's performance in applying the basic study skills. For example, if he is weak in the use of basic references, it may be found, upon observation, that he does not know whether the type of information he desires can be found in an encyclopedia, a dictionary, an atlas, an almanac, a telephone book, a standard text, or some other book. By noting the references he selects when looking for information such as the time of the monsoons in India, the definition of a word, the address of another school, the population of a town, or the location of a country, the teacher can zero in on the problem.

A study of the reader's efficiency in using the particular basic study skill in question is also needed. He may know which reference to use, under which heading to look for the information he wishes to find, and how to estimate pages within the reference, but still, he may be slow and inefficient in using what he knows. Sampling his performance will also give this necessary information.

Which remedial methods to use will usually become apparent when the nature of the difficulty is assessed. The teacher needs to teach the child how to perform the procedures that cause him difficulty. If he does not know how to alphabetize words, it is relatively easy to teach him the order of the letters and that words are arranged in lists in this order by their first letters, then by the second letters, and so on. This is a different and much simpler type of learning than is, for example, word recognition, in which few such rules apply.

Location of Sources of Information

Skill in finding sources of information is helpful in most study activities. The child who knows how and when to use a table of contents, an index, and a computer data base is better equipped for independent study than is the one who does not think of doing these things or is not as skillful at them. Among the most frequent limitations found in locational skills are (1) the inability to decide which references contain the information wanted; (2) not knowing how to use such tools as an index, a table of contents, a reader's guide, and the like; (3) difficulties estimating the probable key words under which information is classified or inflexibility in selecting other references when the first one does not contain the information wanted; (4) inefficiency in finding words in alphabetical listings, especially in those lists with major and subordinate subdivisions; (5) the inability to find specific pages in a book; and (6) not knowing how to skim material, making it hard to find exact information.

The teacher must establish which of the preceding skills the child needs to improve in and then give her instruction and practice in the use of those skills. For example, if the child shows poor judgment as to which book might contain information she desires, the teacher can teach her how to choose a good source by working through the process with her. If her weakness is in not knowing whether to use the table of contents or the index of a book, the teacher can explain and demonstrate the use of each and give her experience in using them. If determining key words causes her difficulty, the teacher can choose several topics to demonstrate how they are listed, from general to specific, from common to unusual, or from major to related headings.

If the child has difficulty finding words in an alphabetical list, she must practice working with the alphabet, with estimating how far through the alphabet a given letter is, and with placing words in alphabetical order. The child who has insufficient skimming ability should be given many activities that require her to locate specific facts within a page or on several pages. It might be well to start with the location of a date, since numbers on a page of print can readily be found.

Use of Basic References

The child who is capable of finding information in general may find using basic reference material confusing. Usually, his difficulty is not knowing what kind of information each reference contains. To assist him, the teacher should find out which references are causing him difficulty, explain what kind of information they contain, and give him experience in using them. The child may be uncertain about the difference between an encyclopedia and a dictionary and what type of information is found in each. He may be equally confused about what can be obtained from other reference books. After the teacher pinpoints the nature of the problem, an explanation of the contents of the different basic references and some experience in using each will usually correct the difficulty. At times, it is necessary to have the child tell in which of the common reference books he would look to find such things as, for example, facts about Columbus, the meaning of the word *Troy*, and the amount of wheat grown in Kansas last year. Each time the child should check the accuracy of his answer by looking up the topic.

Interpretation of Pictorial and Tabular Materials

Skill in reading maps, graphs, charts, and tables is important in understanding printed material. The child who fails to develop such skills will fall behind in reading in the various fields of study during her school years and also as an adult. If a student is weak in interpreting pictorial and tabular materials, the teacher should identify which kinds materials are causing her difficulty and determine the exact nature of the trouble.

Again, as with most of the study skills, once the nature of the difficulty is known, the remedial work to be undertaken is defined. The child who has difficulty, for example, reading maps may stumble for a variety of reasons. She may be unaware that different maps use different scales, because she has seen a map of her city that is larger than a map of her state. She becomes troubled about distances and comparative sizes. Or she may get erroneous notions because she does not know that a flat map of a vast area must distort some features in order to show others. For instance, many maps of the United States show the state of Maine closer to the top than the state of Minnesota. As a consequence, some people think that Maine extends farther north than Minnesota, but in reality it does not. Similarly, because wall maps always have north at the top, many children think rivers flow downhill to the south and are surprised to learn that some rivers flow north and empty into Hudson Bay. Many such faulty concepts can be established in trying to read maps.

In reading other types of pictorial and tabular materials, there are also many kinds of confusion. The teacher should first find the source of the difficulty and then give the child systematic instruction and purposeful experiences in order to overcome the weakness. Corrective work is best accomplished in science and social studies materials, and students can obtain practice working with maps, graphs, charts, and tables by completing assignments in the corresponding classes. Since these skills begin to form early in the child's reading experience, map reading may be started by having the child interpret a map the teacher has made to show her safe ways to go home from school. In a similar fashion, examining a chart showing daily temperatures at noon is often one of the child's early school experiences, and the teacher can work with it to improve interpretive skills.

Remedial instruction for children who are weak in interpreting pictorial and tabular materials must progress from simple illustrative maps, graphs, charts, and tables to more complex ones and from representations of things that the child has experienced to more unfamiliar examples.

Deficiencies in Reading Content

In the intermediate grades and at more advanced educational levels, some students lack the flexibility that is necessary to adjust their reading procedures to the distinct purposes and materials of each content field. By a *content field*, we mean any field that employs a specific type of reading that requires unique language structures, vocabularies, or purposes—for example, shop manuals, scientific or mathematical materials, poetry, or even cookbooks. The adjustments required of a student in reading content are numerous and often subtle. Nonetheless, when a specific problem is pinpointed, direct instruction focused on the problem corrects the shortcoming in a given field. Diagnoses of reading difficulties within a content field are accomplished best by informal procedures and firsthand observation. Once the problem is located, the remedial work is done best by the teacher of the specific content field, in collaboration with a reading specialist when necessary.

The curricular materials of every field the child meets impose their own specific and unique demands upon his reading capabilities. Suppose, for example, that a fourth-grade child who has been reading stories for most of his 3 years of reading experience is confronted suddenly with a geography book. He has always read a story uninterrupted, from the top of the first page on through to the end. In the geography book, he starts at the top of the page in the customary manner. He reads about 10 lines and then is told to look at Figure 1 on page 12. He looks at Figure 1 on page 12 and, returning to the page he had just left, starts at the top of the page again. He has always done this. So he again reads 10 lines, which now seem familiar, and is asked to look once more at Figure 1 on page 12. He tells himself that he has already looked at Figure 1 on page 12, so he goes on reading down the page. Somewhat later, he reads, "You noticed in Figure 1 that. . . ." But he has noticed no such thing. No one had told him to look for such a thing, and he was unfamiliar with the ways of the geographer. These kinds of episodes are, of course, minor misunderstandings, but many reading difficulties are caused by an accumulation of just such misunderstandings, each small in itself.

The earliest indication that a student is having trouble reading the materials in a specific subject ordinarily comes from the teacher's observation of his classroom performance. When this happens, the teacher should first check to see that the trouble is not due to a more general problem, but is in fact limited to difficulty reading materials in the specific content field. Then, the teacher should appraise the student's performance and determine what is impeding him. Some of the major difficulties encountered by students reading in the content fields are described in the sections that follow. The specific fields to be discussed are social studies, science, mathematics, and literature. They provide a sampling of the diversified types of reading to which a student must be able to adjust.

Social Studies

The field of social studies can present severe reading problems to certain students. A student's understanding of historic, civic, economic, and geographic facts and their ramifications is often limited to what the student gains through reading, because direct experience, and thus prior knowledge, in these areas tends to be restricted. The variety and amount of reading required in social studies are great. Some reading in the field may be done rapidly, to grasp the main idea. Other times, reading must be slow and careful, with attention to condensed, and sometimes complicated, details. The degree of precision required for a satisfactory understanding of most social studies material, however, falls between these two extremes.

Special Vocabulary

A commonly encountered obstacle in reading social studies material is the specialized terms that are used. These include unique words such as *cuneiform, plateau,* and *integration,* as well as proper names of people, places, and events. There are also words with specialized meanings when they occur in certain contexts. Among these are *mouth, cape, run, court,* and *balance.* Especially difficult are abstract terms such as *democracy, culture,* and *civilization.* Although a student may be able to pronounce some of these words without help, many of their meanings are learned only gradually and with the teacher's aid.

Complex Concepts

It is the concept associated with it that gives meaning to an item of vocabulary. Consequently, the development of vocabulary meanings and the development of concepts progress concurrently. In the social studies, many concepts, and consequently their word meanings, are very complex and difficult to learn. Extensive reading of appropriate materials is useful, but to accomplish this, the number of topics to be covered should be restricted.

Selection, Evaluation, and Organization

The extensive reading that is necessary to achieve satisfactory progress in the social studies requires the application of various comprehension and study skills. The student must be acquainted with source materials and their use in selecting pertinent information, must be able to read critically and evaluate materials that are selected, and must be skillful in organizing the information she finds to use in reports or discussions.

Readability

The style of writing used in social studies textbooks frequently makes them difficult to read. Often, many facts and ideas are expressed in a relatively few paragraphs without sufficient organizational clues in the form of headings, sub-headings, and boldface or italic type to bring out clearly the relative importance of the different facts and ideas. Hence, there is little or no indication as to what is most important to learn. Yet to memorize all the details is neither possible nor desirable. Under such conditions, the student is inclined to blunder along, learning some facts and ideas indiscriminately, or even learning nothing at all.

Content versus Skills

Is it the teacher's responsibility to teach only content in social studies? Or must the teacher also teach skills in the field? Usually, it is assumed that the teacher will provide practice in the skills needed, along with instruction in social studies content. Too frequently, however, this does not happen. Although research has shown that reading is the most important skill necessary for mastering social studies content, most social studies teachers place content first and teach reading skills only if there is time (Berryhill, 1984). Herber (1965) points out that this tension between content and skills is not necessary "if the skills are taught functionally *as* students read the required text, using the text as the vehicle for skills development" (p. 95). When this is done, content and skills are taught simultaneously; skills should not be pulled out of context and taught separately.

History

Certain reading problems in the social studies are particularly apparent in the field of history. Three are of prime importance. First, history texts usually do not make allowance for the fact that the temporal order of events is not sensed readily by many students. Second, writers in general, and historians in particular, do not seem to appreciate students' tendencies to interpret everything in terms of present-day conditions. It is often difficult for students to place historical events in the period when or the place where they occurred. This happens most frequently with the treatment of past methods of communication, transportation, science, or living conditions in general. Good instruction requires that students be taught to interpret the time and the conditions in which events have occurred. Third, reading and interpreting pictures, charts, maps, and related historical materials are specialized kinds of reading that are important because they develop relevant word meanings and concepts, as well as provide information. (Developing skills in this area was discussed earlier.)

Geography

Reading problems common to the social studies in general also occur in geography, as do other problems more specifically related to reading geographical materials. Among the specific problems are the following. First, to understand geographical material requires an appreciation of variation in human circumstances such as in housing, clothing, food, occupations, and traditions, or in natural conditions such as the physical features of regions, climate, and vegetation, or in the relationships between human circumstances and natural conditions. Second, it is necessary for a student to maintain a geographic point of view in absorbing the subject matter, in both verbal and numerical form, that is relevant to a geographical unit. This point of view is established through the introduction of the unit and the definition of its purposes. Third, there is often a problem in teaching the child to think concretely in terms of geographical locations as he reads about different places and events that take place within them. Fourth, a geography text is organized so that it frequently interrupts the child, referring him to material on other pages. Fifth, the child may not be able to comprehend material in the form of a map and integrate it with explanatory text material.

Science

For the child to understand the world in which she lives, she must learn some science. The variety of purposes for which science is read ranges from reading to gain general impressions and grasp relationships, to reading to learn in detail the consecutive steps in an experiment, to reading to evaluate the conclusions arrived at in a class discussion. Many of the difficulties encountered in reading science are due to the inherent complexity of the subject, although, as Holliday (1991) points out, texts "cluttered with recall questions, inadequate explanations, and scientific jargon" (p. 47) contribute to misunderstandings. Numerous problems encountered in reading science are similar to those met in the other content fields, while others are unique due to the specific purposes and emphases of science.

Vocabulary

The language of science is precise and specific. Each branch of science—chemistry, biology, physics, and so on—uses its own technical terms, as well as the basic vocabulary used in more general reading. Since the terms embody scientific concepts, it is necessary for the student to learn the vocabulary of a particular field if he is to comprehend the material in that field. Examples of rather highly specialized scientific terms are *electromagnet*, *molecule*, *gravity*, and *lever*. The student must also learn specialized meanings of general words used in a scientific context. Examples from physics are *scale*, *charge*, and the verb *to conduct*.

Concepts

Even the elementary concepts in science are sometimes complex and difficult to understand. Two examples are the concepts represented by the terms *magnetism* and *photosynthesis*. The degree to which concepts in science are grasped depends upon the student's prior knowledge, the clarity of the context in which the unfamiliar items of vocabulary occur, and the skill of the teacher in demonstrating and explaining the concepts. Many reasonably concrete scientific concepts, such as *electromagnetism* and *surface tension*, are readily demonstrated, explained, and understood. Many others are not subject to direct demonstration and therefore must be handled by means of verbal description and abstract explanation. These are difficult for the student to understand. Models, diagrams, and analogies are sometimes helpful in clarifying such concepts.

Pictures and Diagrams
Reading and interpreting pictures and diagrams in science can be inadequate without assistance from the teacher. Ordinarily, an accompanying legend explains the pictures and diagrams, as does the text itself, in a discussion of facts and principles. Some students, however, fail to relate the verbal discussion properly to the diagrams or pictures. Abstract schematic diagrams are still more difficult to read and interpret.

Following Directions
The directions to be followed in carrying out experiments in science are specific. Both children and adults seem to have great difficulty in following these printed directions. Yet the successful performance of the experiment requires that they be followed very carefully. Reading directions for experiments should therefore be done slowly, meticulously, and thoughtfully, so that the sequential order of the steps described can be followed. Ordinarily, difficulties arise, not because the student cannot read and understand the words and sentences, but rather because she does not follow them correctly, omits steps, or does them in the wrong order. It may be helpful for the teacher to demonstrate an experiment and have the students write down the steps as they are performed.

Comprehension Abilities and Study Skills
Remembering facts encountered is, on the whole, a minor aspect of the successful reading of science materials. More important is the recognition of relationships and the formulation of generalizations. The interpretive comprehension necessary for reading science materials successfully can be achieved only when the student has learned to perceive the proper relationships among the pertinent facts. To foster interpretive comprehension, an approach to science that focuses on discussion, demonstration, and experimentation, as well as text assignments, is helpful, especially when the teacher actively monitors and guides the students' comprehension (Hynd, Qian, Ridgeway, & Pickle, 1991). When the student acquires an interpretive comprehension of science materials, she can proceed to formulate her own statements of relationships—in other words, make generalizations. Ultimately, it is also important that the student learn to reason independently while reading scientific materials. Mallow (1991) suggests that, when reading science texts, students "read slowly and more than once with pencil and

paper in hand, chewing over each new idea" (p. 332). Skill in doing this is developed relatively slowly.

Reading comprehension and study skills are more or less constantly used in reading science materials. The particular skills employed depend upon the nature of the material and the purpose for reading it. The student must be prepared to vary her procedures for the most effective reading. For instance, when working on a topical unit in science, she must read to select, evaluate, and organize material, and she cannot do this unless she can grasp relationships and make generalizations.

Mathematics

Reading mathematical material presents a variety of problems, some of them highly specific. Frequently, there are more reading problems per page in mathematics than in any other subject. Like science, mathematics has its own technical vocabulary (e.g., *numerator, quotient,* etc.). Mathematics also uses common words with a special meaning (e.g., *product, divided,* and *power*), employs complex concepts, and involves the study of relationships and the making of generalizations. Pictures and diagrams must be read and interpreted. Much of this reading is concerned with learning about the processes and procedures involved in solving problems, working through examples, and obtaining directions for assignments.

Meaning of Symbols

In arithmetic and other forms of mathematics, students must learn to attach meanings to highly abbreviated symbols, such as $+$, $-$, $\div$, $=$, $\times$, and $\sqrt{}$. When he first learned to read, the child dealt with words as symbols; now they are condensed to shorthand signs. Thus, "is equal to" is represented by the symbol $=$. Also, students need to learn to recognize promptly many specialized abbreviations, such as lb, ft, yd, cm, and min, to mention only a few. Meanings must be assigned both to numbers encountered in context and to those same numbers isolated in columns (e.g., problems in addition, subtraction, and multiplication). The student must comprehend the place value of numbers such as 429, the significance of 0 in numbers such as 30 and 0.4, and the meaning of common and decimal fractions. One prerequisite for a student to solve a mathematical problem is that he have as accurate a command of all the technical symbols that appear in the problem as he would if the concepts the symbols stand for were expressed uneconomically in words. Without systematic instruction, many students make slow progress in acquiring sufficient skill to understand and properly manipulate these symbols, abbreviations, and numerals.

Word Problems

The statement of a mathematical problem in words ordinarily is succinct, is precise, and involves complex relationships. A satisfactory understanding of word problems is achieved by slow, careful, precise reading, together with rereading and reasoning. Besides having a clear understanding of words and phrases, the student must be able to select relevant facts and relationships among the pertinent words and phrases. Reading mathematical word problems is one of the most difficult reading tasks encountered in the content fields. There is little success without intensive concentration. The teacher should realize fully the difficulty of the task the student faces. To succeed with word problems, students should adopt the following strategy or procedure for solving them: (1) The problem should be read to determine its nature. (2) It should be reread to select the relevant information and the processes to be used to solve it. (3) The problem then should be solved and the answer checked for accuracy. To use this strategy or procedure successfully, the student must understand the number system and know the basic arithmetic facts. She must also possess a vocabulary of fundamental terms for quantitative reasoning and understand the use of mathematical processes.

Literature

No field requires as great a diversity of reading techniques as does literature. Unlike such areas as science, mathematics, and social studies, literature includes many types of writing. A variety of reading skills is necessary to comprehend a group of genres, as well as expository text. Yet, unlike other areas in which rewriting text is often required, literature demands that each author's style and linguistic choices be preserved (Fishel, 1984). In addition, a primary responsibility of teaching literature is the development of reading interests and tastes.

The major purpose for teaching literature is to develop the reading skill necessary for the thoughtful interpretation of an author's meaning, for sharing the moods the author wishes her readers to feel, and for entering imaginatively into whatever experience she creates. Although these skills have usually been emphasized in the reading program already, they are refined, expanded, and perhaps supplemented, with teacher guidance, as children read literature. The better a student's proficiency in general reading comprehension, and the larger his vocabulary, the more success he will have in reading literature. Such success also reflects the student's prior experience in reading narrative material, because literature is primarily narrative.

Reading Ability

The ability to read and appreciate literature depends upon competence in reading. To read literature well at any level, the child relies on his fundamental reading ability. In other words, the child will be able to read literature satisfactorily at the reading level he has reached in general reading, but not much higher. In addition to general reading ability, the two specific types of comprehension closely related to continued growth in reading literature are *reading to interpret* and *reading to appreciate,* both discussed earlier in the chapter. The teacher must observe each of these when diagnosing the student who has difficulty reading and enjoying literature.

Enrichment of Meanings

The benefits gained from reading literature result in great part from the enrichment of meanings the practice brings. Enriched meanings are to be found almost everywhere in literature. One benefit is the development of the reader's appreciation of descriptive words, especially words associated with the sensory impressions of sight, sound, taste, touch, and smell. Meanings are further enhanced as the reader develops skill in interpreting figures of speech and symbolic expressions and learns, with guidance, to draw upon her prior knowledge to interpret an illusion or to gain a keener insight into the substance of a piece. Frequently, the impact of a piece of literature depends on the reader's imagination, as when she realizes the meaning of an author's mere hint or suggestion.

General Comment

Proficiency in oral reading and flexibility in silent reading are both important in the appreciation of literature. Literature—especially drama and poetry—should not be read at a constant rate. For example, to appreciate the phrase, "the murmuring pines and the hemlocks," the student should not read the passage at a constant rate, but should pause and let his imagination take over. He should sense the movement of the trees, smell their aroma, feel the rug of needles underfoot, hear the gentle wind, see the sunlight breaking through the branches, and see the pattern of shadows on the ground as he reads.

The next two chapters will deal with specific difficulties directly related to reading literature. One of these is weakness in rate of comprehension. Another, especially related to drama and poetry, is deficiency in oral reading, and a third deals with the student who does not have a lasting interest in reading or who is a reluctant reader. These three reading difficulties must be corrected if reading literature is to become a permanent accomplishment for personal development and enjoyment.

Summary

Three major groups of individuals with specific remedial problems are readers who are limited in one or more types of comprehension, readers who have failed to develop some of the basic study skills, and readers who are ineffective at reading content materials, but who are competent readers in all other respects.

The usual method of correcting a specific type of comprehension difficulty is to have the student read material at an appropriate level of difficulty. The purposes for reading should emphasize the specific comprehension skill that the student needs to strengthen. The reasons for reading should be understood by the student before reading is begun, and the accuracy of the student's reading should be monitored. Specifically, the comprehension skill in question should be checked. The specific comprehension skills students need to develop are retaining factual information, sensing the organization of information, judging the authenticity and relevance of information, interpreting information read, and appreciating what has been read.

The chief method for correcting limitations in basic study skills is to isolate the specific skill a student needs to improve and teach her that skill, while providing sufficient practice to make it permanent. Among the basic study skills are locating sources of information, using basic references, and interpreting pictorial and tabular materials.

Reading skills and abilities need to be adjusted to each content field. The comprehension abilities employed and the rate of reading applied depend on the nature and organization of the material, its difficulty, and the purpose for which the reading is to be done. The content fields of social studies, science, mathematics, and literature involve a wide range of materials to be read, and somewhat different reading abilities are required in each field. The problems that arise in each are related to the particular abilities that come into play.

Study Questions

1. Why is it that some readers have difficulty locating and retaining information read?
2. What are the similarities and differences between the evaluative and interpretive comprehension abilities?
3. Do you agree or disagree that it is important for a student with serious reading difficulties to appreciate the aesthetic qualities of reading? Support your point of view.
4. How can a teacher help students who are unable to locate sources of information or who are inefficient in using basic references?
5. How do the essential reading skills required for success in social studies, science, mathematics, and literature vary from one of these fields to another?

Selected Readings

Cullinan, B. E. (Ed.). (1992). *Invitation to read: More children's literature in the reading program.* Newark, DE: International Reading Association.

Dupuis, M. M. (Ed.) (1984). *Reading in the content areas: Research for teachers.* Newark, DE: International Reading Association.

Herber, H. L. (1978). *Teaching reading in content areas* (2nd ed.). Englewood Cliffs, NJ: Prentice Hall.

Maggart, Z. R., & Zintz, M. V. (1990). *Corrective reading* (6th ed.) (pp. 334–365). Dubuque, IA: William. C. Brown.

Richek, M. A., List, L. K., & Lerner, J. W. (1989). *Reading problems: Assessment and teaching strategies* (2nd ed.) (pp. 249–270). Englewood Cliffs, NJ: Prentice Hall.

Rubin, D. (1991). *Diagnosis and correction in reading instruction* (2nd ed.) (pp. 322–381). Boston: Allyn and Bacon.

Rupley, W. H., & Blair, T. R. (1989). *Reading diagnosis and remediation* (3rd ed.) (pp. 201–268). Columbus, OH: Merrill.

Santa, C. M., & Alvermann, D. E. (1991). *Science learning: Processes and applications*. Newark, DE: International Reading Association.

Chapter *16*

Correcting Reading Rates and Oral Reading Difficulties

Two reading difficulties that concern many people are how fast they can or should read and an uncomfortable feeling they get upon reading aloud. Both of these may persist in a given individual, even though that person is accomplished in all other aspects of reading. Of course, no one can be a rapid reader or an effective oral reader if he does not possess the basic word-recognition skills and the basic comprehension abilities. But inefficient rates of comprehension and ineffective oral reading may burden individuals who are proficient in all other aspects of reading.

Correcting Inefficient Rates of Comprehension

In recent years, much attention has been devoted to rapid reading in the mass media. Speed reading has become a profitable business, and concern about rates of reading is also reflected in the writings of professional educators. Public interest is heightened by enticing promises to teach people to read 1,000 or even up to 20,000 words per minute with good comprehension. Because of all this, the unsophisticated individual may gain the impression that all she has to do to improve her reading is to read faster.

Since there is so much to read today, and so much pressure to keep informed, the ability to read rapidly is a valuable asset. Increasing one's reading speed by 25 to 50 percent will save much time. Some readers can even improve their rates by 50 to 100 percent.

Most people read unnecessarily slowly. It is best to read any material, whether a novel, business report, medical journal, textbook, or other work, as rapidly as possible with understanding. As we shall see shortly, it is possible to increase one's rate of reading by a considerable degree without loss of comprehension—but not from 12,000 to 20,000 words per minute. The question, "How fast should I read?" can have no single answer. But it is safe to say that most of us should read much faster than we presently do.

Certain writers seem to believe that speed of reading is a valid measure of reading performance in itself, even when it is divorced from comprehension. However, a measure of the rate at which words are recognized as words, with no reference to grasping their meanings and relationships, yields a score of little or no consequence in real life. Put plainly, "reading" without comprehension is not reading. The only practical and adequate definition of rate of reading is *rate of comprehension* of printed and written text. This is the definition followed in this book. To measure speed of reading, therefore, one must measure the rate at which text is comprehended. In addition, comprehension itself must always be considered in relation to the purpose for which reading is done. What this means, then, is that in practice, it becomes important to know the rate at which a particular student grasps the general ideas in a story, or the rate at which he comprehends an exposition of history or science material, or some such similar thing. With regard to tests, rate of reading is rate of comprehending, as measured in the particular test. Consequently, standardized tests of speed of reading have certain limitations. One limitation is that the speed of reading attained is based on unnaturally short passages, compared with the length of passages the student is usually expected to read. A second, even more serious, limitation is that the materials in such tests provide inadequate samples of all the different materials students must read. Thus, speed of reading is measured for one type of material only.

In some discussions, it is assumed that speed of reading is a general ability that somehow transfers readily to the reading of a wide variety of materials. In truth, there is no such general speed of reading ability: Even the most proficient reader's rate of reading is fairly specific to a particular situation.

Every teacher must realize that rapid reading in itself does not produce better understanding. A fast rate of comprehension is possible only if the student already possesses the abilities that are necessary for reading and understanding text clearly and rapidly.

An uninformed person is likely to believe that a fast reader is inaccurate and poor in comprehension, while a slow reader is accurate and comprehends what he reads better. However, research into this question fails emphatically to substantiate this belief. By contrast, some hold the opinion that fast reading is good reading and that slowness makes for poor reading. But, although some fast readers do comprehend better than slow readers, there are many exceptions. Fast readers are not always good readers.

In evaluating the data on the relation between reading rate and comprehension, one should keep in mind that there is no general speed of reading skill nor any one comprehension skill. These skills are specific, varying with the kind of material read and the purpose of reading (Spache, 1976b). Accordingly, improvement in rate in one type of reading is not likely to transfer to any significant extent to all reading. For example, improvement in one's rate of reading literature does not necessarily transfer appreciably and automatically to reading science.

The teacher should realize that neither slow nor fast reading produces proper understanding all by itself. Thus, increasing one's reading speed does not necessarily improve comprehension, and for some students, it may even decrease comprehension. The rate at which a particular child should read a specific set of materials is pretty much an individual matter, to be determined by individual diagnosis. Although among mature readers, the faster readers usually comprehend better, there are exceptions. The best indications are that a program to improve speed of reading would be advantageous to most students who are advanced in the basic reading abilities, provided that speed is not pushed to where adequate comprehension is impossible. Also, any general program for accelerating the reading speed of all students in a class is inadvisable. Finally, the true situation may be that the child who has the skills and abilities that are necessary to comprehend well also has those that are necessary to read faster. So drill on speed of reading per se cannot be expected to be worthwhile. There are students, however, who have habits in silent reading that prevent them from adjusting their rate to the purpose and difficulty of any text they read. These students always read at an undesirably slow rate.

Diagnosing Inefficient Rates of Comprehension

Taking in account what has just been said, it appears hazardous to specify average rates of comprehension for the different grade levels. In a given grade, the average rate may be 290 words per minute for reading in one situation and only 140 words in another. Recall that when average rates are published, they are for reading a specific kind of material for a single, set purpose. Usually, they are taken from a test in which the material is relatively easy to read. They should not be interpreted as norms for diverse types of material read for various purposes. Thus, although standardized tests with norms give some information, most diagnoses of inefficient rates of comprehension must be ascertained from informal appraisals.

Standardized Tests
Standardized tests designed for measuring reading ability in the primary grades are ordinarily not concerned with speed. In fact, it is unwise to stress speed of reading during the first 3 years in school. Rather, emphasis should be placed on such considerations as sight vocabulary, word-recognition techniques, reading by thought units, vocabulary knowledge, and comprehension. Any attempt to measure speed in the primary grades might lead to a misplaced pressure on how fast the child reads before he has acquired the basic techniques upon which smooth, rapid reading depends.

Most standardized tests are designed to measure the child's speed in reading relatively short, easy materials for a set purpose. The vocabulary and sentence structure of these materials are simple. The tests merely provide an opportunity for students to show their maximum speed in reading *specific, easy text.* The tests are useful, therefore, only to gain some preliminary information about the students' speed of reading. They are not appropriate for finding out the speed at which particular classroom materials will be read. Informal diagnosis is needed for this task.

Informal Diagnosis

When the results of tests are desired in order to guide instruction, the teacher will want to know the rate at which a student can read classroom materials. He will also want to know how versatile the student is in adapting her speed to changes in difficulty of the material she reads and to varying purposes for reading. These objectives can be reached only through informal tests.

Informal rate-of-reading tests are constructed easily. The teacher merely selects, from appropriate material, a series of consecutive paragraphs of the difficulty and complexity desired. The length of the test will vary with the type of material, the student's reading level, and the difficulty of the material. Ordinarily, the selection will contain from 400 to 800 words. The longer selections may be used for more accomplished readers and for less exacting reading tasks.

There should be comprehension questions for the student to answer when the reading is completed. The nature and number of the questions should be determined by the purpose for reading. When reading to get the main idea, the student may be asked to indicate the correct answer out of 5 listed. When reading to answer specific questions, there may be 6 or 8 questions. If the purpose is to note important details, there may be 10 or 12 questions. The teacher should be aware that, unless comprehension is monitored, a child may skip through the material in order to make a good showing and not understand it adequately.

The purpose for reading should be understood by the student before she starts to read a passage. If individual diagnosis is done, the student may read directly from a book. The number of words read per minute is computed for 2 or 3 minutes of reading.

If an entire class is to be tested at the same time, the selection should be duplicated. A definite time limit, short enough so that the fast readers cannot quite finish, is set. Each student marks where she is when time is called and then counts the words read. Or all the students may be allowed to finish the selection. Each student copies down the last number that the teacher has listed on the chalkboard, indicating the time that has elapsed. The teacher changes the number on the board at the end of every 10 seconds. This method of timing is preferred, since the questions to be answered cover the entire selection.

Interpretation of Diagnosis

Standard scores, grades, or percentile norms are usually given for standardized tests. By consulting these, the teacher is able to discover whether the student is reading unduly slowly for the type of text used and for the purpose set by the test. The scores identify students who are fast and accurate, fast and inaccurate, slow and accurate, and slow and inaccurate.

In using the informal rate tests, the teacher can take into account both rate of reading and amount of comprehension. After testing several students—good as well as poor readers—the teacher will have data to show whether a particular child reads relatively slowly or fast in a specific reading situation. For the scores on comprehension, he will also be able to note the child's accuracy of comprehension. Good comprehension is represented by about 85 percent accuracy, average comprehension by about 70 percent, and poor comprehension by about 50 percent or less.

Diagnosis should always consider comprehension along with rate. If the rate is high and comprehension low, or both the rate and comprehension are low, increasing the rate is not indicated. But when the rate is average or low and comprehension is high, the student will probably profit from a program to increase her speed of reading.

As already indicated, the proficient reader adjusts her rate to the difficulty and nature of the material and to the purpose for reading. The student who uses only one rate for all materials and purposes encounters many difficulties. If the student's habitual rate is fast, it is not suitable for reading difficult materials in the content areas; if it is a slow, plodding rate, it is not suitable for reading narratives and other easy materials. Similarly, when the purpose is to grasp the main idea of a passage, the rate should be faster than when it is to note the important details of the passage.

The degree of a child's versatility in adjusting her reading rate to different materials and purposes may be ascertained as follows: (1) Through the use of informal tests, as previously described, the rates at which the child reads materials at several levels of difficulty and complexity may be determined. (2) Then the rates at which she reads a single selection for different purposes may be measured. The teacher should have the student read the selection for the general idea, then reread it to find the answers to specific questions, and then read it again to note important details. If the child reads the selection at roughly the same rate (either fast or slow) each time, then remedial instruction is indicated to develop the child's ability to adjust her speed of reading to fit the situation.

General Remediation for Inefficient Rates of Comprehension

To be effective, a program for increasing speed of reading must be organized carefully and must temporarily be the major instructional objective. The program should be confined to those students who show prospects of improving. Attempts to increase the reading speed of students with a mental disability or with a limiting or complex reading disability will most likely lead to confusion, frustration, and discouragement, rather than more efficient reading.

Materials

Relatively easy material should be used, particularly in the early stages of the program. It should contain very few, if any, unfamiliar words. The difficulty level of the material should be one or two grades below the reading level of the student. In general, the material should be selected from books other than classroom texts. Only when there is considerable improvement in the speed of reading the easy materials should the teacher gradually introduce the more diffi-cult types of reading. It is essential, however, to make this transition, so that the student will transfer appropriately rapid reading rates to classroom materials. The transition should be made under the teacher's observation and guidance; otherwise it may be only partial or nonexistent. It is possible for a child to learn to read easy material rapidly, but not transfer the skill to other instructional materials.

In the early stages of the program, there should be little emphasis on moni-toring comprehension. It is enough in these stages merely to ask the student what a selection is about. When rapid recognition of words and smooth phrasing become habitual, comprehension will improve. It will then be important to place more emphasis on monitoring comprehension. Rapid reading with adequate comprehension is, of course, the goal sought.

Motivation

In any program for increasing speed of reading, a variety of incentives is neces-sary if the student is to be motivated. Without motivation, a student does not feel any urgency to read faster and is not likely to do so. Various incentives are suitable:

1. The reading material used should be interesting to the student. An inter-ested student is a motivated one. Other things being equal, she will be anxious to read quickly to the end of an interesting story to find out what happened.

2. A daily record of results should be kept. The teacher should greet any evidence of improvement with enthusiasm; gains that are seen and appreciated motivate a student to even greater effort.

3. Fatigue and boredom should be avoided at all costs. All materials should be introduced with zest and in such a manner that the student will hope and expect to improve. If a student shows signs that she is tired or annoyed, pressure to read faster should be temporarily discontinued, until she shows a more posi-tive attitude.

4. The teacher's cheerful and sympathetic guidance will help maintain moti-vation. At times, this will mean working alone with a student to provide just the help and encouragement she needs. This is particularly important during the periods when no discernible gains can be observed and the student becomes discouraged.

5. Allowing the student to participate with the teacher in organizing her remedial program will aid her motivation. The benefits she will enjoy when she can read faster should be discussed with her. Her special difficulties should be talked over, and plans for improvement should be worked out jointly by the teacher and the student. As obstacles arise or old habits reappear, procedures for eliminating them should also be worked out together. The more enthusiastically the student affirms the benefits of reading faster, and the more she participates in the remedial planning, the better her motivation will be for overcoming her difficulties.

6. The purpose for each practice reading should be understood. Reading without a clearly understood purpose cannot be well-motivated reading. Sometimes, students may be reading with more attention to details than is necessary. A conversation about this with the student will show her how to correct it.

7. When the student's speed has improved through special practice, incentives should be provided to motivate her to transfer the faster reading to leisure reading and to school subjects. All sorts of encouragement should be used—for example, praise for the number of stories or books the student has read for enjoyment, a discussion of the benefits of faster reading, and emphases on doing class assignments speedily. She should be helped to see the benefits of carrying over improved speed to all types of reading.

8. After special instruction to increase the student's rate of reading is completed, the teacher must be alert to relapses to the old, slower rates. Motivation to maintain faster reading can be provided by special speed tests at periodic intervals, together with class discussion on the importance of adjusting one's speed to purposes and materials.

Working Against Time

An effective and much-used technique for increasing a student's speed of reading is to work against time. Relatively easy material—a grade or so in difficulty below the student's achievement level, for example—is selected for the beginning reading selections. These early readings should be about 350 to 400 words long. Each may be reproduced on one page. When the teacher is working with a single student, reading may done directly from a book or magazine. Five or six questions are recorded on a separate sheet. The questions should be relatively easy, dealing with the general ideas in the selection. After the selection is finished, the text is removed and the questions are answered. The student's comprehension may suffer initially, but will improve as time goes on.

Each reading selection should be introduced under as favorable conditions as possible. The purpose for reading should be made clear to the student. The circumstances should be such that the student will be eager to read as fast as possible with understanding. He should expect to improve over previous attempts. The teacher should time the reading and compute the number of words read per minute as his score. The student should be shown how to plot his scores on a simple graph, so that he will see his gains. When little or no gain is achieved for a time, the teacher should be sympathetic and encouraging.

Two exercises per day provide enough challenge for this kind of work, and they should be separated by an hour or so. This *spaced learning* is more effective than several readings, one after another. After the first few readings, the student's comprehension should be adequate. As the program gets well under way, no student should be pushed to read faster than he can comprehend.

Mechanical Devices

A number of mechanical devices have been developed for increasing speed of reading. Special motion pictures, text pacers, short-exposure devices, and computer programs have been used to give children practice in reading faster. Each of these methods presents phrases, lines of print, or words at speeds that may be varied by the teacher. Teacher-constructed flash cards can also be used to present words or phrases rapidly.

Although the use of machines—especially computers—is highly motivational for some students, those taught by regular methods make as great gains as those taught by machines. There is, however, always a possibility that a given child will improve with machine training, but not by ordinary methods.

Programs for improving speed of reading can be satisfactory without the use of machines if the selections are carefully chosen, the program of training properly organized, and the instructions effectively carried out. If the teacher is able to provide incentives that will motivate the student, machines or other gadgets are not necessary to achieve satisfactory gains in speed of reading. In other words, the use of certain machines does increase the child's speed of reading, but is not necessary to produce the same gains.

Two definite drawbacks to mechanical devices in attempting to increase speed of reading are their expense and the fact that their use too often becomes a ritual and overemphasizes the mechanical aspects of reading over the more important processes of comprehension and reflection on content.

Remediation for Specific Types of Inefficient Rates

At least six distinct difficulties are associated with inefficient rates of reading: overanalysis, word-by-word reading, undesirable habits, faulty eye movements, excessive vocalization, and inflexibility. Each is treated in its own, unique way.

Overanalysis

Overanalysis takes two forms: the tendency to analyze words that are already known as sight words and the tendency to segment words into too many parts. The remedial procedures for both types have been presented in the preceding subsection and in Chapter 11. In general, rapid-exposure devices are useful.

Word-by-Word Reading

The word-by-word reader has failed to learn to read in thought units. Consequently, he may not be able to recognize a group of three or four words at a glance. If so, training with rapid-exposure techniques is useful. But, in addition, he may not be able to group words into thought units as he reads connected text. In this case, he should also be given the training suggested in the preceding subsection, as well as that directed at word-by-word reading in Chapter 14, also including rapid-exposure techniques.

Undesirable Habits

Some children have the habit of moving their finger or a pointer along the line of print to guide their reading. Although perhaps justified in the early stages of learning or remedial work, the practice should be discarded as soon as feasible. The best way to break this habit is to discuss the problem with the student and then have her hold the book with both hands. Continuing to point while holding the book with both hands will be awkward for her, and moving her fingers along the line of print will remind her that she is pointing again.

Another undesirable habit is head movements. Instead of sweeping along the line of print with appropriate eye movements, the student moves her head from left to right. This is stopped by explaining the problem to the student and then asking her to rest her chin on one hand as she attempts to read more rapidly. This practice will warn her if she moves her head again.

Many children develop a congenial, meandering style of reading that is considerably below the rate at which they might read with both understanding and pleasure. When this becomes habitual, as frequently happens, it is a handicap to proficient reading. Such easygoing dawdling permits the child's attention to wander and fosters daydreaming. In addition, the child covers an inadequate amount of text in an allotted time. When unduly slow reading is really dawdling, a program to promote an appropriate faster rate should be implemented. In any reading, the correct rate is the fastest for the situation that also produces satisfactory comprehension. The general approaches to increasing rate of comprehension will usually overcome habitual dawdling.

Faulty Eye Movements

Much attention has been focused on the relationship of eye-movement patterns to speed of reading. Because rapid reading is accompanied by few fixations and few regressions per line of print, techniques to train eye movements have been developed for the purpose of increasing reading speed. A more appropriate procedure, however, would be to promote reading efficiency: Whereas eye-movement exercises tend to be mechanical and emphasize speed of reading, following the procedures described in this book to improve one's basic comprehension and rate of comprehension will automatically result in better eye-movement sequences and faster reading.

Excessive Vocalization

In the early stages of silent reading in the primary grades, many children tend to articulate words. At that level, vocalization does not slow down their speed of silent reading, for the child can read no faster than he can talk. Later, as reading skill develops, vocalization becomes an impediment to improving speed of silent reading. With some children, the habit of pronouncing each word is so strong, that it persists into adulthood if not corrected. The words may be whispered, or the lips and vocal organs may form the words without any sound. Whatever form the articulation takes, it is time consuming: As long as the habit persists, silent reading can be no faster than the words can be articulated. Until vocalizing is eliminated, at least in part, there can be little improvement in speed of reading.

A good technique for eliminating vocalization is to give the child reading material that is very easy and extremely interesting, with practically no unfamiliar words. If the material is interesting and exciting, the child will want to read the story rapidly to find out what happens. He is urged to do this, at first with short stories or mysteries and later, after a satisfactory rate of reading is achieved with them, with more diversified materials.

A rapid reader cannot vocalize, because it takes too long to articulate the words. When a child gets a good start in reading easy stories, he should be encouraged to race through them as rapidly as possible. For a while, he may get little meaning, but later, vocalization will be reduced to a minimum and better comprehension will return.

Inflexibility

It has already been noted that reading at as fast a rate as the text can be comprehended is desirable in any content field. Although a properly fast rate of reading mathematical materials is relatively very slow, some students still read such materials at an undesirably slow rate. The same is true for areas such as science and social studies. Whatever the material and purpose, there can be unnecessarily slow or fast rates of reading. A rapid rate of reading in itself has no particular value. Rather, the proficient reader has several speeds, each of which can be used as the occasion demands. An essential part of the instructional program is to ensure that students acquire these speeds and gain skill in using them appropriately. The emphasis should be on teaching students to be adaptable, versatile readers who are able to adjust their rates to the nature and difficulty of text and to their purposes for reading it. The goal is to *comprehend* the material at as fast a rate as possible, and the best way to achieve it is to ensure that the student has the prior knowledge and the reading ability to understand properly what she is to read. When this is done, she will learn to read the material rapidly and with understanding. Several aspects of the problem need attention simultaneously.

First, for effective reading, the rate at which the material is read must be appropriate to the nature and difficulty of the material. The nature of reading material varies widely. At one time, the student may be reading a fast-moving story or an item of general interest in a newspaper. Here, the appropriate rate of reading is relatively rapid. A short time later, the student may be reading geographic text concerned with the concept of erosion by wind and water. In this, a relatively slow rate of reading is necessary to grasp the ideas and relationships. Still later, she may be reading the procedures for solving a mathematical or scientific problem, which requires very slow, analytical reading and often rereading. The student needs to learn how to evaluate the nature of the material so that she may adopt a rate that is appropriate for understanding that particular kind of material.

Adjusting to variations in difficulty is similar. Such variations arise in many ways. Materials in some content fields contain more facts than materials in others—for example, science or mathematics, compared with literature. At times, there is even marked variation in difficulty within the same unit in a single field. Difficulty may occur when unfamiliar vocabulary and concepts, complex sentences and paragraphs, or unusual grammatical constructions are encountered. Increased attention to content necessitates slower reading for adequate understanding. The student should read just as slowly as is needed to grasp what is presented. Any student who attempts to read all materials at the same rate, despite their content or difficulty, will be in trouble. To read with understanding and at an effective rate, the student must be able to modify her rate. Easy material should be read faster than difficult material, and familiar material should be read faster than unfamiliar material.

Perhaps the most important aspect of all is the adjustment of the student's rate of reading to the purpose for which she is reading. This has been stressed throughout. If the student needs to get only a general impression or idea, or if she merely needs to look up a given item on a page, her speed of reading should be relatively rapid. But if she needs to grasp the concepts in a given selection thoroughly, her pace should be relatively slow. Before reading any text, the student should have a clear idea of her purpose for reading. The most satisfactory purpose, of course, is one set by the student herself. When she cannot do this, the teacher's guidance should help provide a purpose that is *acceptable* to her. To be a really good reader, however, she must learn to set her own purposes. Doing so requires discrimination and flexibility. The student must be able to size up the materials and clearly understand the purpose for reading them. Then she must be able to choose the appropriate rate for her to read with understanding. In other words, *the proficient reader is the adaptable, versatile reader.*

To gain flexibility in rate of reading, the child must learn to choose a particular speed for a particular situation and to read at that rate with understanding. This requires the teacher's guidance, because every student reads many kinds of materials for many purposes. The development of flexibility in speed of reading tends to be difficult to learn.

Opportunities for guidance in adjusting the student's speed of reading to the different kinds of materials she reads are abundant when teaching units in the content fields. Preparation for each unit should include a discussion of the right reading procedures. Another approach is to have students read the same material several times, each time for a different purpose, such as (1) to grasp the main idea, (2) to note important details, (3) to answer questions given in advance, and (4) to evaluate what is read.

There is always opportunity to guide the development of flexibility when teaching the specific comprehension abilities and study skills described in the previous chapter. Any instruction designed to develop comprehension in reading necessarily involves guiding the students to discover the most effective rate at which to read specific textual material.

Gains to Be Expected

In the primary grades, while the mechanics of reading are being mastered and where much of the reading is oral, the rates of silent and oral reading are about the same. But in the fourth grade, children are ready to learn to read silently faster than they can read orally.

As noted earlier, the first step in organizing a program to increase speed of reading is to reduce to a minimum any habits that may hinder or obstruct gains in speed. When this is done, a teacher can expect practically all students to increase their rates with training, although there will be individual differences in the rates achieved. There is ample evidence that training produces greater gains among the faster readers than among the slower ones.

In a properly conceived and executed program for a group at any school level, a few children achieve relatively small gains, many make moderate gains, and a few achieve large gains. An occasional child will make truly exceptional improvement. Ordinarily, students are given special practice periods of 10 to 30 minutes. The program usually extends over several weeks, with a total of 15 to 18 hours of training. Representative average gains for groups vary greatly. Harris and Sipay (1975) reported gains of 39 percent. If a school training program extends over 2 months or so, the teacher can expect an average gain of 40 to 50 percent. There is little evidence concerning the transfer of the rate one achieves with certain reading materials to other materials or the extent to which the gains are maintained after the training stops.

In most programs to improve reading rates, comprehension is maintained at an adequate level (75 percent or higher). If speed alone is emphasized, however, comprehension may decrease. No student should be pushed to this stage.

How fast can a person be expected to read? Since many factors affect one's rate of reading, no single answer to this question can be given. The available data usually pertain to reading fairly easy material. With such material, 400 words per minute is very high for a seventh-grade student, and 600 words per minute is very high and 850 exceedingly rare for college students. It is not uncommon for some well-educated adults who are superior readers to attain rates of 500 to 600 words per minute. There is, however, a physiological limit beyond which one cannot read any faster. Harris and Sipay (1990) point out that this limit is around 800 to 900 words per minute when one reads most of the words on a page. Reports of rates between 1,200 and 1,500 or more words per minute refer only to partial reading, or skimming. Any claim that a person can be taught to read 10,000 or even 20,000 words per minute is false. Words simply cannot be seen at that rate.

As mentioned, in the primary grades, there should be no stress placed upon the children to improve their rates of reading. For a majority of students up through about the fifth grade, a satisfactory rate can be expected as a result of a good reading program. But some pupils in the intermediate grades (1–4) can benefit from a specialized program to improve their rates of reading. Among these students are the dawdlers and those who persist in their habits of slow reading after the major causal factors (vocalization, poor recognition of words, a small sight vocabulary, etc.) have been reduced or eliminated. Flexibility in one's reading rate should also be taught in the intermediate grades and beyond. Although attention is sometimes given to improving reading rates in the early intermediate grades, provisions for developing appropriate rates seem desirable from the beginning of the sixth grade through high school and into the college years.

Overcoming Ineffective Oral Reading

The ultimate aim of instruction in oral reading is to enable the reader to interpret a passage for others. The effective oral reader learns to interpret text for an audience in a relaxed and fluent manner. At the start, all oral reading should be prepared, but as a child matures in both silent and oral reading ability, he will become increasingly adept at reading orally at sight. The amount of preparation needed for oral reading depends on the circumstances and the maturity of the reader. The parent who reads a story to her child is probably reading it at sight. Sharing a book by reading aloud is also done at sight. In most other instances, oral reading is prepared, interpretive reading, rather than sight reading. Both types of oral presentation should be among the outcomes of a reading program.

There are many adults who dislike to read orally. This probably is because of unpleasant, early reading experiences they have had and a failure to develop oral reading ability. A good deal of instructional time spent having children read selections orally at sight, while the rest of the group follows silently, each in his or her own book, is destructive to poor oral readers. As the better readers read ahead silently or supply words to their less fortunate classmate, the poor oral reader stumbles along, with each of his errors apparent to all.

It should be noted that there are some children who are good silent readers and who have developed all the basic reading proficiencies, but have a serious disability in oral reading. These children constitute a group having a specific reading difficulty. If their poor oral reading is the result of some basic difficulty, the major problem is correcting that difficulty. When there is no such underlying difficulty, but the child is still an ineffective oral reader, his problem should be diagnosed. The child who is poor in oral reading, but is otherwise an able reader for his general reading level, may be experiencing one of the following difficulties: (1) He may have an inappropriate eye-voice span; (2) he may lack proper phrasing in oral reading; (3) his rate and timing in oral reading may be inappropriate; or (4) he may become frustrated while reading aloud.

Eye-Voice Span

Many children with problems in oral reading have difficulty because their eye-voice span, the distance that the readers' eyes are ahead of their voices, is inappropriate. They may be focusing their attention exclusively on the word they are speaking, or they may be trying to maintain an eye-voice span that is too great for their general reading maturity. In the former case, the child reads aloud in a halting and stumbling fashion, with little expression and many pauses. She cannot anticipate the meaning of what she is reading and, therefore, cannot express it with her voice. Very likely, she will read in a monotone. Each word she fails to recognize at sight causes her to halt to inspect it, whereas with a longer eye-voice span, she should have time to identify words before pronouncing them.

If the child is trying to maintain too great an eye-voice span in oral reading, then she is probably an able silent reader who is transferring her silent reading habits to oral reading. She races ahead silently, perhaps at the rate of 300 to 400 words a minute, but can pronounce words orally at only 140 words a minute. Such a child may try to maintain an eye-voice span of 8 to 10 words. As a result, she will likely omit many words or read so rapidly that she can give but little expression to what she is reading aloud.

The diagnosis of eye-voice span is easy to make. The child is given a book at a level of difficulty at which she will encounter few word difficulties reading orally. She is given time to prepare the material, and then she is asked to read it aloud to the examiner, who is at the child's right. As the child reads aloud, the examiner reads along silently with her. At intervals, the examiner covers the child's page with a 3" × 5" card in order to find out how many words the child is able to say after she can no longer see the print. This should be done preliminarily several times before the examiner starts keeping an actual record. The examiner should cover the rest of the line of print when the child is pronouncing a word that comes about one-third of the way through the line. The same testing should also be done with unprepared, or sight, oral reading. In this way, the examiner obtains information on the eye-voice span of a child in both prepared and sight oral reading. Children in the early grades, with a first- or second-grade reading ability, cannot maintain an eye-voice span of more than a word or two in prepared oral reading. In sight oral reading, they can be expected to be little more than word callers. Instruction in sight oral reading should be delayed until they have greater competency in reading.

Remedial instruction for the child with a narrow eye-voice span should always be done using prepared, and never sight, oral reading. Conversational passages are best for developing fluent oral reading in such a child. The material should be easy, with few, if any, unfamiliar words. The child should be encouraged to try to look ahead on the line of print. Special attention should be given to phrasing. The purpose for oral reading should be authentic, such as preparing to read something aloud that she is going to read to others. She should rehearse until she is satisfied that she is ready to read orally.

The child who is trying to maintain too long an eye-voice span needs to be taught to use one that is more appropriate. At the start of remedial training, she should be given an opportunity to read prepared material before an audience. Her oral reading should be recorded with a tape recorder so that she can develop an awareness of any pattern she might have and consider how to improve it. She should be taught how to pause from time to time while reading aloud, and she should be encouraged to look at her audience frequently. The problem with teaching the child who has too long an eye-voice span is getting her to use her otherwise superior reading ability effectively in oral reading.

Phrasing Ability

A student who is a poor oral reader may lack proper phrasing ability and tend to read aloud either word by word or by clustering words into groups, disregarding the thought units involved. In either circumstance, attention to the meaning of what is read is neglected. The word-by-word reader can be detected immediately as he reads orally. Each word is pronounced unrelated to any other. The words are read in much the same manner as a mature reader might read a grocery list. When a child reads in this way, he may be directing his attention to the meaning of each word, but he is paying little attention to the interrelationships among them. More difficult to detect when one is listening to his oral reading is the child who clusters words without regard to the real thought units they comprise. This child's reading may seem rather fluent, but it does not make sense.

The remedial training for children who lack proper phrasing in oral reading is the same for both types. Word-by-word reading is often brought about in the first place by having children read text that is too difficult for them or that repeats words in a mechanical and more or less senseless way.

The material used to correct the tendency toward inappropriate phrasing in oral reading should be easy for the child, avoid inane repetition, and include a considerable amount of conversation. Dramatic readings, tape recordings, dummy or live microphone readings, and other such activities encourage proper phrasing. No sight oral reading should be attempted until growth in phrasing is well established.

Rate and Timing in Oral Reading

Many children who lack ability in oral reading attempt to read too rapidly or have a poor sense of timing. They may start out reading at a reasonable rate, but then they read increasingly faster, until little of what is read can be understood. The good oral reader at any level reads at a rate that is relatively slow. She has a moderate degree of flexibility in her rate, so that she may express different moods by altering her rate of reading. She learns to use pauses effectively to hold the attention of her audience and also to emphasize important points.

One of the best ways to help a child improve her oral reading is to devote attention to her rate and timing. The child will profit from studying good oral readers on television and trying to emulate their performances. Tape recordings of the child's own reading will demonstrate her present pattern to her. Oral reading conditions best suited to the child's needs are those related to class or small-group activities. Having her be a "news reporter" during sharing periods is excellent because the news is made of short paragraphs giving accounts of different unrelated events. Each "news item" is read, and then the child pauses before going on to the next. The pauses are short enough so that she does not accelerate her reading. Similarly, participating in a small group to read a play aloud is useful. Reading long selections from a story should be avoided until the child has her speed and timing under control.

Frustration in Oral Reading

Some children who have had frequent disagreeable experiences in oral reading become insecure or even frightened when they have to read aloud. The child who is experiencing frustration during oral reading is easily detected. If his voice gets increasingly higher as he reads, he is becoming more and more frustrated. His errors increase as he reads. He tries to avoid reading aloud. Few classroom situations are more highly emotionally charged than is oral reading for the poor reader. Everything that can be done to relieve his stress in such situations should be done. To help the easily frustrated oral reader, have him read text that he has prepared so well that he can feel confident. Make sure to be near at hand and ready to prompt him if he gets into difficulty. Having the child read out of sight of his audience helps him establish confidence. Reading offstage as a narrator in a play or reading behind the screen for a puppet show often helps. Reading an announcement over a microphone placed in another room offers a good opportunity for the child to read, free from self-consciousness. If, under these conditions, the material is well prepared and relatively easy to read, progress can be expected. As soon as possible, the child should discard these devices and learn to read before his audience.

In working with an easily frustrated oral reader, certain precautions should be taken. The child's early oral reading experiences should grow out of a desire to share a story with others. He should be encouraged to tell the major part of the story in his own words and read aloud only a small section—a paragraph or two is enough. He should select the part that he would like to read and prepare it in advance, even rehearsing it aloud with the teacher. Then, when he reads aloud to the group, if he gets into difficulty with a word, the teacher should supply it immediately. If, while reading, the child uses a high-pitched or strained voice, reads at an unusually rapid rate, or shows any other sign of stress, he should finish by telling, rather than reading, the rest of the story. Gradually, he can increase the length of the selection he prepares for oral reading. Only after he becomes confident reading aloud to the group should he attempt to read aloud at sight. In all oral reading, the material should be relatively easy and free from words the child is likely to find difficult.

General Methods for Developing Fluency in Oral Reading

Much practice with appropriate text is necessary to develop fluency in oral reading in nonfluent young readers. Henk, Helfeldt, and Platt (1986) describe several useful methods for improving fluency. One technique is imitative reading, in which the teacher reads a portion of text aloud as the child reads it silently, followed by the child reading the portion aloud. Another method is radio reading, in which each student reads from a separate script while the teacher monitors the performance from a master script. Repeated readings can also be used. In this method, children reread a selection many times as they chart decreases in the time they require and in the errors they commit. An individual method can be used in which teacher and student read aloud together, or a choral reading method can be employed in which the children read aloud together. To promote fluent reading, children should be urged to read material that they have practiced with "just as you would say it."

Self-Improvement in Oral Reading

As soon as children are old enough to recognize that they have problems in oral reading, they can be guided to want to improve their own oral reading abilities. For self-improvement of oral reading, children can use a checklist. Each child monitors her own progress. In this way, one child may be working on rate of reading, another on phrasing, and a third on accuracy. Pairs of children may, under congenial circumstances, judge the oral reading of each other. When this is done, each child should tell her partner what she liked about the way the partner read, how well she thinks her partner did on what he was working on, and any ways in which she thinks her partner might do even better. A list such as the following will prove helpful in this regard:

1. Did my partner select interesting material?
2. Was he well prepared?
3. Did he read loud enough?
4. Did he read the material "just as he would say it"?
5. Did he read fast enough, but not too fast?
6. Did he read so that I understood the meaning?
7. Did he look relaxed with good posture?
8. Did he use marks of punctuation to help him?
9. Did he make me feel he wanted to read to me?

When a child improves her oral reading, not only is her interpretive reading enhanced, but her oral language is enhanced as well. As a result, her silent reading improves, too. The child who is accustomed to and enjoys reading aloud will use some of the expressions she likes in her spoken language. She will gain confidence before groups and will sense the importance of adequate preparation. Her silent reading will improve because, in preparing for oral reading, she will be concerned with the meanings, the characterizations, and the actions that she is to interpret to others. Her concern with thought units in oral reading will teach her to cluster words together suitably in silent reading. Current approaches to oral reading appear to be vastly superior to the "round-the-room" reading of earlier days that produced so many insecure oral readers among the adults of today.

Case Study of a High School Student with a Basic Comprehension Limitation and Poor Rate of Reading

John, a ninth-grade student, was referred to a university clinic for work in reading during a 10-week summer period. He came from a distant state and stayed with his grandparents during his remedial work. He also registered in a summer reading improvement class. He had attended a school system in one of the mountain states during his elementary and junior high school years.

School History. At the time John was admitted to the clinic, he was 16 years and 5 months old. His school record showed that he had repeated the second grade because of an illness that kept him out of school for the last 2 months of the school year. John's work up until that time seemed to be progressing well, except for a notation that he was having some difficulty in oral reading.

The rest of the elementary-grade years of the record showed that he was progressing with somewhat below-average success in social studies and reading, but maintained good achievement in arithmetic and science. John was known to be a bright, cooperative boy, although his teachers noted that he was somewhat shy and withdrawn. They had made a special effort to get him to participate in class activities. During his junior high school years, John continued to do reasonably well in mathematics courses, somewhat poorly in science, and very poorly in social studies and English.

As a result of a conference with John, it was found that he had received instruction at a reading center during the preceding year to increase his speed of reading. He said that he had improved a little, but try as he would, he could not seem to read fast enough to keep up with his assignments. John indicated that he took his books home and read his regular texts with great care, but could not find the time to do the extra reading required in the English and social studies courses. He found the mathematics and science courses easier to cover. He also said that he did not like to participate in class discussions.

Physical Status. John's physical status was excellent and there was no indication of any sensory limitation. He liked to go hiking in the mountains and was very fond of skiing, which he did often. His shyness seemed to be limited to the classroom, since he participated in skiing, swimming, and tennis with his friends.

Abilities. John was found to be an intellectually able boy. He was measured on the Wechsler-Adult Intelligence Scale—Revised and was found to have a verbal I.Q. of 114, a performance I.Q. of 126, and a full-scale I.Q. of 120. This would place his reading expectancy at a beginning college freshman level $(1.20 \times 10) + 1$, or grade 13.

John was given the Woodcock Reading Mastery Tests—Revised, Form G. His grade scores follow:

Word Identification	9.0
Word Attack	9.7
Word Comprehension	10.0
Passage Comprehension	4.9
Total Reading	8.4

These results show that word recognition was not John's basic problem. His pronunciation of common words, ability to work out the pronunciation of new words, and his understanding of the meanings of words were adequate. A comparison of his general reading vocabulary, science-mathematics vocabulary, social studies vocabulary, and humanities vocabulary showed each to be reasonably well developed. John's comprehension of passages, on the other hand, was very poor. Since the Woodcock Reading Mastery Tests—Revised are administered individually and allow adequate time for each response, John's poor comprehension of passage was judged to be the result of a basic comprehension problem, not simply a reflection of his generally slow reading rate.

John's oral and silent reading ability was then appraised by informal techniques (Chapter 8). He was found to read orally and silently at approximately the same rate—about 90 words a minute. He could read seventh-grade material aloud without excessive word-pronunciation errors; but when he answered questions about the content, even of fourth-grade material, he was inaccurate and asked to be allowed to reread to find the answers. This he could do reasonably well. John was a word-by-word reader who gave no indication of reading in thought units and had little sense of sentence organization. His eye-voice span was limited to one or two words.

In silent reading, John could be seen to make many eye fixations per line of print, and he made many large regressions. This indicated that he was using much the same single-word techniques in silent reading that he had used in oral reading. The examiner also noted that while John was reading silently, he was, in fact, reading aloud to himself. This showed up in lip movements and other indications of excessive vocalization. John was reading silently, word by word, vocalizing what he read and then rereading to understand the meaning of what he had read.

The diagnostic questions raised in Chapter 7 and the answers to them were as follows:

1. Is John correctly classified as having a reading disability? The results of the diagnosis showed that he definitely had a reading disability, a limiting condition that would have to be overcome before he could become an able reader and achieve at a level that was in keeping with his intellectual capacity. John's tendency to withdraw in the classroom was felt to be a symptom, and not the cause, of his problem. Rather, it led one to believe that he was aware of his reading inadequacy.

2. What is the nature of the training needed? The remedial program designed for John had the following components: (1) practice in rapid recognition of phrases, including flash drills, as discussed in Chapter 14; (2) prepared oral reading, with emphasis on proper phrasing and oral expression of sentence meanings to improve reading in thought units; (3) steps to overcome the vocalization John used in reading activities; (4) the use of contextual clues and other meaning clues as an aid to comprehension (see Chapter 14).

3. Who can give the remedial work most effectively? On the basis of the diagnosis, it was decided that work with an individual remedial reading teacher, plus a reading-improvement class, was the best arrangement that could be made for John during the summer period.

4. How can improvement be brought about most efficiently? At the start, the clinician selected materials with high interest and at a low reading level. These materials required a reading ability at the level of about the end of the fourth grade, but had the interest level and format of a seventh-grade book. In addition, independent reading of suitable materials, such as those discussed in Chapter 9, was encouraged. The remedial reading teacher gave John many opportunities to do prepared oral reading, with emphasis upon proper phrasing and oral expression of sentence meanings. This was thought to be justified in spite of John's vocalization tendencies, since the failure to read by thought units and sentence meaning is more limiting to total reading growth than is vocalization. The remedial reading teacher developed exercises to help train him in locating thought units within sentences, as described in Chapter 14. Flash drills, using flash cards, were developed for rapid phrase-recognition exercises.

The teacher of the reading improvement class was informed of the findings of the diagnosis, and she adjusted her instruction for John in order to achieve the same remedial objectives. Her help was especially effective in helping John overcome his tendency to withdraw when working in groups.

John took home relatively easy books for independent reading. He was told to read these books as rapidly as he could for 3-minute periods, as measured by a timer on the electric stove. Then he was to note, for each 15-minute period, the number of pages read, such as "from the top of page 21 to the middle of page 29." He was also told to write, in not more than three short sentences, the major ideas presented. Each day he would bring the results of his independent reading to the remedial reading teacher. Using his "major ideas" sentences as notes, he would discuss the independent reading he had done at home the day before. He also kept a daily rate chart, calculated on the results of his final 15-minute timed period of reading. John was, of course, free to read the books taken home for leisurely, untimed reading, and he was encouraged to do so. During his home reading, as in all other reading activities, John was told to try to limit vocalization. This home practice was reinforced by the flash drills used to develop phrase recognition, which also helped in overcoming vocalization.

5. Does the child have any limiting conditions that must be considered? John was not limited in any sensory or physical way that would contribute to the complexity of his reading problem. His tendency to withdraw in school situations and his lack of confidence, while thought to be a direct outgrowth of his reading frustrations, were taken into account in formulating the remedial plans. John's confidence was bolstered by the acceptance of himself and his reading problem by the remedial reading teacher. His withdrawal tendencies were recognized quickly by the high school corrective-reading teacher. At the very start of instruction, she provided John with a story to report on about delivering the mail on skis and encouraged him to tell about his own skiing experiences. This approach quickly established John favorably among his classmates.

6. Are there any environmental conditions that might interfere with the child's progress in reading? The environment in which John was placed during the summer period was thought to be ideal. His grandparents were cooperative and knowledgeable. They made certain that he had an enjoyable summer vacation, including opportunities to swim and play tennis with his classmates. They also provided John with a suitable place for leisure reading and took a healthy interest in what he was reading.

Results. John was given remedial instruction as outlined previously, and he also enrolled in the reading improvement class for the 10-week period. The results were thought to be outstanding. Of course, John was an able boy with no limiting physical conditions and was helped under ideal circumstances. His problems were of a type in which rapid correction often takes place. Nonetheless, the results were gratifying to all persons concerned.

The Woodcock Reading Mastery Tests—Revised, Form H, were repeated at the end of the 10-week period, with the following results:

Word Identification	9.3
Word Attack	9.4
Word Comprehension	10.8
Passage Comprehension	10.7
Total Reading	10.5

The limiting condition of word-by-word reading and his excessive vocalization had been overcome. John was now able to couple his skill in word recognition with his able intellect to read slightly better than a typical beginning 10th-grade student, even though he was still not reading up to his reading expectancy level. John had also overcome the insecurity in reading situations that had previously inhibited his performance. This gain in confidence undoubtedly helped to improve his measured reading capabilities. John's interest in reading and his ability to concentrate on what he was reading developed to the point that, while reading a book on his way to school on the bus one morning, he missed his stop and rode all the way to the downtown area before he looked up from his book to check on his whereabouts.

An informal evaluation showed that John was able to read high school material for varied purposes at from 300 to 400 words a minute, with a high degree of accuracy. It was felt, at the end of the session, that his reading would no longer interfere with his future progress.

Summary

A good speed of reading is that rate at which text is comprehended according to the purpose for which it is being read. For the proficient reader especially, speed of reading is fairly specific to a particular reading situation. In general, the goal is to comprehend the text at as fast a rate as possible. To achieve this goal, the student must learn to adjust his rate of reading to fit the material he is reading and his purpose for reading it. General methods for determining deficiencies in rate of reading include standardized tests and informal tests. Each type of test should supplement the other in diagnosis.

A complete diagnosis of difficulties in speed of reading must include an analysis of possible limiting conditions, such as difficulties with the basic word-recognition skills and basic comprehension abilities, which preclude rapid reading. These must be corrected before the specific types of inefficient rates can be overcome. Among the specific rate problems are overanalysis, word-by-word reading, undesirable habits, faulty eye movements, excessive vocalization, and inflexibility.

Any program for improving rate of reading must include (1) the use of appropriate materials, (2) proper incentives to develop and maintain motivation, (3) techniques for increasing the rate, and (4) an emphasis on adjusting the rate to different kinds of text and different purposes.

Two general techniques are used to increase speed of reading: working against time and using various machines. Just as much gain in speed can be obtained by well-organized, less complicated, and less expensive procedures as by machines.

Ineffective oral readers need to be given text that is relatively easy for them to read, and they must have ample opportunity to prepare to read orally. The major problems in oral reading are an inappropriate eye-voice span, lack of proper phrasing, an undesirable rate and timing in reading orally, and frustration in doing so.

Study Questions

1. How should the child's reading rate be assessed?
2. What incentives should be considered when trying to help a student improve her reading speed?

3. What is meant by "a flexible reader"? What characteristics of the reading task determine the appropriate reading rate?
4. What are the causes of poor oral reading? What are some general practices that promote good oral reading?

Selected Readings

Burmeister, L. E. (1983). *Foundations and strategies for teaching children to read* (pp. 444–467). Reading, MA: Addison-Wesley.

Durkin, D. (1987). *Teaching young children to read* (4th ed.) (pp. 124–149). Boston: Allyn and Bacon.

Harris, A. J., & Sipay, E. R. (1990). *How to increase reading ability* (9th ed.) (pp. 632–654). New York: Longman.

McCormick, S. (1987). *Remedial and clinical reading instruction* (pp. 343–355). Columbus, OH: Merrill.

Spache, G. D., & Spache, E. B. (1986). *Reading in the elementary school* (5th ed.) (pp. 303–323). Boston: Allyn and Bacon.

$$Chapter \quad 17$$

Encouraging Continued Growth in Reading

After a child has overcome a reading difficulty sufficiently to allow him to discontinue relying on remedial instruction, he should be placed in classroom situations in which he will gain increasing independence in reading. He must be carefully aided and assisted by the classroom teacher. This child needs the support and encouragement necessary to ensure that he will continue to improve in reading, and he also needs opportunities to develop real self-sufficiency and independence in reading.

If the results of remedial training are to become permanent, and if continuous growth in reading is to occur in the classroom, the child should develop a permanent interest in reading, establish independence in reading, and continue to progress in reading after remediation.

Developing a Permanent Interest in Reading

Throughout the remedial treatment programs discussed in this book, attention has been focused on getting the child with reading difficulties to become independent in his reading. The development of reading interests and the desire to use reading as a source of information and enjoyment were considered essential to reading growth. If remedial instruction is to establish permanent learning, an appreciation of reading as a worthwhile activity must be cultivated.

Of great importance in establishing a continuing appreciation for and utilization of reading is to provide the child with selections and materials that appeal to his interests. Whether in a remedial reading setting or in a classroom, nothing is more important to ensuring continued growth in reading than maintaining strong motivation. There is ample evidence that children make greater progress in their reading when they read about things that are highly interesting to them.

According to research by Greenlaw (1983), children at the primary level select as most preferred, books that are classified as funny, followed by books about make-believe situations, books about people, and animal stories; books about real things, rhymes, and mystery books were third most popular. Fairy tales, sports, and how-to-do-it books were chosen least often. Intermediate-level children selected, as their most preferred books, adventure stories, books on jokes and humor, and informational books. Second most popular were fantasies, mysteries, sports books, and books on the supernatural. How-to-do-it books, biographies, historical fiction, and poetry were chosen third most frequently, and science fiction and romance were chosen least often. October issues of the *Reading Teacher* and the *Journal of Reading* provide current bibliographies of books that are most preferred by children and young adults. *Kid's Favorite Books* (1992) supplies a list of over 300 recent titles selected by 10,000 children ages 5–13.

When Wolfson, Manning, and Manning (1984) had fourth-grade children respond to a reading interest inventory, they found that more boys than girls expressed interest in reading about adventure, machines and applied science, and animals. More girls than boys, however, expressed interest in multiethnic family life and children and fine and applied arts. Boys and girls showed little or no difference in interest in their preferences for fantasy, sports, social studies, famous people, and plants. Fantasy was the most popular category studied among boys and girls combined, whereas plants was not a popular topic for either.

A review of research on children's leisure reading interests by Greaney (1980) revealed that children at the end of elementary school read the most, girls read more books than did boys, children from higher socioeconomic classes read more than did children from lower socioeconomic classes, good students read more and better quality materials than did poor students, and many readers at the secondary level seemed to have abandoned reading altogether. Mellon (1987) studied the leisure reading of rural secondary students and found that over 25% of low-achieving students indicated that they did no leisure reading. Further, twice as many males as females said that they did not read in their spare time. The two most frequently given reasons for not reading were working after school and hatred of reading. Among males who did leisure reading, the three most preferred types of reading were magazines, sports and sports biographies, and comic books. For females, the three most preferred categories were romance, mystery, and magazines.

In general, the foregoing research suggests that there are differences in reading preferences, depending upon the age and sex of the reader. A decline in leisure reading with age, accompanied by the complete rejection of reading by many older, poor-achieving students, is a cause for concern.

Identifying Specific Interests of a Child with a Reading Disability

Studies of children's reading interests are valuable for suggesting what types of books might appeal to children of a certain age and sex, as well as what books might appeal to a given child. When teaching an individual child, however—especially one who is resistant to reading—it becomes necessary to identify and evaluate her own particular interests. This may be done through several devices.

Questionnaires

Information may be gained from simple questionnaires. Often, the best questionnaire is one devised by the teacher himself, for it can apply specifically to a particular child or group of children. For children with reading difficulties, the teacher must often read the items of the questionnaire to the child and write in her responses.

Interview

As the remedial reading teacher works with a child with reading difficulties, she should be alert to the child's interests. When the child seems to be comfortable in the remedial reading setting, the teacher should have a relaxed, conversational interview with the child. Informal conversation, recommended by Norton (1987, p. 101), is a simple, natural, and effective way to uncover a child's interests.

The interview may supplement the questionnaire or, for some children, substitute for it. During the interview, every effort is made to help the child feel comfortable, so that he will want to talk freely about his activities in and out of school, the kind of reading he likes, his favorite television programs, and so on. The teacher may use a mimeographed outline to guide the interview and to record the information. It should not be used if it breaks the rapport between teacher and student. Jotting down such items as his favorite sports, movies, books, or suggestions for future reading does not ordinarily disturb a child. But sometimes, the relaxed, personal give-and-take of a quiet interview is ruined by following a schedule. Note that although an interview may be time consuming, so much information is usually gained that it is worthwhile.

Observation

A relatively simple and effective way to find out what interests a child is to watch her daily activities. When children are free to express themselves in talk, play, drawing, and other activities, the alert teacher will find many opportunities to jot down an anecdotal note for later reference. The child who draws dogs is probably interested in reading about dogs. The child who loves to play truck driver usually enjoys reading about trucks. Many possible reading interests are discovered in this way.

Methods for Developing the Desire to Read

Children with reading difficulties, nearly all of whom, at the start of remedial treatment, dislike reading, present special complications. The teacher's first task is to identify the child's interests, as previously described. Then the child should be introduced to voluntary reading with a book on a topic of major interest to him. This book should be easy to read, short, and well written and should have lots of pictures. More books should be supplied as needed. The first several books may all be on one subject—perhaps animals if they are what the child likes. It is important to keep within the area of his known interests until the habit of voluntary reading is established, even if those interests are very narrow. He may refuse to read anything but animal stories, or space stories, or basketball stories. But in time, his interests will expand gradually. The main problem with children with reading disabilities is to teach them to read at an appropriate level. Enrichment and expansion of interests can come later, gradually.

To develop an interest in reading, conditions in school and at home must be favorable to reading. Reading is encouraged in school settings by (1) teachers who are enthusiastic about books, (2) classrooms and resource rooms that are full of well-selected, easily accessible books, (3) enough time provided to look through, choose, and read books, (4) specific recommendations given by teachers and peers, and (5) teachers who read aloud every day. (For more information about school settings that encourage reading, see Hickman (1983); to learn more about reading aloud to children, *The Read-Aloud Handbook* (Trelease, 1985) is highly recommended.) Reading is encouraged at home by (1) parents who are supportive of the activity, (2) books and magazines made available that are appropriate to the child's reading level and interests, (3) parents who converse with their child about what the child has read, and (4) parents who read aloud to their children. To be effective, all of these activities must be spontaneous, rather than staged to snare the child into reading. Many children want to be like their parents in ways that are genuine and worthwhile. Under such favorable conditions, most children will lengthen their leisure-time reading and broaden their reading interests.

Although the real motivation for reading must come from the child himself, the teacher can help the child pursue established interests and discover new ones. The child is not born with interests; rather, they are acquired and can be encouraged by guidance. One interest can lead to another. For example, a child may be interested in baseball. This may lead to reading newspaper accounts of baseball games, which in turn may lead to reading biographies of baseball heroes, which may lead to reading about—who knows what? Some suggestions for developing and extending the child's permanent interests in reading are discussed in the following subsections.

Build Interest by Reading to Children

The remedial reading teacher who reads stories aloud with real enthusiasm so that they fascinate children will have little difficulty stimulating interest in reading. Reading aloud also helps the teacher demonstrate an appreciation for good literature (Marino, 1991). An entertaining story that the teacher has read to a group will be reread by many children when it is placed in the reading corner and when attention is called to it. Or, some of the more advanced readers may read a prepared selection from a story aloud to the group. When reading aloud to others, the reader is motivated to do her best, and her listeners become interested in the story and will probably wish to read it all.

Build Interests That Are Free from Instruction in Skill Development

There should be a clear-cut distinction between reading done in the remedial program to develop skills and abilities and reading to expand interests, much of which is achieved during time devoted to personal reading. McKee (1948) emphasized this point when he said that "methods used to help children build an abiding interest in good reading material and a taste for such material must be inherently informal," enabling children to approach a selection as something to be enjoyed in its own right. There is no surer way to stifle expanding interests than to stop the ongoing enjoyment of a story or selection in order to engage in drill upon a fundamental of reading or to attempt to extract an analysis of content, plot, or characterization. It is unwise to probe and quiz, implying that nothing can be learned unless the teacher asks questions and the children answer them. However, as Indrisano and Paratore (1992) suggest, children can be encouraged to respond to text in an unstructured manner, and later, rereading can be done to meet specific goals or complete defined tasks. When a child needs help in recognizing a word or comprehending a concept, it should be given freely and quickly, so that he can continue to communicate with the author actively and with interest.

To instill in a child the interest and desire to do extensive reading—to be a reader—is a leading goal of any reading program. The beauty and the wonder of reading are lost when it becomes nothing more than a forced and unpleasant classroom exercise. All of the reading skills combined are of little use to the child who does not read.

Present Systematic Lessons

Lessons designed to expand the child's reading interests should be planned carefully and systematically. Based upon knowledge of each child's reading abilities and interests, the remedial reading teacher can design experiences to expand the children's interests. One way of doing so is to integrate the ideas found in reading with the children's daily experiences. Careful integration of ideas, of course, requires considerable thought and attention.

Any subject has the potential for deepening and expanding the child's reading interests. It is often assumed that the development of those interests is limited to reading juvenile fiction. Such an assumption should not be made; it should be recognized that, currently, children's interests are being expanded beyond juvenile fiction. It is equally important to recognize that children are interested in the wonders of the world about them. Expository text provides a basis for questioning that stimulates a deeper understanding of what it means to exist in the world (McClure & Zitlow, 1991). The concept of children's literature has broadened to include materials from many genres, both expository and narrative.

Use Hobbies to Stimulate Reading Interests

Teachers have found that allowing children time to pursue hobbies in school is worthwhile. One child's enthusiasm may spark others' interest in a particular hobby. Often, the teacher can suggest some type of related reading that will be valuable to the young enthusiasts. Especially at the secondary level, many students participate in optional after-school activities that stimulate a strong interest in reading. Books directed toward specialized interests often have great appeal to students who devote their time and energy to the areas presented.

Other methods of stimulating interest in reading include (1) displays of book jackets and book advertisements, (2) a book club with its own student officers, (3) carefully organized and regularly changed book exhibits in a corridor display case, (4) an attractive wall chart on which each student can list books he has read, and (5) book talks, in which a small group of students discusses books informally. Students most enjoy discussing books with a few classmates who share similar interests. In general, the enthusiastic teacher who promotes "real" reading and plans systematically for developing interests will find success.

Perhaps the most effective incentive for broadening one's interests comes from feeling the enthusiasm of the teacher and of other students for stories and books that do *not* deal with what one thought was the only interesting area. Judicious use of all of the methods discussed can be applied to expand reading interests, as well as to deepen them. The alert teacher will know which method or methods to use with a particular student.

We have pointed out the strong influence of a teacher's enthusiasm. It is well known that the teacher who is most successful in developing an interest in reading in a specific area is herself interested in that area, lives it, appreciates it, and shares her enjoyment with the children whom she teaches. It should be noted that interaction among students also generates far-reaching reading interests.

The goal of continued growth in reading by a particular student will have been achieved when she has acquired broad and permanent interests and socially desirable tastes. Although growth in reading interests and tastes is gradual, proper guidance throughout the grades can accomplish much. Besides providing a strong motivation for learning to read, interests determine what is read and how much is read voluntarily.

There is no such thing as a criterion of good taste that is applicable to all children. Children don't make appropriate choices for reading materials naturally, but develop this ability in a supportive environment (Marino, 1991). Improvement in taste is relative to the level of a particular child. Although improvement may be slow, well-organized guidance can lead to a better choice of reading materials for all children. The gains will be large for some students and small for others. A remedial reading program to broaden interests and cultivate tastes is essentially the same as a nonremedial reading program. The main difference is that the remedial program is more intensive and more highly individualized.

Establishing Independence in Reading

When a child begins remedial reading instruction he is often insecure and lacks self-confidence and independence. A important part of helping such a child improve his reading is helping him to become increasingly more independent.

Developing Initial Independence

In initial remedial reading instruction, it is often wise to intersperse short, easily accomplished reading activities with other types of activities that are more appealing to children with reading difficulties. Eventually, as a student gains confidence and improves her reading skills, it becomes desirable to devote more of the instructional period to reading. In addition, the student should be asked to read increasingly longer selections and should be given less direct assistance. Both of these tend to increase the student's reading independence. Allowing a student to take an appropriate book home to read is a similar aid to independence. Although oral reading is valuable for many children with reading difficulties, silent reading must receive a good deal of emphasis in order to help establish skills for independence in reading. Allowing a student to select her own reading material fosters independence in reading, as does encouraging her to use reading for her own reasons. The independent reader reads books of her own selection for such reasons as pure enjoyment, because her friends are talking about a certain book, or because she needs information for a project or activity.

The older student benefits from some direct instruction in functional reading of such materials as newspapers, telephone books, television guides, catalogs, and promotional pamphlets. Most students enjoy reading these materials, especially when they are free to read according to their own interests, and most learn to use the materials in an independent manner to gather useful information.

Learning to Use Library Resources

Children with reading difficulties often do not make successful use of the school library and therefore can benefit from direct assistance in this area as a part of their remedial instruction. The organization of the library and library procedures can be discussed with the child on an individual basis by the school librarian. The reading teacher can help the child practice such procedures as using the card catalog or computer system, finding books, and checking them out, until the student becomes quite skillful and confident in obtaining books from the library.

Use of the public library should also be encouraged. Often, upon the remedial reading teacher's suggestion, parents take their children to the public library and assist them in selecting a book and obtaining a library card. With encouragement from teachers and parents, these children can become proficient in the use of both the school and the public library and will begin to use both with independence.

Exploring Other Sources of Reading Material

When other children in the school can purchase inexpensive editions of well-liked books through the school book club, children with reading difficulties should be assisted in doing so, too. The remedial reading teacher can compile an appropriate list of choices for the child who reads poorly, and his parents can encourage him to choose a book or two.

In addition, parents can point out to their children the many displays of books and magazines in stores. If a child shows an interest in a magazine from a store display shelf, a parent should feel free to buy it for the child, even though it may seem too advanced for him. Although the child may not be able to read every word, or even understand every idea in the magazine, it is a step toward independence in reading to have a magazine of one's own.

It is also valuable for a child with reading difficulties to be introduced to a bookstore and see the many different books offered for sale there, such as attractive oversized picture books, inexpensive paperback books, and fat hardcover books. It is good for the child to observe that people come to the store to select and purchase books. Perhaps when looking through the books in the store, the child might decide that he wants a book of his own. Such a decision is part of reading independence.

Continuing Progress in Reading after Remediation

When a child has shown sufficient growth in reading to enable her to discontinue remedial assistance, it is important that the remedial reading teacher and the classroom teacher plan together to accomplish a smooth transition for the child. During remediation, a good deal of communication between the classroom teacher and the remedial reading teacher has served to coordinate efforts on the child's behalf. At the termination of remediation, the remedial reading teacher will want to share some insights and suggestions with the classroom teacher that can help him assist the child to continue to improve in reading.

The classroom teacher should support the child so that she can maintain confidence in her reading now that she will be without the reassurance of the remedial reading teacher. The classroom teacher should also be alert to signs of difficulty in reading so that the child does not experience immediate frustration in classroom reading situations. In some instances, children may revisit the remedial reading teacher once a week or twice a month for the purpose of a little additional support. On occasion, these children benefit from being enrolled in a summer program designed to enhance reading improvement.

It is also important for parents to continue to encourage their child's reading efforts and be aware of and support the child's reading program. Communication with the classroom teacher is worthwhile. Occasionally, parents can continue to provide home assistance in reading under the classroom teacher's guidance. Sometimes, they will want to communicate to the teacher about signs of tension they detect in their child or to mention how much better their child seems to like school now that her reading is more successful.

When a child with a reading disability has overcome the difficulties that were impeding her reading and educational growth, when she has developed a real desire to read, and when she has established independence and self-sufficiency in the use of reading as a tool of learning at her level of reading expectancy, her chances for continued growth in reading become excellent. If, in addition, her teachers continue to give instruction suited to her individual learning characteristics, her successful reading development will be practically ensured. Such diagnostic teaching will make success possible for many students who otherwise would be unable to realize their complete educational potential. This kind of teaching takes the highest level of professional dedication, but therein lies the educational future of many children.

Study Questions

1. How can one identify specific interests of children with reading difficulties?
2. What can be done to help children with reading difficulties develop an interest in reading?
3. How do parents and teachers guide a child to reading independence?
4. Why make an effort to ensure continuing progress in reading after remediation?

Selected Readings

Children's Book Council, Inc. (1992). *Kids' favorite books*. Newark, DE: International Reading Association.

Harris, A. J., & Sipay, E. R. (1984). *Readings on reading instruction* (3rd ed.) (pp. 344–382). New York: Longman.

Trelease, J. (1985). *The read-aloud handbook* (2nd ed.). New York: Viking Penguin.

References

Ackerman, P. T., Anhalt, J. M., & Dykman, R. A. (1986). Inferential word-decoding weakness in reading disabled children. *Learning Disability Quarterly, 9,* 315–324.

Aram, D. M., Kelman, B. L., & Nation, J. E. (1984). Preschoolers with language disorders: 10 years later. *Journal of Speech and Hearing Research, 27,* 232–245.

Armbruster, B. B. (1992). On answering questions. *The Reading Teacher, 45,* 724–725.

Austin, M. C., Bush, C. L., & Huebner, M. H. (1961). *Reading evaluation.* New York: Ronald Press.

Bader, L. A. (1983). *Bader reading and language inventory.* New York: Macmillan.

Bakker, D. J., Bouma, A., & Gardien, C. J. (1990). Hemisphere-specific treatment of dyslexia subtypes: A field experiment. *Journal of Learning Disabilities, 23,* 433–438.

Bakker, D. J., Teunissen, J., & Bosch, J. (1976). Development of laterality. In R. M. Knights & D. J. Bakker (Eds.), *The neuropsychology of learning disorders: Theoretical approaches.* Baltimore: University Park Press.

Balow, B., Rubin, R., & Rosen, M. J. (1975). Perinatal events as precursors of reading disability. *Reading Research Quarterly, 11,* 36–71.

Bannatyne, A. (1974). Diagnosis: A note on recategorization of the WISC scaled scores. *Journal of Learning Disabilities, 7,* 272–273.

Barnitz, J. G. (1980). Syntactic effects of the reading comprehension of pronoun referent structures by children in grades two, four, and six. *Reading Research Quarterly, 15,* 268–289.

Bender, L. (1957). Specific reading disability as a maturational lag. *Bulletin of the Orton Society, 9,* 9–18.

Berryhill, P. (1984). Reading in the content area of social studies. In M. M. Dupuis (Ed.), *Reading in the content areas: Research for teachers* (pp. 66–81). Newark, DE: International Reading Association.

Betts, E. A. (1957). *Foundations of reading instruction.* New York: American Book Company.

Beverstock, C. (1991). *Your child's vision is important.* Newark, DE: International Reading Association.

Birch, H. G., & Gussow, J. D. (1970). *Disadvantaged children: Health, nutrition, and school failure.* New York: Grune and Stratton, Inc.

Blachman, B. A. (1984). Relationship of rapid naming ability and language analysis skills to kindergarten and first-grade reading achievement. *Journal of Educational Psychology, 76,* 601–622.

Black, F. W. (1973). Neurological dysfunction and reading disorders. *Journal of Learning Disabilities, 6,* 313–316.

Black, F. W. (1974). Self-concept as related to achievement and age in learning disabled children. *Child Development, 45,* 1137–1140.

Black, F. W. (1976). Cognitive, academic, and behavioral findings in children with suspected and documented neurological dysfunction. *Journal of Learning Disabilities, 9,* 182–187.

Blaha, J. (1982). Predicting reading and arithmetic achievement with measures of reading attitudes and cognitive styles. *Perceptual and Motor Skills, 55,* 107–114.

Blair, J. C., Peterson, M. E., & Viehweg, S. H. (1985). The effects of mild sensorineural hearing loss on academic performance of young school-age children. *Volta Review, 87,* 87–93.

Blake, M. E. (1985). The relationship between field dependance-independance and the comprehension of expository and literary text types. *Reading World, 24,* 53–62.

Blanchard, J. S., Mason, G. E., & Daniel, D. (1987). *Computer applications in reading* (3rd ed.). Newark: International Reading Association.

Bloomfield, L, & Barnhart, C. (1961). *Let's read: A linguistic approach.* Detroit: Wayne State University Press.

Bockmiller, P. R. (1981). Hearing-impaired children: Learning to read a second language. *American Annals of the Deaf, 126,* 810–813.

Bond, G. L. (1935). *The auditory and speech characteristics of poor readers.* New York: Teachers College, Columbia University.

Bond, G. L., & Dykstra, R. (1967). *Coordinating center for first grade reading instruction programs.* Final Report of Project No. X-001, Contract No. OE-5–10–264. Minneapolis, MN: University of Minnesota.

Bond, G. L., & Wagner, E. B. (1966). *Teaching the child to read* (4th ed.). New York: Macmillan.

Bormuth, J. R. (1976). Comparable cloze and multiple-choice test comprehension scores. *Journal of Reading, 10,* 295.

Bow, J. N. (1988). A comparison of intellectually superior male reading achievers and underachievers from a neuropsychological perspective. *Journal of Learning Disabilities, 21,* 118–123.

Bowers, P. G., Steffy, R., & Tate, E. (1988). Comparison of the effects of IQ control methods on memory and naming speed predictors of reading disability. *Reading Research Quarterly, 23,* 304–319.

Brady, S. (1986). Short-term memory, phonological processing, and reading ability. *Annals of Dyslexia, 36,* 138–153.

Bristow, P. S. (1985). Are poor readers passive readers? Some evidence, possible explanations, and potential solutions. *The Reading Teacher, 39,* 318–325.

Brock, H. (1982). Factor structure of intellectual and achievement measures for learning disabled children. *Psychology in the Schools, 19,* 297–304.

Brown, J. I., Bennett, J. M., & Hanna, G. (1981). *Nelson-Denny reading test.* Chicago: Riverside.

Bryan, T. H., & Bryan, J. H. (1978). *Understanding learning disabilities* (2nd ed.). Port Washington, NY: Alfred.

Burmeister, L. E. (1983). *Foundations and strategies for teaching children to read.* Reading, MA: Addison-Wesley.

Buttery, T. J., & Mason, G. E. (1979). Reading improvement for mainstreamed children who are mildly mentally handicapped. *Reading Improvement, 16,* 334–337.

Camp, B. W., & Zimet, S. G. (1975). Classroom behavior during reading instruction. *Exceptional Children, 42,* 109–110.

Carbo, M. (1983). Research in reading and learning style: Implications for exceptional children. *Exceptional Children, 49,* 486–494.

Carbo, M. (1985). Research in learning style and reading: Implications for instruction. *Theory into Practice, 23,* 72–76.

Carner, R. L. (1981). Physiological variables and reading disability. *Journal of Research and Development in Education, 14,* 24–34.

Catts, H. W. (1986). Speech production/phonological deficits in reading-disordered children. *Journal of Learning Disabilities, 19,* 504–508.

Catts, H. W., & Kamhi, A. G. (1986). The linguistic basis of reading disorders: Implications for the speech-language pathologist. *Language, Speech, and Hearing Services in Schools, 17,* 329–341.

Cegelka, J. A., & Cegelka, W. J. (1970). A review of research: Reading and the educable mentally retarded. *Exceptional Children, 37,* 187–200.

Chapman, J. (1979). Confirming children's use of cohesive ties in text: Pronouns. *The Reading Teacher, 33*, 317–322.

Chapman, J. W., Silva, P. A., & Williams, S. M. (1984). Academic self-concept: Some developmental and emotional correlates in nine-year-old children. *British Journal of Educational Psychology, 54*, 284–292.

Children's Book Council, Inc. (1992). *Kid's favorite books*. Newark, DE: International Reading Association.

Chomsky, C. (1969). *The acquisition of syntax in children from 5 to 10*. Cambridge, MA: M.I.T. Press.

Clymer, T. W. (1952). *The influence of reading ability on the validity of group intelligence tests*. Unpublished doctoral dissertation, University of Minnesota, Minneapolis.

Cohen, S. A. (1969). *Teach them all to read*. New York: Random House.

Cohen, S. A., & Cooper, T. (1972). Seven fallacies: Reading retardation and the urban disadvantaged reader. *The Reading Teacher, 26*, 38–44.

Cole, L. (1938). *The improvement of reading*. New York: Holt, Rinehart, and Winston.

Collins, M. D., & Cheek, E. H. (1989). *Diagnostic-prescriptive reading instruction* (3rd ed.). Dubuque, IA: Wm. C. Brown.

Conoley, J. C., & Kramer, J. J. (Eds.). (1989). *The tenth mental measurements yearbook*. Lincoln, NE: University of Nebraska Press.

Cooper, E. J., & Sherk, J. (1989). Addressing urban school reform: Issues and alliances. *Journal of Negro Education, 58*, 315–331.

Cooter, R. B. (1990). *The teachers guide to reading tests*. Scottsdale, AZ: Gorsuch Scarisbrick.

Crane, J. A. (1950). *Reading difficulties as a social work problem*. Unpublished master's thesis, McGill University, Montreal, Canada.

Crawley, S. J., & Merritt, K. (1991). *Remediating reading difficulties*. Dubuque, IA: Wm. C. Brown.

Critchley, M. (1970). *The dyslexic child*. Springfield, IL: Charles C. Thomas.

Cruickshank, W. M. (Ed.). (1971). *Psychology of exceptional children and youth* (3rd ed.). Englewood Cliffs, NJ: Prentice Hall, Inc.

CTB/McGraw-Hill. (1986a). *California achievement tests*. Monterey, CA: Author.

CTB/McGraw-Hill. (1986b). *California achievement tests, reading*. Monterey, CA: Author.

Cullinan, B. E. (Ed.). (1992). *Invitation to read: More children's literature in the reading program*. Newark, DE: International Reading Association.

Cummins, J. P., & Das, J. P. (1980). Cognitive processing, academic achievement, and WISC-R performance. *Journal of Consulting and Clinical Psychology, 48*, 777–779.

Dale, E., & Chall, J. (1948). Formula for predicting readability. *Educational Research Bulletin, 27*, 11–20 and 37–45.

Dalgleish, B. W. J., & Enkelmann, S. (1979). The interpretation of pronominal reference by retarded and normal readers. *British Journal of Educational Psychology, 49*, 290–296.

Dechant, E. V., & Smith, H. P. (1977). *Psychology of teaching reading* (2nd ed.). Englewood Cliffs, NJ: Prentice Hall.

DeHirsh, K., Jansky, J. J., & Langford, W. S. (1966). *Predicting reading failure: A preliminary study*. New York: Harper & Row.

Denckla, M. B. (1987). Application of disconnection concepts to developmental dyslexia. *Annals of Dyslexia, 37*, 51–61.

Dolch, E. W. (1945). *A manual for remedial reading.* (2nd ed.). Champaign, IL: Garrard Press.

Dolch, E. W. (1951). *Psychology and teaching of reading* (2nd ed.). Champaign, IL: Garrard Press.

Dolch, E. W. (1960). *Teaching primary reading* (3rd ed.). Champaign, IL: Garrard Press.

Dorman, C. (1985). Defining and diagnosing dyslexia: Are we putting the cart before the horse? *Reading Research Quarterly, 20*, 505–508.

Duane, D. D. (1983). Neurobiological correlates of reading disorders. *Journal of Educational Research, 77*, 5–15.

Dunn, R. (1988). Teaching students through their perceptual strengths or preferences. *Journal of Reading, 31*, 304–309.

Dunn, R., Price, G. E., Dunn, K., & Saunders, W. (1979). Relationship of learning style to self concept. *The Clearing House, 53*, 155–158.

Dupuis, M. M. (Ed.). (1984). *Reading in the content areas: Research for teachers*. Newark, DE: International Reading Association.

Durkin, D. (1987). *Teaching young children to read* (4th ed.). Boston: Allyn and Bacon.

Durrell, D. D. (1955). *Improving reading instruction.* New York: Harcourt Brace Jovanovich.

Durrell, D. D., & Catterson, J. H. (1980). *Durrell analysis of reading difficulties* (3rd ed.). San Antonio, TX: The Psychological Corporation.

Eames, T. H. (1935). A frequency study of physical handicaps in reading disability and unselected groups. *Journal of Educational Research, 29,* 1–5.

Edmiaston, R. K. (1984). Oral language and reading: How are they related for third graders? *Remedial and Special Education, 5,* 33–37.

Ekwall, E. E. (1986). *Teacher's handbook on diagnosis and remediation in reading* (2nd ed.). Boston: Allyn and Bacon.

Eldredge, A. R. (1981). An investigation to determine the relationships among self-concept, locus of control, and reading achievement. *Reading World, 21,* 59–64.

Engle, P. L. (1975). Language medium in early school years for minority language groups. *Review of Educational Research, 45,* 283–325.

Englemann, S., & Bruner, E. C. (1983). *Reading mastery: DISTAR reading I.* Chicago: Science Research Associates.

Erickson, M. E. (1987). Deaf readers reading beyond the literal. *American Annals of the Deaf, 132,* 291–294.

Evans, R. V. (1979). The relationship between the reading and writing of syntactic structure. *Research in the Teaching of English, 13,* 129–135.

Feagans, L. V., & Merriwether, A. (1990). Visual discrimination of letter-like forms and its relationship to achievement over time in children with learning disabilities. *Journal of Learning Disabilities, 23,* 417–425.

Featherstone, W. B. (1951). *Teaching the slow learner* (rev. ed.). New York: Bureau of Publications, Teachers College, Columbia University.

Feldhusen, J. F., Thurston, J. R., & Benning, J. J. (1970). Longitudinal analysis of classroom behavior and school achievement. *Journal of Experimental Education, 38,* 4–10.

Felton, R. H., & Wood, F. B. (1989). Cognitive deficits in reading disability and attention deficit disorder. *Journal of Learning Disabilities, 22,* 3–13.

Fernald, G. M. (1971). *Remedial techniques in basic school subjects.* New York: McGraw-Hill.

Fishel, C. T. (1984). Reading in the content area of English. In M. M. Dupuis (ed.), *Reading in the content areas: Research for teachers* (pp. 5–20). Newark, DE: International Reading Association.

Fletcher, J. M., Satz, P., & Scholes, R. J. (1981). Developmental changes in the linguistic performance correlates of reading achievement. *Brain and Language, 13,* 78–90.

Foorman, B. R., & Liberman, D. (1989). Visual and phonological processing of words: A comparison of good and poor readers. *Journal of Learning Disabilities, 22,* 349–355.

Fries, C. C. (1963). *Linguistics and reading.* New York: Holt, Rinehart, and Winston.

Frost, B. P. (1965). Some personality characteristics of poor readers. *Psychology in the Schools, 2,* 218–220.

Gardner, E. F., Rudmen, H. C., Karlsen, B. A., & Merwin, J. C. (1983a). *Stanford achievement tests.* New York: Psychological Corporation.

Gardner, E. F., Rudmen, H. C., Karlsen, B. A., & Merwin, J. C. (1983b). *Stanford achievement tests: Reading tests.* New York: Psychological Corporation.

Gates, A. I. (1947). *The improvement of reading* (3rd ed.). New York: Macmillan.

Gates, A. I., McKillop, A. S., & Horowitz, E. C. (1981). *Reading diagnostic tests* (2nd ed.). New York: Teachers College Press.

Gaver, M. V. (1961). Effectiveness of centralized library services in elementary schools (phase 1). *Library Quarterly, 31,* 245–256.

Geneva Medico-Educational Service. (1968). Problems posed by dyslexia. *Journal of Learning Disabilities, 1,* 158–171.

Gentile, L. M., & McMillan, M. M. (1987). *Stress and reading difficulties: Research, assessment, intervention.* Newark, DE: International Reading Association.

Gillet, J. W., & Temple, C. (1990). *Understanding reading problems: Assessment and instruction* (3rd ed.). Glenview, IL: Scott Foresman.

Gillingham, A., & Stillman, B. W. (1960). *Remedial training for children with specific disability in reading, spelling, and penmanship.* Cambridge, MA: Educators Publishing Service, Inc.

Glavin, J. P., & Annesley, F. R. (1971). Reading and arithmetic correlates of conduct-problem and withdrawn children. *Journal of Special Education, 5,* 213–219.

Glazer, S. M., & Morrow, L. M. (1978). The syntactic complexity of primary grade children's oral language and primary grade reading materials: A comparative analysis. *Journal of Reading Behavior, 10,* 200–203.

Glazer, S. M., Searfoss, L. W., & Gentile, L. M. (Eds.). (1988). *Reexamining reading diagnosis.* Newark, DE: International Reading Association.

Goodman, K. S. (Ed.). (1973). *Miscue analysis: Applications to reading instruction.* Urbana, IL: National Council of Teachers of English.

Goodman, Y. M., Watson, D. J., & Burke, C. L. (1987). *Reading miscue inventory: Alternative procedures.* New York: Richard C. Owen.

Goswami, U., & Bryant, P.(1990). *Phonological skills and learning to read.* East Sussex, UK: Lawrence Erlbaum.

Graubard, P. S. (1971). The relationship between academic achievement and behavior dimensions. *Exceptional Children, 37,* 755–756.

Gray, R. A., Saski, J., McEntire, M. E., & Larsen, S. C. (1980). Is proficiency in oral language a predictor of academic success? *The Elementary School Journal, 80,* 260–268.

Greaney, V. (1980). Factors related to amount and type of leisure time reading. *Reading Research Quarterly, 15,* 337–357.

Greenlaw, M. J. (1983). Reading interest research and children's choices. In N. Roser and M. Frith (Eds.) *Children's choice: Teaching with books children like* (pp. 90–92). Newark, DE: International Reading Association.

Grohens, J. (1988). Nutrition and reading achievement. *The Reading Teacher, 41,* 942–945.

Hallahan, D. P., & Kauffman, J. M. (1991). *Exceptional children* (5th ed.). Englewood Cliffs, NJ: Prentice Hall.

Halpern, H. G. (1984). An investigation of reading and conceptual tempo measures. *Reading World,* 24(1), 90–96.

Hammill, D. D, & McNutt, G. (1980). Language abilities and reading: A review of the literature on their relationship. *The Elementary School Journal, 80,* 269–277.

Hardman, M. L., Drew, C. J., Egan, W., & Wolf, B. (1990). *Human exceptionality: Society, school, and family* (3rd ed.). Boston: Allyn and Bacon.

Hare, B. A. (1977). Perceptual deficits are not a cue to reading problems in second grade. *Reading Teacher, 30,* 624–627.

Harris, A. J. (1970). *How to increase reading ability* (5th ed.). New York: David McKay.

Harris, A. J., & Jacobson, M. D. (1972). *Basic elementary reading vocabularies.* New York: Macmillan.

Harris, A. J., & Sipay, E. R. (1975). *How to increase reading ability* (6th ed.). New York: David McKay.

Harris, A. J., & Sipay, E. R. (1980). *How to increase reading ability* (7th ed.). New York: Longman.

Harris, A. J., & Sipay, E. R. (1984). *Readings on reading instruction* (3rd ed.). New York: Longman.

Harris, A. J., & Sipay, E. R. (1990). *How to increase reading ability* (9th ed.). New York: Longman.

Harris, W. J., & King, D. R. (1982). Achievement, sociometric status, and personality characteristics of children selected by their teachers as having learning and/or behavior problems. *Psychology in the Schools, 19,* 452–457.

Hart, B. O. (1976). *Teaching reading to deaf children.* New York: Alexander Graham Bell Association for the Deaf.

Hegge, T. G., Kirk, S. A., & Kirk, W. D. (1945). *Remedial reading drills.* Ann Arbor, MI: Wahr.

Heilman, A. W., Blair, T. R., & Rupley, W. H. (1986). *Principles and practices of teaching reading* (6th ed.). Columbus, OH: Merrill.

Heimlich, J. E., & Pittelman, S. D. (1986). *Semantic mapping: classroom applications.* Newark: International Reading Association.

Helfeldt, J. P. (1983). Sex-linked characteristics of brain functioning: Why Jimmy reads differently. *Reading World, 22,* 90–96.

Henk, W. A., Helfeldt, J. P., & Platt, J. M. (1986). Developing reading fluency in learning disabled students. *Teaching Exceptional Children, 18,* 202–206.

Herber, H. L. (1965). Reading study skills: Some studies. *Reading and Inquiry, 10,* 94–96.

Herber, H. L. (1978). *Teaching reading in content areas* (2nd ed.). Englewood Cliffs, NJ: Prentice Hall.

Herbert, D. J. (1968). Reading comprehension as a function of self concept. *Perceptual and Motor Skills, 27,* 78.

Hermann, M. A. (1987). *Tiger's tales: A reading adventure* [computer program]. Pleasantville, NY: Sunburst Communications.

Hewett, F. M., & Taylor, F. D. (1980). *The emotionally disturbed child in the classroom: The orchestration of success* (2nd ed.). Boston: Allyn and Bacon.

Hickman, J. (1983). Classrooms that help children like books. In N. Roser & M. Frith (Eds.) *Children's choices: Teaching with books children like* (pp. 1–11). Newark, DE: International Reading Association.

Hieronymus, A. N., Hoover, H. D., & Lindquist, E. F. (1986). *Iowa tests of basic skills.* Chicago: Riverside Publishing Company.

Holliday, W. G. (1991). Helping students learn effectively from science text. In C. M. Santa & D. E. Alvermann (Eds.), *Science learning: Processes and applications.* Newark, DE: International Reading Association.

Horn, W. F., & Packard, T. (1985). Early identification of learning problems: A meta-analysis. *Journal of Educational Psychology, 77,* 597–607.

Hoskins, S. B. (1986). Text superstructures. *Journal of Reading, 29,* 538–543.

Howell, M. J., & Manis, F. R. (1986). Developmental and reader ability differences in semantic processing efficiency. *Journal of Educational Psychology, 78,* 124–129.

Huelsman, C. B., Jr. (1970). The WISC subtest syndrome for disabled readers. *Perceptual and Motor Skills, 30,* 535–550.

Hynd, C. R. (1987). Instruction of reading disabled/dyslexic students. *Teacher Education and Practice, 3,* 17–33.

Hynd, C. R., Qian, G., Ridgeway, V. G., & Pickle, M. (1991). Promoting conceptual change with science texts and discussion. *Journal of Reading, 34,* 596–601.

Idol, L. (1987). Group story mapping: A comprehension strategy for both skilled and unskilled readers. *Journal of Learning Disabilities, 20,* 196–205.

Indrisano, R., & Paratore, J. R. (1992). Using literature with readers at risk. In B. C. Cullinan (Ed.), *Invitation to read: More children's literature in the reading program* (pp. 138–165). Newark, DE: International Reading Association.

Isom, J. B. (1968). Neurological research relevant to reading. In H. K. Smith (Ed.), *Perception and reading.* Newark, DE: International Reading Association.

Jewell, M. G., & Zintz, M. V. (1986). *Learning to read naturally.* Dubuque, IA: Kendall/Hunt.

Jobe, F. W. (1976). *Screening vision in schools.* Newark, DE: International Reading Association.

Johnson, D. J., & Myklebust, H. R. (1967). *Learning disabilities: Educational principles and practices.* New York: Grune & Stratton.

Johnson, M. S., Kress, R. A., & Pikulski, J. J. (1987). *Informal reading inventories* (2nd ed.) Newark, DE: International Reading Association.

Jorm, A. F., Share, D. L., Matthews, R., & Maclean, R. (1986). Behavior problems in specific reading retarded and general reading backward children: A longitudinal study. *Journal of Child Psychology & Psychiatry & Allied Disciplines, 27,* 33–43.

Kamhi, A. G., & Catts, H. W. (1986). Toward an understanding of developmental language and reading disorders. *Journal of Speech and Hearing Disorders, 51,* 337–347.

Karlsen, B., Madden, R., & Gardner, E. F. (1984). *Stanford diagnostic reading test.* San Antonio, TX: The Psychological Corporation.

Kaufman, A. S. (1975). Factor analysis of the WISC-R at 11 age levels between $6\frac{1}{2}$ and $16\frac{1}{2}$ years. *Journal of Consulting and Clinical Psychology, 43,* 135–147.

Kaufman, A. S., & Kaufman, N. L. (1985). *Kaufman test of educational achievement, brief form.* Circle Pines, MN: American Guidance Service, Inc.

Kavale, K. A. (1981). The relationship between auditory perceptual skills and reading ability: A meta-analysis. *Journal of Learning Disabilities, 14,* 539–546.

Kavale, K. A. (1982). Meta-analysis of the relationship between visual perception skills and reading achievement. *Journal of Learning Disabilities, 15,* 42–51.

Kendler, J. P. (1972). Is there really a WISC profile for poor readers? *Journal of Learning Disabilities, 5,* 397–400.

Kent, C. E. (1984). A linguist compares narrative and expository prose. *Journal of Reading, 28,* 232–236.

Kephart, N. C. (1971). *The slow learner in the classroom* (2nd ed.). Columbus, OH: Merrill.

Kirby, J. R., & Robinson, G. L. W. (1987). Simultaneous and successive processing in reading disabled children. *Journal of Learning Disabilities, 20,* 243–252.

Kirk, S. A. (1940). *Teaching reading to slow-learning children.* Boston: Houghton Mifflin.

Kirk, S. A., & Elkins, J. (1975). Characteristics of children enrolled in the Child Service Demonstration Centers. *Journal of Learning Disabilities, 8,* 630–637.

Kirk, S. A., & Gallagher, J. J. (1989). *Educating exceptional children* (6th ed.). Boston: Houghton Mifflin.

Kirk, S. A., Kliebhan, J. M., & Lerner, J. W. (1978). *Teaching reading to slow and disabled learners.* Boston: Houghton Mifflin.

Kirk, U. (1989). Neurological aspects of learning difficulty. In R. Roswell & G. Natchez, *Reading disability* (4th ed.) (pp. 17–40). New York: Basic Books.

Klein, R. S., Altman, S. D., Dreizen, K., Friedman, R., & Powers, L. (1981). Restructuring dysfunctional attitudes toward children's learning and behavior in school: Family-oriented psychoeducational therapy. *Journal of Learning Disabilities, 14,* 15–19.

Knox, G. E. (1953). Classroom symptoms of visual difficulty. In *Clinical studies in reading: II* (Supplementary Educational Monographs no. 77), Chicago: University of Chicago Press.

Kogan, N. (1980). Cognitive styles and reading performance. *Bulletin of the Orton Society, 30,* 63–78.

Kozlowski, L. J. (1968). Identifying visual problems by teacher observation. In *Clinical Studies in Reading: III* (Supplementary Educational Monographs no. 97), Chicago: University of Chicago Press.

Larsen, J., Tillman, C. E., Ross, J. J., Satz, P., Cassin, B., & Wolkin, W. (1973). Factors in reading achievement: An interdisciplinary approach. *Journal of Learning Disabilities, 6,* 636–644.

Lebauer, R. S. (1985). Nonnative English speaker problems in content and English classes: Are they thinking or reading problems? *Journal of Reading, 29,* 136–142.

Lenchner, O., Gerber, M. M., & Routh, D. K. (1990). Phonological awareness tasks as predictors of decoding ability: Beyond segmentation. *Journal of Learning Disabilities, 23,* 240–247.

Leong, C. K. (1989). The locus of so-called IQ test results in reading disabilities. *Journal of Learning Disabilities, 22,* 507–512.

Leslie, L., & Caldwell, J. (1990). *Qualitative reading inventory.* Glenview, IL: Scott Foresman/Little Brown Higher Education.

Lloyd, H. M. (1965). What's ahead in reading for the disadvantaged? *The Reading Teacher, 18,* 471–476.

Lundsteen, S. W. (1976). *Children learn to communicate.* Englewood Cliffs, NJ: Prentice Hall, Inc.

Lyle, J. G. (1970). Certain antenatal, perinatal, and developmental variables and reading retardation. *Child Development, 41,* 481–491.

MacGinitie, W. H., Kamons, J., Kowalski, R. L., MacGinitie, R. K., & MacKay, T. (1978). *Gates-MacGinitie reading tests.* Chicago: Riverside Publishing Company.

Maggart, Z. R., & Zintz, M. V. (1990). *Corrective reading* (6th ed.). Dubuque, IA: Wm. C. Brown.

Mallow, J. V. (1991). Reading science. *Journal of Reading, 34,* 324–338.

Margolis, H., Peterson, N., & Leonard, H. S. (1978). Conceptual tempo as a predictor of first-grade reading achievement. *Journal of Reading Behavior, 10,* 359–362.

Marino, M. (1991). Weaving threads: Creating a tapestry for learning through literature. In J. T. Feeley, D. S. Strickland, & S. B. Wepner (Eds.) *Process reading and writing.* New York: Teachers College Press.

Martin, H. P. (1971). Vision and its role in reading disability and dyslexia. *The Journal of School Health, 41,* 468–471.

McClure, A. A., & Zitlow, C. S. (1991). Not just the facts: Aesthetic response in elementary content area studies. *Language Arts, 68,* 27–33.

McConaughy, S. H. (1985). Good and poor readers' comprehension of story structure across different input and output modalities. *Reading Research Quarterly, 20,* 219–232.

McCormick, S. (1987). *Remedial and clinical reading instruction.* Columbus, OH: Merrill.

McDermott, J. C. (1983). Physical and behavioral aspects of middle ear disease in school children. *Journal of School Health, 53,* 463–466.

McGee, R., Silva, P. A., & Williams, S. (1984). Behaviour problems in a population of seven-year-old children: Prevalence, stability and types of disorder—a research report. *Journal of Child Psychology and Psychiatry, 25,* 251–259.

McGee, R., Williams, S., & Silva, P. A. (1984). Slow starters and long-term backward readers: A replication and extension. *British Journal of Educational Psychology, 58,* 330–337.

McKee, P. (1948). *The teaching of reading in the elementary school.* Boston: Houghton Mifflin.

McKinney, J. D., Mason, J., Perkerson, K., & Clifford, M. (1975). Relationship between classroom behavior and academic achievement. *Journal of Educational Psychology, 67,* 198–202.

McMichael, P. (1979). The hen or the egg? Which comes first—antisocial emotional disorders or reading disability? *British Journal of Educational Psychology, 49,* 226–238.

Melekian, B. A. (1990). Family characteristics of children with dyslexia. *Journal of Learning Disabilities, 23,* 386–391.

Mellon, C. A. (1987). Teenagers do read: What rural youth say about leisure reading. *School Library Journal, 33,* 27–30.

Miller, K. L., & George, J. E. (1992). Expository passage organizers: Models for reading and writing. *Journal of Reading, 35,* 372–378.

Minnesota Educational Computing Corporation. (1985). *Word munchers.* [Computer program]. St. Paul, MN: Author.

Miramontes, O. (1987). Oral reading miscues of Hispanic students: Implications for assessment of learning disabilities. *Journal of Learning Disabilities, 20,* 627–632.

Monroe, M. (1932). *Children who cannot read.* Chicago: University of Chicago Press.

Moore, D. W., & Wieland, O. P. (1981). WISC-R scatter indexes of children referred for reading diagnosis. *Journal of Learning Disabilities, 14,* 511–514.

Moore, D. W., & Wilson, B. J. (1987). On the search for a characteristic WISC-R subtest profile of reading/learning disabled children. *Reading Research and Instruction, 26,* 133–140.

Moores, D. F. (1982). *Educating the deaf: Psychology, principles, and practices* (2nd ed.). Boston: Houghton Mifflin.

Morice, R., & Slaghuis, W. (1985). Language performance and reading ability at 8 years of age. *Applied Psycholinguistics, 6,* 141–160.

Mueser, A. M. (1981). *Reading aids through the grades* (4th ed.). New York: Teachers College Press.

Myers, P. I., & Hammill, D. D. (1976). *Methods for learning disorders* (3rd ed.). New York: John Wiley and Sons.

Naslund, R. A., Thorpe, L. P., Lefever, D. W. (1983, 1984). *SRA achievement series.* Chicago: Science Research Associates.

National Institute of Education (1985). *Becoming a nation of readers.* Washington, DC: Author.

Neuman, S. B. (1986). The home environment and fifth grade students' leisure reading. *Elementary School Journal, 86,* 335–343.

Nichols, E. G., Inglis, J., Lawson, J. S., & MacKay, I. (1988). A cross-validation study of patterns of cognitive ability in children with learning difficulties, as described by factorially defined WISC-R verbal and performance IQs. *Journal of Learning Disabilities, 21,* 504–508.

Nolte, R. Y., Singer, H. (1985). Active comprehension: Teaching a process of reading comprehension and its effects on reading achievement. *The Reading Teacher, 39,* 24–31.

Norton, D. E. (1987). Evaluating and selecting literature for children. In *Through the eyes of a child: An introduction to children's literature* (2nd ed.). Columbus, OH: Merrill.

Olson, R., Wise, B., Conners, F., Rack, J., & Fulker, D. (1989). Specific deficits in component reading and language skills: Genetic and environmental influences. *Journal of Learning Disabilities, 22,* 339–348.

Paradise, L. V., & Block, C. (1984). The relationship of teacher-student cognitive style to academic achievement. *Journal of Research and Development in Education, 17,* 57–61.

Poostay, E., & Aaron, I. E. (1982). Reading problems of children: The perspectives of reading specialists. *School Psychology Review, 11,* 251–256.

Pratt, A. C., & Brady, S. (1988). Relation of phonological awareness to reading disability in children and adults. *Journal of Educational Psychology, 80,* 319–323.

Prendergast, M. A., & Binder, D. M. (1975). Relationships of selected self concept and academic achievement measures. *Measurement and Evaluaton in Guidance, 8,* 92–99.

Prentice Associates, Inc. (1986). *Trickster coyote.* Bridgeport, CT: Queue, Inc.

Prescott, G. A., Balow, I. H., Hogan, T. P., & Farr, R. (1987). *Metropolitan achievement tests: Reading diagnostic tests.* New York: Psychological Corporation.

Price, G. E., Dunn, R., & Saunders, W. (1981). Reading achievement and learning style characteristics. *The Clearing House, 54,* 223–226.

Quinn, L. (1981). Reading skills of hearing and congenitally deaf children. *Journal of Experimental Child Psychology, 32,* 139–161.

Rabinovitch, R. D. (1962). Dyslexia: Psychiatric considerations. In J. Money (Ed.), *Reading disability: Progress and research needs in dyslexia* (pp. 73–79). Baltimore: Johns Hopkins Press.

Readence, J. E., & Baldwin, R. S. (1978). The relationship of cognitive style and phonics instruction. *Journal of Educational Research, 72,* 44–52.

Reid, D. K., & Hresko, W. P. (1981). *A cognitive approach to learning disabilities.* New York: McGraw-Hill.

Reutzel, D. R. (1985). Reconciling schema theory and the basal reading lesson. *The Reading Teacher, 39,* 194–197.

Richardson, E., & DiBenedetto, B. (1985). *Decoding skills test.* Parkton, MD: York Press.

Richek, M. A., List, L. K., & Lerner, J. W. (1989). *Reading problems: Assessment and teaching strategies* (2nd ed.). Englewood Cliffs, NJ: Prentice Hall.

Rist, R. C. (1970). Social class and teacher expectations: The self-fulfilling prophecy in ghetto education. *Harvard Educational Review, 40,* 411–451.

Roberge, J. J., & Flexer, B. K. (1984). Cognitive style, operativity, and reading achievement. *American Educational Research Journal, 21,* 227–236.

Roberts, T. (1983). Factors of intelligence in the reading comprehension of learning disordered/reading disordered youngsters. *Reading Improvement, 20,* 91–95.

Robinson, H. A., Faraone, V., Hittleman, D. R., & Unruh, E. (1990). *Reading comprehension instruction 1783–1987: A review of trends and research.* Newark, DE: International Reading Association.

Robinson, H. M. (1972). Visual and auditory modalities related to methods for beginning reading. *Reading Research Quarterly, 8,* 7–39.

Rosenblum, D. R., & Stephens, M. I. (1981). Correlates of syntactic development in kindergartners: Deficiency vs. proficiency. *Brain and Language, 13,* 103–117.

Rosenthal, A. S., Baker, K., & Ginsburg, A. (1983). The effect of language background on achievement level and learning among elementary school students. *Sociology of Education, 56,* 157–169.

Roswell, F. G., & Natchez, G. (1989). *Reading disability* (4th ed.). New York: Basic Books.

Rourke, B. P. (1975). Brain-behavior relationships in children with learning disabilities. *American Psychologist, 30,* 911–920.

Rubin, D. R. (1982). *Diagnosis and correction in reading instruction.* New York: Holt, Rinehart and Winston.

Rubin, D. (1991). *Diagnosis and correction in reading instruction* (2nd ed.). Boston: Allyn and Bacon.

Ruddell, R. B. (1979). Early prediction of reading success: Profiles of good and poor readers. In M. L. Kamil & A. J. Moe (Eds.). *Reading research: Studies and applications.* Twenty-eighth yearbook of the National Reading Conference.

Rugel, R. P. (1974). WISC subtest scores of disabled readers: A review with respect to Bannatyne's recategorization. *Journal of Learning Disabilities, 7,* 48–64.

Rupley, W. H., & Blair, T. R. (1989). *Reading diagnosis and remediation* (3rd ed.). Columbus, OH: Merrill.

Rutherford, W. L. (1967). Vision and perception in the reading process. In J. A. Figurel (Ed.) *Vistas in reading.* Newark, DE: International Reading Association.

Rystrom, R. (1973). Reading, language, and nonstandard dialects: A research report. In J. L. Laffey & R. Shuy (Eds.), *Language differences:*

Do they interfere? (pp. 86–90) Newark, DE: International Reading Association.

Rystrom, R. (1977). Reflections of meaning. *Journal of Reading Behavior, 9,* 193–200.

Samuels, S. J. (1988). Decoding and automaticity: Helping poor readers become automatic at word recognition. *The Reading Teacher, 41,* 756–760.

Samway, K. D., Whang, G., Cade, C., Gamil, M., Lubandina, M. A., & Phommachanh, K. (1991). Reading the skeleton, the heart, and the brain of a book: Students' perspectives on literature study circles. *The Reading Teacher, 45,* 196–205.

Sannomiya, M. (1984). Modality effect on text procesing as a function of ability to comprehend. *Perceptual and Motor Skills, 58,* 379–382.

Santa, C. M., & Alvermann, D. E. (1991). *Science learning: Processes and applications.* Newark, DE: International Reading Association.

Sattler, J. M. (1982). *Assessment of children's intelligence and special abilities* (2nd ed.). Boston: Allyn and Bacon.

Savage, J. F., & Mooney, J. F. (1979). *Teaching reading to children with special needs.* Boston: Allyn and Bacon.

Searls, E. F. (1985). *How to use WISC-R scores in reading/learning disability diagnosis.* Newark, DE: International Reading Association.

Seaton, H. W. (1977). The effects of a visual perception training program on reading achievement. *Journal of Reading Behavior, 9,* 188–192.

Seigler, H. G., & Gynther, M. D. (1960). Reading ability of children and family harmony. *Journal of Developmental Reading, 4,* 17–24.

Serwatka, T. S., Hesson, D., & Graham, M. (1984). The effect of indirect intervention on the improvement of hearing-impaired students reading scores. *The Volta Review, 86,* 81–86.

Shapiro, K. L., Ogden, N., & Lind-Blad, F. (1990). Temporal processing in dyslexia. *Journal of Learning Disabilities, 23,* 99–107.

Siegel, L. S. (1989a). IQ is irrelevant to the definition of learning disabilities. *Journal of Learning Disabilities, 22,* 469–486.

Siegel, L. S. (1989b). Why we do not need intelligence test scores in the definition and analyses of learning disabilities. *Journal of Learning Disabilities, 22,* 514–518.

Silva, P. A., Chalmers, D., & Stewart, I. (1986). Some audiological, psychological, educational and behavioral characteristics of children with bilateral otitis media with effusion: A longitudinal study. *Journal of Learning Disabilities, 19,* 165–169.

Silva, P. A., McGee, R., & Williams, S. (1985). Some characteristics of 9-year-old boys with general reading backwardness or specific reading retardation. *Journal of Child Psychology and Psychiatry, 26,* 407–421.

Simons, H. B. (1973). Black dialect and learning to read. In J. L. Johns (Ed.), *Literacy for diverse learners* (pp. 3–13). Newark, DE: International Reading Association.

Sinatra, R. (1989). Verbal/visual processing for males disabled in print acquisition. *Journal of Learning Disabilities, 22,* 69–71.

Singer, M. (1990). *Psychology of language.* Hillsdale, NJ: Lawrence Erlbaum.

Smith, F. (1978). *Reading without nonsense.* New York: Teachers College Press.

Smith, P. L., & Friend, M. (1986). Training learning disabled adolescents in a strategy for using text structure to aid recall of instructional prose. *Learning Disabilities Research, 2,* 38–44.

Snowling, M. (1987). *Dyslexia: A cognitive developmental perspective.* New York: Basil Blackwell.

Snowling, M., Goulandris, N., Bowlby, M., & Howell, P. (1986). Segmentation and speech perception in relation to reading skill: A developmental analysis. *Journal of Experimental Child Psychology, 41,* 489–507.

Sornson, H. H. (1950). *A longitudinal study of the relationship between various child behavior ratings and success in reading.* Unpublished doctoral disseration, University of Minnesota, Minneapolis.

Spache, G. D. (1953). A new readability formula for primary-grade reading. *Elementary School Journal, 52,* 410–413.

Spache, G. D. (1963). *Toward better reading.* Champaign, IL: Garrard.

Spache, G. D. (1965). *A study of a longitudinal first grade reading readiness program* (Cooperative Research Project 2742). Tallahassee, FL: Florida State Department of Education.

Spache, G. D. (1970). *Good reading for the disadvantaged reader.* Champaign, IL: Garrard.

Spache, G. D. (1975). *Good reading for the disadvantaged reader: Multi-ethnic resources.* Champaign, IL: Garrard.

Spache, G. D. (1976a). *Diagnosing and correcting reading disabilities.* Boston: Allyn and Bacon.

Spache, G. D. (1976b). *Investigating the issues of reading disabilities.* Boston: Allyn and Bacon.

Spache, G. D. (1978). *Good reading for poor readers* (rev. ed.). Champaign, IL: Garrard Publishing.

Spache, G. D. (1981). *Diagnostic Reading Scales.* Monterey, CA: CTB/McGraw-Hill.

Spache, G. D., & Spache, E. B. (1986). *Reading in the elementary school* (5th ed.). Boston: Allyn and Bacon.

Spache, G. D., & Tillman, C. E. (1962). A comparison of the visual profiles of retarded and non-retarded readers. *Journal of Developmental Reading, 5,* 101–109.

Spreen, O., & Haaf, R. G. (1986). Empirically derived learning disabililty subtypes: A replication attempt and longitudinal patterns over 15 years. *Journal of Learning Disabilities, 19,* 170–179.

Stanovich, K. E. (1985). Explaining the variance in reading ability in terms of psychlogical processes: What have we learned? *Annals of Dyslexia, 35,* 67–96.

Stanovich, K. E. (1989). Has the learning disabilities field lost its intelligence? *Journal of Learning Disabilities, 22,* 487–492.

Stanton, W. R., Feehan, M., McGee, R., & Silva, P. (1990). The relative value of reading ability and IQ as predictors of teacher-reported behavior problems. *Journal of Learning Disabilities, 23,* 514–517.

Stevens, D. O. (1971). Reading difficulty and classroom acceptance. *The Reading Teacher, 25,* 52–55.

Strickland, D. S., Feeley, J. T., & Wepner, S. B. (1987). *Using computers in the teaching of reading.* New York: Teachers College Press.

Sullivan Associates. (1973). *The programmed reading series.* New York: McGraw-Hill.

Swanson, B. (1982). The relationship between attitude toward reading and reading achievement. *Educational and Psychological Measurement, 42,* 1303–1304.

Swanson, B. B. (1984). The relationship of first grades' self report and direct observational attitude scores to reading achievement. *Reading Improvement, 21,* 170.

Szeszulski, P., & Manis, F. R. (1987). A comparison of word recognition processes in dyslexic and normal readers at two reading-age-levels. *Journal of Experimental Child Psychology, 44,* 364–376.

Taylor, B., Harris, L. A., & Pearson, P. D. (1988). *Reading difficulties: Instruction and assessment.* New York: Random House.

Templeton, S., & Mowery, S. (1985). Readability, basal readers, and story grammar: What lies beneath the "surface"? *Reading World, 24,* 40–47.

Thayer, J. A. (1970). Johnny could read—what happened? *Journal of Reading, 13,* 501–506, 561.

Thonis, E. W. (1976). *Literacy for America's Spanish speaking children.* Newark, DE: International Reading Association.

Torgesen, J. K. (1989). Why IQ is relevant to the definition of learning disabilities. *Journal of Learning Disabilities, 22,* 484–486.

Trelease, J. (1985). *The read-aloud handbook* (2nd ed.). New York: Viking Penguin.

Vacca, J. A., Vacca, R. T., & Gove, M. K. (1987). *Reading and learning to read.* Boston: Little, Brown.

Vellutino, F. R., & Scanlon, D. M. (1986). Experimental evidence for the effects of instructional bias on word identification. *Exceptional Children, 53,* 145–155.

Vellutino, F. R., & Scanlon, D. M. (1987). Phonological coding, phonological awareness, and reading ability: Evidence from a longitudinal and experimental study. *Merrill-Palmer Quarterly, 33,* 321–363.

Venezky, R. L., & Chapman, R. S. (1973). Is learning to read dialect bound? In J. L. Laffey & R. Shuy (Eds.) *Language differences: Do they interfere?* (pp. 62–69). Newark, DE: International Reading Association.

Vernon, M. D. (1960). *Backwardness in reading.* New York: Cambridge University Press.

Vernon, M. D. (1969). *Visual perception and its relation to reading.* Newark, DE: International Reading Association.

Vick, M. L. (1973). Relevant content for the black elementary school pupil. In J. L. Johns (Ed.),

Literacy for diverse learners (pp. 14–22). Newark, DE: International Reading Association.

Voeller, K. K. S., & Armus, J. (1986). A comparison of reading strategies in genetic dyslexics and children with right and left brain deficits. *Annals of Dyslexia, 36,* 270–286.

Wagner, R. K. (1986). Phonological processing abilities and reading: Implications for disabled readers. *Journal of Learning Disabilities, 19,* 623–630.

Walberg, J. J., & Tsai, S. (1985). Correlates of reading achievement and attitude: A national assessment study. *Journal of Educational Research, 78,* 159–167.

Wasson, B., Beare, P., & Wasson, J. (1990). Classroom behavior of good and poor readers. *Journal of Educational Research, 83,* 162–165.

Wattenberg, W. W., & Clifford, C. (1966). Relationship of self-concept to beginning achievement in reading. *Childhood Education, 43,* 58.

Weinberg, W., & Rehmet, A. (1983). Childhood affective disorder and school problems. In D. F. Cantwell and G. A. Carlson (Eds.), *Affective disorders in childhood and adolescence: An update* (pp. 109–128). New York: SP Medical & Scientific Books.

Weintraub, S. (1972). *Auditory perception and deafness.* Newark, DE: International Reading Association.

Weintraub, S., & Cowan, R. J. (1982). *Vision/Visual perception: An annotated bibliography.* Newark, Del.: International Reading Association

Werner, P. H., & Strother, J. (1987). Early readers: Important emotional considerations. *The Reading Teacher, 40,* 538–543.

Westman, J. C. (1990). *Handbook of learning disabilities: A multisystem approach.* Boston: Allyn and Bacon.

Wharry, R. E., & Kirkpatrick, S. W. (1986). Vision and academic performance of learning disabled children. *Perceptual and Motor Skills, 62,* 323–336.

Wiess, M. J. (1982). Children's preferences for format factors in books. *The Reading Teacher, 35,* 400–406.

Wilkerson, A. (1971). *The foundations of language.* London: Oxford University Press.

Wilson, R. M., & Cleland, C. J. (1985). *Diagnostic and remedial reading for classroom and clinic* (5th ed.). Columbus, OH: Merrill.

Winograd, P., & Niquette, G. (1988). Assessing learned helplessness in poor readers. *Topics in Language Disorders, 8*(3), 38–55.

Wolfson, B. J., Manning, G., & Manning, M. (1984). Revisiting what children say their reading interests are. *Reading World, 23,* 4–10.

Woodcock, R. W. (1986). *Woodcock reading mastery tests, revised.* Circle Pines, MN: American Guidance Service.

Woodcock, R. W., & Johnson, M. B. (1989). *Woodcock-Johnson psycho-educational battery, revised.* Allen, TX: DLM Teaching Resources.

Woods, M. L., & Moe, A. J. (1985). *Analytical reading inventory* (3rd ed.). Columbus, OH: Merrill.

Young, F. A. (1963). Reading measures of intelligence and refractive errors. *American Journal and Archives of American Academy of Optometry, 40,* 257–264.

Zinkus, P. W., Gottlieb, M. I., & Schapiro, M. (1978). Developmental and psychoeducational sequelae of chronic otitis media. *American Journal of Diseases of Children, 132,* 1100–1104.

Author Index

Subject Index